Research Reports ESPRIT



Project Group Speech Technology · Volume 1

Edited in cooperation with the European Commission

K. Varghese S. Pfleger
J.-P. Lefèvre (Eds.)

# Advanced Speech Applications

## European Research on Speech Technology

Springer-Verlag
Berlin Heidelberg New York
London Paris Tokyo
Hong Kong Barcelona
Budapest

**Volume Editors**

Kadamula Varghese, European Commission
Rue de la Loi 200, B-1049 Brussels, Belgium

Silvia Pfleger
Technical University Munich, Dept. of Computer Science
Orleansstr. 34, D-81667 Munich, Germany

Jean-Paul Lefèvre
AGORA Conseil, 185 Hameau du Château
F-38360 Sassenage, France

This volume gives an overview of the results of advanced European research on speech technologies and its applications in the multilingual framework of the European Union.

The technical papers present advanced experimental results obtained in the Sub-programme "Information Processing Systems and Software" in the first two phases of ESPRIT, the European Specific Programme for Research and Development in Information Technology supported by the European Commission.

CR Subject Classification (1991): J.1, K.3, H.1.2, H.4.3, H.5.2, I.2.7, I.3.6

ISBN 3-540-58142-1 Springer-Verlag Berlin Heidelberg New York
ISBN 0-387-58142-1 Springer-Verlag New York Berlin Heidelberg

Publication No. EUR 15871 EN of the
European Commission,
Dissemination of Scientific and Technical Knowledge Unit,
Directorate-General Information Telecommunications, Information Market and
Exploitation of Research,
Luxembourg.



Typesetting: Camera-ready by the editor
SPIN: 10472411 45/3140-543210 – Printed on acid-free paper

# Foreword

Traditionally, the European-based biannual international conference "EUROSPEECH" dealing with all aspects of speech science and technology is preceded by an "ESPRIT Speech Projects Days", which presents a particularly well timed opportunity to measure progress in speech technology and applications in Europe. The last venue was held in Berlin, Germany, on September 20th, 1993. The success of this workshop encouraged the major European experts in the field to contribute to this volume. Published in the ESPRIT Research Report series, it presents the results of advanced European research on speech technologies and its applications in the multilingual framework of the European Union.

Speech is an important factor in building an integrated European communication platform. Strong links exist between speech and natural language processing, and human computer interaction. Recent experimental results on multilingual conversion between both speech and text show the advantage of integrating phonetic, lexical, and syntactic knowledge, and also demonstrate the feasibility of multilingual voice systems in the human-computer interface applications. Multilingual queries use natural language-based co-operative dialogue as an interface to the computer services in the information applications. Continuous and robust speech understanding is here addressed for both speaker-independent and speaker-adaptive processing, together with dialogue modelling and management. Such technologies are then used in the design of computer workstations with a speech-based human interface for a large range variety of information technology applications (e.g. in the office, telecommunications, and computer aided education).

This volume brings together a valuable collection of experiences in advanced speech technologies, and their integration in a large application domain with the aim of increasing human comfort and security when dealing with computer-based information systems.

May 1994 D.E. Talbot

# Preface

Speech is undoubtedly the most natural and spontaneous means of human communication. However, in our communication with machines, which are more and more present in our daily environment, we have never been able to integrate completely this favourite medium. Industrial and scientific research has been performed over the last five years with the aim of improving man-machine communication, mainly through applications involving speech compression, synthesis, recognition, and in some cases speech understanding. Embracing a large number of industrial and scientific applications, the speech-based communication involves now strongly related areas such as natural language processing and knowledge representation, additionally to acoustic signal processing. In fact, speech and natural language are so closely connected and embedded in many applications, that it might be difficult to make a formal - and to some extent - artificial separation.

Europe has always been an excellent area for the promotion of speech technology, due to its heritage in cultural diversity. Compared to countries in which a unique language is pre-eminent, such as Japan or the USA, speech diversity in Europe imposes the existence of a multilingual communication platform common to all European communities, while preserving their specific cultural heritage. At the European level, many of the efforts, driven by industrial and academic experts, are strongly supported by the European Commission itself, through programmes such as ESPRIT, RACE, TELEMATICS and others, with a considerable commitment to the development of advanced applications. At the present time, most of these speech-based applications are still in the process of maturation. This leads to a lack of visible exploitation results and products based on existing speech technologies, which gives a widespread impression of non-marketable speech technologies. In fact, a reliable basis exists for the development of commercial products, and there is a clear demand for speech technologies, provided that an efficient and robust performance is available under realistic conditions of use.

Speech and natural language techniques, profitably coupled with other technologies, can provide simple solutions in large markets. The efficient integration of the most advanced speech technologies in real products is still a world-wide research topic of considerable interest. Also the transfer of the available research results and existing technologies from the laboratories to the market place, as suitable systems in the real application environment, continues to remain a challenge in this field. Including contributions from senior European experts in the field, this volume describes advanced speech applications currently developed as advanced results of European research on speech technology.

A large variety of experiences are here presented, ranging from long-term research motivations to industry-driven applications through standardisation activities. Groups of experts involving large-scale collaborations at the European level are directed to the definition of multilingual standards and to the specification of databases, speech and language descriptive methods, and quantitative tools for assessment. As discussed in the fundamental research oriented papers, on the one side a coherent description of the interactions between speech perception and speech production including other media, such as visual information or gestures, and on the other side the development of discourse representations and structure, taking into account both linguistic and non-linguistic information, can be seen as two ultimate research goals. In terms of technology, experimental results on multilingual conversion, between both speech and text, show the advantage of integrating phonetic, lexical, and syntactic knowledge, while integration of the same knowledge in speech recognition leads to improved robustness against inter- and intra-speaker changes in articulation and against ambient noise. Other technology oriented contributions deal with continuous speech recognition as well as dialogue aspects. Both speaker-adaptive and speaker-independent systems are described, together with dialogue modelling, with the aim of designing spontaneous conversational interactions with a machine. All these technologies associated with already available results are widely integrated in the reported applications, which include access to telephone services involving speech recognition and synthesis, aid for foreign language learning based on analysis of the speech characteristics of non-native speakers, access to large databases using natural language, real-world dictation characterised by a large and open vocabulary and allowing the speaker to dictate with a natural speaking style, control of a robot for hospital service tasks, and a multilingual lexical learning system for disabled persons.

This book provides details about the practical use of speech technology in interaction with computers, as well as results of field tests along with experience gained from working prototypes, and state-of-the-art information which will be of great interest for the reader. Both specialised scientists and industrial developers can benefit from reading the volume. Results described in this book represent a unique picture of the most advanced speech applications available in Europe, covering a large number of information technology areas, including industry, telecommunication, office, aids for the handicapped, and computer aided education. This set of experiences forms a valuable and comprehensive foundation for a better understanding of the current state of speech technology, and paves the way for future products on the market, illustrating the strength, the vitality, and the potentiality of an industrial sector of considerable interest.

May 1994

K. Varghese
S. Pfleger
J.-P. Lefèvre

# Contents

# Advanced Speech Technologies in the ESPRIT Programme

J. Mariani
LIMSI-CNRS
BP 133, F-91403 Orsay Cedex, France

## Abstract

The effort on research and development in the field of Speech Technologies is very large in Europe, with the automation of communication as the major challenge in a multilingual framework. Advanced speech techniques, integrated in the multilingual European environment, ensure the communication platform which is necessary in order to build the community of countries, while preserving their cultural heritage. This paper provides an overview of the main ESPRIT projects on speech technologies, and their applications in the European Union environment.

## 1. Introduction

### 1.1 The ESPRIT Program

At the European level, the Spoken Language Technology has been addressed in several projects mainly funded by the ESPRIT programme of the CEC, but a substantial national support can also be reported. ESPRIT *(European Strategic Programme for Research and development in Information Technology)* has following important objectives:

- to provide the European Information Technology industry with the technologies it needs to meet the competitive requirements of the 1990s,
- to promote European transnational cooperation in information technology, and
- to contribute toward the development and implementation of international standards.

ESPRIT is a long-term research programme, and two phases have already been successfully finished: ESPRIT I (1984-1989), and ESPRIT II (1988-1993). In ESPRIT I, five main research sectors have been selected: Microelectronics, Software Engineering, Advanced Information Processing, Office Systems, and Computer Integrated Manufacturing. In ESPRIT II, research work was mainly concentrated to three main sectors: Microelectronics, Information Processing Systems, and Integrated Systems (including Office Systems and Computer Integrated Manufacturing). A complementary basic research programme (Basic

Research Actions) was also initiated. The new phase ESPRIT III (1992-1997) is in progress.

For each phase, a workprogramme has been proposed and a Call for Proposal launched. Each submitted proposal has been reviewed by a team of experts, and the decision of acceptance has been made by the Commission on the basis of this scientific expertise. In contrast to some of the national programmes, ESPRIT projects are usually funded 50% of the total cost. During the phase ESPRIT I the 50% funding rule was the same for industry and universities. Starting with phase ESPRIT II, universities and research institutions could be funded 100% of the marginal cost. Two rules apply to the participants to an ESPRIT project: (1) at least two countries of the European Union should be represented, and (2) at least two independent companies should be involved. This second rule does not apply to ESPRIT "Basic Research Action" (BRA) projects.

During the phase ESPRIT I only European companies could build of consortium, but consortia have been opened to EFTA (European Free Trade Association) countries starting with the phase ESPRIT II. However, EFTA-partners are not funded by the CEC, but by their own country.

In ESPRIT I, Speech Technology was the main topic of 7 projects: 2 projects in the area "Advanced Information Processing" and 5 projects in the area "Office Systems". Speech also has been present in other areas, in 6 additional projects. In ESPRIT II, Speech Technology was the main topic of 11 different projects: 8 projects in Information Processing Systems, and 3 projects in Basic Research. An exploratory action in Information Processing Systems, and a Network of Excellence in Basic Research Actions should also be added. Speech is also indirectly present in 9 additional projects (3 in Information Processing Systems, 3 in Integrated Systems and 3 in Basic Research) which deals with human-machine interface including speech, or natural language processing.

## 1.2 Language Processing and ESPRIT

Based on the previous experience, the recommendation in the ESPRIT III Basic Research workprogramme has been to strengthen the links not only between speech processing and natural language processing, but also with other closely related areas, like vision, knowledge representation and human-computer interaction. The accent was put on the integration of linguistic and non-linguistic information, on speaker characterization and voice representation methods (i.e. that can deal with prosodics and speaking styles), on using contextual information and discourse structure, and on the development of dedicated hardware architectures, including VLSI. The use of self organizing methods, and the study of the resulting organization have been encouraged. Integration of speech, text, gesture, visual information, temporal coordinating of speech, and transmodal semantic co-reference should have been the ultimate goal.

ESPRIT I has been a major event in the European Information Technology R&D community, as it has started links between researchers or laboratories that could not have met in conferences organized at national level, or even in the US, before ESPRIT I was launched. ESPRIT I was mainly technology driven, and so was ESPRIT II at its beginning. During the phase ESPRIT II, a strong request for the projects to be more oriented towards industrial applications was raised by the CEC, probably based on the evaluation of the low amount of products which have been marketed as a result of the projects financed in ESPRIT I. This request resulted in some wavering within the consortia, which had to adapt their initial programme to the new guidelines. The IT industrial crisis also added some problems in the involvement of companies, especially in long term R&D such as speech or language processing.

The relationship between the subsequent phases has been questionable, as it is necessary for each call for proposal to resubmit a new proposal, and the evaluation is made in the same way, should it be the continuation of an existing project, or a completely new one. Also, several projects were accepted for a long duration (up to 3 years), for their technical contents, but not budgetized accordingly. The concequence was the necessity to redo parts of the administrative formalities several times for all partners of a consortia, without having any insurance that the project would last its initial planned duration, which was considered as necessary for a successful completion. This is also incompatible with long term research areas, such as speech and language processing, and would plea for a larger scale specific programme in these areas.

The projects which have been conducted within the ESPRIT programme cover a large area, from Basic Research to practical applications, through technological improvement, both in terms of hardware and software.

## 2. Basic Research on Speech Communication

While ESPRIT I did not consider Basic Research as a specific area, two projects started within the BRA initiative of ESPRIT II. They addressed the problems of speech production and perception. One project is concerned to Auditory Modelling for speech recognition, the other one addresses the Articulatory Modelling for speech synthesis, as follows.

The project ACTS (High-resolution Speech Recognition: Auditory Connectionist Technologies for Speech) was managed by the Applied Psychology Unit (APU) of the Medical Research Council (MRC) in Cambridge (UK). It addresses the computer modelling of auditory processing and connectionist systems for speech recognition. It is based on research into peripheral auditory processing and cognitive research on speech perception and memory. The first goal was to develop a recognition system that benefits from the pre-processing embodied in current models of the human auditory system, and in accordance with the psycholinguistic research. A computer simulation of cochlea processing has been implemented. The connectionist recogniser has been compared with the Hidden Markov Models approach, and the auditory model has been compared to an FFT filterbank.

The purpose of the project ACCOR (Articulatory-Acoustic Correlation in Coarticulatory Processes: a Cross-Language Investigation) is to undertake the physiological and linguistic constraints on the dynamics of articulation during speech production phases. A cross-language study of articulation identifies the major language-independent universal regularities of the phenomenon, and how they interact with language-specific factors. Investigations of coarticulatory regularities are integrated with new and improved ways of exploiting these regularities in deriving articulatory representations from the acoustic analysis of speech.

A large corpus containing multimodal speech information has been investigated and appropriate solution hve been implemented, e.g. for the acoustic signal and articulatory parameters (EPG-Electropalatography, laryngograph, nasal and oral volume velocity of air, also some EMA-Electromagnetic Articulography parameters).

The research work performed within the ACCOR project has been continued by the ACCOR II Working Group, which has been started in ESPRIT III, and which combines the use of EPG and EMA parameters. It worked in close relationship with the ESPRIT III SAM A project, and BRA VOX working group.

The VOX research work is concerned with the analysis and synthesis of speaker characteristics. It is based on the fact that the problem of taking into account speaker characteristics in speech processing is often underestimated, as a second order type of information, while being of major importance for obtaining high quality systems. The VOX working group gathers an interdisciplinary team of specialists in speech science, speech technology and experimental psychology. It seeks to investigate the acoustic, articulatory and perceptual correlates of speaker type (i.e. voice type), speaker state (i.e. emotion and attitude) and speaker style (i.e. careful versus casual speech), with the goal of improving speech technology systems, especially the speech recognition and synthesis, and speaker identification.

The speech project MAPS (Mapping of Action and Perception) running in ESPRIT III is concentrated on the sound-to-gesture inversion in speech (i.e. that is how to find back the articulatory parameters from the acoustic signal). This work is conducted with methods already applied successfully to robotics, the total system being called an "Articulotron". This robotic approach allows for the unification of perception and action in speech, with a specific study of the coarticulation problem, and of adaptive behaviour to compensate for perturbations.

While these projects are basic research, other ones are more driven by technological improvement, based on the study of different methods, like artificial intelligence techniques, statistical modelling, or neural networks.

## 3. Technology Improvements

The objective of the project SIP (Advanced algorithms and architectures for Speech and Image Processing), co-ordinated by CSELT (Italy) in ESPRIT I, was to develop the algorithmic and architectural techniques required for recognising and understanding spoken and visual signals, taking advantage of the similarities between the two domains), and to demonstrate these techniques by means of suitable applications in several areas ( e.g. medical , industrial).

The goal on speech processing was the recognition of continuous speech, with constrained syntax, for a 1000 word vocabulary. Progress was made along two complementary lines: a statistical approach (using Hidden Markov Models), and a knowledge-based approach (using Artificial Intelligence techniques).

Starting at the end of the ESPRIT I phase, the IKAROS project (Intelligence and Knowledge-Aided Recognition of Speech), was a related project to the SPIN project of ESPRIT I, with Alcatel-Laboratoires de Marcoussis as a prime contractor, while being also the prime contractor in SPIN. The aim was to evaluate artificial intelligence techniques for speech understanding. The final demonstrator was planned to be a continuous speech recognition system, with a vocabulary of 1000 words, multi-speaker, multi-lingual (French, English, German), for natural-type spoken languages with dialogue management. Initially planned for 4 years, it was stopped after 2 years, with the conclusion that Artificial Intelligence techniques wouldn't bring better results than statistical ones. The Artificial Intelligence techniques competed a lot with Pattern Matching techniques, based on statistical methods.

The neural network approach was also investigated in two ESPRIT II and two ESPRIT III projects, and an overview of these projects is given below.

The aim of the SPRINT BRA project (Speech Processing and Recognition using Integrated Neurocomputing Techniques), is to address various unsolved problems in speech recognition, taking advantage of the apparent distinctive features of neural networks (i.e. non-linearity, self-organization, and paralellism). The problems are in relationship with speech variabilities: adaptation to new speakers or new environments, noise immunity, classification of speech parameters using a set of phonetic symbols, and recognition of isolated words (lexical access). The speech representation levels considered are signal, parameter, phonetic and lexical, and the transition from one level to the next one has been investigated.

In the more general PYGMALION project on Neurocomputing, and its application to speech recognition, the goal is to develop a portable European Neural Network Specification Language, and to demonstrate the potential of a neural network approach through industrial applications, mainly on image and speech processing. A cascadable VLSI demonstrator has been produced, and a speech recognition OEM product has been built at Alcatel-SEL, in Germany, based on a neural network methodology .

The HIMARNET project (ESPRIT III) is related to the development of hybrid Artificial Neural Networks (ANN) and uses Hidden Markov Models (HMM) algorithms for robust speech recognition. The target is here the isolated word speaker-independent recognition of medium size vocabularies (50-100 words) for telephone transmission quality speech, with applications in this area. The weakness of both approaches (i.e. lack of discriminating abilities for simple HMM approaches, and difficulty to deal with time modeling for ANN) are especially studied.

A similar approach is used in the WERNICKE project (ESPRIT III BRA), where an hybrid ANN-HMM approach is developed for large vocabulary, speaker independent, continuous speech recognition. In this project, a laboratory located in the US, but having European funding (ICSI), participates as a subcontractor. Each partner experiments different approaches: hybrid HMM/MLP (multilayer perceptron), recurent neural networks, and speaker adaptation in Artificial Neural Networks. A special hardware (RAP- Ring Array Processor) is developed at ICSI. Comparative testing are here made on international speech databases.

## 4. System Assessment and Evaluation

In order to assess the quality of recognition, or synthesis systems, and to compare different methodologies, the MULTILINGUA project (on Multilingual Speech Input-Output Assessment Methodology and Standardisation) was launched in early ESPRIT I, and was quickly renamed SAM (Speech Assessment Methodology). It was headed by University College of London (UK), and included a lot of European laboratories. The objective of the project was to provide a pan-European basis for the assessment of speech technology devices. The definition phase was allied with the SPIN project. Initially in the Office and Business systems sector, it was translated later to the Information Processing sector. Work has been conducted on the definition of standards, the collation of speech material existing in different countries (English, Italian, German, French, Dutch, Danish, Swedish) and the definition of a language-independent methodology for assessing speech input and output systems. The multilingual EUROM database has been developed and distributed on CD-ROM format.

This first project was followed by SAM 2, where the activities focused on following major areas:

- speech input assessment (recogniser tests run on a PC-based workstation called Sesam),
- speech output assessment (both objective and subjective methods have been developed), enabling new technologies (i.e. the specification of uniform protocols do speech databases collection and management across the project languages).

The Sesam workstation has been provided with tools for speech labeling, analysis and Input-Output assessment.

In ESPRIT III, two projects were proposed as a continuation of SAM. These are SAM A ("A" for Application), which was accepted in the main ESPRIT programme, and SAM R ("R" as Research), which was rejected as a Basic Research Action. The work in SAM A is based on the results of SAM 2, and added three new languages (Greek, Spanish and Portuguese).

Apart from those SAM projects, aiming at evaluating the technical quality of speech Input-Output systems, the 449 project (ESPRIT I) has been performed. It was concerned with the investigation into the effective use of speech at the human-machine interface) . The main objectives were to determine the current state of the art in speech technology, to explore the potential for future applications, and to determine the additional new requirements, so that a number of potential applications can be realised. Several results were presented at the end of this 2-year project, which ended in 1987. Continuous speech recognition could not be obtained and a knowledge-based approach was needed.

It appears that continuous speech recognition is not available commercially, but neither are the systems ideas or designs that could make efficient use of it, while interesting applications can be developed with simple recognition systems.

Two areas of system developments (see [15], [24]) can also be identified: one related to the relationship between speech and text, and one related to spoken dialogue, both in a multilingual framework.

## 5. Multilingual Coversion Systems: Speech-to-Text and Text-to-Speech

The relationship between speech and text, both in terms of Text-to-Speech synthesis, and Speech-to-Text recognition (i.e. Voice Activated Typewriting) is a specific task. It has the advantage of a rather well defined area, as it is possible to use very large amount of textual data, already available on electronic support. The study of the specifities of the textual information and its relationship with speech is of major importance. As it is possible to build easily a lexicon and a language model from existing data, it is possible to process large vocabularies, in a multilingual framework.

Two successive projects addressed these issues: the projects 291 and 860 (ESPRIT I) on "Linguistic Analysis of the European Languages" have been initiated by Olivetti. They produced the software necessary to perform grapheme-to-phoneme and phoneme-to-grapheme conversion at word level, without considering the speech signal itself. The project covered the following languages: Dutch, English, French, German, Greek, Italian, and Spanish.
Reference corpora of about 200,000 words plus dictionaries and list of ambiguities (homographs and homophones) were extracted from common European Community texts and newspapers. A linguistic model, based on typical syntactic patterns extracted from texts by statistical analyses, has been developed to deal with ambiguous solutions.

The Polyglot project is a continuation of this research work in the ESPRIT II, also with Olivetti as a prime contractor. The goal of Polyglot (Multilanguage Speech-to-Text and Text-to-Speech system) is to demonstrate the feasibility of multi-language voice input-output for several applications, by integrating phonetic, lexical and syntactic knowledge common to text-to-speech and speech-to-text. It resulted in a large vocabulary speaker adaptive isolated speech recognition and high quality text-to-speech synthesis for six European languages. The feasability of large vocabulary continuous speech recognition was also studied, and tools for extending easily speech recognition and synthesis to other languages have been designed. The applications address remote access to an electronic mailbox and voice access to a telephone directory.

## 6. Spoken Dialogue

A first trial on spoken dialogue took place within the PALABRE project (ESPRIT I), on the "Integration of artificial intelligence, vocal Input-Output and natural language dialogue, with application to directory services". This project had a duration of 12 months (while 48 months were initially targeted). Its goal was to define and realise an acquisition, management and interrogation system in natural language for a large and evolving knowledge database. The Inputs-Outputs were to be either textual or vocal. The feasibility was to be demonstrated through a phone directory "Yellow Pages" application. The architecture was based on a blackboard approach, and two approaches were proposed to parse a query started by the user:

- a deterministic parser for written input, and
- an augmented transition network for spoken input.

The knowledge was represented using the KL-ONE language. PALABRE served as a preliminary study for subsequent projects in the field of speech and natural language processing (especially SUNDIAL and PLUS).

The SUNDIAL project (ESPRIT II) on Speech Understanding and Dialogue is an attempt to address the problem of spoken language dialogue in real conditions. It is a 5-year project, which addresses the problem of speech-based cooperative dialogue as an interface for computer applications in the information services domain. The technologies that are developed are speaker-independent or speaker-adaptive continuous speech recognition and understanding, and oral dialogue modeling and management. Speech input consists of naturally spoken utterances of telephone quality, with a vocabulary of 1000 to 2000 words, for 4 different languages (English, French, German and Italian). Three information service applications have been identified initially: intercity train timetables (German), Flight enquiries and reservations (English and French), and a hotel database (Italian). The spoken phenomena to be covered in the dialogue are studied through the analysis of both human-human and human-machine simulated by human (called the Wizard of Oz method) dialogue databases. Recognition is based on Hidden Markov Models.

The PLUS project ("A Pragmatic-Based Language Understanding System") can be considered as a follow-on of the PALABRE project, but mainly oriented towards written language. PLUS aims to achieve robustness in natural language understanding by considering natural language as a communicative activity whose essential characteristics is to convey a meaning that is both appropriate and contextually relevant. It exploits both linguistic and pragmatic phenomena (such as interpretation with respect to context and inference tools derived from non linguistic problems. The first demonstrator is be developed for telephone "Yellow Pages" queries, in both French and English.

## 7. Robust Speech Input-Output Systems

One of the main conclusions of ESPRIT I was the necessity to realize robust systems, that still behave in an acceptable way, when used in a real (not laboratory) environment. This problem was considered in 3 projects within ESPRIT II.

The objective of the project ARS (Adverse Environment Recognition of Speech) was to develop improved algorithms for speech recognition in the presence of noise, and to build a real-time demonstrator. Two application environments have been chosen: namely vehicles and factories. A multilingual database has been collected in noisy environment. It serves in order to compare baseline systems. From that, advances have been made on speech signal preprocessing, speech pattern matching in noisy environments, speaker adaptation and error correction strategies. Those improvements have been installed on a real-time hardware for mobile radio communication on cars.

The ROARS project aimed at the design of a Robust Analytical Speech Recognition System. its goal is to increase the robustness of existing analytical speech recognition system (i.e. one using knowledge about syllables, phonemes and phonetic features), in order to achieve speaker independent continuous speech understanding with dialogue capabilities. The starting point is an already existing system for French, which is adapted for Spanish. The robustness of this existing system is improved regarding intra and inter-speaker changes in articulation, and various ambient noises. The aim of the second phase is the implementation of a system for air traffic control, and the integration of other devices, such as keyboard, tracker ball and screen, with a vocabulary of 100 to 200 words.

The aim of the explanatory action ROBUST (Robust speech understanding) was to organise workshops in order to evaluate results and ongoing work in the field of robust speech understanding and to propose directions for future work.

In the ESPRIT III programme, that started in 1992, the workprogramme qualifies robust speech recognition as a priority area, in the framework of a speech activated information server robust to noise. The system has to be speaker independent, or speaker adaptive. This aspect appears in the Freetel and Himarnet projects.

Other projects directly considered the integration of speech Input-Output systems in applications, especially for the design of advanced computer workstation in the office, for telecommunication and for computer education applications (e.g. language training).

# 8. Speech Applications

## 8.1 Speech in Office Environment

The project SPIN (Speech Interface at Office Workstation) was a 5-year project, started very early, as a pilot speech project in ESPRIT I. It was headed by Alcatel-Laboratoires de Marcoussis. The overall aims of the project were to make significant advances in speech Input-Output algorithms, to study ergonomic aspects of integrating speech in the office environment, and to build a demonstrator. It addressed speech coding, where three coding methods (MPLPC, TDHS and RELP) have been investigated. It also addressed speech recognition, where the production of a demi-syllable lattice was produced from continuous speech, text-to-speech synthesis for French, Italian and Greek, and speaker verification. A three DSP-based modular hardware has been developed, and the different algorithms have been implemented. There was a strong connection with the IKAROS project, also headed by Laboratoires de Marcoussis, but based on novel Artificial Intelligence techniques.

In the ESPRIT I "Intelligent Workstation System (IWS)" project, headed by Bull, and in the ESPRIT II MULTIWORKS project, headed by Olivetti, speech was considered as one of the possible means to build the interface between the user and the workstation. The goal of MULTIWORKS is to develop an office workstation that manipulates video, graphics, text, voice and sounds. This project included the use of enhanced user interfaces, including new interaction devices such as voice input and electronic paper.

## 8.2 Telecommunication Applications

The objective of the ESPRIT II SUNSTAR project (Integration and Design of Speech Understanding Interface) is to show the benefits and enhancements that human computer interfaces can offer when they are based on speech Input-Output.

Two fields of applications, which represent market sectors of rapidly growing importance, have been chosen:

- a professional, office-type environment, and
- a public telephone network environment.

The project is application driven, in the sense that it concentrates on the integration of available speech functions into demonstrator systems, rather than on fundamental research issues leading to the development of new speech systems.

The objectives of the FREETEL project in Esprit III is to enhance the quality of hands-free communication via various terminals (telephones, videophones and mobile phones). The problems which are here addressed are the adaptation to the acoustic environment, the echo cancellation, the voice activity detection and the noise reduction. The specifics characteristics of each application have to be dealt with (e.g. background noise, transmission delays and interactions with the system in the case of mobile phones, and longer echoes and possibily wideband signals in the case of telephones or videophones).

### 8.3 Computer-Aided Education Application

The ESPRIT II SPELL project aims at designing an Interactive System for Spoken Language Training. Its aim is to analyse the speech characteristics of non-native speakers and to develop tools to improve their spoken language skills. Research topics include phonetic analysis, phonetic distance metrics, multilingual systems, linguistics and computer-aided instruction, in 3 languages: English, French and Italian. SPELL has been continued in the ESPRIT III phase (SPELL II), in order to bring the resulting product closer to market.

## 9. Speech and Natural Language

Starting in ESPRIT II, a major trend is to consider speech together with natural language processing.

### 9.1 The Network of Excellence in Speech and Natural Language (ELSNET)

The Network of Excellence in Speech and Natural Language (ELSNET), created in 1991, has been assigned the task of providing an infrastructure for coordinating research and postgraduate training facilities on a European scale, with the long-term goal of contributing towards the construction of an integrated model of the "cognitive chain" linking speech to reasoning via natural language. The major goal is to strengthen the links between the "Speech Communication" and the "Natural Language Processing" communities. The actions are related to the organisation of workshops dealing with Spoken Language Processing (i.e. the Integration of Speech and Natural Language), postgraduate exchange programs, reusability and systems assessment methods for speech, natural language, and spoken language, and also the improvement of the links between industry and academic institutions.

## 9.2 Basic Research in Language Processing

The project DYANA (Dynamic Interpretation of Natural Language) addresses the question of the integration of logic, natural language and speech, focusing on the themes of partial information and dynamic interpretation in natural language processing, with particular attention to developing a computational and cognitively motivated model of how spoken language is understood. The work is divided in four interdependent themes:

- Grammar Development, Speech and Prosody,
- Meaning, Discourse and Reasoning, and
- Logic and Computation.

This project publishes a Newsletter. It has been extended in ESPRIT III with Dyana II, where three interdependent themes are identified (Grammar Architecture, Interpretation in Context, and Implementation and Integration).

The DANDI (Dialogue and Discourse) working group coordinates and stimulates scientific cooperation between European research centres involved in studying the question of how informaton is encoded and extracted from discourse. It is divided in four special interest groups: Discourse relations and their linguistic expression, questions, communication failure and repair, accomodation and presupposition. It organizes workshops in those areas.

The project DANDELION (ESPRIT III) is focused on the development of a language-independent theory of discourse. It is based on linguistic analysis and psycho-linguistic experimentations. The specifications have to be neutral with respect to generation, interpretation and translation, with a special emphasis on the study of contextual factors and linguistic phenomena.

## 9.3 Multilingual Natural Language Processing

The project TWB (Translator's workbench project) aims at the development and integration of computer-based tools for multilingual text processing for the conversion of documents to/and from a number of Community languages. These tools include spelling, grammar, style and layout checkers.

The project INTREPID (Innovative Techniques for Recognition and Processing of Documents) aims at developing new techniques for document recognition and processing. It includes a linguistic contextual post-processing (lexical, grammatical and semantic analysers) for three European languages (English, Italian, Spanish).

The project EMIR (European Multilingual Information Retrieval) completes a feasability study into the automatic indexing of free text and the multilingual querying of text databases. The indexing is based on statistical methods. The initial prototype addresses English/French. It could be extended to English/German, and finally to French/German, resulting in a trilingual query system.

### 9.4 Lexicons

Research work on lexicons is also very important, and appears in several projects, as follows.

The Multi-Purpose standard lexicon project MULTILEX, headed by Olivetti, is an answer to the need for a universal, standardised format and software conversion packages, leading to a general reusability of lexical resources, in a number of applications including publishing, machine translation, optical character recognition (OCR), speech recognition and information retrieval. It covers 7 European languages.

The aim of the projects ACQUILEX ("Acquisition of Lexical Knowledge for Natural Language Processing Systems") in ESPRIT II, and ACQUILEX II in ESPRIT III is to develop techniques and methodologies for using existing machine-readable dictionaries in the construction of components for natural language processing systems. The main focus of attention is here concentrated on the extraction of lexical information from multiple machine-readable sources, in a multilingual context, with the overall goal of constructing a single multilingual lexical knowledge-base.

## 10. Other European Programmes

Apart from ESPRIT, Speech Communication is addressed in the CEC/DGXIII Computerised Language Processing Division (Luxembourg), in the EUROTRA programme on machine translation, and in the LIFE initiative (Language Industry For Europe). A market study has been conducted by Ink International and AEG-Olympia.

Starting from this study, and based on the results and on the experience of EUROTRA, a "Linguistic Research and Engineering" (LRE) programme has been launched, within the Telematics area. The objective of this programme is the development of a basic linguistic technology which can be integrated in a large variety of applications involving natural language components, and aiming at the improvement of the interlinguality of the linguistic representation of text or discourse, reflecting the multilinguality of Europe. The domain specific knowledge is used to constrain possible linguistic interpretations.

The interface with speech technology is also part of the programme. Here both topics are investigated the use of linguistic knowledge to improve the performance of speech analysis and synthesis, and the integration of speech Input-Output in linguistic applications. Also the use of advanced computational technologies, like parallelism, and the study of the economic and social impact of new linguistic technologies are included in this programme. The creation of common methods, tools and linguistic resources, such as software tools, grammars, dictionaries, terminological collections, annotated written and spoken language and standards is another important part of this programme. The applications that would be taken into consideration are: multilingual machine translation, multilingual abstracting and indexing, aids for monolingual and multilingual document generation, speech analysis and synthesis, human-machine communication, knowledge acquisition from natural language text and computer-aided instruction. Language Training is also identified as a field where a large effort should be put. As a response to the LRE 1993 "Call for Proposals", 3 projects dealing with speech processing have been selected, and started in early 1994. These projects are listed below.

The SQUALE project studies the possibility of using the evaluation paradigm, that has been used in the DARPA Language Processing programme of the European framework, with the necessity to extend it to a multilingual environment. The tests will be conducted by 3 European research laboratories, which are familiar with conducting and reporting test experiments within DARPA. The tests are organized by an independent laboratory.

The EUROCOCOSDA project ensures the participation of Europe in the international COCOSDA committee ("Coordinating Committee on Speech Databases and Speech I/O System Assessment"). Apart from the organizational aspects, several actions are also present in the project: coordinating the European effort related to the building of a very large telephone speech database (Polyphone), recording and distributing the "Translanguage English Database" (TED), consisting of talks in English, with a large variety of dialects and accents, in the area of speech science (all recordings were made at the Eurospeech'93 conference which took place in Berlin in September 1993). Other databases are considered in the area of newspaper read texts, and for speech synthesis systems development and evaluation purposes. The project RELATOR aims at creating a Network of Repository for Linguistic Resources, both written and spoken. The legal, commercial and structural aspects are here studied.

In the project PROMETEUS (EUREKA), and in the CEC/DRIVE programme concerning the car industry, as well as in the CEC/RACE programme on telecommunications, and in the CEC/TIDE programme on aids to the handicaped, speech technologies are also used for different applications.

Most of these research results conduct to a specific programme in the area of Linguistic Engineering (LE), in the 4th Framework Program.

## 11. The European Forces in the Field of Spoken Language Processing

A study of the number of publications in the US IEEE-ICASSP conference during 15 years, i.e. 1976-1991 (see [21]) shows that, on a total of 2200 published papers, the European laboratories are in the second position, with about 25% of the number of papers, behind the US (50%), but well ahead Japan (12%). A total of at least 260 laboratories can be identified at the European level (160 public and 100 industrial laboratories), in 17 European countries (230 laboratories in the European Union), with about 3000 researchers and engineers.

### 11.1 The European Speech Communication Association (ESCA)

The creation of the ESCA scientific society has been initiated in 1988 by the CEC, and by several scientists, including the representatives of the French Acoustical Society, and of the British Institute of Acoustics. It organizes an European conference on Speech Communication and Technology, called Eurospeech

(Eurospeech'89 in Paris, Eurospeech'91 in Genova, and Eurospeech'93 in Berlin with about 850 visitors), and regular ESCA Tutorial and Research Workshops (12 ETRWs have been already organized since 1989) on various topics in the field of Speech Communication. The Journal of the Association is the "SPEECH COMMUNICATION" journal, and a Newsletter (NESCA) is also published regularly.

### 11.2 Other European Societies and Journals

There are several Scientific Societies and groups which operate at the European level:

- the FASE (Federation of National Acoustics Societies),
- the Eurasip Association which is generaly devoted to Speech Processing and organizes conferences on this topic (EUSIPCO), and also has a journal published by North-Holland "Signal Processing" (M. Kunt, Editor), and
- the COST 209 (a research group on Telecommunications (see [25]).

The ECCAI (European Coordinating Committee on Artificial Intelligence) organizes regularly the ECAI (European Conference on Artificial Intelligence), and the ACL (Association for Computational Linguistics), which is a US Society with a set of European members (EACL), organizes regularly a European Conference. Acta Acustica is published by the European Acoustics Associations (EAA). "Computer Speech and Language" is published by Academic Press.

### 11.3 European National Programms

At the national level, some countries have scientific associations, or coordinated activities on Speech Technologies (see [5], [16], [17], [20], [22], [23], [25], [27], [28], [29], [30]).

In **France** [16] the GDR/CNRS-PRC "Human-Machine Communication" is coordinating the national effort on Human-Machine Communication, including speech activities. It has four poles: Speech Communication, Natural Language Processing, Machine Vision, and Multimodal Interfaces. It has its own budget from CNRS (Franch National Research Agency), and the ministry of Research and Technology (see [9], [2]). A subgroup of the French Society of Acoustics (SFA/GCP) organizes an Annual Conference on Speech (JEP), and specialised workshops on different topics related to Speech Processing.

The AFCET association for Computer Science has a Working Group on "Speech Hardware and Software Architectures". The ARC (Association for Cognitive Research) organizes specialized workshops and has interest in Speech and Natural Language processing. The SEE (French Society of Electrical and Electrotechnical Engineers) has also a Group on Signal Processing, including speech. The "Tenor" association liaises industrial companies working in the area.

In the UK the national research (see [6], [10]) is co-ordinated by the Alvey Programmme. Here 6 projects involving Speech Technology have been developed putting together public research and industrial laboratories (see [10], [6]).

These projects are listed below:

- VODIS (limited dialog),
- SYNDAX (recognition of chinese),
- SPAR software (UCL, GEC, ICL) for research environment,
- STA (Logica, NPL, RSRE, Smiths Industries, UCL) on performance assessment of speech recognition systems,
- WOZ experiments using Palantype for VAT (Dundee University), and
- the Speech Demonstrator (Marconi, CSTR and Husat).

In the ITI programme (Information Technology Initiative) 3 projects have been now started:

- SYLK (Statistical Syllabic Knowledge) by the Universities of Sheffield and Leeds) with GEC Marconi, RSRE and Artificial Intelligence Ltd. as "uncles",
- SRT (Speech Recognition Techniques) by Marconi, RSRE, PARSYS and Cambridge Algorithmica on speech recognition based on recognition-by-synthesis, and
- "Pre-Scribe" (Cambridge University, CSTR, UCL, RSRE, NPL) on collecting spoken language data.

Two other projects were started later.

The SALT work on Speech & Language Technology is based on the SALT 2000 report (R.K Moore 1988, RSRE), and helped the creation of the SALT Club, gathering researchers both in speech and natural language. The Institute of Acoustics organizes conferences on Speech. It has a special group on the Assessment of Speech Technology (STAG). The IEE (Institute of Electrical Engineers) has also activities in the field.

In **Germany** the large project SPICOS (Siemens-Philips-IPO COntinuous Speech Recognition) involves several European companies as follows: Philips Laboratory in Hamburg, Siemens Laboratory in Munchen, and IPO in Eindhoven. This project aims at providing joint research activities on Continuous Speech Recognition (see [14]).

A new project, called ASL (Architectures for Speech and Language Research) has been launched in January 1991 by the German Ministry of Industry (BMFT). This 4-year project has a budget in the range of 60 Mio DM (about 30 Mio ECU). The ASL project is divided in two subprojects:

- ASL North project, which involves Hamburg University (coordinator), Berlin University, Bielefeld University, Dusseldorf University, Bochum University, Bonn University, IBM Stuttgart, DFKI Saarbrucken, and Siemens. Its title is "Innovative concepts for integrative architectures, tests with small vocabulary"; and
- ASL South project on the "Improvement of existing stochastic algorithms with large vocabularies", with Siemens as coordinator, Philips Aachen, SEL-Alcatel, Daimler Benz, and Erlangen University.

This project can be considered, in some ways, as a follow-on of the SPICOS project; plus a third one; Phondat, with the University of Munchen as coordinator, and the Universities of Braunschweig, and Kiel, on the design and realization of speech databases (including recording and labelling), and text databases.

This project has been followed by an even larger one one machine translation of speech input in real time, called VERBMOBIL. Taking into account the difficulty of the task, this project would last 20 years, and will benefit for a very large budget. The definition phase has been conducted in 1991. Siemens, IBM, IAI Eurotra-D Saarbrucken, DFKI Saarbrucken, Technical Univ. Berlin, and the universities of Hamburg, Karlsruhe and Stuttgart participated in that pilot phase. The DAGA (German Acoustics Society) organizes conferences on speech.

In **The Netherlands** (see [26], [28]) the SPIN programme on "Analysis and Synthesis of Speech" (ASSP) was conducted from 1985 to 1991. It included 5 academic partners (Phonetic Institutes of Amsterdam, Leiden, Nijmegen, Utrecht, and IPO in Eindhoven) and the PTT Dr Neher Research Laboratory. This is a coordinated research programme. A second programme (ASSP-2) was proposed as a 5-year programme (1991-1995).

The SPEX initiative (Speech Expertise Center) for the collection of speech data, and the assessment of speech systems has been here created. In a related field, the CELEX (Centre for Lexical Information) project is intended to offer an efficient access to multilingual lexical databases. A phonetic society exists with about 80 members (see [26]). An acoustical society (NAG) has also workshops in this domain.

In **Denmark** a project on Speech Recognition has been supported since 1983 by the Danish Council for Scientific and Industrial Research, with 3 major Danish industrial partners (Elbau, Jutland Telephone, and STL), and the Speech Technology Center of the Universty of Aalborg (see [3]).

The Danish Teletechnical Society has also been involved in scientific activities related to speech activities (like organizing the ESPRIT Aarhus Workshop in 1987). Presently, the strategic research programme "Processing of Natural Language in Application Orientated Dialogue Systems" is funded by the Danish Technological Research Council and conducted in cooperation between three centres for Speech Technology located at Aalborg University, at the Language Technology Department of the University of Copenhagen, and at the Cognitive Science Department of the Roskilde University. The programme has the aim of developing prototype systems that handle speech input and have sufficient linguistic and domain knowledge to conduct an intelligent dialogue with the user.

## 11.4 Programmes in other Countries

There are similar programmes in other countries (see [12], [13]), all around the world (see[15]). The largest one is the US DARPA programme (see [1], [19], [31], [32]) on Human Language Technology. This programme was started in 1984 (that coincides with the beginning of the ESPRIT programme), as a component part of the Strategic Computing Program. The HLT programme (see [8]) includes both spoken and written language processing. There is a goal to address Multilingual Language Processing by the year 2000. It is different from the ESPRIT programme in many aspects. The participants are usually funded 100%. The programme is driven by the improvement of the technology on generic tasks. There is no cooperation between the participants, but rather a competition, based on the evaluation paradigm. This paradigm implies that all participants (called "the players") have to test their system on the same data, at a given time. They are expected to report during a workshop the obtained results on the tests which have been performed, and they compare the advantages and drawbacks of different methods or approaches.

The organization of the tests (gathering of very large quantities of speech and text data, distribution of the training data, of the test data and of the format that should be used to report the obtained results) are taken care by an independent body (NIST, the National Institute fo Science and Technology, formerly National Bureau of Standards (NBS)).

This paradigm has been used first for medium size vocabulary (1000 words) speaker dependent or independent continuous speech recognition, with read sentences in the area of Naval Resource Management. It was followed by two new tasks consisting of read newspaper texts from the Wall Street Journal (about 20,000 words), and of spontaneous speech in dialogues extracted from an Air Traffic Information System (ATIS). Non-US laboratories have been invited to participate in the test campaign since 1992. Three laboratories (Cambridge University (UK), LIMSI-CNRS (France) and Philips (Germany)) also participated to this campaign. They achieved very good results, and were among the top ranks in the testing.

The same paradigm was applied to text understanding (MUC), database query in natural language (TREC), and machine translation. This programme is now accompanied by a basic research programme in cooperation with NSF. DARPA also supported the launching of the "Linguistic Data Consortium" (LDC), which has the task of gathering and distributing huge amounts of written and spoken data.

There is also a strong effort in **Japan**, with a national program (see [4], [7], [11]), where many institutions participate in the various working groups. At the ATR company a specific action (which started in 1986 for a duration of 15 year) is devoted to the task of "Interpreting Telephony", which aims at allowing a human speaker to speak in his own language, and have it recognized, translated and synthesized for other people in different language. Large programs (see [18]) are also going on in **Australia** and **Corea**.

## 12. Conclusions

It appears that the research on speech communication in Europe involves today a large number of public research laboratories, working both on language independent and language specific (their mother language) aspects, funded by national programs. A rather large number of industrial research groups are working on language independent aspects, and on one or two languages, and several European transnational research and development projects, especially within the ESPRIT programme and in large industrial co-operating groups.

It may be said that we obtain an impressing figure if we add all the budget allocations which are presently devoted in Europe for speech and language technology. However, it is necessary to spend a large part of this budget for cooperative efforts in order to use it optimally. This implies a strong transnational coordination between research and industry, aiming at a precise industrial long-term goal. The way to reach it practically is through an efficient cooperation between the programmes of the European Union and the national research programmes.

## References


1. J. Baker "State-of-the-Art Speech Recognition, US Research and Business Update", First European Conference on Speech Technology, Edinburg, Sept. 1987.
2. R. Carré "The French National Project on Speech Communication Research : An Overview", Danish Teletechnical Society Conference on Speech Technology, Aarhus, May 1987.
3. P. Dalsgaard, "The Danish and the Nordic Project on Speech Technology : Status and Future Activities", Danish Teletechnical Society Conference on Speech Technology, Aarhus, May 1987.
4. M. Eskénazi, J. Mariani, S. Bornerand, "Report on the ICSLP Satellite Workshop on Assessment in Kobe (Japan) and Visits to several Japanese laboratories working on Speech Communication", Speech Communication, Vol. 10, N.2, June 1991.
5. ESPRIT, The Synopses I, II, III, October 1992.
6. F. Fallside, "Speech Technology in the UK : The Alvey Programme", Danish Teletechnical Society Conference on Speech Technology, Aarhus, May 1987.
7. H. Fujisaki, "Overview of the Japanese National Project on Advanced Man-Machine Interface through Spoken Language", First European Conference on Speech Technology, Edinburg, September 1987.
8. G. Doddington, "ARPA HLT Overview", HLT Workshop, Princeton, March 6-8, 1994.
9. J.P. Haton, "The French National Project on Speech Communication Research. An Overview", Speech Tech'86 Conference, New-York, April 1986.
10. J. Holmes, "Speech Technology in the UK Alvey Program", Speech Tech'86 Conf., New-York, April 1986.
11. A. Kurematsu, "Automatic Telephone Interpretation : A Basic Study", Internal Report, ATR Laboratories (Osaka), May 1987.
12. J. Laver, "Worldwide Survey on Speech Technology", Danish Teletechnical Society Conference on Speech Technology, Aarhus, May 1987.
13. J. Laver, "Speech Technology in Perspective", Eurospeech'89, Paris, September 1989.
14. H. Mangold, "The German National Speech Projects. An Overview", Danish Teletechnical Society Conference on Speech Technology, Aarhus, May 1987.

15. J. Mariani, "Les ordinateurs de la cinquième génération. Reconnaissance vocale : des objectifs relativement modestes", La Recherche N.154, April 1984.

16. J. Mariani, "Speech Technologies in Western Europe : A review. Part I : France and the UK", Speech Technology Magazine, Vol.3 N.1, Aug./Sept. 1985.

17. J. Mariani, "Speech Technologies in Western Europe . Part II : The rest of Western Europe", Speech Techn. Magazine, Vol.3, N.2, March/Apr. 1986.

18. J. Mariani, "National and International Programmes on Speech Technology", Speech Tech'86 Conference, New-York, April 1986.

19. J. Mariani, "Speech Technology Activities in the USA", Danish Teletechnical Society Conference on Speech Technology, Aarhus, May 1987.

20. J. Mariani, "Speech Technology in Europe", European Conference on Speech Technology, Edinburgh, September 1987.

21. J. Mariani, "La Conférence IEEE ICASSP de 1976 à 1990: 15 ans de recherches en Traitement Automatique de la Parole", LIMSI Internal Report 90-8, September 1990.

22. J. Mariani, "Speech Research and Technology: Advances in Europe", Eurospeech'91 Conference, Genoa, September 1991.

23. G. Modena, "Speech Processing : An outlook on ESPRIT funded European Research" in "Recent Advances and Applications of Speech Recognition", International Workshop, Roma, May 1986.

24. T. Moto-Oka, "Les ordinateurs de la cinquième génération", La Recherche N.154, April 1984.

25. G. Pirani, "COST 209 : Linking Different European Languages", Speech Tech'86 Conference, New-York, April 1986.

26. L. Pols, "The Netherland National Speech Technology Project", Danish Teletechnical Society Conference on Speech Technology, Aarhus, May 1987

27. J. Roukens, "European Cooperative Research in Speech Technologies", Speech Tech'86 Conference, New-York, April 1986.

28. J. Roukens, "The ESPRIT Programmes on Speech Technology Now and in the Near Future", Danish Teletechnical Society Conference on Speech Technology, Aarhus, May 1987.

29. J. Roukens, "Speech Technology Within the ESPRIT Programme", First European Conference on Speech Technology, Edinburg, September 1987

30. J. Roukens, J. Mariani, D. Bouis, "Programme of the European Communities for the European Speech Technology.", ASA Conference. Honolulu, Hawaii. November 14-18, 1988.

31. A. Sears, "DARPA/ Information Processing Techniques", Speech Tech'86 Conf., New-York, April 1986.

32. C. Wayne, "A snapshot of two DARPA speech and natural language programs", 4th DARPA Workshop on Speech and Natural Language, Pacific Grove, February 1992.

## Annex 1:
## Speech Projects in ESPRIT I

291/860: Linguistic Analysis of the European Languages
Olivetti, CSATA (Italy), LIMSI (France), Ruhr Univ. (Germany), Madrid Univ., UNED (Spain), Patras Univ. (Greece), ACORN (UK), Nijmegen Univ. (The Netherlands), duration: 50 months.

449: Investigation into the effective use of speech at the human-machine interface
British Maritime Technology, Voice Systems International, ICL (UK), Fincantieri (Italy), duration: 13 months.

IKAROS: Intelligence and Knowledge-Aided Recognition of Speech
CGE-LdM (France), GEC Research (UK), Stuttgart Un., Fraunhofer Inst. (Germany), duration: 38 months

SAM 1 (MULTILINGUA): Multilingual Speech Input-Output Assessment Methodology and Standardisation
Univ. College of London (UK), CSELT (Italy), JYSK Telefon (DNK), Amsterdam Univ. (The Netherlands), CNET (France), then Univ. College of London (UK), NPL, Smiths Industries, RSRE, Logica (UK), CSELT (Italy), JYSK Telefon (DNK), TNO-Amsterdam Univ., Dr Neher Lab. (The Netherlands), GRECO (CNET, CRIN, CERFIA, ENST, LIMSI, IPA, ICP) (France), duration: 12 months.

PALABRE: Integration of artificial intelligence, vocal Input-Output and natural language dialogue: application to directory services
SESA, CNET, ERLI, LIMSI (France), SARITEL, Politecnico di Torino (Italy), British Telecom (UK), duration: 12 months (48 months initially targeted).

SIP: Advanced algorithms and architectures for speech and image processing
CSELT (Italy), AEG (Germany) , Strasbourg Un., Thomson (France), Torino Un. Politecnico di Torino (Italy), HITEC (Greece), GEC (UK), duration: 60 months.

SPIN: Speech Interface at Office Workstation
CGE-LdM, OROS, CEA, SESA (France), AEG, Nixdorf (Germany), CSELT, SNS PISA (Italy), Amsterdam Univ. (The Netherlands), Athens Un. (Greece), duration: 60 months.

**Other projects with speech topics in ESPRIT I:**

ACORD: Construction and Interrogation of Knowledge Bases using Natural Language Text and Graphics
CGE-LdM, BULL, Un Clermont-Ferrand (France), Triumph-Adler, Fraunhofer IAO, Un. Stuttgart (Germany), Univ. Edinburgh (UK).

IWS: Intelligent workstation
BULL, INRIA (France), Forth Res. Center of Crete (Greece), OCE-Nederland, Un. Nijmegen (The Netherlands).

HERODE: "Handling Mixed Text/ Image/ Voice Documents based on a Standardised Office Document Architecture
Siemens (Germany), Alcatel TITN, CRIN (France).

HUFIT: Human Factors Laboratories in Information Technologies
Fraunhofer IAO, Siemens, Munster Un. (Germany), BULL (France), ICL, HUsat Res. Center (UK), Olivetti (Italy), Philips (The Netherlands), Un. do Minho (Portugal), Un. College Cork (Irland).

PODA: Piloting of the Office Document Architecture
Siemens, Nixdorf (Germany), BULL, Alcatel TITN, PTT (France), Olivetti, Syntax (Italy), ICL, UCL (UK), Oce-Nerthelands (The Netherlands).

SOMIW: Secure, Open, Multimedia Integrated Workstation
BULL, INRIA (France), AEG (Germany), INESC (Portugal), Iselqui, Saritel, Italtel (Italy), Prodata, Sema Group Belgium, SCK-CEN (Belgium).

## Annex 2: Speech Projects in ESPRIT II

ARS: Adverse Environment Recognition of Speech
CSELT, Politechnico di Milano (Italy), ENST, Matra (France), Logica, Univ. Cambridge, Univ. Keele (UK), Madrid Univ., Page Iberica (Spain), duration: 36 months.

POLYGLOT: Multilanguage Speech-to-Text and Text-to-Speech system
Olivetti, Software Sistemi (Italy), LIMSI, BULL (France), Ruhr Univ., Triumph-Adler, Philips-Kommunications, Siemens (Germany), Madrid Univ., UNED (Spain), Patras Univ. (Greece), CSTR (UK), Nijmegen Univ., Philips-IPO (The Netherlands), duration: 36 months.

ROARS: Robust Analytical Speech Recognition System
Thomson-CSF/Sintra-ASM, CRIN (France), University of Valencia, ENA Telecommunicaciones (Spain), duration: 36 months.

ROBUST: Robust speech understanding
Page Iberica (Spain), Lernout and Hauspie (Belgium), Knowledge (Greece), duration: 15 months.

SAM 2: Speech Assessment Methodology
Univ. College of London (UK), NPL, Smiths Industries, RSRE, Logica (UK), CSELT, CNR, Fondazione Hugo Bordoni (Italy), JYSK Telefon (DNK), TNO-Amsterdam Univ., Dr Neher Lab. (The Netherlands), GRECO (CNET, CRIN, CERFIA, ENST, LIMSI, IPA, ICP) (France), AEG, RUB, Bielefeld Univ. (Germany), Televerket, KTH (Sweden), ELAB (Norway), duration: 36 months.

SPELL: Interactive System for Spoken Language Training
OROS (France), Alcatel-FACE, University of Roma, CSATA (Italy), CSTR (UK), duration: 24 months.

SUNDIAL: Speech Understanding and Dialogue
Logica, Univ. Surrey (UK), AEG, Erlangen Univ., Siemens (Germany), CNET, IRISA, CAP-SESA (France), SARIN, CSELT, Politechnico di Torino (Italy), duration: 60 months.

SUNSTAR: Integration and Design of Speech Understanding Interface
JYSK Telefon (Dnk), Stuttgart University IAT, Fraunhofer Gesellschaft IAO (Germany), Telefonica (Spain), Alcatel-Face (Italy), INESC (Portugal), duration: 60 months.

## Speech Projects in Basic Research of ESPRIT II

ACCOR: Articulatory-Acoustic Correlation in Coarticulatory Processes: a cross-Language Investigation
IPA-CNRS (France), CNR-Padova (Italy), Siemens, Maximilians Univ. (Germany), Un. Valencia, Un. Politecnica Barcelona (Spain), Un. Reading (UK), Univ. Dublin (Ireland), Univ. Stockholm (Sweden), duration: 30 months.

ACTS: High-resolution Speech Recognition: Auditory Connectionist Technologies for Speech
MRC, Univ. Cambridge, Un. Edinburgh (UK), ICP (France), INESC (Portugal), Un. statale di Milano (Italy), duration: 30 months.

SPRINT: Speech Processing and Recognition using Integrated Neurocomputing Techniques
CAP SESA, ENST, IRIAC (France), RSRE (UK), SEL (Germany), UPM (Spain), duration: 30 months.

## Other projects with speech topics in ESPRIT II:

EMIR: European Multilingual Information Retrieval
CEA-CEN, SYSTEX (France), Univ. de Liège (Belgium), Transmodul (Germany), duration: 36 months.

INTREPID: Innovative Techniques for Recognition and Processing of Documents
Un., PACER Systems (UK), duration: 30 months.

MULTILEX: The Multi-Purpose standard lexicon
Triumph-Adler (Germany), CAP-SESA, ASSTRIL, IMAG (France), Univ. Pisa, Lexicon (Italy), L-Cube (Greece), Philips, Vrije Univ. Amsterdam (The Netherlands), Siemens-Nixdorf, Univ. Munster, RUB (Germany), Univ. of Surrey, Univ. of Manchester (UK), Systems Spain (Spain), duration: 36 months.

MULTIWORKS: Multimedia Workstation
Chorus Systems (France), ICL, ACORN, Harlequin (UK), Philips Consumer Electronics (The Netherlands), duration: 24 months.

PLUS: A Pragmatic-Based Language Understanding System
CAP SESA, LIMSI (France), Univ. Pisa, Omega (Italy), Philips UK, Univ. of Bristol, UMIST (UK), SCS (Germany), ITK (The Netherlands), Un. of Göteborg (Sweden), duration: 48 months.

PYGMALION: Neurocomputing, and application to speech recognition
THOMSON (France), CSELT, Politecnico di Torino (Italy), Computer Technology Inst. (Greece), INESC (Portugal), IRIAC, PHILIPS-LEP, ENS, CEA-LETI, INPG, Concept Logiciels Expert, Sextant Avionique (France), UCL (UK), UPM (Spain), SEL (Germany), duration: 24 months.

TWB: Translator's workbench
Triumph-Adler, Daimler-Benz, Siemens, Fraunhofer IPA, University Heidelberg (Germany), L-Cube (Greece), Univ. of Surrey (UK), Siemens SA, Un. Politecnica de Catalunya (Spain), duration: 36 months.

*The projects on natural language processing in ESPRIT II / BRA:*

ACQUILEX: Acquisition of Lexical Knowledge for Natural Language Processing Systems
CNR/Un. di PISA (Italy), Un. Amsterdam (The Netherlands), Un. Cambridge, Cambridge Univ. Press (UK), Un. College Dublin (Ireland), Un. Politecnica de Cataluna (Spain), duration: 30 months.

DANDI: Dialogue and Discourse
Center for Cognitive Science Univ. Edinburgh, UMIST, Univ. Cambridge, Un. Essex (UK), Copenhagen School of Economics (Denmark), Ecole Polytechnique (France), Istituto dalle Molle (Switzerland), Inst. für Deutsche Sprache, Univ. Saarlandes (Germany), BIM, Univ. Antwerpen, Univ. Liège (Belgium), Linguistics Int. of Ireland (Ireland), Max-Planck Inst. für Psycholinguistik Nijmegen, Univ. Nijmegen, Univ. Tilburg (The Netherlands), Univ. di Milano (Italy), duration: 30 months.

DYANA: Dynamic Interpretation of Natural Language
Center for Cognitive Science Un. of Edinburgh (UK), Un. Amsterdam (The Netherlands), Un. Stuttgart, Tübingen, München (Germany), duration: 30 months.

ELSNET: Network of Excellence in Language and Speech
Center for Cognitive Science/Un. Edinburgh (UK), main nodes: LIMSI-CNRS (France), Univ. Stuttgart (Germany), Roskilde University (Denmark), INESC (Portugal), Univ. Pisa (Italy), OTS-Utrecht, Univ. Amsterdam (The Netherlands), KTH (Sweden) on 40 academic/public research nodes, and 50 industrial nodes.

## Annex 3: Speech Projects in ESPRIT III

FREETEL: Enhancement of Hands-free Telecommunications
Matra Communications, ENST, Philips-LEP, University of Rennes (France), Page Iberica (Spain), Imperial College of Science, Technology and Medicine (UK), ILSP (Greece), duration: 36 months.

HIMARNET: Study of Hidden Markov Models and Neural Networks for Robust Isolated Word Recognition
Faculté Polytechnique de Mons, Lernout & Hauspie Speech Products (Belgium), TEDAS (Germany), Iselqui (Italy), Ascom (Switzerland), duration: 36 months.

SAM A: Speech Technology Assessment for Multilingual Applications
Logica, NPL, DRA, (UK), CSELT, Fondazione Hugo Bordoni (Italy), JYSK Telefon (DNK), TNO, (The Netherlands), Vecsys-LIMSI, ENST, ICP (France), RUB, Bielefield Univ. (Germany), Televerket (Sweden), INESC (Portugal), Patras University (Greece), Polytechnic University of Catalunya (Spain), duration: 36 months.

SPELL II: Interactive System for Spoken European Language Training
Agora Conseil, OROS (France), Alcatel-FACE, University of Roma, CSATA (Italy), CSTR (UK), duration: 24 months.

*Speech Projects in Basic Research (ESPRIT III):*

SPEECH MAPS: Sound-to-Gesture Inversion in Speech: Mapping of Action and Perception
ICP, ENST (France), Univ. Lausanne (Switzerland), Inst. Studis Catalan (Spain), KTH (Sweden), Univ. Leeds (UK) + Univ. Köln (Germany), Univ. Strabourg (France), Univ. Genoa (Italy), Dublin City Univ. , Trinity College Dublin (Ireland), Univ. Lund (Sweden), Univ. Southampton (UK).

VOX: The analysis and Synthesis of Speaker Characteristics
CSTR, Univ. of Cambridge, Reading, Sheffield (UK), IKP-Univ. Bonn (Germany), IPA, LIMSI (France), Trinity College Dublin (Ireland), Univ. Geneva (Switzerland), KTH (Sweden).

WERNICKE: A Neural Network Based Speaker Independent, Large Vocabulary, Continuous Speech Recognition System
Lernout & Hauspie (Belgium), INESC (Portugal), Univ. Cambridge (UK).

*The projects on natural language processing in ESPRIT III / BRA:*

ACQUILEX II: Acquisition of Lexical Knowledge
Univ. Cambridge , Cambridge University Press (UK), CNR/ Univ. di PISA (Italy), Univ. Amsterdam, Van Dale Lexicografie (The Netherlands), Univ. College Dublin (Ireland), Univ. Politecnica de Cataluna, Biblograf (Spain).

DANDELION: Discourse Functions and Discourse Representation: an Empirically and Linguistically Motivated, Interdisciplinary Approach to Natural Language Texts
CLS (The Netherlands), GMD-IPSI, Univ. Saarlandes (Germany), Univ. Complutense Madrid (Spain), Univ. Edinburgh (UK).

DYANA II: Dynamic Interpretation of Natural Language
Univ. Amsterdam , Univ. Utrecht (The Netherlands), Center for Cognitive Science, Univ. of Edinburgh (UK), Univ. Stuttgart, Tubingen, Munchen (Germany), Univ. Oslo (Norway).

# A Common European Approach to Assessment, Corpora and Standards

Richard Winski *
Vocalis Ltd,
Chaston House, Mill court,
Cambridge, CB2 5LD, UK

Adrian Fourcin
University College London,
Wolfson House, 4 Stephenson Way,
London, NW1 2HE, UK

## Abstract

The 'Speech Assessment Methods' ESPRIT projects 1541, 2589 (SAM) and 6819 (SAM-A) have been directed towards the definition and application of multilingual standards to assist in the assessment, evaluation, cross-comparison and further advance of spoken language technology with immediate and long-term industrial benefits. The SAM group has involved collaboration among thirty-one laboratories in twelve countries, nine within the EU and three within EFTA.

The work has been concerned with the establishment of databases, speech and language descriptive methods, and quantitative tools for the assessment both of speech input systems (including recognition and verification) and speech output (synthesis) systems. The project activities have primarily involved the eleven languages of the consortium but have been conceived so as to facilitate the introduction of other member states' languages. Standard European databases in eleven languages have been completed and are progressively available on compact disc (EUROM 0 and EUROM 1). Common workstation facilities using a standard configuration (SESAM) hosted on low-cost IBM PC computers are being used in the laboratories of the project. These provide a reference for the application of a comprehensive range of software packages designed for input and output assessment in addition to the provision of supporting linguistic analysis software. Common methods of linguistic standardisation have been evolved and a common

* Prepared on behalf of the ESPRIT SAM and SAM-A projects. See Section 8 for a full list of participants.

computer compatible phonemic notation (SAMPA) has been introduced for European languages.

## 1 Historical context

The SAM ['Speech Assessment Methods'] Projects have been dedicated to the definition and application of multilingual European standards and resources. The aim in respect of standards has been to develop practical tools and de facto protocols which might eventually lead to International Standards. The emphasis in respect of resources has been towards the provision of a coherent multilingual infrastructure designed to assist and inform use, development and research in speech technology. In total the SAM group has involved the collaboration of thirty-one laboratories in twelve countries, nine within the EU and three within EFTA. The consortium has spanned a broad range of interests and has comprised leading industrial, academic and government laboratories in the fields of speech technology research and manufacture, phonetics, linguistics and acoustics.

The ESPRIT SAM 2589 project ['Multi-lingual Speech Input/Output Assessment, Methodology and Standardisation'] completed its three-year ESPRIT II Main Phase in 1992. This followed a preliminary 'Definition Phase' (ESPRIT 1541) which commenced in 1987 in which the state of the art, and the requirements in Europe and the rest of the world were investigated, and a 'bridging' 'Extension Phase', in which preparatory work for the Main Phase was undertaken. A subsequent project SAM-A (ESPRIT 6819) ['Speech Technology in Multilingual Applications'] was planned and undertaken as a three year follow-on project to consolidate the previous work and extend its application further especially towards industrial requirements and coverage of the additional EU languages - Greek, Portuguese and Spanish. Funding provision was eventually only provided for an initial one year period, and the original objectives were, in consequence, only partially attained. The community resources allocated to these last two projects have totalled 3.7 MECU, corresponding to a total manpower of 61 person-years over the six years of the projects' active history. It is important to recognise however that many achievements of the project have been obtained for all or a substantial number of the community languages represented. A high degree of parallel activity and national effort and investment has been involved. These EU resources may therefore be seen to be relatively modest when viewed as an average for each national group or language.

Work in the SAM project has been divided into three inter-connected working areas, and these are used to structure the description in the following sections of this chapter:

I Speech Recognition and Speaker Verification Assessment (Input)
II Speech Synthesis Assessment (Output)
III Enabling Technology and Research (ETR)

In overviewing the achievements of the SAM projects it is perhaps helpful to summarise the state of progress in this field before the commencement of the project. Prior to the last decade performance assessment had been an active concern of many individual groups world-wide with specialised projects, workshops and interest groups and a developing literature and methodology. There were few publicly available resources or agreed conventions regarding assessment methodology. In spite of the progression towards digital methods, there were few generally agreed formats for recording, formatting, or exchange of speech data (with the possible exception of VCR/PCM tape formats), and these were frequently difficult to use in practice for realistic assessment activities. Many existing databases had been recorded in analogue form and were consequently difficult to access and distribute. There were no large corpora of multilingual speech data available to act as reference data or to permit effective cross language comparisons to be performed.

Although a number of performance assessment methods had been developed there were virtually no publicly available tools for speech input or output assessment. Assessment of speech input technology products was generally based on a few publicly available test corpora providing inadequate representation of even the main European languages, mostly referencing American English material as a standard. These were generally restricted to small vocabularies: digits, common words, etc., in many ways a reflection of the predominant technology of the time, although some corpora of application-specific data were also in existence. There were, similarly, virtually no multilingual evaluation methods for speech synthesis. Those which existed were mainly developed for American English, such as the Diagnostic Rhyme Test and the Modified Rhyme Test. These segmental tests were not easily transferable to other languages. The 100 fixed semantically anomalous, so-called Haskins sentences are another example of an existing but insufficient American English test at the sentence level.

The prevailing situation in some respects was an inevitable consequence of the large storage requirements that speech technology development and assessment demands. Whilst background technological advances in effective low-cost computing hardware and mass storage (in particular CD-ROM), and standardisation resulting from the increasing availability of personal computing hardware have doubtless been a major factor in the world-wide move towards common standards for data exchange, the importance of co-ordinated groups of active researchers spanning different disciplines such as within the SAM project should not be underestimated. Indeed in its first year of existence, in what was primarily a definition phase, the SAM project pioneered the use of CD-ROMs for speech (following the example of GRECO in France) and produced the first co-ordinated multilingual speech corpus on CD-ROM (EUROM 0). However technological advance alone does not guarantee progression towards standards, and the process of obtaining convergence of working methods is equally important if advances in technology are to be effectively harnessed. The diversity of working methods is a typically human phenomenon and necessarily requires considerable human effort and resources to establish norms and standards. The SAM project has had a predominant role in defining and encouraging their use, both in Europe and further afield, often through painstaking processes of negotiation. In much less than a decade the situation today has been substantially transformed, such that previously unimagined quantities of reference speech data are now routinely accessed world-wide and supported by an emerging body of useful application tools and recommended practices. The SAM projects have contributed both to these developments in Europe and to the international collaboration in this area.

## 2 Input assessment

The project has been concerned with several different aspects of speech input assessment. At the outset there was a concern to establish reference data and methods which could be routinely applied to a wide variety of recognition systems and applications. The scope of interest in speech input assessment is however potentially extremely diverse, and spans the range of classes of recogniser from simple small-vocabulary speaker-dependent isolated-word devices to vocabulary-independent, speaker-independent continuous-speech systems. Application areas similarly can span simple voice command tasks to complex tasks such as the speech typewriter or dialogue-based information retrieval systems where significant human factors issues are involved. Systems can also be operative in a wide variety of acoustic environments from the relatively benign quiet room or office through telephony-based applications to adverse or hazardous environments such as the factory floor, in-vehicle systems or military applications where the use of special noise-cancelling techniques is essential.

The extreme diversity of these methods and applications clearly prevented them all from being addressed effectively within the given resource constraints and it was therefore necessary to focus on a few immediately relevant and realisable goals and to prepare a relevant groundwork of basic speech knowledge. Activities were initially focused on small-medium vocabulary systems operating in low-noise conditions, with increasing attention on more complex systems such as large vocabulary, adaptive, adverse-environment or word-spotting systems as the project progressed.

A state of the art review of international progress in speech input assessment was performed during the definition phase of the project [1]. This identified the priority objectives for the project. Its conclusions showed that there were:

- continuing practical difficulties arising from non-standard data representations
- limited guidelines for conducting testing, restricted mostly to documentation
- a variety of proposed assessment methods and measures, but inadequately supported by theoretical or experimental verification or cross-comparisons to provide standards or recommendations
- a need for effective analytic methods of assessment related to fundamental speech knowledge
- limited use or availability of automatic testing methods or supporting real-time tools
- few speech corpora designed and recorded in a disciplined manner for assessment
- very little multilingual recorded material and few procedures for performing multilingual assessments

The project goals aimed to address these priority requirements, and identified two complementary aspects of assessment to motivate the work: device assessment and methodology development. The first has been concerned with satisfying the immediate practical need for a common base of standard tools and methods which can be readily and routinely applied for straightforward evaluation and comparison of ASR (automatic speech recognition) devices e.g. from different manufacturers or for different end-user applications. The second concern was to advance the state of the art in assessment methodology itself. There is considerable scientific and practical motivation to develop testing methods which make explicit use of speech knowledge. These can potentially provide greater diagnostic information to aid system designers, may provide prediction possibilities, for example, for different application areas, vocabularies, accents and speaker types, and are fundamentally necessary for principled cross-language comparisons. The first method relies upon laboratory-based testing using large pre-recorded speech databases, and the second upon analytic determination or prediction of performance through appropriate techniques which make use of carefully parametrised test data. There are of course many common requirements in each of these approaches, and the practical activities of the project were designed to serve both approaches. Activities have therefore focused on the provision of:

- large multilingual speech databases as assessment references to support methodology research and as speech knowledge sources
- tools to conduct automatic testing of systems using standardised test methodologies, documentation and a reference workstation (SESAM) to ensure experimental repeatability

- experimental investigations of advanced knowledge based assessment methodologies

It is important to clarify what the project did not attempt to address. As mentioned, the practical emphasis was initially on developing real-time assessment tools as required to assess existing or near-product commercial systems. Laboratory systems can also be assessed using the same approach, but these are frequently non real-time software programs which in practice can be efficiently assessed using pre-computed data files storing the parametric speech representations rather than the acoustic signal itself. No attempt was therefore made to define standard assessment methods for these systems, nor for recognition-based products or embedded applications, where hardware or application constraints make it difficult or impossible to test using these approaches. In-situ field trials are frequently mandatory or more appropriate in these latter cases. Although no attempt was made to define general recommendations within the available project resources the tools and general approaches adopted in the project can frequently be applied in these situations also.

## 2.1 Multilingual Assessment Database - EUROM 1

The provision of a large multilingual database was essential to a number of activities in all three areas of speech input assessment, output assessment and enabling technologies, and its definition and later collection was defined as a major activity of the project. Corpus design principally centred on satisfying the requirements of the two primary approaches to speech input assessment investigated in the project. The following requirements were identified:

- multilingual, spanning all the representative languages
- homogeneous design and collection to provide a reference standard
- adequate acoustic/linguistic representation with controlled coverage of all major phonological phenomena in each language, to support analytic assessment and cross-language investigations
- recorded in quiet, acoustically neutral environment to ensure uniformity and to permit subsequent addition of post-production phenomena by post-processing
- representative of variability in speech production forms, from speakers of both sexes, a wide age range, and contrasting dialectal representations
- representative speech data for different task complexities, including isolated words, connected-word phrases, continuous speech passages
- suitable for testing different classes of ASR, although not primarily providing training material
- sufficiently large to permit statistically significant testing to be performed

These multiple requirements were difficult to satisfy within the limited project resources, however a multi-tiered design was chosen, described in detail later. In order to serve as a useful long-term reference for technology which is both currently available and in development, the database includes number phrases and general-purpose application-related sentence sequences. The provision of assessment consonant-vowel material covering the major phonemic contrasts and contexts for each language was specifically designed to support phonetically-motivated approaches to assessment, whilst permitting direct testing of isolated word systems to be performed with greater sensitivity. This data complements the more limited isolated and connected digit material and read passages recorded for 5 languages in EUROM 0.

## 2.2 Speech Input Assessment Workstation

A standard test software suite for recognition assessment has been developed and implemented on the SESAM workstation and tested in multi-lingual, multi-laboratory trials. All the modules are written in Microsoft C and interconnect using standard SAM ASCII files, illustrated schematically in Fig.1. The basic test suite comprises an optional DBMS interface for automatic selection of test utterances; a recogniser assessment control module which performs the assessment of a device to which it is interfaced; and a separate scoring module which computes and reports standard performance statistics. The results of the scoring program can be analysed to identify interactions between recognition performance and test data characteristics. A calibration procedure has been specified which uses a low-cost recognition module and specified test data on the EUROM 0 to provide a degree of assurance that the test equipment is correctly set up. These software modules are described in detail in the SAM User Guide to Speech Input Assessment [8].

### Assessment Control Module

The SamPac software component is designed to perform the assessment of isolated or continuous word recognisers controlled by several user-defined files. These files can be generated automatically, e.g. using the RISE database access tool described in section 4.2 with which users can generate and edit lists of test utterances using a simple forms-based approach. SamPac has been designed to work continuously to permit correct execution of tests that can run for many days if necessary. It handles all interactions with the recogniser, including training, and a windows-based user interface permits monitoring of the workstation activity and on-line performance figures. The program supports two modes of testing: presentation of individual utterances synchronously with the recogniser responses, and continuous playout of extended speech samples without artificial deep silence between tokens, as required when testing recognisers in noise. SamPac uses resident drivers to control the analogue interface board and the individual recognisers. In this way, the greater part of the software is quite independent of the analogue interface board which is utilised, and it is easier to develop new recogniser drivers which can have separate communication protocols.

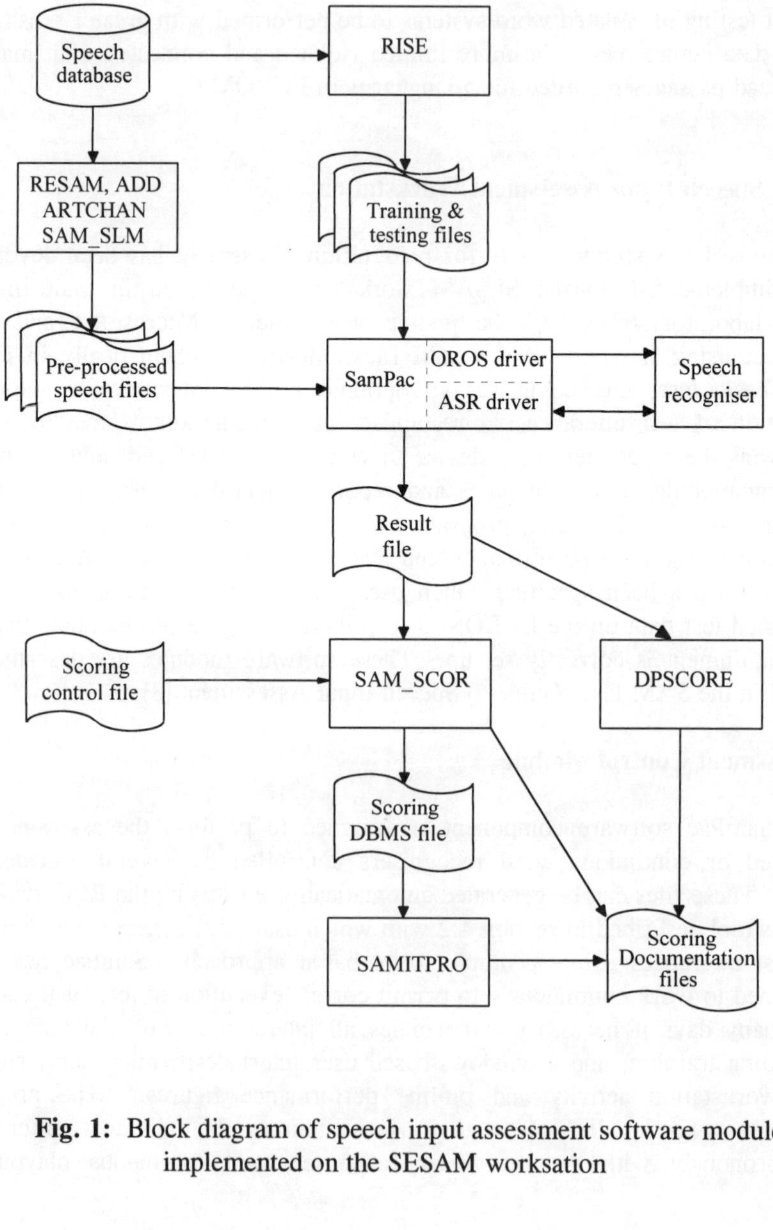


**Fig. 1:** Block diagram of speech input assessment software modules implemented on the SESAM worksation

## Scoring

The SAM_SCOR program scores results produced from the automated tests of recognisers and can be used with the main classes of recogniser, from small vocabulary speaker-dependent isolated word systems to medium/large vocabulary speaker independent continuous speech recognisers. It provides a range of recognition performance measures - hit; miss; substitution; correct rejection; false alarm. In addition, at the isolated word level, confusion and similarity matrices, confidence analyses, and the application of the McNemar test are standard facilities. Special scoring facilities are provided for the EUROM 1 CVC (consonant-vowel-consonant) test data. For connected word and continuous speech recognisers the program acts as a pre-processor for running the NIST string alignment and scoring routines which have been implemented on the SESAM workstation and distributed with their kind permission. An alternative alignment scoring algorithm DPSCORE has been developed to score the SamPac recogniser output which also includes response time statistics.

The output of the scoring software is designed to provide uniform presentation of the assessment results that are easy to understand and cross-compare. SAM_SCOR generates a file which can subsequently be fed back into the DBMS to make it possible to relate speech material characteristics to recogniser performance measures. It is also possible to perform further analysis of the interactions between recognition performance and test data characteristics using the software tool SAMITPRO (SAM Iterative Proportional Fitting). Performance can thus be related to speaker characteristics such as sex, age, dialectal category or to recogniser type, testing-site, microphone and noise-level.

## Test data preparation

There are several support tools useful in preparation of test data for assessment purposes. The Speech Level Measuring program, SAM_SLM determines the speech level of a signal file. It implements a method of measuring the signal level based on a level distribution histogram after squaring and low-pass filtering the signal wave form, and the RMS and DC-offset values are calculated from this. RESAM is a set of tools for processing speech files prior to testing. It supports re-sampling of speech at different sample rates, design and application of FIR filters, and addition of noise. These are useful when using noise files from sources such as the Noise-ROM and the EUROM 0 CD-ROMs which were recorded at differing sample rates. A software package (ARTCHAN) has been developed for off-line simulation of speech communication channels for use in both speech input and output assessment. The system is focused on telephone communication systems. The following transmission properties can be included: band-pass limiting, additive noise, non linear distortion, echoes, and quantization errors. The transfer-function related parameters for these channels can be varied. The parameter values are defined and calibrated for a number of representative telephone channels, which constitute a database of post production factor conditions.

### Analytic assessment tools

A speech parameter analysis package has been developed from work in the UK STA project resulting in a software package, SAM-SPEX. Currently six speaker-dependent parameters are measured. The aim is to make it possible for speech databases eventually to be calibrated in terms of factors which show a sensitivity in respect of recogniser performance to support analytic methods of assessing recognition performance. An additional software tool implements the HENR (Human Equivalent Noise Ratio) model of human word recognition capabilities. This provides a facility for estimating vocabulary difficulty in any putative application.

### Auxiliary tools

There are in addition two software recognisers which can act as a calibration reference: SAM_REC0 is a DTW-based isolated word which can be run on the SESAM, and a similar connected-word recogniser SAM_REC1 enables accelerated recognition to be obtained on a TMS320C30 DSP board.

## 2.3 Standard test protocols and resources for recogniser assessment

### Recogniser testing

A range of recognisers are now supported with compatible driver software and experiments have been conducted using these. They encompass a wide range of representative classes of device, both commercial and proprietary, covering the main classification features: isolated, connected word and continuous speech; speaker-trained, speaker-adaptive and speaker-untrained; small-, large- and vocabulary-independent systems. The list of recognisers tested includes: CSELT ESPRIT SUNDIAL recogniser, Datavox, Dragon Dictate, DRA AURIX, ENSIGMA SRS1E_ED, ESPRIT ARS recogniser, ESPRIT SUNSTAR 3R and SUNCAR, Infovox RA201, Jutland Telefon SAPCA, LIMSI-LV-CSR and LIMSI-VI-CSR, Marconi Macrospeak and MR8, SAM_REC1, Scott Instruments SIR-20, VCS Telerec and VR/40, Votan. Protocols used for testing some of these recogniser classes and illustrative results are detailed in the SAM User Guide to Speech Input Assessment [8].

**Standard database material**

The test workstation has been designed to be used with speech databases collected according to SAM protocols. However it is not difficult to make use of data recorded using other formats, and the CONVERT software for example enables the large number of North American DARPA/NIST corpora to be used with the SAM workstation. In addition to EUROM 0 and EUROM 1, there are increasing numbers of databases available in SAM format, including major national databases for France, Germany, Italy, Netherlands, Spain, the UK and several East European countries, including Bulgaria and Poland. Reference noise recordings are available on CD-ROM (Noise-ROM 0 and SUNROM-1) for a range of domestic, commercial, telecommunications and military environments, and a reference database of EUROM 0 data with a range of added noise conditions is available on CD-ROM (NOISEX 92).

The suite of SAM tools available can also be used to efficiently collect large speech databases to establish a complete, automatic procedure for performance assessment entirely within the SAM framework. Thus there is full support at all levels: for a user wishing to perform an off-the-shelf standard test using the available EUROM and noise data; to customise such a test to their particular requirements; or to create a different test set altogether, perhaps in a different language or for a specific application. Finally, the EUROM 1 data collection has been arranged so that post-production factors can be incorporated by simulation into the (originally anechoically recorded) speech data, and this also has been the object of concerted activity within the project.

**Telephone-based recogniser assessment and environmental factors**

Several activities have focused on the assessment of recognisers operating over the telecommunications network as this is one of the major application areas for the technology. Studies have been performed to support the definition of appropriate recommendations. One important finding is that recognisers behave very differently if the speech is presented bracketed by artificial deep silence, and assessment should be performed using the continuous mode of presentation which preserves the inter-utterance acoustic background during testing. These results have been presented for consideration by the ITU-TS (CCITT). Studies have also been performed to identify procedures which ensure that speech data recorded over the telephone channel for later laboratory testing yield results which match those for on-line assessment.

The SAM tools were developed interactively with requirements in the ESPRIT ARS project for performing assessment of a speech recognition application operating in adverse noise conditions, specifically hands-free voice dialling in a car. Work performed in parallel with this project investigated techniques of modelling the Lombard effect. This work follows the approach initially adopted in the project of using transformation techniques with respect to a clean reference database, for investigating environmental or channel factors. Subsequent work in this regard is supported by a software simulation tool of a number of common channel transmission factors such as band-pass limiting, additive noise, non linear distortion, echoes and quantization errors. These are intended to provide a useful analytic means of investigating post-production factors without having to invest in a separate data collection activity.

## 2.4 Analytic assessment methods

In parallel with the practical activities designed to serve the immediate needs of recogniser testing, activities have focused on developing more advanced, analytic techniques of assessment. There are a number of motivations underlying this work, principally concerned with establishing techniques which are more accurate, reliable, informative and efficient. Current methods of assessment are most frequently based on the direct presentation of relatively large numbers of speech tokens representing general purpose or task specific test vocabularies. These can consume considerable resources both in their creation and application in assessment, and frequently yield misleading results if they do not adequately represent the normal range of variability encountered in the target user population and application environment. Even if the results are representative of the target requirements it is not usually possible to extrapolate the results to other situations, such as the use of alternative dialogue elements, or different user groups, regions or languages.

We have therefore been faced with the need to develop a more fundamental and comprehensive approach towards the investigation and the evaluation of input assessment methodologies when the needs have to be met not only of operating with a range of speakers, accents and dialects, but also languages. Such an approach is designed to provide a more principled basis for both mono- and multi-language assessment. By applying techniques which ensure that the test conditions are representative of the target, more accurate and reliable performance figures should be obtained. The use of a phonetically motivated test database provides a basis for vocabulary-independent assessment and yields increased sensitivity with fewer test tokens. This approach is intrinsically capable of providing valuable diagnostic information leading to advances in recogniser design, through important insights gained into both automatic speech recognition and the nature of speech itself. A significant operational benefit of such a technique arises if it is possible to characterise the recognition process sufficiently well to enable prediction of performance to occur. This would permit exploratory determination of one or several recognition approaches to a range of application-related dimensions, including for example vocabulary difficulty, speaker or environmental characteristics, without having to perform an actual field trial in each case. A final motivation for these investigations is that test procedures are expected to be more efficient, requiring smaller databases and shorter tests.

The SAM projects have supported ongoing investigations into several analytic assessment approaches summarised below, specifically performance modelling, predictive assessment using the RAMOS and RSA approaches and vocabulary difficulty measurement using HENR. These methods are complementary, and a series of investigations have been defined which are aimed ultimately to realise an integrated method for predictive assessment. This work has been substantially advanced during the course of the SAM and SAM-A projects, however sustained funding for research is essential for the long-term potential of these methods to be realised.

**RAMOS**

RAMOS (Recogniser Assessment by means of Manipulation Of Speech) is a diagnostic method under development based on a test vocabulary of CVC-words. The aim of this approach is to characterise the performance of a recognition system as a function of the controlled variation of specific speech production and transmission parameters. An analysis of a reference database is first performed to determine the representative range of variability of a number of such parameters, e.g. the first two formants. Test tokens are drawn from the reference database and presented to the recogniser after manipulation of the specific parameters to be controlled. (The CVC lists of the EUROM 1 database are designed to be used with this method; the database also includes CVC tokens embedded in carrier phrases to permit the effect of context in continuous speech utterances to be addressed.) This data can also be used directly in the present SESAM workstation as a sensitive test using minimal pair comparison, similar to the intelligibility tests with nonsense CVC words and using an open response scoring format. It provides diagnostic information obtained from the confusions between phonemes. The method has been investigated using both Dutch and Danish subsets of the EUROM 1 database.

**RSA**

RSA (Recogniser Sensitivity Analysis) was originally investigated for English speech in the UK Alvey STA project. This method is potentially complementary to RAMOS in that it permits a recogniser to be characterised in terms of measured properties of the speech signal, but relies on characterising a sufficiently large database in terms of factors which show a sensitivity in respect of recogniser performance, rather than manipulating these parameters artificially. The EUROM 1 database was intended to capture a relatively high degree of speech production variability to support investigation into this method. Currently six speaker-dependent parameters are measured: speaking rate; energy; larynx frequency; 'voice quality'; vocal tract area estimate; and (temporal) pattern congruence. These can be derived using the SAM-SPEX software package.

**HENR**

A reference method of assessing performance has been proposed by calibrating a recogniser or recognition task against the equivalent human performance. The HENR (Human Equivalent Noise Ratio) is a measure of the difficulty of a recognition task defined in terms of the level of noise required to degrade the test data to obtain equivalent performance to that of a model of human perception. A software tool is available on the SESAM to implement the HENR model of human word recognition capabilities which provides a facility for estimating vocabulary difficulty in any putative application. Currently the model is available for English only, and requires the vocabulary to be specified phonetically.

### 2.5 Speaker verification

A comprehensive state-of-the-art review of speaker verification systems and techniques for their assessment has been completed. This has included a survey of existing commercial systems and applications. Initial experimental work has been performed to identify suitable algorithms for use in reference speaker verification systems. Some preliminary recommendations are also made regarding assessment, however it is shown that the lack of common databases and experimental protocols makes it difficult to objectively compare the various systems at present. This work was part of a fuller investigation planned to take place within the SAM-A project, and intended to provide practical recommendations and guidelines for performing assessment of speaker verification systems.

## 3 Output assessment

In the first year of the project an extensive overview of progress in the assessment of text-to-speech systems was performed, reported in the first SAM book [1]. This overview was performed as part of the definition phase of the project which identified a number of important areas for future investigation within the project. Subsequent work within the SAM-A project has extended the review to include a survey of standard tests, with special reference to subjective listening tests performed according to ITU-TS (CCITT) recommendations. The basic principles that were initially specified for future co-operative work, are still valid:

- multilingual approach
- appropriate not just for present systems, but also for the evaluation of future text-to-speech systems
- not limited to segmental intelligibility, but also addressing naturalness, quality, and acceptability, including adverse conditions
- integration of activities in various laboratories and aiming at international standardisation

Standard word-level and sentence-level segmental multi-lingual intelligibility tests have now been defined. The test material is automatically generated by software on the SESAM workstation in the languages of the project using phonotactic and word frequency constraints. Compatible software provides for response collection, collation and scoring. These tests and tools are fully described in the SAM User Guide to Speech Output Assessment [9]. In addition to the standard SAM tests that have been developed, a handbook in [12] was in the course of development in the SAM-A phase and currently overviews the range of available assessment methods with particular reference to ITU recommended approaches. This summarises various factors that can influence the choice of assessment method and underlying metrics so as to guide a user in the selection of appropriate tests.

### 3.1 Segmental Assessment

The SAM segmental test has defined guidelines for the automatic generation of nonsense-word lists for the initial SAM eight partner languages, using a set of fixed word structures and phoneme lists. The test material is language specific in that phoneme combinations respect phonotactic constraints for the languages in which they are prepared. The SAM group has chosen to use nonsense words in its definition of this standard with an open response set in order to get an intelligibility score which is not influenced by contextual information or semantically restricted answer choices. This type of material is the most relevant when an analysis of phoneme confusions is required, and in application, for instance, to synthetic material where error patterns may be quite device-specific.

The proposed standard segmental test is straightforward and simple. It consists of maximally three word types (CV, VC, and VCV) in which all existing (and reasonably frequent) initial, medial, and final consonants in a specific language are combined with the three vowels /i u a/ (SAMPA). This word material has been used in several languages (English, German, Swedish,

Dutch) to evaluate the segmental intelligibility of a number of different rule synthesisers. Despite its relative simplicity of design, the results have proved to be very useful, informative, and diagnostic. So far no rule synthesiser is capable of achieving a 100% correct score.

## 3.2 Suprasegmental Assessment

The importance of word-intelligibility at the sentence level is in regard to the fuller information it provides on a wider range of contextual effects. These are key factors in overall intelligibility, and deficiencies in this area of synthesis probably contribute to the reduced comprehension of synthesised messages in noise. In order to test word intelligibility in sentence context it was clear that the project should choose several different grammatical structures, but no fixed test material. This led to the development of semantically unpredictable sentences, or SUS. Five different grammatical structures and word lists are defined for the initial eight languages of the consortium to permit the generation of an unlimited number of test sentences. These represent the most common structures in the languages concerned with the necessary restriction to not more than about seven words per sentence (because of memory limitations of the listener in reproducing the sentence heard). The use of 'number of sentences correct' is proposed as the basic score. The word score might potentially be more accurate, but is strongly related to the sentence score anyway and requires far more complicated response storage and scoring facilities. The SUS test material has already found wide acceptance outside ESPRIT and has been successfully used in several languages. It has been recommended to the ITU; the National Bureau for French Standards AFNOR has also shown an interest in this approach.

## 3.3 Prosody assessment

Although the SUS-sentences might themselves present a possibility to evaluate the prosodic capabilities of a synthesiser at the sentence-type level, the project has adopted a more basic approach. A first proposal has been formulated and a suite of tests has been investigated in which both form and function of particular prosodic contours are judged in terms of naturalness and acceptability. If, for instance, the slope of a falling contour is too shallow, this should become apparent from a test on prosodic *form*. The appropriateness, however, of such a contour in a given semantic/pragmatic context, or its success in signalling morphological and syntactic functions by intonational means, would result from *functional* tests. Both form tests, using mono- and multi-syllabic words in English and Italian in which the monotone version is used as a reference, and prosodic function tests have taken place. Tests have been performed in collaboration with the ESPRIT SUNDIAL project, in which human-machine dialogue situations are created, and the appropriateness to context of different prosodic contours is judged. The SESAM workstation and the SOAP software have been used for these tests.

Work performed in the SAM-A project has investigated prosody in text-to-speech systems operating in interactive situations. The effects of different groups of speakers (interactive listeners, naive listeners and experts) and different categories of speech material were tested in two separate laboratories. A methodological study of assessment has been pursued using a modified MOS technique never previously applied in SAM although often used in several standardisation commissions for the assessment of natural or artificial voice. Of the various methodologies that were considered, the use of MOS offered significant experimental advantages. It proved to perform consistently among the three groups of listeners and two separate laboratories. The experiments have shown that the methodology can offer a simple and valid means to assess overall speech output quality in an interactive situation, but it seems to be not particularly suitable for diagnostically assessing specific prosodic cues of speech when only one voice is being evaluated.

## 3.4 Overall quality assessment

Right from the very beginning of the project, overall quality assessment has been approached in a very systematic way with many specific experiments. Several methods, such as magnitude estimation, categorical estimation, paired comparison, and reaction time measurements, have been compared. Within each method several variables have been studied, such as scale size, whether an external or internal reference is used, and scale terminology. The experiments have been carried out for several languages (French, Swedish, Italian, and Dutch) and with a number of different synthesisers, including natural speech and masked conditions. Some work has additionally been performed on comprehension of natural and synthetic speech in Italian. Different subject groups, in terms of experience, amount of training, or hearing impairment have been used. Finally the response means have been varied, from using scoring forms, and keyboard input, to line segment control on a video screen. The objective has been to find one or a few methods, that

- provide for the best inter-laboratory and inter-language agreement
- have excellent test-retest reliability
- have the highest validity
- are sensitive and efficient
- are least subject to various stimulus context effects
- have learning effects that could be controlled

Present recommendations imply two scaling methods: A magnitude estimation procedure where the subject adjusts the length of a line segment on a computer screen to match his judgement, as well as a 20-point categorical estimation procedure. Reaction time may not measure quality per se but intelligibility or other factors such as processing load, and it is therefore suggested to explore this measure as an index of communication difficulty.

## 3.5 Analytic assessment

Although the human listener is the ultimate judge of the quality of the speech produced by a rule synthesiser, acquiring these subjective judgements for each new condition is very laborious and time consuming. There is a strong desire to simplify and automate these measurements. There is also a potentially very beneficial point in this approach: it can be analytic and predictive. In analogy to the objective (physical) measures sometimes used in evaluating speech communication channels (such as the articulation index AI or the speech transmission index STI), SAM has studied the possibilities for doing something similar for the objective evaluation of the quality of synthetic speech. However, there are several complicating factors: firstly there is no unique, best, reference realisation for each word or sentence, and secondly not only are the acoustic characteristics of the speech signal important, but also text preprocessing and linguistic realisation in determining the final speech quality

So far several overall characteristics of synthetic speech have been compared with those for natural speech, from one or more speakers and languages. These overall characteristics have been based on F0 and pause distributions, long-term average spectra and its variation over time, and correlation patterns reflecting the statistics of the dynamics of speech in the frequency and in the time domain. The level up to which these measures actually define the naturalness of speech is still a widely open point for research.

## 3.6 Listener variability and listener dimensions

In most subjective evaluation tests several listeners are used to acquire statistically reliable results. The variability between listeners is then ‘averaged out’, although it might contain systematic effects, for example if individual behaviour were predictable (from psycho-acoustic and/or audiometric tests), if it were consistent over various tests (from phoneme intelligibility to prosodic adequacy judgements), if training had not been consistent, or if certain listeners were more sensitive to specific speech deficiencies than others. The standard segmental test (with CV, VC, and VCV) was used to collect individual data in several languages. Results have been collected from 60 listeners on several types of sentences and VCVs for synthetic and natural speech in quiet and in noise. These results provide a basis for a quantification of listener variability and specification of listener dimensions.

## 3.7 Speech Output Assessment Software

### Speech Output Assessment Package (SOAP)

A system has been implemented on the SESAM workstation to support the automatic assessment of synthesisers using the standard tests developed on the project. The present form of this system, called SOAP, uses a modular architecture where the separate modules are linked by user-accessible ASCII files. This enabled a flexible system to be produced by several partners working simultaneously. At the centre of SOAP is the test module, which prompts the listener to listen to synthetic speech and make a response in an appropriate manner. These results are then processed and scored. The test modules supplied with SOAP offer an extensive variety of methods by which to collect the listener's response, and this allows the implementation of a variety of test protocols. These are illustrated diagrammatically in Fig 2. The four levels of testing, presently implemented in SOAP are: segmental, suprasegmental, prosodic, and overall quality. These are each described in the following paragraphs.

The segmental test software controls the playing of sampled synthetic speech tokens in a sequence determined by a definable test file. The subject responds using the keyboard or a mouse-driven graphical interface, and these responses are stored together with details describing the test. Keyboard responses (which permit the subject to enter almost any characters) may be transcribed into an unambiguous SAMPA form which is listener-independent, using a pre-processing module which applies a SAM-defined protocol. Processed keyboard responses and responses from the mouse/screen interface can then be automatically scored using a module for segmental scoring which produces percentage scores, confusion matrices, feature matrices and scores weighted by frequency of occurrence. The analysis can be performed in terms of certain types of phonetic feature (e.g. place of articulation and voicing), and the effect of vowel environment together with other statistics. The SOAP system has been used in commercial evaluation at the segmental level.

Suprasegmental tests using sentence material have been implemented on SOAP however responses have to be scored by hand since the complexity of interpreting sentence length responses makes automatic procedures inappropriate. A user-friendly program SUSGEN was developed to generate the SUS sentences in several different languages. Five different grammatical structures and word lists are defined for the initial eight languages of the

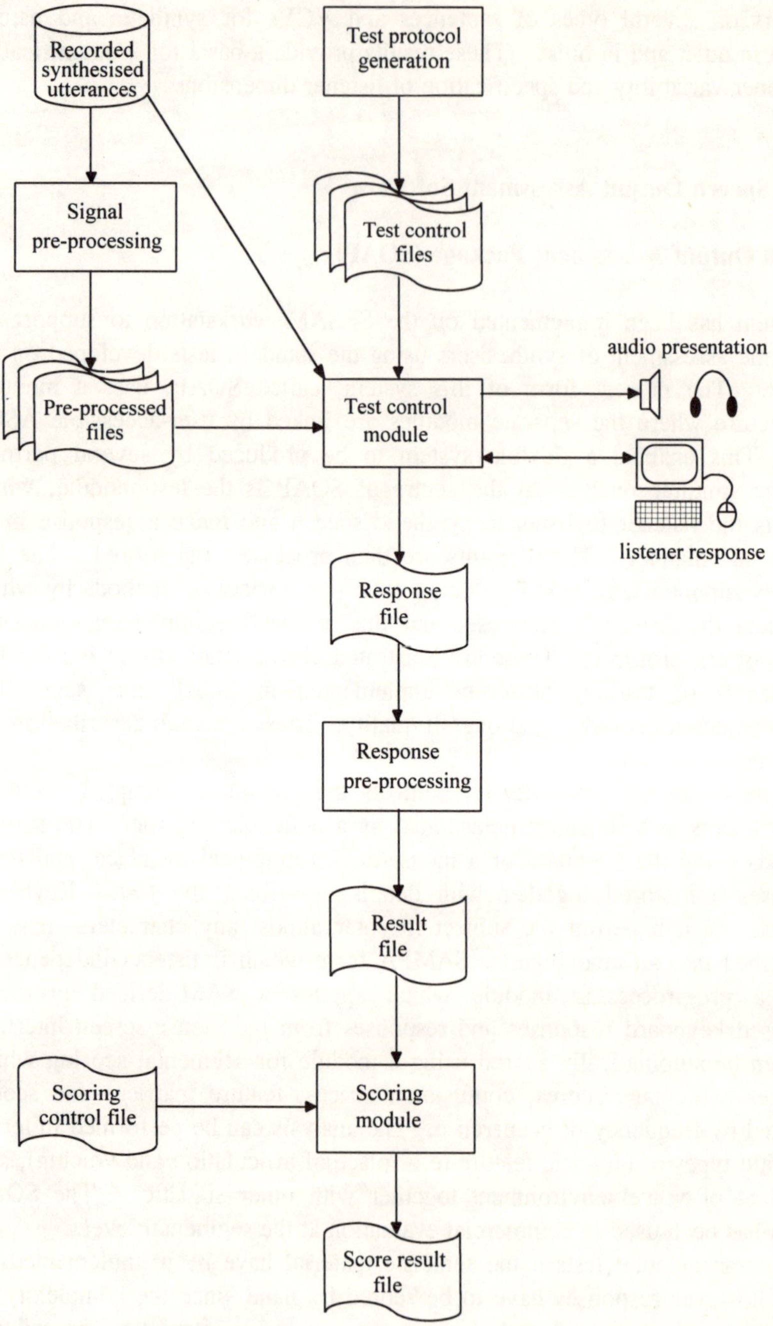


**Fig 2:** Block diagram of SOAP synthesis assessment software package implemented on the SESAM workstation

consortium to permit the generation of an unlimited number of test sentences. These represent the most common structures in the languages concerned.

Protocols for assessing the prosodic quality of synthetic speech have been implemented on SOAP, together with automatic scoring of responses to give geometric means of the results in terms of synthesiser, intonation pattern, etc. Prosodic testing has been carried out by the ESPRIT SUNDIAL project using the SOAP system.

Four methods of psychophysical scaling of global quality are available on SOAP. Interactive screen graphics allows categorical scaling using 10 and 20 point scale, magnitude estimation by free numbers and by line length. Automatic scoring of results to give the overall geometric mean score associated with each synthesiser is provided. Eight lists of twenty sentences (adapted from the read sentences on EUROM 1) are provided in all languages of the consortia.

A variety of utility programs have also been written for SOAP. These include programs to add noise to speech files, to automatically generate test sequences, to randomise test sequences and to equalise speech levels. The system comes with demonstrations that illustrate SAM protocols and with complete documentation (contained in the SAM User Guide to Speech Output Assessment [9]). Modification of SOAP to run intelligibility tests, with synthetic speech produced on-line instead of via stored speech files, could easily be accommodated.

**Parametric Test Manager (PTM)**

Following the experience with the SOAP package, a software tool has been developed during the SAM-A project to provide facilities for those who wish to run generalised speech assessment tests without being restricted to pre-defined test conditions. The Parametric Test Manager (PTM) features an integrated design which permits all aspects of the definition, execution and analysis of the tests to be managed and performed within the package using a unified software structure and user-interface. In order to be able to deal with a wide variety of test methods and speech material the software has been functionally designed with a high degree of flexibility and makes use of careful structuring of data and methods to implement the tests. The use of object-oriented approaches and a standard graphical user interface are at the heart of the implementation. The functional architecture is shown in Fig. 3 where a database system forms the kernel of the system and manages all the data required by different applications, including subject descriptions, test definitions and responses.

PTM applications are divided into four classes: data maintenance, test management, sub-system software and tools. Data maintenance applications provide an interactive access to the database, for data acquisition, input, editing and manipulation, e.g. for input of symbolic (linguistic) stimuli data and their appropriate test-set groupings. Test management applications handle test definition (involving selection of the desired stimuli and subjects) and test execution (stimulus presentation and recording of responses). Sub-system software includes all driver software to provide access to video and audio hardware. Finally auxiliary applications are provided e.g. to simplify importing large amounts of data. At present the system implements assessment using categorical estimation, but other tests can be readily implemented as a result of its general architecture.

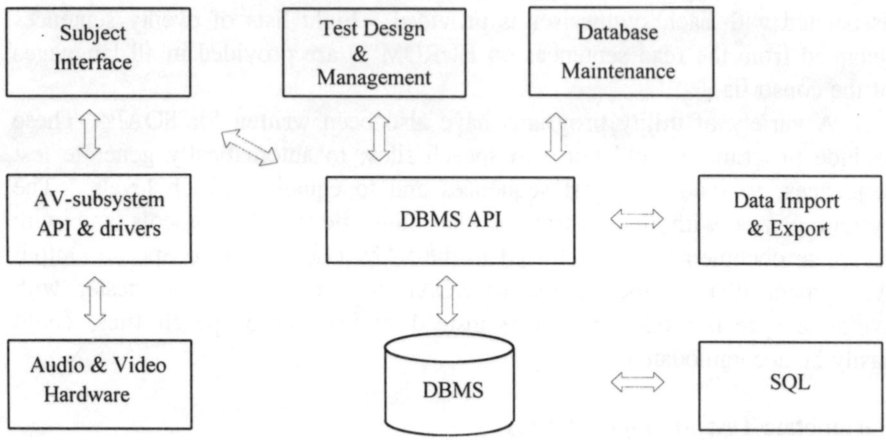


**Fig. 3:** PTM software architecture overview

## 4 Enabling technology and research

The third area of activity in the SAM project, ETR, was designed to give infrastructure support to work in both input and output assessment by the provision of basic tools, corpora and speech knowledge. Its primary tasks involved: data collection, management, labelling; the development of linguistic tools; and the coherent development within the project of the core workstation SESAM. SESAM, has been specified and implemented both for input and output assessment and evaluation, and also for data collection following standard protocols, database management, and speech signal labelling. A phonemic notational system for all European languages, SAMPA, has been developed and is in use both for manual labelling and, currently, for semi-automatic label alignment. Phonemic level structural constraints across the languages of the project have been compiled and are used in corpus definition. Broader descriptors have also been investigated for multi-lingual application. Other, physical, levels of description are being quantified as a contribution to analytic methods of assessment and information on cross-language lexica has been compiled.

## 4.1 SESAM Workstation

At the very beginning of the SAM Project, the need to ensure a practical basis for ready collaboration between so many different laboratories in different countries was met by the definition of a standard reference workstation. SESAM was originally conceived as a common tool at most giving limited test-bed facilities and acting as interface in networking with more practical, more powerful, mainframes. It has emerged, however, both as a means of fulfilling these reference facilities and as a workstation in its own right. It has been adopted as a common tool within the SAM laboratories, and used increasingly in other European projects and programmes as well as a bridge between US and EU speech standards. SAM software ('CONVERT') has been incorporated into some DARPA CD-ROMs so that American speech material can be used on SESAM in the same way as SAM-standard files.

The minimum hardware requirements for SESAM defined early in the project to support all software were an IBM PC-AT or compatible computer using DOS V3.0, an analogue interface board (OROS AU21 or AU22), 1 Mbyte of extended memory, 20 Mbyte hard disk, and means for accessing recorded speech data (e.g. CD-ROM reader). This constituted the 'low-level SESAM'. Improvements in personal computing have resulted in more powerful implementations, typically 386 or 486 processors, RAM size of 2 or 4 Mbytes, hard disk sizes of 100 Mbytes or greater, and VGA graphic display, which constitute the standard SESAM configuration suitable for running nearly all SAM software. The ready availability of such systems in most labs ensures that SAM tools can be applied widely. Mass storage devices are essential for speech corpus collection and interchange activities, and standards were agreed for the latter. While CD-ROM has been considered the best choice for archival and transmission of completed databases, intermediate requirements have been served using Exabyte tape though DAT systems are proposed as the preferred technical solution. These specifications and related developments are detailed in the SAM User Guide to Enabling Tools [10].

Recent work on the SAM-A project has reviewed the requirements and capabilities of the SESAM workstation specification, in particular with regard to alternative audio boards and operating systems, including Microsoft Windows and Windows/NT. It was concluded that the SESAM specification based on DOS and the OROS AU21/22 speech interface board were sufficient for most existing tools, however a restructured speech output assessment tool

(PTM) was developed within the project to take advantage of the flexibility and standardisation offered by the Windows Multimedia environment. An upgraded definition of requirements, including the option of digital speech output, has been derived and specified in the most recent project documentation as a basis for future software developments.

## 4.2 Standard workstation tools

Hardware and software specifications were defined and widely applied in regard, for example, to the structure and code normalisation of software; the formatting of data and organisation of databases; and the provision of interfaces. A baseline document was produced to define software production standards with Microsoft C specified as the standard programming language. All software was designed to be modular in function, and to allow inter-communication via standardised ASCII files offering maximum flexibility for development, use and exchange. Speech sample files have been standardised as a header-less binary file containing 16 bit speech data only, and an associated description file containing recording conditions, speaker characteristics, orthographic transcription and other information in ASCII. Label files have also been defined to support the associated transcription requirements at different levels of phonetic resolution. Standard filename recommendations are provided. These recommendations define a base set of European conventions for organisation and exchange of speech data which can be universally applied without limitation in regard to the diversity of existing systems or foreseen advances in computing technology.

Three software packages provide key support facilities to the use of the workstation within the project. These are illustrated in Fig. 4. The first is EUROPEC, which is designed to provide for the realisation of large speech databases. Two-channel acquisition (e.g. for microphone and laryngograph signals) and monitoring is possible which may be manually controlled or automatically triggered as a function of signal level, with visual prompting for the speaker. Automatic end-point detection facilitates the handling and recording of large organised corpora. This is also substantially assisted by the automatic inclusion in the database of description text files in standard form with header and body, so that the orthographic prompt can be routinely incorporated together with complete sessional and recording item and condition information. In addition complementary utility programs provide support in corpus integration and management.

The second important package, PTS, is designed to display and handle speech signals, related contexts and annotations, and can be used with data acquired via EUROPEC. Its primary function is to enable the labelling of speech data files with either SAMPA (see below) or IPA notations, using window-based displays of waveform and spectrograms of the signal. A range of manipulation functions has been incorporated for viewing and editing (e.g. cut, paste, copy, save), measurement, monitoring and saving both signal and label files. The software is available in two versions, one running on standard configurations of SESAM, and a second which provides increased capabilities but requires a DOS/16M extender card.

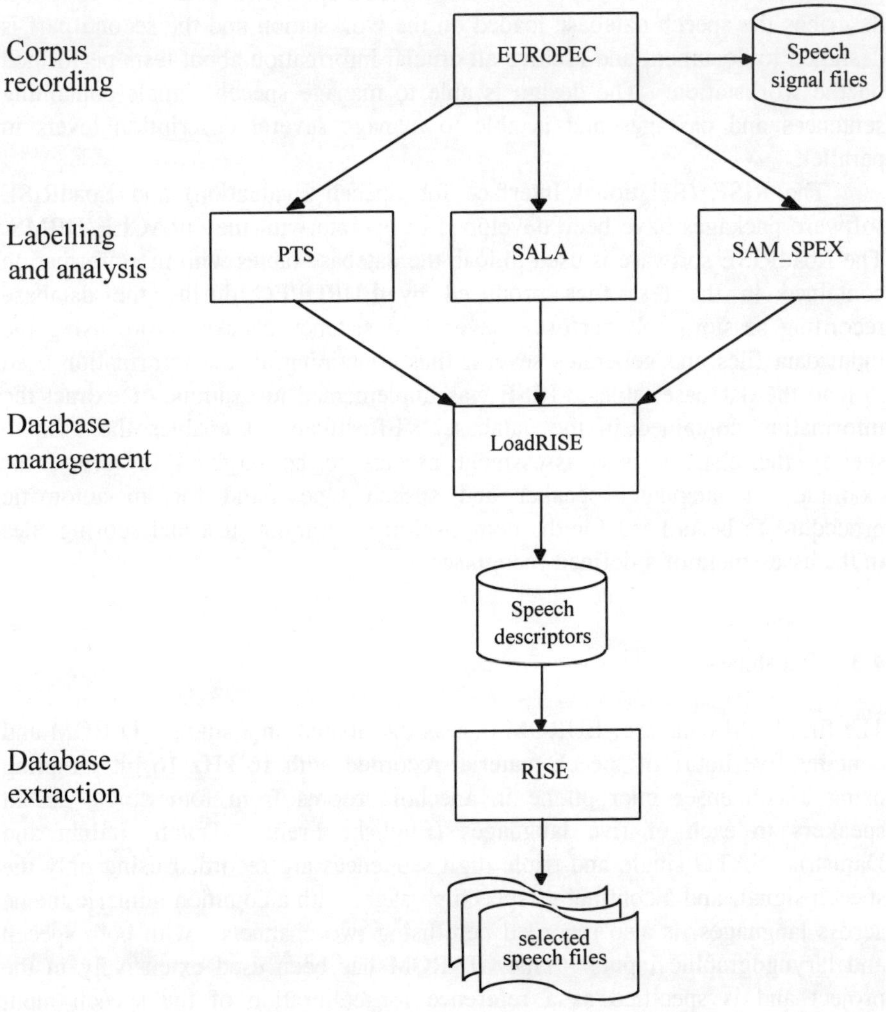


**Fig 4:** Block diagram of software packages used in corpus creation implemented on the SESAM workstation

The third centrally important package is in regard to data management and is based on a commercially available relational DBMS (Database Management System), ORACLE. This has been chosen to cater for the major needs of data retrieval and data archiving for all languages and all speakers in the SAM project, based on performance comparisons of several systems undertaken during the Extension Phase. The data management structure has been designed to allow the integration of important characteristics of both present and future SAM speech databases and is in two parts: the first one describes the speech database loaded on the workstation and the second part is designed to document and archive all crucial information about tests performed on the workstation. The design is able to manage speech signals containing sentences and passages and is able to manage several description levels in parallel.

The RISE (Relational Interface for Speech Evaluation) and LoadRISE software packages have been developed to operate with the ORACLE DBMS. The LoadRISE software is used to load the database tables with the information contained in the text files produced by EUROPEC during the database recording sessions. It performs several consistency checks before using the input data files and generates several files containing all the information used to load the database tables. RISE was implemented to examine or extract the information contained in the database. Effectively, it enables the user to specify the characteristic assessment aspects to be targeted in terms, for example, of language, speaker and speech types, and for an automatic procedure to be utilised for the composition of training, test and scoring files in the assessment of a defined recogniser.

## 4.3 Databases

The first SAM database, EUROM 0, was distributed on a single CD-ROM and contains five hours of speech material recorded with 16 kHz 16 bit sampling using a condenser microphone in anechoic rooms from four single accent speakers in each of five languages (English, French, Dutch, Italian and Danish). NATO single and triple digit sequences are recorded using only the speech signal, and a continuous speech passage, with a common numeric theme across languages, is also recorded here using two channels - with both speech and laryngographic inputs. This CD-ROM has been used extensively in the project and is specified as a reference for calibration of the speech input assessment tools.

A second major data collection activity has resulted in the collection of a very substantial amount of data which is unique in the size and the breadth of its coverage of different European languages. The EUROM 1 database contains more than twelve hours of data for each of the eleven European languages covered: Danish, Dutch, English, French, German, Greek, Italian, Norwegian, Portuguese, Spanish and Swedish. The material is of high acoustic quality, and was selected specifically for use in the assessment of speech technology devices. The control software used in making the recordings provided for orthographic labelling of the data and alignment of the text and signal portions at the level of the prompt units. Phonotypical transcriptions have been made separately for all languages and broad phonetic labelling using SAMPA (SAM Phonetic Alphabet) has been applied to some parts of the database. Language subsets of EUROM 1 are now available on CD-ROM, and the provision of EU funding is planned to ensure availability of all recorded material of this important reference resource. A minimum of three CD-ROMs are planned for each language.

Very careful consideration was given to the homogeneity of the data across languages. This was achieved by the use of identical recording protocols, which were specified earlier in the project and applied using standard software tools, and by a careful definition of the speech content, such that each language was represented in the same way wherever possible. The speech (and calibration) recordings were made in acoustically treated rooms using calibrated condenser microphones and, in addition to the acoustic signal, larynx activity was recorded simultaneously, using a laryngograph, for samples of the speech in each language. The use of anechoic condenser microphone recordings permit the subsequent imposition of post-production effects. The recordings were made using the SAM agreed standard of 20 kHz 16 bit sampling to ensure optimal signal representation; inter-utterance acoustic background signals were also preserved. The protocols defined for collection of database materials have been developed to provide guidelines on recording procedures and quality criteria for use in the wider European Speech Community.

The database material specification for each language is as follows:

- C(C)VC(V) material in isolation and in context, in the range 60-100 items per language
- 100 selected numbers from 0 - 9999, providing complete coverage of the phonotactic possibilities of the language number system
- 40 short passages comprised of five thematically linked sentences
- 50 sentences composed to compensate for phonemic frequency imbalance in the passages
- 5 pairs of context words for use with C(C)VC(V) material

The database has been designed with a hierarchical structure to maximise its usefulness both for training and testing different types of speech technology device, as described in section 2.1, and for more basic research including inter-language comparisons. In each language, material was recorded by 60 subjects, 30 female and 30 male, each of whom recorded 100 numbers, 3 passages and 5 sentences. Of these a "few talker" subset of 5 females and 5 males made extended recordings: isolated C(C)VC(V) items, 500 numbers, 15 passages, 25 sentences. A further "very few talker" subset of one female and one male, selected from the 10, additionally recorded the contextualised C(C)VC(V)s and the 5 context words, using both acoustic and laryngographic signals. A total of 660 speakers thus recorded over 130 hours of data, making this a very substantial multi-lingual resource with many different applications.

## 4.4 SAMPA

The SAM Phonetic Alphabet (SAMPA), which defines a standard keyboard based notation (ASCII) corresponding to the relevant International Phonetic Association symbols for each of the languages represented in the project, was agreed very early in the project, and has now been extended to cover all the major European languages. As an *information interchange* code, SAMPA is defined as an ASCII encoding of a subset of the symbols of the International Phonetic Association; it is not intended to replace other encodings of the IPA, nor was it intended to be a substitute for the IPA. As a *phonetic representation system*, SAMPA is designed as a broad phonetic transcription alphabet to provide conventional symbols for representing the phonemes and their major variants in all languages dealt with in the SAM project; since the phoneme is a non-transferable language specific unit, phonetic values associated with the symbols vary somewhat from language to language. The basic SAM transcription system was originally intended to evolve as a multi-tier labelling tool and work has been directed towards the introduction of prosodic and acoustic element levels of description.

One of the tangible achievements of the SAM project has been the universal adoption of SAMPA in other ESPRIT projects and in all major speech laboratories in partner countries. It has been utilised in both the British and German national speech databases. This means that SAMPA has already become the *de facto* computer compatible representation system for the major Western European languages. This consensus for the representation of phonemic contrasts in all the languages of the group provides a common labelling basis for cross-comparison and for a structured multi-lingual approach to database specification in the development of standard methods of assessment and detailed evaluation.

## 4.5 Labelling

Multi-lingual labelling, in which phoneme categories are assigned to successive regions of the speech signal, has always been an important part of the SAM group's activity. This is because overall assessment, detailed evaluation and the processes of training themselves can most fundamentally be performed using accurate descriptions of speech given in phonetic and orthographic terms. So, although the precise assignment of discrete categories, for different sound classes, to the continuous speech signal is an impossible task - since the subjective level of segmental labelling is not compatible with any physical set of exact temporal stretches of the signal - their consistent correlation is of real value. The SESAM workstation is designed to support this work, and manual labelling in all the languages of the project has provided essential reference material. Transcription verification (consistency and normalisation checking) and statistical analysis (diphoneme distribution) software is available (SAMTRA).

A further development of this work involves semi-automatic label alignment (SALA) using several approaches (ELABSEG, DKI_SALA, SAPHO). In this way the larger quantities of speech material generated by current database gathering, and which are in need of labelling, can be accommodated without imposing an impossibly large manual labelling task - simply by using an ordinary transcription made without reference to signal details. This has been done for texts in Norwegian, French, Danish and English as an exercise across the whole of the SAM project. Automatic scoring software (ELSA) has been written and, although it is still necessary for an expert labeller to check the setting of the label time boundaries, this provides a common basis for evaluation.

In addition to the automatic labelling performed within EUROPEC, some broad phonetic labelling has been carried out on English continuous-speech recordings. Initially, this activity was combined with a trial of the semi-automatic labelling systems, using auditorily transcribed input strings. For this purpose, broad phonetic SAMPA transcriptions were produced for all the English Few Talker (FT) recordings of the 5-sentence passages. Examples of these are provided as part of the EUROM 1 Data Documentation [7]. Also, manual alignment of inter-pausal sections of the FT passage recordings was performed to define the segments required by the semi-automatic labelling systems. Manual labelling of the English FT passages was carried out in parallel with the trials in automatic alignment, but the demands on man-power of this labelling mode means that only nine recorded passages of one FT set were completed.

An extension of work on SAMPA and the growing need in the context of spoken language for linguistic knowledge and tools on prosody has led to the design of criteria for and a survey on prosodic labelling. This area is still in its infancy, and work in this area has stimulated international discussion and information interchange on the problem. Two of the substantive results in the area however deserve particular mention. First, concrete proposals have been made for the establishment of symbol inventories for prosodic labelling and discussed in some detail; it was considered premature to present any one of these as a standard at the present time. Two complementary proposals were put forward: SAMSINT, a purpose-designed system for transcription and spline interpolation based semi-automatic prosodic labelling, and SAMPROSA, a flexible general purpose set of prosodic transcription and labelling symbols, designed to allow selection of subsets covering level based, tonetic, and pitch accent oriented and other prosodic transcription conventions. Second, in collaboration with work in speech output evaluation at the suprasegmental and prosodic levels, a consistency test on prosodic transcription was conducted and demonstrated the value of the methods.

### 4.6 Speech and Language Material Complexity

The increasing development of databases and of detail in speech technology processing itself, leads to the need for the specification of speech and language material along additional dimensions to those discussed above. A set of dimensions for defining the linguistic properties of speech databases has been produced, based on a distinction between the notion of "system complexity" (of grammars, lexica, and processors) for phonetic and linguistic knowledge based constraints on database design, and the notion of "corpus complexity" for the *post hoc* analysis of existing databases. Work performed during the SAM project addresses some of these issues in regard to: the further collation of phonotactic information; the measurement of basic physical speech parameters (using SAM_SPEX for example) to tie in with the analytic procedures discussed above; the use of more representative speech; and the gathering of information on computer compatible lexica. Software for quantitative transcription based analysis of corpus complexity in terms of phonotactic constraints was developed (SAMTRA), and a qualitative classification system was developed and applied to the EUROM 0 database in terms of linguistic descriptors. A cross-linguistic investigation which may have fundamental application in the engineering of complete multi-lingual systems, comes from the further application within SAM of the tools developed for automatic label alignment. Here, phonetic feature search in databases coming from different speech/language sources than those used in the original training will provide a further means for the appraisal of language independent speech-specific dimensions.

## 5 Relationship with other projects and programmes

There have been a number of important interactions with projects, in EU programmes and elsewhere in the world. The ESPRIT ARS, SUNSTAR and SUNDIAL projects in particular have made significant use of SAM protocols and tools for assessment of both speech input and output systems, and have contributed to their development. Correlated activities in these projects resulted in helpful exchanges of information. Interactions with the NATO/RSG10 group were instrumental in the definition of the EUROM0, and also resulted directly in the production of the noise ROM. Contacts with the DARPA/NIST assessment activities have ensured that exchanges of relevant procedures, software and data have taken place. The EAGLES project (Expert Advisory Group in Linguistic Engineering Resources) has recently been formed to establish concensual modes of working in Europe with regard to resources and assessment, involving both natural and spoken language. One of the five working groups is devoted to spoken language methodology and resources and will extensively draw from the work of the SAM project. The activities of the SAM group have been directly instrumental in the formation of COCOSDA (International Committee for Co-operation in Speech Assessment and Databases) which aims to provide a focus for co-ordinated activities world-wide. Both of these latter initiatives receive support by the CEC through the LRE program.

## 6 Conclusion

Work in the SAM group was specifically oriented towards European needs, and has resulted in the implementation of standard tests, new testing procedures, and the development of standard controlled databases. SAM work has led to widely adopted de facto standards for the acquisition, formatting and multi-level annotation of multi-lingual spoken corpora, and to methods of system assessment and evaluation for the present generation of speech recognition and synthesis devices. The impact of its work however has extended beyond Europe itself, as evidenced by its influence on other related programmes, and in the recent establishment of working groups formed to encourage common approaches at an international level.

The SAM group has provided a concrete foundation for future European work in Spoken Language and has demonstrated that a specifically European concept is feasible. Beyond this, the group has provided systematic pointers for the development of future Spoken Language resources. Obvious immediate future needs, which increase the dimensionality of the resource development and assessment problems and need careful co-ordination, lie in the provision of Spoken Language databases for the assessment of more complex systems, for instance in respect of speaker and dialect range, multi-lingual applicability, cognitive content, dialogue structure and environment. The further development of assessment techniques themselves is necessary in order to provide analytic, user-related bases for performance quantification, explanation, and prediction to ensure further progress in research, development, and application in respect of Spoken Language resources. This work is dependent both upon the substantial national support provided by the individual partners and on the coherence coming from sustained funding of adequate programmes of research and technology application as have been, until recently, supported by the EU in the ESPRIT programme.

## 7 SAM resources

| | | |
|---|---|---|
| ARTCHAN | V1.0 | Mar 1994 |
| DKI_SALA | V1.1 | Mar 1992 |
| DPSCORE | V1.0 | Oct 1993 |
| ELSA | V2.4 | Dec 1990 |
| ELABSEG | V2.5 | Apr 1992 |
| EUROPEC | V4.11 | Sep 1991 |
| HENR | V2.0 | Oct 1993 |
| LOADRISE | V1.104 | Feb 1992 |
| PTM | V1.0 | Mar 1994 |
| PTS | V4.40 | Mar 1992 |
| RESAM | V1.1 | Nov 1991 |

| | | |
|---|---|---|
| RISE | V1.3 | Jun 1991 |
| SAM_REC0 | V1.0 | Nov 1990 |
| SAM_REC1 | V2.0 | May 1992 |
| SAM_SCOR | V4.0 | Sep 1993 |
| SAM_SLM | V3.0 | Dec 1993 |
| SAM_SPEX | V2.0 | Feb 1992 |
| SAMITPRO | V1.1 | Mar 1992 |
| SAMPAC | V3.26 | Nov 1992 |
| SAMTRA | V1.0 | Jun 1991 |
| SAPHO | V2.0 | Dec 1990 |
| SOAP | V4.0 | Mar 1992 |

## 8 List of SAM and SAM-A partners

Denmark: Institute of Electronic Studies, Aalborg University; Jydsk Telefon
France: CNRS/GRECO (Aix, CERFIA, CRIN, ENST, ICP, LIMSI); VECSYS
Germany: Daimler-Benz; Bochum University; University of Bielefeld
Greece: University of Patras
Italy: CNR; CSELT; Fondazioni Ugo Bordoni
Netherlands; PTT-RNL; TNO; University of Amsterdam
Norway: ELAB, University of Trondheim
Portugal: INESC
Spain: Universitat Politecnica de Catalunya
Sweden; KTH; Telia Research AB
Switzerland: Institut Dalle Molle d'Intelligence Artificielle Perceptive
UK: Defence Research Agency (RSRE); Logica UK Ltd; National Physical Laboratory; Smiths Industries Aeronautics and Defence Systems; University College London; Vocalis Ltd

Further information can be obtained from the authors (email addresses: cocos@phonetics.ucl.ac.uk; richard@vocalis.demon.co.uk) or from these national institutions.

## 9 References

The activities of the projects have resulted in approximately 350 internal and external reports and publications. The most recent references should be consulted for the most up-to-date descriptions of project outputs. In particular the User Guides to Assessment contain both introductory material and detailed information required to implement and use the standard SAM tools and tests.

### SAM and SAM-A General Publications

1. ESPRIT 1541 (SAM) Fourcin, A.J., Harland, G., Barry, W. and Hazan, V., "Speech Input and Output Assessment", Ellis Horwood, 1989.
2. ESPRIT 1541 (SAM) Extension Phase Final Report. University College, London, February 1989
3. ESPRIT 2589 (SAM) "Support available from SAM project for other ESPRIT Speech and Language work", Ref. SAM-UCL-G001, University College, London, July 1989.
4. ESPRIT 2589 (SAM) Interim Report, Year 1, Ref. SAM-UCL-G002. University College, London, February 1990.
5. ESPRIT 2589 (SAM) Interim Report, Year 2. Ref. SAM-UCL-G003. University College, London, February 1991.
6. ESPRIT 2589 (SAM) Interim Report, Year 3. Ref. SAM-UCL-G004. University College, London, February 1992.
7. ESPRIT 2589 (SAM): "Guide to EUROM1 Speech Database", Ref. SAM-NPL-102, NPL, Teddington, March 1992.
8. ESPRIT 2589 (SAM): "User guide to input assessment", Ref. SAM-UCL-G005, University College, London, April 1992.
9. ESPRIT 2589 (SAM): "User guide to output assessment", Ref. SAM-UCL-G006, University College, London, April 1992.
10. ESPRIT 2589 (SAM): "User guide to ETR tools", Ref. SAM-UCL-G007, University College, London, April 1992.
11. ESPRIT 6819 (SAM-A): Periodic Progress Report, Year 1. Ref. SAM-A/G001. Vocalis Ltd, Cambridge, April 1993.
12. ESPRIT 6819 (SAM-A): Periodic Progress Report, Year 1. Ref. SAM-A/G002. Vocalis Ltd, Cambridge, October 1993.

**Input Group's External Reports**


13. Barry, W.J., "Critical parameters in the definition of speech recogniser performance", Proc. XII International Congress Phonetic Sciences, Aix-en-Provence 1991, Vol 5, pp 66-69.
14. Capman F. & Chollet G. "SAMREC0: a C30 based reference connected word recogniser for the evaluation of speech data bases.", ASA meeting, Baltimore, April 1990.
15. Chollet G. & Gagnoulet C. "On the evaluation of speech recognisers and data bases using a reference system.", IEEE ICASSP 1982.
16. Chollet G. "Reconnaissance automatique de la parole: evaluation des techniques et des systemes". Minis et Micros, No. 232, May 1985.
17. Chollet G. "Reference systems for speech recognition research, development and evaluation.",NATO-ASI, Bad Windsheim, July 1987.
18. Danielsen, S., "Standardisation of speech input assessment with the SAM ESPRIT project", Presented at Kobe, 1990, 6 Jan 1990.
19. Steeneken, H. & Geurtsen, F., Description of the RSG.10 Noise Database. Report IZF 1988-3 (1988), TNO Institute for Perception, Soesterberg.
20. Steeneken, H. & Geurtsen, F., "Description of the RSG10 noise database", 1 March 1988.
21. Steeneken, H., M. Tomlinson, J-L Gauvain, Assessment of two commercial recognisers with the SAM Workstation and EUROM 0 - Proceedings of ESCA Workshop Speech Input/Output Assessment and Speech Databases 6.7.1. Sept 1989 Noordwijkerhout.
22. Steeneken, H. & Van Velden, J., RAMOS-Recogniser Assessment by means of Manipulation of Speech. Proc. ESCA 1989-Paris: 316-319.
23. Steeneken, H. & Van Velden, J., Objective and diagnostic assessment of (isolated) word recognisers. IEEE Proc. ICASSP, Glasgow (1989), 540-543.
24. Steeneken, H. & Houtgast, T., "On the mutual dependency of octave-band-specific contributions to speech intelligibility", Presented at Eurospeech '91, 1 Sept 1991.
25. Steeneken, H., Quality Evolution of Speech Processing Systems, "Speech Analysis, Synthesis and Man-Machine Speech Communications for Air Operations", Kluwer Norwell, 1991.
26. van Velden, J. & Smoorenburg, G., "Vowel Recognition in Noise for Male, Female and Child Voices", Presented at ICASSP 91 53, 1 June 1991.

27. Winski, R. & Kordi, K., "Assessment of continuous speech recognisers using recogniser sensitivity analysis", Proc. Eurospeech '91, Genoa, Vol. 2, pp 521-524.

**SAM Output Group's External Reports**

28. Barry, W.J., Grice, M., Hazan, V. & Fourcin, A.J., "Excitation distributions for synthesised speech", J.P. Tubach & J.J. Mariani (eds) Eurospeech '89, Vol 1, Proc. European Conference on Speech Communication and Technology, Paris. Edinburgh: CEP Consultants, 1989, pp 353-356.
29. Benoit, C., "Intelligibility test for the assessment of French synthesisers using Semantically Unpredictable Sentences", Proc. ETRW on Speech I/O Assessment and Speech Databases, Noorwijkerhout, Holland, pp 171-174 (1989).
30. Benoit, C., "Variabilite de l'intelligibilite d'un synthesiseur de parole par diphones", Proc. "Variabilite et Specificite du locuteur, Societe Francaise d'Acoustique, Marseille-Luminy, pp 164-169 (1989).
31. Benoit, C., "An intelligibility test using Semantically Unpredictable Sentence: Towards the quantification of linguistic complexity", Speech Communications 9, pp 293-304 (1990).
32. Benoit, C., "Dix listes phonetiquement equilibrees de dix phrases semantiquement impredictibles", Journal d'Acoustique 3, pp 69-74 (1990).
33. Benoit, C., "On the assessment of audio-visual speech synthesis", Proc. Workshop on International Cooperation and Standardisation of Speech Databases and Speech I/O Assessment Methods, Chiavari, Italy (1991).
34. Benoit, C. & Pols, L., "On the assessment of synthetic speech", Talking Machines: Theories, Models and Design, G.Bailly, C. Benoit Eds, Elsevier North-Holland, pp 439-446 (1992).
35. Benoit, C. Boyer, M., Emerard, F. & Hamon, C., "Comparaison de qualite subjective de trois synthesiseurs de parole", Proc. 16th JEP of the SFA, Hammamet, Tunisia, pp 310-313 (1987).
36. Benoit, C., Chanard, C., Rissoan, V. & Tchagbale, Z., "Intelligibilite comparee du francais de France et d'Abidjan", Actes des 19 Jounees d'Etude sur la Parole, Bruxelles, May 1992 (In SAM-UCL-G004, Appendix II.f).
37. Benoit, C., van Erp, A., Hazan, V. & Jekosch, U., "Multi-lingual synthesiser assessment using Semantically Unpredictable Sentences", Proc. Eurospeech '89 Conf., Paris, pp 633-636.
38. Bezooijen, R. van & Pols, L.C.W. (1990), "Evaluating text-to-speech systems: Some methodological aspects", Speech Communication 9(4), 263-270.

39. Carlson, R., Granstrom, B. & Hunnicutt, S., "Multi-lingual text-to-speech development and applications", Advances in speech, hearing and language processing, A.W. Ainsworth (ed), JAI Press London (1990).
40. Carlson, R., Granstrom, B. & Nord, L., "Evaluation and development of the KTH text-to-speech system on the segmental level", Speech Communication, Vol.9, pp 271-277 (1990).
41. Carlson, R., Granstrom, B. & Nord, L., "Segmental intelligibility of synthetic and natural speech in real and nonsense words", Proc. International Conference on Spoken Language Processing, Nov 1990, Kobe, Japan.
42. Carlson, R., Granstrom, B. & Nord, L., "Segmental evaluation using the ESPRIT/SAM test procedures and mono-syllabic words", Talking Machines: Theories, Models and Applications (G. Bailly & C. Benoit eds), June 1990.
43. Delogu, C., Paoloni, A. & Pocci, P., "Quality evaluation experiments of Italian speech synthesisers", Proc. ECCE-5 Fifth European Conference on Cognitive Ergonomics, Urbino, Italy, Sept 1990.
44. Delogu, C., Paoloni, A. & Pocci, P., "Applicazione della "Magnitude Estimation" come guidizio di qualite de segnale vocale sintetizzato", Proc. AIA-91 Associazione Italiana di Acustica, Napoli April 1991.
45. Delogu, C., Paoloni, A. & Pocci, P., "New directions in the evaluation of voice input/output systems", IEEE Journal on selected areas in Communications Vol.9, No.4 May 1991.
46. Fourcin, A.J., "Assessment of synthetic speech", Talking Machines: Theories, Models and Design, G. Bailly, C. Benoit Eds, Elsevier North-Holland, pp 431-434, Jan 1992.
47. Granstrom, B., "The use of speech synthesis in exploring different speaking styles", Proc. ESCA Workshop on the Phonetics and Phonology of Speaking Styles: Reduction and Elaboration in Speech Communication, Barcelona, Oct 1991.
48. Granstrom, B. & Nord, L., "Neglected dimensions in speech synthesis", Proc. ESCA Workshop on the Phonetics and Phonology of Speaking Styles: Reduction and Elaboration in Speech Communication, Barcelona, Oct 1991, 1 Jan 1991.
49. Granstrom, B. & Nord, L., "Ways of exploring speaker characteristics and speaking styles", XIIth International Congress of Phonetic Sciences, Aix-en-Provence, Aug 1991.
50. Grice, M., "Syntactic structures and lexicon requirements for Semantically Unpredictable Sentences in a number of languages", Proc. ETRW on Speech I/O Assessment and Speech Databases, Noordwijkerhout, Holland, pp 171-174 (1989).

51. Hazan, V. & Grice, M., "The assessment of synthetic speech intelligibility using Semantically Unpredictable Sentences", Proc. ETRW on Speech I/O Assessment and Speech Databases, Noordwijkerhout, Holland, pp 171-174.
52. Hegehofer, T., Jekosch, U. & Holstein, D., "Beurteilungen des Natuerlichkeitsgrads synthetischer Sprache mit semantisch anormalen Satzen", Proc. DAGA '91, Bochum.
53. Jekosch, U., "Maschinelle Phonem-Graphem-Umsetzung fur unbegrenzten deutschen Wortschatz", Published by Herne, July 1989.
54. Jekosch, U., "The cluster-based rhyme test: A segmental synthesis test for open vocabulary", Proc. ESCA Tutorial Day and Workshop on Speech Input/Output Assessment and Speech Databases, Noordwijkerhout, pp 1.4.1-1.4.4. (1989).
55. Jekosch, U., "A weighted intelligibility measure for speech assessment", Proc. ICSLP '90, Kobe, Vol 2. pp 973-6.
56. Jekosch, U. & Belhoula, A., "Rechnergestuetzte Generierung von Testmaterialien zur Sprachguetebeurteilung", Proc. DAGA '91, Bochum.
57. Jekosch, U., Belhoula, A., Hegehofer, T. & Marianak, A., "Verwendung von sinnleeren Woerten und -texten zur Sprachguetebeurteilung", Proc. DAGA '91, Bochum.
58. Mariniak, A., Jekosch, U., Belhoula, A. & Maris, C., "Ein spektrales Aehnlichkeitsmal als Hilfsmittel fur objektive Verfahren zur Sprachguetemesssung", Proc. DAGA '91, Bochum.
59. Pavlovic, C., "Derivation of primary parameters and procedures for use in speech intelligibility predictions", J. Acoust.Soc.Am. 82, pp 413-422 (1987), 1 Jan 1987.
60. Pavlovic, C.V., Rossi, M. & Espesser, R. (1990), "Use of the magnitude estimation technique for assessing the performance of text-to-speech synthesis systems", J. Acoust. Soc. Amer. 87(1), 373-382.
61. Pavlovic, C., Rossi, M. & Espesser, R., "A pilot study on the possibility of using the ESNR method for assessing text-to-speech synthesis systems", 1 Jan 1989.
62. Pavlovic, C., Rossi, M. & Espesser, R., "Methods for reducing context effects in the subjective assessment of synthetic speech", Proc. XIIth ICPhS Vol 3 82-85, 20 July 1991.
63. Pavlovic, C., Sorin, C., Roumiguiere, J.P. & Lucas, J.P., "Cross validation between a magnitude estimation technique and a pair comparisons technique for assessing quality of text-to-speech synthesis systems", J.d'Acoustique 3, pp 75-83 (1990).
64. Pavlovic, C.V., Rossi, M. & Espesser, R., "Use of the magnitude estimation technique for assessing the performance of text-to-speech synthesis systems", J.Acoust. Soc. Amer. 87(1) pp 373-382 (1990).

65. Pols, L., ""Standardised synthesis evaluation methods", Proc. International Workshop on International Coordination and Standardisation of Speech Database and Assessment Techniques for Speech Input/Output, Kobe, pp 53-60 (1990).
66. Pols, L., "Assessing the speech quality of text-to-speech synthesisers", Proc. VERBA-90, International Conference on Speech Technology, Rome, pp 295-302 (1990).
67. Pols, L., "Does improved performance also contribute to more phonetic knowledge?", Proc. ESCA Tutorial Day on Speech Synthesis, Autrans, pp 49-54 (1990).
68. Pols, L., "Guest editor of special issue on Speech Input/Output Assessment and Speech Databases", Speech Communication 9 (4) pp 263-388; Editorial/Biography, v-vi,(1990).
69. Pols, L., "Improving synthetic speech quality by systematic evaluation", Recent Research toward Advanced Man-Machine Interface through Spoken Language, H.Fujisaki (ed), Tokyo, pp 445-453, (1990).
70. Pols, L., "Evaluating the performance of speech technology systems", Inst. of Phonetic Sciences Proc. 15, pp 27-41, (1991).
71. Pols, L., "Gaining phonetic knowledge whilst improving synthetic speech quality?", J.Phon 19 (1), pp 139-146 (1991).
72. Pols, L., "Quality assessment of text-to-speech synthesis-by-rule", Advances in Speech Signal Processing, S. Furui & M.M. Sondhi (eds), Marcel Dekker Inc., Chapter 13, pp 387-416, (1991).
73. Pols, L., "Speech perception in the next ten years: Technological solutions vs. acquiring actual speech knowledge", Proc. XIIth International Congress of Phonetic Sciences, Aix-en-Provence, France, Aug 19-24, Vol. 1, pp 130-133, (1991).
74. Pols, L., "Evaluating the performance of speech input/output systems - a report on the ESPRIT-SAM project", Proc. DAGA '91, Bochum, pp 139-150 (1991).
75. Pols, L.C.W. (1990), "Assessing the speech quality of text-to-speech synthesizers", Proceedings VERBA-90, International Conference on Speech Technology, Rome, 295-302.
76. Pols, L.C.W. (1990), "How useful are speech databases for rule synthesis development and assessment?", Proceedings Int. Conf. Spoken Language Processing ICSLP 90, Kobe, Vol. 2, 1289-1292.
77. Pols, L.C.W. and SAM partners. (1992) "Multi-lingual synthesis evaluation methods", in Proceedings of ICSLP 92 (Banff, Canada), pp 181 - 184.
78. Rossi, M., "Peut-on predire l'organisation prosodique du langage spontane?" (1988)

79. Rossi, M., Espesser, R. & Pavlovic, C., "The effects of internal reference system and cross-modality matching on the subjective rating of speech synthesisers", Proc. Eurospeech '91 273-276, 1 Sept (1991)
80. Santi, S & Grenie, M, "Individual strategies in synthetic speech evaluation", Proceedings ESCAM Workshop Autrans 25/9/90 pp 265-268, (1991).
81. Studebaker, G.A., Pavlovic, C. & Sherbecoe, R.L., "A frequency importance function for continuous discourse", J. Acoust.Soc.Am. 81 1130-1138 (1987).
82. van Bezooijen, R. & Pols, L., "Evaluation of a sentence accentuation algorithm for a Dutch text-to-speech system", Proc. Eurospeech '89, Vol. 1, pp 218-221 (1989).
83. van Bezooijen, R. & Pols, L., "Evaluation of text-to-speech conversion for Dutch: From segment to text", Proc. ESCA Workshop on Speech Input/Output Assessment and Speech Databases, 3,4.1-3.4.4 (1989).
84. van Bezooijen, R. & Pols., "Evaluation text-to-speech systems: Some methodological aspects", Speech Communication 9 (4), pp 263-270 (1990).
85. van Bezooijen, R. & Pols, L., "Evaluation of allophone and diphone based text-to-speech conversion at the paragraph level", Proc. XIIth International Congress of Phonetic Sciences, Aix-en-Provence, France, Aug 19-24, Vol.3, pp 498-501 (1991).
86. van Bezooijen, R. & Pols, L., "Performance of text-to-speech conversion for Dutch: A comparative evaluation of allophone and diphone based synthesis at the level of the segment, the word and the paragraph", Proc. Eurospeech '91, Genova, Vol. 2, pp 871-874.

**SAM ETR Group's External Reports**

87. Andersen, O., Cosi, P. & Dalsgaard, P., "A SONN-based architecture for automatic speech segmentation and alignment", Proc. Primo Workshop Italiano su "Le Reti Neuroniche per il Trattamento del Parlato", Fondazione Ugo Bordoni, Rome, Nov 1990.
88. Autesserre, D., Perennou, G. & Rossi, M., "Methodology for the transcription and labelling of a speech corpus", Journal of the International Phonetic Association, (1989) 19 (1), 2-15.
89. Baekgaard, A. & Dalsgaard, P., "A tool for designing dialogues in speech understanding interfaces", Proc. ICSLP '90, Kobe.
90. Barry, W.J., Hazan, V. & Fourcin, A.J., "Speech technology assessment in Europe and the UK Proceedings of Speech-Tech '88, New York", New York: Media Dimensions Inc. pp 260-262 (1988).
91. Barry, W.J. & Fourcin, A.J., "Levels of labelling", Computer Speech and Language 6, pp 1-14 (1992).

92. Barry, W.J., Goldsmith, M., Fourcin, A. & Fuller, H., "Larynx analyses of normative reference data", 1 June 1990.
93. Barry, W.J., Goldsmith, M.J., Fourcin, A.J. & Fuller, H.C., "Stability of voice frequency measures in speech", Proc. XIIth International Congress of Phonetic Sciences '91, Vol.5, pp 38-41.
94. Bourjot, C., Boyer, A, Fohr, D. and Haton, J-P., "Tools for phonetic labelling and phonetic assessment", Proc. Workshop on Speech Input/Output Assessment and Database Management, Leeuwenhorst (Netherlands, Sept 1989.
95. Bourjot, C., Boyer, A. & Fohr, D., "Phonetic decoder assessment", Proc. Workshop on Speech Input/Output Assessment and Database Management, Leeuwenhorst (Netherlands), Sept 1989, 1 Jan 1989.
96. Bourjot, C., Boyer, A., Fohr, D. & Haton, J-P., "Methodologies pour l'evaluation phonetique", Proc. 18emes Journees d'Etudes sur la Parole, Montreal, May 1990, 1 May 1990.
97. Caerou, J-C., Dolmazon, J-M & Lunati, J-M, "SESAM - A low cost workstation for speech assessment", Proc. of ESCA Workshop on Speech Input/Output Assessment and Speech Databases Noorwijkerhout Sept 1989, 1 Sept 1989.
98. Cosi, P., Falavigna, D. and Omologo, M., "A preliminary statistical evaluation of manual and automatic segmentation discrepancies", 177, 1 June 1991.
99. Dalsgaard, P., "Phoneme label alignment using acoustic-phonetic features and Gausian probability density functions", To be published in Computer Speech and Language, Academic Press, Hartcourt Brace, Jovanovich Publishers, 1 Jan 1992.
100. Dalsgaard, P. & Barry, W.J., "Acoustic-phonetic features in the framework of neural network multi-lingual label alignment", Proc. International Conference on Spoken Language Processing, Nov 1990, Kobe, pp 945-948, 18 Nov 1990.
101. Dalsgaard, P., Andersen, O. & Barry, W.J., "Multi-lingual acoustic-phonetic features for a number of European languages", Proc. Eurospeech, Genoa, Sept 1991, pp 685-688.
102. Dalsgaard, P., Andersen, O. & Barry, W.J., "The cross-language validity of acoustic-phonetic features in label alignment", Proc. XII International Congress Phonetic Sciences, Aix-en-Provence 1991, Vol 5, pp 382-385.
103. Dalsgaard, P., Andersen, O., Barry, W.J. & Jorgensen, R., "On the use of acoustic-phonetic features in interactive labelling of multi-lingual speech corpora", ICASSP, San Francisco, March 1992.
104. Dalsgaard, P., Anderson, O. & Barry, W.J., "Multi-lingual label alignment using acoustic-phonetic features derived by neural-network technique", Proc. ICASSP, May 1991, Toronto, pp 197-200. (1991)

105. Dolmazon, J-M., Benoit, C., Gauvain, J-L. & Perennou, G., "Le projet europeen SAM: evaluation multilingue des dispositifs d'entree-sortie" (1987).
106. Dours, C., de Calmes, M., Kabre, H., Pecatte, J.M., Perennou, "A multi-level automatic segmentation system: SAPHO and VERIPHONE", Proc. Eurospeech '89, Paris, Vol 2. pp 83-86 (1989).
107. Fuller, H.C., Fourcin, A.J., Goldsmith, M.J. & Keene, M., "A database of normative speech recordings", Proc. Institute of Acoustics, 12 (1990).
108. Fourcin, A. J. & Dolmazon, J-M. (on behalf of the SAM project) (1991). "Speech knowledge, standards and assessment" in Proceedings of the XII International Congress of Phonetics (Aix en Provence), pp 430-433.
109. Gibbon, D., "Intonation and discourse", Text and Discourse Constitution, de Gruyter, Berlin, pp 2-25 (1988).
110. Gibbon, D., "German intonation", To appear in: D.Hirst & A. di Cristo, Intonation Systems, Cambridge, C.U.P., (1991).
111. Gibbon, D. & Braun, G., "Phonologische Netze", Proc. the Connectionism Workshop, GMD, Schloa Birlinghoven, (1988).
112. Goldsmith, M.J., "Speech databases for UK speech technology research: a survey of resources and future needs" (1989).
113. Kabre, H., Pérennou, G. & Vigouroux, N., "A non-linear filtering method applied to automatic segmentation of multi-lingual speech corpora", Proc. Eurospeech '91, Genoa, Sept 1991, Vol 2, pp 689-693, (1991).
114. Kabre, H., Pérennou, G. & Vigouroux, N., "Automatic labelling of speech signal into phonetic events", Proc. ICPhS, Aix-en-Provence, (1991).
115. Kvale, K. & Foldvik, A.K., "Manual segmentation and labelling of continuous speech", Proc. ESCA Workshop on Phonetics and Phonology of Speaking Styles: Reduction and Elaboration in Speech Communication, Barcelona (1991).
116. Pérennou, G., de Calmes, M., Pecatte, J., Vigouroux, N., "Phonetic-string alignment for an automatic labelling of speech corpora", Proc. ESCA Workshop on Speech Input/Output Assessment and Speech Databases, Noordwijkerhout, The Netherlands, Sept 89, paper 5.4, 01 Sept 1989.
117. Pérennou, G. & Vigouroux, N., "L'indication de l'accent dans les transcriptions peut-elle faciliter l'alignement automatique?", 1 Dec 1990.
118. Pérennou, G., Thihoni, J., Karouby, H-P. & Vigouroux, N., "Generation de corpus phonetiques et prosodiques destines aux systemes de reconnaissance analytique", 1 March 1990.

119. SAM, Linguistic engineering and speech assessment (presented by Fourcin, A.J). Proceedings of Le Genie Linguistique, Versailles, Jan 1991.
120. Svendsen, T. & Soong, F.K., "On the automatic segmentation of speech signals", Proc. ICCASSP '87, 1 Jan 1987.
121. Svendsen, T., "A two-pass semi-automatic algorithm for segmentation and labelling"
122. Svendsen, T. & Kvale, K., Automatic Alignment of Phonemic Labels With Continuous Speech. Proc. ICSLP, Kobe, Nov 1990.
123. Tomlinson, M. & Ponting, K., "Annotation at the Speech Research Unit, RSRE, Malvern", 10 Aug 1989.
124. van Erp, A., Barry, W.J., Grice, M., "A unified approach to the labelling of speech: first multi-lingual results", Proc. Europspeech 1989, Paris, Vol 2, pp 88-91, 01 Jan 1989.

**SAM-A External Publications**

125. Bimbot F. and Mathan., "Text-free Speaker Recognition using an Arithmetic-Harmonic Sphericity Measure." Eurospeech 1993.
126. Castagneri G. "Comparison of two methods of performance assessment of commercial Speech Recognition Systems operating in telephone environment." CCITT document. Question 5/XII, D.13/(sg12), Source: CSELT (Italy). May 1993
127. Castagneri G., Di Fabbrizio G., Massone A.and Oreglia M. "SIRVA - A large speech database collected on the Italian telephone network " EUROSPEECH '93 proceedings.
128. Castagneri G., Di Fabbrizio G., Massone A.and Oreglia M. "TESCOS - an integrated workstation" AVIOS '93 proceedings
129. Chollet, G. "Evaluation of ASR systems, algorithms and databases." Proc. NATO ASI, Bubion 1993
130. Danielson, S., "Enhanced Direct Assessment of Speech Input systems within the SAM-A ESPRIT Project", Eurospeech 1993, Berlin.
131. Delogu,C., Conte S., Paoloni A., Sementina C., "Comprehension of Synthetic Speech in Good and Adverse Conditions." Cannes (1991)
132. Delogu, C., Falcone M., Paoloni A., Ridolfi P., Vagges K. "Intelligibility of Italian TtS synthesisers in Adverse Conditions." Proc. of ETRW on "Speech Processing in Adverse Conditions." Cannes (1991)
133. Delogu, C., Conte S., Paoloni A., Sementina C. "Two Different Methodologies for Evaluating the Comprehension of Synthetic Speech." Proc. of ICSPL 92.
134. Delogu, C., Paoloni A., Ridolfi P., and Vagges K. "Intelligibility of Italian Text-to-Speech Synthesisers over Ortophonic and Telephonic Channel", Eurospeech 1993, Berlin.

135. Delogu, C., and Sementina C., "Towards a more realistic evaluation of synthetic speech: a cognitive perspective", Proc. NATO ASI 93, pp. 109-112 Bubion (SPAIN).
136. Goldman J.Ph. and Chollet G. "Voice Transformations for the Evaluation of Speaker Verification Systems." NATO-ASI, Bubion '93.
137. Homayounpour M.M., Goldman J.Ph. and Chollet G. "Machine vs Human Speaker Verification". IAFP 1993.
138. Steeneken, H J M., and Varga A.,. "Comparison of Recogniser Assessment Methods." Proc. ETRW "Speech processing in Adverse Conditions." Carmen Mandelieu (1992).
139. Steeneken H J M.,"Subjective and Objective Intelligibility Measures." Proc. ETRW "Speech Processing in Adverse Conditions", Carmen Mandelieu, Tutorial 1. (1992)
140. Steeneken, H.J.M. and Varga, A. (1993). "Assessment for automatic speech recognition (I): Comparison of assessment methods". Accepted for publication in Speech Communication.
141. Steeneken, H J M and Varga., A., (1993). "Assessment for automatic speech recognition (II): NOISEX-92: A database and an experiment to study the effect of additive noise on speech recognition systems". Accepted for publication in Speech Communication.
142. Varga, A., Steeneken, H.J.M., Tomlinson, M., and Jones, D., (1992). "The NOISEX - 92 Study on the effect of additive noise on automatic speech recognisers." Description of RSG.10 and ESPRIT SAM experiment and database, DRA Speech Research Unit, Malvern, England.

**SAM Input Group's Official SAM Reports**

143. Americo, A., "Factors conditioning a speaker's recognition", FUB-15, 20 June 1991.
144. Andersen O, & Lindberg B., "Implementation of tools for analysis of variance", SAM-IES-056, Jan 1991.
145. Barry, W.J., "Analytic phonetic study of SAMSPEX parameters for use in RSA", SAM-UCL-024, 28 Feb 1991.
146. Castagneri, G., Chollet, G., Lindberg, B., Danielsen, S., Ga, "Assessment of EUROM 0 in recogniser comparison tests", SAM-CT-64, 23 Feb 1989.
147. Castagneri, G., Senia, F. & Di Carlo, A., "Overview on the control files generator", SAM-FB-01, 9 Jan 1990.
148. Castagneri, G. & Senia F., "Specification of DBMS system", SAM-CT-97, Feb 1990.
149. Castagneri, G. & Senia, F., "Setting up DBMS on standard workstation", SAM-CT-103, 31 Aug 1990.

150. Castagneri, G. & Senia F., "Oracle installation guidelines", SAM-CT-100, May 1990.
151. Castagneri G., Oreglia M., "Experience using SAS" Report SAM-CT-104 Sept 1990.
152. Castagneri, G. & Senia F., "Proposal for a connected recogniser evaluation system", SAM-CT-109, Jan 1991.
153. Castagneri, G. & Oreglia, M., "Evaluation of scoring methods - Part 1", SAM-CT-110, 6 March 1991.
154. Castagneri, G. & Senia, F., "Review of specification of DBMS System", SAM-CT-111, 15 March 1991.
155. Chollet, G., Capman, F. & Daoud, J., "On the evaluation of recognisers - statistical validity of the tests", SAM-ENST-02, 11 March 1991 (In SAM-UCL-G004, Appendix I.b).
156. Chollet, G., Capman, F. & Daoud, J., "SAMREC0 - implementation of the ENST-ARECOM baseline system on a TMS320C30-based DSP board - present state", 11 March 1991.
157. Chollet, G., Capman, F., Bardaud, P. & Tadj, C., "Measurements of the limits of the reference recogniser SAM_REC1: noise addition and simulation of the Lombard effect", SAM-ENST-03, 25 March 1992 (In SAM-UCL-G004, Appendix I.c).
158. Christensen, H. & Lindberg, B., "A preliminary evaluation of LoadRISE applied to the Danish part of EUROM 1", SAM-IES-058, 1 Nov 1991.
159. Danielsen, S., "Speech parameter extractor", SAM-JT-119, 1 Sept 1990.
160. Delogu, C. & Paoloni, A., "Human factors for automatic speech recognition", FUB-21, 1 March 1992.
161. Di Carlo, A. & Paoloni, A., "Review on continuous speech recognition assessment", FUB-14, 11 June 1991.
162. Falcone, M. & Di Carlo, A., "Assessment of the VOTAN recogniser with SAM workstation and EUROM 0 digits for five European languages (short form)", 25 Jan 1992.
163. Falcone, M. & Di Carlo, A., "Assessment of the Votan recogniser with SAM workstation and EUROM 0 digits for five European languages (complete form)", SAM-FUB-16, 25 Jan 1992.
164. Lindberg, B. & Danielsen, S., "Proposal for scoring software on SESAM", SAM-SC-21, 1 Feb 1989.
165. Lindberg B., Andersen O. & Danielsen S. "Input Assessment Scoring Methods on SESAM", Document SAM-IES-31, Oct 1989.
166. Lindberg, B. & Danielsen, S., "Specification of the low level SESAM", SAM-JT-045, 15 Feb 1989.
167. Lindberg, B. and Danielsen, S., "Specification of SESAM Assessment Workstation and EUROM 0", 1 Jan 1989.
168. Lindberg, B., Andersen, O. & Danielsen, S., "Input assessment scoring methods on SESAM", SAM-IES-047, 29 Jan 1990.

169. Lindberg, B., Andersen, O & Danielsen, S., "Final SAM standard input assessment test procedures. Milestone i.7", March 1992.
170. Lindberg, B., Danielsen, S., Jorgensen, R. & Dalsgaard, P., "CVC testing of the 3R recogniser on the Danish part of EUROM 1", SAM-IES-060, 15 March 1992 (In SAM-UCL-G004, Appendix I.a).
171. Prouts, B., Djoudadi, S. & Messaoudi, A., "Description of the driver RSDTVX and assessment of the DATAVOX recogniser", SAM-LI-31, 4 Feb 1992.
172. Sherwood, T., "Ensigma Test Procedures", SAM-NPL-101, 28 Jan 1992.
173. Sherwood, T., Fuller, H. & Danielsen, S., "Test procedures for the Ensigma Speech Recogniser", SAM-NPL-101, 9 March 1992.
174. Steeneken, J. M. & van Velden, J. G., "Recogniser assessment by means of CVC words as available in the EUROM 1 database", SAM-TNO-040, 28 October 1991.
175. Steeneken, J.M, "Speech level and noise level measuring method", SAM-TNO-042, 28 October 1991.
176. Steeneken, J.M. & Varga, A., "Design of an experiment on the effect of additive noise on automatic speech recognition", SAM-TNO-041, 28 October 1991.
177. Tomlinson, M. & Whittaker, D. & Jones, D., "Protocols for testing Dragon Dictate", SAM-RSRE-021, 27 March 1992.
178. Tomlinson, M., Whittaker, D. & Jones, D., "Assessment of ENSIGMA digit and Dragon Dictate recognisers - results of experiments using English digits in quiet and noise," SAM-RSRE-020, 27 March 1992.
179. van Velden, J. G., "SAMPAC with remote DAC-driver interface", SAM-TNO-045, 03 Nov 1991.
180. Winski, R. & Kordi, K., "Assessment of connected speech recognisers using recogniser sensitivity analysis", SAM-LO-0281, 15 Feb 1991.
181. Winski R & Kordi K., "Extension of RSA to evaluation of connected/continuous speech recognition", SAM-LO-028, Feb 1991.

**SAM Output Group's Official SAM Reports**

182. Autesserre, D., Meunier, C. & Malet, J.F., "French corpus adapted from the SAM English version", 20 April 1990.
183. Autesserre, D. & Meunier, C., "Segmentation criteria and labelling conventions", , 25 Feb 1991.
184. Benoit, C., "A pair comparison test for the overall quality assessment of speech synthesisers in Italian and in German", 27 July 1990.
185. Benoit, C. & Grice, M., "A manual for the SUS test: a unified methododology for multi-lingual text-to-speech synthesis assessment at the sentence level", SAM-ICP-UCL-001, 6 March 1991.

186. Delogu, C. & Paoloni, A., "The use of reaction-time for evaluating the overall quality of synthetic speech", FUB-09, 1 May 1991.
187. Delogu, C. Paoloni, A., "A magnitude estimation experiment to evaluate "quality" of Italian text-to-speech synthesisers", FUB-11, 1 May 1991.
188. Delogu, C., Falcone, M. & Paoloni, A., "Proposal for a reaction time assessment on SESAM workstation", FUB-13, 1 June 1991.
189. Delogu, C., Paoloni, A. & Sementina, C., "Comprehension of natural and synthetic speech: preliminary studies", FUB-19, 1 Feb 1992 (In SAM-UCL-G004, Appendix II.c).
190. Delogu, C. & Paoloni, A., "A comparison between different methodologies for evaluating the quality of text-to-speech synthesis systems", FUB-12, 1 June 1991 (In SAM-UCL-G004, Appendix II.d).
191. Djarangar, D., "CV, VC and CVC French tests", 1 Aug 1990.
192. Falaschi, A., "Proposal of a pseudo-word generation method for speech synthesiser segmental quality assessment", 1 May 1990.
193. Gibbon, D., "SAMPROSA (SAM PROSodic alphabet)", 22 June 1991.
194. Goldstein, M., "Subjective assessment of speech synthesisers: some guidelines when setting up experiments", SAM-STA-06, 1 Dec 1989.
195. Goldstein, M., Lindstrom, B. & Till, B., "Addendum to SAM-STA-07 and preliminary results from graphic scaling of qualitative terms", 7 Jan 1991.
196. Goldstein, M., Lindstrom, B. & Till, O., "Assessing global performance of speech synthesisers: Context effects when assessing naturalness of Swedish sentence-pairs generated by 4 systems using 3 different assessment procedures free number magnitude estimation, 5- and 11-point category scales)", SAM-STA-07, 15 Jan 1992 (In SAM-UCL-G004, Appendix II.a).
197. Goldstein, M., "Assessing segmental intelligibility of two rule-based synthesisers and Natural Speech using the ESPRIT/SAM VCV test procedures (SOAP v3.0) in Swedish", 23 August 1991 (In SAM-UCL-G004, Appendix II.b).
198. Grice, M., "SAM prosody group results of transcription exercise", SAM-UCL-031, 20 June 1991.
199. Grice, M. & Hirst, D., "The evaluation of prosody in text-to-speech systems in a number of languages", SAM-UCL-023, 19 Feb 1991.
200. Grice, M. & Vagges, K., "The assessment of intonation in text-to-speech systems - A pilot test in English and Italian", 10 June 1991.
201. Grice, M., Vagges, K. & Hirst, D., "Prosodic form tests", SAM-UCL-038, 10 March 1992 (In SAM-UCL-G004, Appendix So.5 - Part One).
202. Grice, M., Vagges, K. & Hirst, D., "Prosodic function tests", SAM-UCL-039, 17 March 1992 (In SAM-UCL-G004, Appendix So.5 - Part Two).

203. Hazan. V, "Review of word lists for British and American English", 5 May 1989.
204. Hazan, V., "Quantification of listener variability", SAM-UCL-041, 25 March 1992 (In SAM-UCL-G004, Appendix So.8 - Part Two).
205. Houtgast, T. & Verhave, J., "An objective approach to speech quality", 20 March 1992 (In SAM-UCL-G004, Appendix So.9).
206. Howard-Jones, P., "Consideration of software requirements for speech output evaluation", SAM-UCL-011, 5 Jan 1990.
207. Howard-Jones, P., "Proposal for a small cross-laboratory assessment of VCV intelligibility", SAM-UCL-028, 7 Jan 1991.
208. Howard-Jones, P., "NADSAM - a small programme to add noise to speech files", SAM-UCL-029, 20 March 1991.
209. Howard-Jones, P., "Specification of listener dimensions", SAM-UCL-040, 28 Feb 1992 (In SAM-UCL-G004, Appendix So.8 - Part One).
210. Howard-Jones, P. et al, "Midterm SAM standard output assessment procedures", SAM-UCL-021, 20 Dec 1990.
211. Jekosch, U., "Introduction of four different approaches for the word level and prosodic assessment", 11 Sept 1989.
212. Jekosch, U., "The cluster-identification test", 14 Feb 1992 (In SAM-UCL-G004, Appendix II.e).
213. Pavlovic, "Information on a new ANSI standard on speech intelligibility tests", CP_05_89.AIX, 15 Nov 1989.
214. Pavlovic, C, Sorin, C., Roumiguiere, J-P & Lucas, J-P, "Cross validation between a direct magnitude estimation technique and a pair comparisons technique for assessing the quality of text-to-speech synthesis", CP_08_89.AIX, 27 Nov 1989.
215. Pavlovic, C., "Use of the magnitude estimation technique for assessing the performance of text-to-speech synthesis systems", CP_07_89.AIX, 27 Nov 1989.
216. Pavlovic, C., "An investigation of some methods for obtaining contextual invariance and subject invariance in the subjective assessment of speech quality", CP_02_90.AIX, 31 July 1990.
217. Pavlovic, C., "Overview of multi-lingual output assessment", CP_05_90.AIX, 13 Nov 1990.
218. Pavlovic, C., "Scaling of speech intelligibility by elderly individuals using magnitude estimation, category estimation and pair comparisons", CP_05_91.AIX, 1 April 1991.
219. Pavlovic, C., "Physical ("objective") measures of speech quality", CP_11_91.AIX, 16 Aug 1991.
220. Pavlovic, C., "Overall quality", CP_01_92.AIX, 9 Jan 1992.

221. Pavlovic, C. & Rossi, M., "Quality assessment of synthesised speech: status report, systematisation, and recommendations", CP_06_89.AIX, 25 Nov 1989.
222. Pavlovic, C. & Rossi, M., "Methodological issues in speech quality assessment: topics requiring a prompt group discussion and further experiments", CP_09_89.AIX, 26 Nov 1990.
223. Pavlovic, C., Rossi, M. & Espesser, R., "Definition of assessment methodology for overall quality of synthetic speech", CP_02_91.AIX, 29 Jan 1991.
224. Pavlovic, C., Rossi, M. & Espesser, R., "Methods for reducing context effects in the subjective assessment of synthetic speech", CP_04_91.AIX, 1 April 1991.
225. Pavlovic, C., Rossi, M. & Espesser, R., "Perceived spectral energy distribution for EUROM 0 speech and for some synthetic speech", CP_03_91.AIX, 1 April 1991.
226. Pavlovic, C., Rossi, M. & Espesser, R., "Overall quality", CP_02_92, 22 Jan 1992.
227. Pols, L., "SAM main phase planning for segmental synthesis tests", 25 Feb 1989.
228. Pols, L., "Manual for running presently available tests to evaluate the speech quality of text-to-speech synthesisers", 12 June 1989.
229. Vagges, K. & Cosi, P., "CV and VCV segmental test: Pilot experiment", 1 March 1990.

**SAM ETR Group's Official SAM Reports**

230. Barry, W.J, SAM Labelling Criteria, SAM-UCL-026, Oct 1990.
231. Barry, W.J., SALA Labelling Tests, SAM-UCL-019.
232. Barry, W.J., "SALA labelling tests", SAM-UCL-020, 28 Feb 1991.
233. Barry, W.J. & Fourcin, A.J., "Selection of speakers", SAM-UCL-030, 20 May 1991.
234. Barry, W.J., Dalsgaard, P. & Andersen, O., "Implementation of Label-Alignment Methodologies and Multi-lingual Labelling (Milestone e.11)", SAM-UCL-036, 28 Feb 1992 (In SAM-UCL-G004, Appendix Se.11).
235. Blomberg, M. & Nord, L. "Comparison between manually and automatically labelled speech files." KTH, Oct 1990.
236. Bourjot, C., Boyer, A. & Fohr, D., ELSA label-testing software, CRIN, Aug 1990
237. Bourjot, C., Boyer, A. & Fohr, D. "Evaluation of ELABSEG SALA on Italian Files, CRIN-INRIA, Oct 1990.
238. Braun, G. & Gibbon, D., "Outline of specifications for an automatic test sentence generator for use in speech output assessment", UBI-SAM-1, 22 July 1988.

239. Braun, G., Gibbon, D. & Johanntokrax, M., "German transcriptions (pre-EUROM-n)", UBI-SAM-4/89, 23 Jan 1989.
240. Braun, G., Gibbon, D & Johanntokrax, M., "Bielefeld linguistic generator for unpredictable intelligibility test sentences", UBI-SAM-5/89, 27 Jan 1989.
241. Braun, G., Gibbon, D. & Johanntokrax, M., "SAM phonemic transcription analysis specifications", 14 Nov 1989.
242. Caerou, J-C, Gauvain, J-L, Winski, R. & Blauert, J. et al, "Definition of software production, documentation etc", SAM-ICP-033, 11 Jan 1990.
243. Caerou, J-C., Dolmazon, J-M. & Schoutens, M.C., "Evaluation of DAT as mass storage", SAM-ICP-032, 17 Jan 1990.
244. Caerou, J-C. & Dolmazon, J-M., "Mass data storage: review of the present state and first draft of proposal", SAM-ICP-047, 24 June 1991 (In SAM-UCL-G004, Appendix III.a).
245. Castagneri, G. & Senia, F., "Setting up DBMS on standard workstation", SAM-CT-103, 31 Aug 1990.
246. Castagneri, G. & Vaccheta, L., "Documentation of the Italian EUROM 1 database", SAM-CT-122, 9 March 1992.
247. Cosi, P. & Vagges, K. "SALA Labelling Tests. SAM-CSRF (CNR)-06 CSRF-CNR, Oct 1990.
248. Cosi, P., "General considerations on semi-automatic segmentation and labelling", SAM-CSRF-01, 6 Dec 1989.
249. Dalsgaard, P., "Brief technical report on the Danish approach to semi-automatic labelling of speech data using a Self-Organising Neural Network", SAM-IES-039, 1 Nov 1989.
250. Dalsgaard, P., "Tools for semi-automatic label alignment and their evaluation", , 05 Dec 1990.
251. Dalsgaard, P. & Andersen, O., "Status of Danish work on semi-automatic label alignment as per 8 May 1990", SAM-IES-050, 8 May 1990.
252. Dalsgaard, P., Andersen, O. & Barry, W.J., "Implementation of label-alignment methodologies and multi-lingual labelling (milestone e.11)", SAM-UCL-036, 28 Feb 1992.
253. Dalsgaard, P., Andersen, O. & Dyhr, N., "Labelling criteria for Danish EUROM 0 database", SAM-IES-055, 1 March 1992.
254. Dalsgaard, P., Svendson, T. & Perennou, G., "Tools for semi-automatic label alignment", SAM-UCL-019, 25 Feb 1991.
255. Dalsgaard, P., Svendsen, T. & Pérennou, G., Tools for semi-automatic alignment, SAM-UCL-019.
256. Dolmazon, J-M., Caërou, J-C. & Barry, W, Initial development of SAM standard workstation, SAM-UCL-022, Dec 1990.
257. Gibbon, D., "Survey of prosodic labelling for EC languages", SAM-UBI-1/90, 12 Feb 1989.

258. Gibbon, D., "Linguistic aspects of speech material complexity", UBI-SAM-1/91, 15 Feb 1992 (In SAM-UCL-G004, Appendix Se.8).
259. Gibbon, D., "SAMPROSA Notes", UBI, Jan 1991.
260. Grice, M. & Barry, W., Prosodic Transcription and Labelling, UCL, Sept 20 1990.
261. Hendriks, J. "SALA Labelling Tests - RNL", PTT-RNL, Oct 1990.
262. Howard, D. & Howard-Jones, P., "Dictionary of software mnemonics", UCL, July 17, 1990.
263. Grice, M. & Barry, W.J., "Levels of transcription (as defined by ETR linguistic tools group on Nov 16 & 17 1989", SAM-UCL-009, 16 Jan 1990.
264. IRIT, "Semi-automatic labelling", SAM-CERFIA-01, 23 Oct 1989.
265. Lindberg, B. & Christensen, H., "Documentation of the Danish Eurom.1 database", SAM-IES-53, 7 Feb 1992.
266. Lindberg, B. & Danielsen, S., "Proposal for scoring software on SESAM", SAM-SC-21, 01 Feb 1989.
267. Lindberg, B. & Danielsen, S., "Specification of the low level SESAM", SAM-JT-045, 15 Feb 1989.
268. Lindberg, B. and Danielsen, S., "Specification of SESAM Assessment Workstation and EUROM 0", 1 Jan 1989.
269. Michel, D., "Microphone and recording environments for high quality speech recordings", 6 Jan 1989.
270. Nord, L., Report on manual labelling criteria used on the Swedish EUROM.0 material, KTH, Sept 1990.
271. Pérennou, G. & Vigouroux, N., "Transcription and notation of EUROM 0 corpora using SAMPA French sentences, Version 4", 1 Oct 1989
272. Pérennou, G., Malet, J.F., "Questionnaire on a computer-readable lexical material for the SAM project", 25 Jan 1990.
273. Pérennou, G. & Malet, J., "An analysis of responses to the questionnaire on computer-readable lexical material for the SAM project", 10 June 1990.
274. Pérennou, G. & Vigouroux, N., "SAPHO multi-lingual performance", SAM-IRIT-02, 18 March 1991.
275. Pérennou, G., Kabre, H. & Vigouroux, N., "Automatic SAPHO system segmentation of EUROM 0 multilingual speech corpora into phonetic events", SAM-IRIT-03, 18 June 1991 (In SAM-UCL-G004, Appendix III.b).
276. Tomlinson, M., Recording Protocol Final Version, SAM-RSRE-015, Jan 1991.
277. UCL et al, "Initial development of SAM standard workstation milestone e.10", SAM-UCL-022, 20 Dec 1990.
278. van Erp, A., "Transcription of the Dutch Eurom 0 speech material", SAM-581RNL/89, 10 Jan 1989.

279. Wells, J., Barry, W.J., Grice, M. & Fourcin, A.J., "Standard computer-compatible transcription (En.3)", SAM-UCL-037, 28 Feb 1992 (In SAM-UCL-G004, Appendix SEn.3).
280. Zeiliger, J., Serignat, J-F & Dolmazon, J-M., "File specification for corpus recording", 25 March 1989.
281. Zeiliger, J., Serignat, J-F. & Dolmazon, J-M., "Format proposal for description files associated to speech files", SAM-ICP-125, 9 Oct 1989.
282. Zeiliger, J. & Serignat, J.F, EUROPEC Software, Multi-channel Recording. Prompting and Recording Strategies, SAM-ICP-035, March 1990.

**SAM Software Documentation**

283. Andersen, O. & Dalsgaard, P., "DKISALA V1.1 - User's Guide", , SAM-IES-059, 9 March 1992.
284. Andersen, O. & Lindberg, B., "SAMITPRO software version 1.1", , SAM-IES-065, 9 March 1992.
285. Back, C. & Hult, G., "SAM_REC0 isolated word recogniser v 1.0 software documentation and user's manual", Incorporated in Annual Report 1991 (R1), SAM-TVT-003, 13 Nov 1990.
286. Braun, G., "SAMTRA (Vs1.0) Transcription verification and phoneme/diphoneme analysis software adapted for the purposes of ESPRIT 2589 (SAM)", 1 April 1991.
287. Caerou, J-C., Dolmazon, J-M. & Badmoussi, A., "PTS software V.4.40, user manual" 13 March 1992.
288. Castagneri, G. & Senia F., "SAM-RISE V1.1 - User Guide. Relational interface for speech evaluation", Document SAM-CT-105, Sept 1990.
289. Castagneri, G., Di Fabrizzio, G & Senia, F., "SAMPAC v 3.10 documentation", , SAM-CT-120, 9 March 1992.
290. Castagneri, G. & Senia, F., "LoadRise V1.0 - User's Guide", SAM-CT-111, 17 March 1992.
291. CRIN & UCL, "ELSA - ESPRIT labelling system assessment software. User's guide for V2.3", SAM-UCL-027, 7 March 1991.
292. Danielsen, S., "Speech level meter, Version 1.0", SAM-JT-149, 29 Oct 1991.
293. Danielsen, S., "Speech parameter extractor version 2.0", , SAM-JT-163, 24 Feb 1992.
294. Gibbon, D. & Braun, G., "SAMTRA (SAM Transcription Analysis) V1.0", SAM-UBI-3/91, 22 June 1991.
295. Ha, H.T.H. & Benoit, C., "SUSGEN: Semantically unpredictable sentence generation - user's guide", 1 June 1991.
296. Hegehofer, T., "Segmental scoring: documentation", 12 Feb 1992.

297. Howard-Jones, P., "SOAP, Speech Output Assessment Package, Version 4.0", SAM-UCL-042, 28 Feb 1992.
298. Jekosch, U. & Belhoula, K., "Documentation for Wordgenerator", 3 Feb 1992.
299. Lindberg, B., Andersen, O., Jorgensen, R. & Danielsen, S., "SAM_SCOR V.3.1 reference guide", SAM-IES-066, March 1992.
300. Svendsen, T. & Kvale, K., "ELABSEG v2.5 User's Manual", 4 March 1992.
301. van Velden, J., "Speech level measurement V2.0, SAM_SLM", SAM-TNO-043, 6 Nov 1991.
302. Verhave, J., "RESAM, programs for adding signals sampled with a different sample rate", SAM-TNO-044, 12 Nov 1991.
303. Vigouroux, N. & Malet, J.F., "Installing and running IRIT-SALA (DSP Step, SAPHO Step) Version 2", , SAM-IRIT-10, 26 July 1991.
304. Zeiliger, J. & Serignat, J., "Europec software V4.0 user's guide", SAM-ICP-045, 25 Sept 1990.

## SAM-A Internal Reports

305. Bimbot F. (ed.). "Assessment Methodology for Speaker Identification and Verification Systems." SAM-A/ENST
306. Blauert, J. "Current Standardisation Activities in the field of SAM-A.", SAM-A/RUB. April, 1993
307. Buckland A.P. "Assessment of Marconi MR8 and DRA AURIX recognisers: results of multi run experiments using English digits in noise (NOISEX CD-ROMs)." SAM-A/DRA/002. 19 October, 1993
308. Caerou J.C., Dolmazon J.M. and Zeiliger J. "I2: Review of SAM tools and software development strategy." SAM-A/ICP/002/V2. 2 October 1993.
309. Caerou J.C., Dolmazon J.M. and Zeiliger J. "I6: Hardware and Software Requirements Specifications." SAM-A/ICP/003/V2. 6 October 1993.
310. Castagneri G, Senia F. and Fontana M. "Italian EUROM 1 Database Structure." SAM-A/CSELT/006/V1. 22 September 1993
311. Castagneri G. and Di Fabrizzio G. "Telephone Boards for Voice Processing and Telephone Applications. A first overview on hardware and software experience in CSELT." SAM-A/CSELT/003. 10 February 1993.
312. Castagneri G. and Senia F. "Initial Specification to Update SamPac". SAM-A/CSELT/004/V1. 10th March, 1993.
313. Castagneri G. and Senia F. "Specification of Assessment Methodology and Requirements for testing of the SUNDIAL/CSELT and AURIS recognisers at CSELT". SAM-A/CSELT/002. 24 February, 1993

314. Castagneri G. and Steeneken H. "Asessment of telephone based recognisers. Review of first year project activities." SAM-A/CSELT/008. October 1993.
315. Danielsen, S.W. "Initial Specification of Recognisers, Assessment Methodology and Database Requirements." SAM-A/I3 in SAM-A/G002. 25 March, 1993
316. Danielsen S. and Lindberg B. "Specification of Assessment Methodology and Requirements for Testing of the SUNCAR Recogniser at JT/IES." SAM-A/JT/001. 5 March 1993
317. Delogu C., Falcone M. and Sementina C. "Structured Analysis of Subjective SO Assessment; Part One (the measuring methods)." SAM-A/FUB/002/V1. December 31, 1992
318. Falcone M. "Evaluation of Two Algorithms for Text Dependent Speaker Verification on real telephone speech for the Italian Language." SAM-A/FUB/006/V1. 30th September, 1993
319. Falcone M. "Experiments where subjective tests are used: a survey from publications in the speech field, in the last few years." SAM-A/FUB/003. 10 March 1993
320. Falcone M. "Playing Speech Files using the OROS AU21 and AU22 under the WINDOWS Environment: A Demo System." SAM-A/FUB/005/V1. 10th May, 1993.
321. Falcone M. "Software/hardware Review and Future Requirements." SAM-A/FUB/001/V1. December 31, 1992
322. Falcone M. "WDSK21: a WINDOWS audio tool for the AU21 board based on the WABI software approach." SAM-A/FUB/007/V1. October 1993
323. Falcone. M. "New Encode/Decode Programs to Transmit any files via the E-mail Service: an ANSI C Implementation." SAM-A/FUB/004/V1. April1993.
324. Fourcin A.J. and Winski. R. "Creation of Dissemination Centres and Supporting Dissemination Activities." SAM-A/I4 in SAM-A/G002. 18th October, 1993
325. Goldstein M., and Lindstrom B. "Assessment Methods when Evaluating Synthetic Speech." SAM-A/TRAB/01/93. January 1993
326. Goldstein M. "Handbook on Assessment of Text to Speech (TTS) systems." Third draft version. 14 SAM-A/TRAB/01.93. November 1993
327. Hegehofer T., Jekosch U. and Marianik A. "Description of a Test Catalogue." SAM-A/RUB/001/V1. January 1992.
328. Hegehofer T. "Description of the Prototype Parametric Test Manager." SAM-A/RUB/004/V1. October 1993

329. Hegehofer T. "Report I7: Description and Implementation of Audio Interface Hardware and Software Components." SAM-A/RUB/002/V1. June 2, 1993
330. Hegehofer T. "Report I8: Description of Unified Architecture, Data Structures and User Front-End Concept." SAM-A/RUB/003/V1. June 30, 1993
331. Langlais P. "Collection of Speech Database". SAM-A/IDIAP/001. October 1993.
332. Lindberg B. "Considerations regarding EUROM-1 and CDROM's ." SAM-A/IES/001/V2. February 23, 1993
333. Lindberg B. and Danielsen S. "Assessment of the SUNCAR recogniser on the CVC part of the EUROM.1 speech database. SAM-A/JT/IES/T2100009. October 1993.
334. Lindberg B. and Danielsen S.W. "SAM_SCOR Version 4.0 Reference Guide ." SAM-A/IES/005. 30 September 1993
335. Llisterri J., Lourdes A., Blecua B., Machuca M.J., de la Mota C., Rios A, Moreno A. and Salavedra J. "Spanish EUROM 1: Phonetic contents." SAM-A/UPC/002/V1. (1993)
336. Llisterri J. and Marino J.B. "Spanish adaptation of SAMPA and automatic phonetic transcription." SAM-A/UPC/001/V1. 20th April, 1993
337. Moore R., Buckland A.P., Steeneken H.J.M. and Lindberg B. "Initial Report on Indirect Speech Input Assessment." SAM-A/I10 in SAM-A/G002. October 1993
338. Moreno A. "EUROM-1 Spanish Database." Report D6, SAM-A/UPC/003. September 1993
339. Moreno. A. and Lleida E. "Specification of assessment methodology and requirements for testing of the TELEMACO word spotter at UPC". SAM-A/UPC. 5 March 1993.
340. Prouts. B. "Specification of Assessment Methodology and Requirements for Testing of the LIMSI Recognisers at VECSYS." SAM-A/VECSYS/001/V3. 5th March, 1993
341. Salza P.L., Di Fabrizzio G., Oreglia M., Falcone M., Sementina C. and Delogu C. "Development of a context dependent methodology for Text-to-Speech Synthesis evaluation in interactive Dialogue Systems." SAM-A/CSELT/007/V1. October 1993
342. Salza P.L. "Questionnaires Proposal for the Assessment of Prosody in an Interactive Application" SAM-A/CSELT
343. Salza P.L. "Selection of Methodologies for Prosody Assessment of Speech Output Systems in Interactive Applications." SAM-A/CSELT/001/V1. 18th January, 1993

344. Till O. "Relevant Information in CCITT P&G Recommendations and ETSI STC TE4 (92) 49 draft standard regarding factors that influence speech quality." SAM-A/TRAB/002/V1. 19 April 1993.
345. Tomlinson M. "Specification of Recognisers to be tested at DRA, Malvern." SAM-A/DRA/001/V3. January 1993.
346. Wells, J.C. "Revised SAM-PA Notation." SAM-A/D1 in SAM-A/G002. October 1993.
347. Zeiliger J. "Publishing CD-ROMS from EUROM_1." SAM-A/ICP/004/V1. 17th March, 1993
348. Zeiliger J. and Caerou J.C. "Hardware and Software Review." SAM-A/ICP/001. January 9th, 1993

## Acknowledgements

The achievements summarised in this chapter represent the coordinated work of the SAM group involving the collaboration of over 100 individuals in the project consortia. This chapter has been produced with special reference to the final reports of the SAM and SAM-A projects [6, 12]. The authors wish to acknowledge the contribution of all colleagues to this text, and in particular to the SAM and SAM-A work group coordinators: Jean Claude Caerou, Giuseppe Castagneri, Gerard Chollet, Sven Danielsen, Jean Marc Dolmazon, Mauro Falcone, Ute Jekosch, Roger Moore and Louis Pols. The authors wish to acknowledge the high degree of co-operation and commitment of the participating colleagues and institutions which have made this a rewarding as well as scientifically and technically fruitful project.

# Robust System to Access Large Databases in Natural Languages

E. Bilange, L. Horel, G. Tabuteau
CAP GEMINI INNOVATION
86-90, rue Thiers
F-92513 Boulogne-Billancourt Cedex, France

## Abstract

This paper describes a robust natural language and interactive interface for accessing large databases. The aim is to provide an intuitive tool to naive users especially when they do not know exactly what is in the database and how to formulate their queries. This application is not a "natural" SQL-like interface, it is truly natural language and natural dialogue oriented. The pilot application is the Electronic Telephone Directory: Yellow Pages access.

The main assumption of our work is that accessing databases consists in negotiating about semantic spaces, whatever the application is. The ultimate goal is to find a specific object, the one the user is looking for. This space is a shared knowledge between the user and the system. We present here how this space is built thanks to a huge conceptual dictionary (with more than 250 000 links) and how it serves to initiate and proceed the dialogue with the user. The negotiation on this space to find a specific object can also trigger inferences rules derived from the ontology structure in the dictionary.

The system interface is intuitive in its design and users naturally find how to dialogue with the system without any training. It provides a robust and co-operative interaction. The user can choose either natural language or mouse clicks for accessing the database. The user is helped in any situation - unknown words or expressions, misunderstandings, and is also given a regular feedback on the system's interpretations.

This operational system is very near to full natural language coverage (about 100 000 words and expressions are recognised) and offers repair mechanisms and backtracking possibilities.

The work presented here has been partially funded by the CEC in the PLUS ESPRIT Project 5254. The partners of the project are CAP GEMINI INNOVATION (Coordinating contractor), CAP debis, ITK, LIMSI, Omega Generation, UMIST, University of Bristol, and University of Göteborg.

# 1. Introduction

Providing an intuitive access to large databases is difficult since we all have our own mental models about information and these models are different from the real systems. A natural language-based, or a mixed natural language and menu-driven (and mouse click) system for accessing large databases should not ignore users' mental models and therefore it should not impose its own model on users otherwise it is not usable. We do not speak here about the multimodality due to the fact that even if we use different modes, they do not cooperate in one turn.

Our assumption is that a computer is supposed to be helpful. The key point then is to build a system able to give interesting information and to which one can freely talk (i.e. express goals). In our scope of information retrieval, our aimed system is supposed to give any requested information from the database with sufficient efficiency. This efficiency basically comes out with natural interaction, i.e. when you can freely express yourself (without following a constrained sub-language nor a rigid behaviour) and when you understand the limits of your dialoguee so that you can't expect more. In other words, we expect the system to have a large coverage of the language and to apply interaction principles [8] that render explicit to the user its limits and skills.

Two main principles guided us for building our system. They concern first the NLP input and second the dialogue management. These principles are:

- Understanding natural language should be based on an encyclopaedic source of knowledge. This large amount of knowledge [3] can be found in editorial thesaurus and dictionaries since they are based on work of ages. This is the reason why we chose an existing conceptual dictionary as the unique semantic knowledge resource.
- Dialogue is a recursive mechanism whatever the application is. A dialogue is always a cascade of embedded and/or non-embedded negotiations which is precisely a recursive mechanism. A negotiation aims at sharing an object between dialogue participants. Obviously, for information retrieval, negotiations can be about a database object (the object or one of its parts being retrieved) or about the dialogue itself in case of clarifications.

On these principles, we built a French Electronic Yellow Pages access system. The following sections describe these two principles and their implementation. Then we describe how these two points coexist in the system. The last section illustrates the dialogues for accessing the Yellow Pages.

# 2. Wide NL and Conceptual Coverage

## 2.1 Semantic Analysis

As said earlier, the semantics and therefore the ontology of our system is the one of our conceptual dictionary, *Dicologique* [6]. This conceptual dictionary contains more than 117 000 entries which consist in, approximately:

- 17 500 concepts,
- 74 200 words, and
- 25 300 locutions.

Structurally, this conceptual dictionary is a directed acyclic graph (DAG) which implies following two assumptions: no infinite loops exist when travelling through it, and there is a root from which each concept inherits.

With respect to a network structure, it has been easy to simulate logic inferences with efficient algorithms. In fact, there is a hierarchy of concepts which can be compared with inheritance systems [9]. Whatever the hierarchy is, from the implementation point of view, we consider it as a graph with nodes of two types, concepts which are non-terminals, and words and locutions which are terminals.

Several types of *links* exist from concepts to concepts. We use following types:
- ***Theme:*** generic concept which groups a set of related concepts.
- ***Class:*** this corresponds to the usual link ISA or SORT-OF.
- ***List:*** it groups words and locutions which are quasi-synonymous.
- ***Description:*** similar to the usual PART-OF link.
- ***Characteristic:*** groups words which have one characteristic in common.
- ***Linked-terms:*** it contains words that are semantically linked or morphologically linked.

Travelling inside the conceptual dictionary is always „understandable" and paths reflect some concrete or abstract relations between concepts that people can grasp. On the other hand travelling inside a conceptual model of a database is often obscure to naive users. This is precisely why we anchored the conceptual model of the database in the conceptual dictionary.

The underlying idea is clearly that an intuitive travel through the conceptual dictionary is naturally equivalent to a travel through the database. Figure 1 shows the principle of our approach.

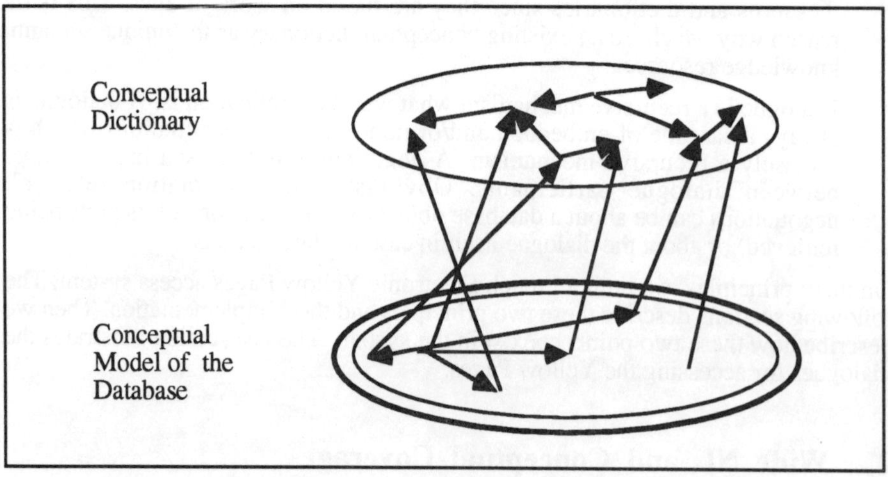


**Fig. 1:** Anchoring the database inside the conceptual dictionary

This anchoring is made easier by treating a concept of the database in the same way than a concept of the conceptual dictionary. So the methodology consists in creating a "new" concept (the concept of the database) which reflects what conceptual domain is involved in this new concept.

For instance, car rental is a concept of the database. Therefore, we will create it as a new concept which covers the car concept and the rent concept. When the new concept requires a complex anchoring (for instance, barrister registered to a foreign bar), the granularity of the conceptual representation will be enforced. But most of the times, the conceptual dictionary itself guarantees the wide NL and conceptual coverage. The effort to anchor these database concepts depends on the application. The ratio for the Electronic Yellow Pages is 30 database concepts per day. This is done with a software tool called Lexilog (i.e. Lexilog is a registered mark of Memodata Inc.). Our assumption is that semantics plays the main role in accessing large databases. Altogether, information coming from the syntactic level and the pragmatic level is used to improve the relevance of interpretation.

### 2.2 Syntactic Analysis

The syntactic analysis is at least required to disambiguate roles of lemma in the query. The second requirement is that it can depict clauses in order to assign scopes of some quantifiers. In order not to loose our wide coverage and genericity we designed and applied a bigram analyser for the purpose of word's role disambiguation. The whole syntactic processing is decomposed as follows:

1. morphological analysis plus spell checking,
2. clause boundaries identification, and
3. syntactic disambiguation.

### 2.3 Degraded Pragmatic Analysis

In NL queries some words (and therefore concepts) are relevant for the query and some others are relevant for the dialogue. For example:

„*I would like to go to an* ***Indian restaurant***"

contains *Indian* and *restaurant* concepts which are relevant for the information retrieval purpose, whereas *I would like to* is relevant to the level of discourse.

The purpose of this step in the query processing is to split up the query into pieces and assign them their function (i.e. dialogue and application). For this task, we automatically extracted specific words and expressions (generated from the concept hierarchy of the conceptual dictionary) that we consider only relevant for the dialogue, such are modals, thoughts, etc. Our former example is now split up into two pieces:

{ *I would like to* | *go to an Indian restaurant* }

Finally, the semantic representation is no more than concepts in the conceptual dictionary. Thus our example will be represented as:

{ *I*, *like* | *go*, (*Indian*, *restaurant* ) }

## 3. Dialogue Mechanisms

The main dialogue mechanism, the recursive principle, is that the two dialoguees are always looking for an object: either to obtain it or to inform about it. This means that at any stage in the conversation an object is searched and therefore partially defined. This may then generate multiple hypotheses about this object. This principle is recursive since an object is viewed as a structured object with facets and each of these facets may be in turn an searched object. Making this principle explicit is of prime importance since this fits well the notion of tracking and making explicit the context of the conversation. For us, the theme of the conversation is a structured tree of hypotheses and searched objects.

This principle suits well various theoretical propositions in dialogue management. For example, the structure of the conversation is then the recursion itself across object facets and then it perfectly reflects the structure of the task as [7] proved. Moreover, meta-communicative phenomena are handled the same way. They mainly occur because of misunderstandings such as a misspelled word, confusion about something, etc. These clarification subdialogues still follow the rule of searching for an object except that this time the object is a dialogue object and not a task or domain object.

### 3.1 Dialogue Representation

We made explicit the representation of the conversation itself in the system. Doing this is crucial for dealing correctly with meta-communicative phenomena [1, 2].

The dialogue is a structure of *exchanges*. An exchange is the structural unit involving both participants as opposed to *moves* which involve one participant for performing it and the other to receive it. Exchanges are made of three components: an *initiative* phase, a *reactive* phase and an *evaluative* phase; one phase is either a move or an exchange. The need for such a triplet organisation is discussed and justified in [1].

Since an exchange is viewed as a discourse segment [7] it has an attention and an intent[1]ion. The initiative makes explicit the attention and the intention of the agent who opened the exchange. The reaction is the response to the intention (which may be negative). Then the evaluation is an optional phase which makes explicit the achievement(s) in the exchange (it can also be negative).

A *move* is a dialogue action, i.e. an action performed at the level of the interface by the user or by the system. An action can be linguistic, i.e. a NL utterance, or extra linguistic, i.e. a mouse click. Interpretation of actions takes place in the context, i.e. the current exchange, of the interaction. Two main types of actions exist: *inform* and *request*. They are contextually refined according to their role in the exchange: initiative, reactive or evaluative (e.g. we can inform about a correction, about a value of a slot or about a set of database solutions).

Each category follows a surface behaviour, i.e. a presentation in the sense of [5], which is performed on the interface. The screen of the application in section 5 illustrates this.

We identified five types of exchanges: simple exchanges whose purpose is to establish a simple fact (i.e. find a simple object which means obtaining an atomic value for an object), complex exchanges to find complex objects (i.e. objects made of atomic objects), initiative, reactive and evaluative exchanges. For example, the following dialogue will have the representation given in figure 2:

S1: please, formulate your query
U1: I would like a cra
S2: a. *proposition of correction: CAR instead of CRA*
b. *show the list of Yellow Pages entries which are related to cars.*
c. would like to rent or buy a car ?
U2: rent
S3: a. *show the list of car rentals*
**b. chauffeur driven or not?**
U3: *click on Hertz*
...

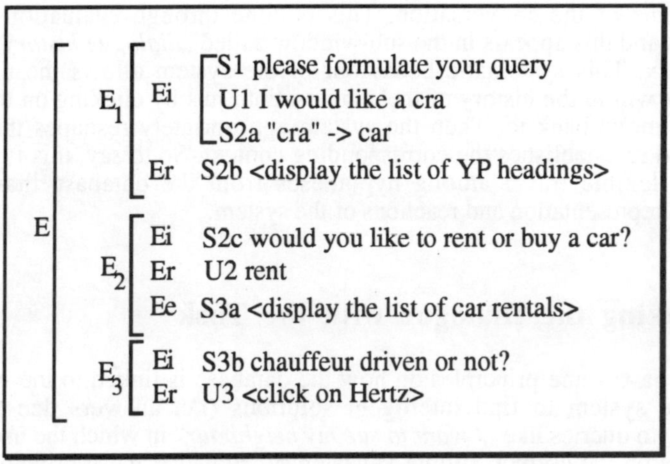


**Fig. 2:** Dialogue representation

*E* is the main exchange, a complex one, which aims at finding the object. $E_1$, $E_2$ and $E_3$ are simple exchanges which respectively aim at getting a description of the object, getting the action the user wants to perform on the object and getting other features about the object. Simple exchanges are made of initiative, reactive and evaluative segments. "Segment" here means that they can be either a move or a simple exchange. Moves can be either performed as natural language utterances (S1, U1 etc.) or as clicks. So moves can be multimodal, i.e. both user and system can choose the mode(s) to perform a move.
The appendix shows the state of the system interface after the bolded utterance S3b.

## 3.2 Discourse Principles and Rules

The principle that the system is always looking to narrow a searched object is guided by the application management in the system (see next section). However, there are other principles in the system which are called pure discourse principles.

Since our implementation is object oriented, it is easy to conceive that each dialogue entity, moves and exchanges, has its own behaviour. One may observe this in our dialogue example above. For example, spelling corrections are just notified to the user as an evaluation of the segment but the system does not stop the dialogue on this clarification, there is an implicit resolution. We have the following principle:

*Evaluations of reactive and initiative segments by the system are not blocking.*

It is then fairly simple in our system to attach different behaviours to different types of object. These behaviours are parameterized and can be switched. For now they are switched off-line and a future extension of the system will be to switch them dynamically during the conversation.
Above all, one important behaviour of the system is that it makes explicit the track

of the theme of the conversation. This is done through evaluation of simple exchanges and this appears in the sub-window called „*dialogue history*" as shown in appendix. This systematic behaviour of the system allows the user the go backwards within the history of the conversation, just by clicking on the step she wishes to move back to. Then the system appropriately reshapes the dialogue history and re-establishes the corresponding context. So to say, this functionality allows a flexible travel among hypotheses from the database thanks to the contextual representation and reactions of the system.

## 4. Linking the Dialogue with the Task

Section 2 gave some principles on how the database is linked to the world. This allows the system to find intelligent solutions (i.e. answers due to indirect reasoning) to queries like „*I want to sue my neighbour*" in which the user has no *a priori* idea on the correct Yellow Pages entry. However these principles are not sufficient when we want to apply mechanisms presented in the previous section.

The searched object is represented as a frame in the system, i.e. a list of slots and values. So we have to map the database entries onto a frame-like representation. In our application, we identified following generic slots for frames:

- *Action,*
- *Object,*
- *Agent,*
- *Type/feature.*

Consequently, each Yellow Pages (YP) entry is represented as a frame with these four slots. Since we wanted to keep our wide coverage and genericity, we **automatically** built these frames. This is done for each slot by applying travel rules through the graph.

The DAG structure enabled us to do it in a quite efficient way. For example, the *object* slot collects all concepts, starting from those of the YP entry, that inherit from the dictionary concept *inanimate object*. When anchoring the YP heading *garages,* we connected it to the concepts *car, vehicle, engine, repair, park..*

The automatic extraction of the *object* slot implies to:

1. select the concepts *car, vehicle* and *engine* because they inherit of both concepts *garages* and *inanimate object,*
2. collect all the daughters of the extracted concepts,
3. extract a subgraph of the conceptual dictionary. In this subgraph, we weight nodes according to their power of expression (i.e. computed according a number of parameters available in the graph structure).
4. From this subgraph, extract the highest weighted concept which corresponds to the best representative concept for the slot (its *prototype*). In figure 3, the prototype of *Action* will be *repair*, and the prototype of *Object* will be *vehicle*.

This is how the system can ask whether one wants to rent, buy or repair a car. This slot filling task is done off-line. It gives good results and can be used as such. However, reviewing of the produced frames increases the performances of the system. Furthermore, depending of the application, it could be interesting to add as many slots as needed (for instance, *Location*, *Time*, *Part of object*, and so on), which is still compatible with the use of a conceptual dictionary. Finally, the type of links helped us to set up inferences on real world like in number of semantic networks (see as an example KL-ONE [4]). For instance, let's have three concepts $C_1$, $C_2$ and $C_3$ such that:

$$C_1 \underset{\textit{is a}}{\supset} C_2 \underset{\textit{part of}}{\supset} C_3$$

then, according to a number of laws of composition, we can automatically infer that:

$$C_1 \underset{\textit{part of}}{\supset} C_3$$

From figure 3 and according to these rules, we can naturally infer that an engine is a part of a vehicle. So the search algorithm consists in the following mechanism:

- whenever some slots of the searched object are filled in,
- then find the most relevant (YP) frames, and
- evaluate the solutions by making hypotheses on missing slots of the object defined by the user.

In our case, this is precisely how the system knows that asking „*would you like to rent or buy a car ?*" is a relevant question since it could decrease significantly the number of answers from the database, and this question is triggered by the filling of the *action* slot.

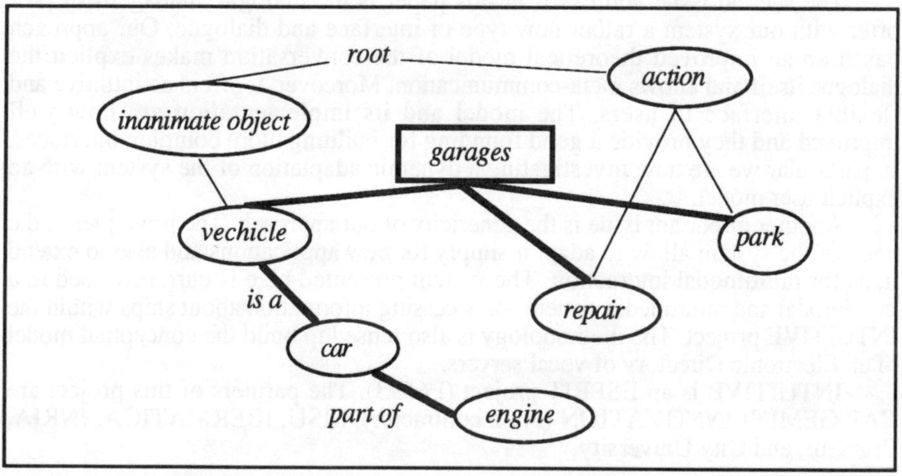


**Fig. 3:** Example of anchoring showing inheritance

## 5. Performances

Here are some results (see figure 4) obtained with respect to:

- answer times of the system which depends on the complexity and the correctness of the user input,
- numbers of hypotheses due to the vagueness of the query, and
- indirectness of answers.

| | *Answer Time* | *Number of Hypotheses* | *Indirect Answer* |
|---|---|---|---|
| *I would like a car* | 0,3 s | > 10 | no |
| *my doll is broken* | 0,2 s | 1 | yes |
| *I want to sue my neighbour* | 0,2 s | 2 | yes |
| *I would like to organize a party* | 0,1s | 6 | yes |

**Fig. 3:** Experimental Results

## 6. Conclusions

The system presented in this paper illustrates a strong improvement on the use of natural language. These improvements rely mainly on the range of semantics the system can understand and on the flexibility it can offer during a session.

The wide coverage of semantics comes from the intuition that a conceptual dictionary covers the semantics of the world (and still captures the subjectivity of semantics). Hence we avoid two classical problems in semantic representation: partiality and exhaustivity.

The second issue addressed in this paper is the dialogue management. We offer with our system a rather new type of interface and dialogue. Our approach based on an improved theoretical model of the conversation makes explicit the dialogue itself and allows meta-communication. Moreover, it offers an intuitive and flexible interface to users. The model and its implementation are now well improved and they provide a good founding for building more complex interfaces. In particular we are now investigating a dynamic adaptation of the system with an explicit user model.

Another important issue is the genericity of our approach. The principles at the heart of the system allow to adapt it simply for new applications and also to extend it, as for multimodal interaction. The system presented here is currently used in a multimodal and multimedia system for accessing information about ships within the INTUITIVE project. The methodology is also reused to build the conceptual model of an Electronic Directory of vocal servers.

INTUITIVE is an ESPRIT project (P6593). The partners of this project are CAP GEMINI INNOVATION (main contractor), SISU, IBERMATICA, INRIA, Brameur, and City University.

## Acknowledgements

The authors would like to thank Christophe Godin who helped very much in the starting of this project, and Françoise Lemercier for her collaboration.

## References


1. Bilange E. "Dialogue Personne-Machine", Hermès, Paris, 1992.
2. Bilange E. "A Task independent Oral Dialogue Model", In Proceedings of the European ACL, pp. 83-88, Berlin, April 1991.
3. Bilange E., M. Guyomard and J. Siroux "Separating Task Knowledge from Dialogue Knowledge for Oral Dialogue Management", Proceedings of COGNITIVA, pp. 135-142, Madrid, November 1990.
4. Brachman R. and J. Shmolze "An Overview of the KL-ONE Knowledge Representation System", Cognitive Science, Vol.9, No.2, pp. 171-216, 1985.
5. Coutaz J. "PAC: an Implementation Model for Dialog Design", Proceedings of Interact'87, Stuttgart, pp. 431-436, Sept. 1987.
6. Dutoit D. "A Set-theoretic Approach to Lexical Semantics", Proceedings of COLING 1992.
7. Grosz B.J. and C. Sidner "Attention, Intentions and the Structure of Discourse". Computational Linguistics, Vol.12, No.3, pp. 175-204, July-Sept. 1986.
8. Lancel J.M., X. Briffault , F. Dols, C. Godin, L. Horel, K. Jokinen, and G. Tabuteau "Architectural Design for the PLUS Dialogue System", *(in this volume).*
9. Touretzky D.S. "The Mathematics of Inheritance Systems", Los Altos, Morgan Kaufmann, 1986.

# SPELL: A Pronunciation Training Device Based on Speech Technology

J.-P. Lefèvre
AGORA Conseil
185 Hameau du Château, F-38360 Sassenage, France

## Abstract

This paper reports the achievements of a project whose primary aim is the development of a workstation designed to improve the pronunciation of foreign languages by non-native speakers. The SPELL (Interactive System for Spoken European Language Learning) workstation is intended to be a self-instructional device aimed at intermediate ability foreign language learners. The research is based primarily on the analysis of the speech characteristics of non-native speakers and on the development of tools to be used in the automated assessment and improvement of non-native language pronunciation. The SPELL project, partly funded by the Commission of the European Communities through the ESPRIT programme, has been split into two phases of two-year each. The result of the completed first one (P5192) is an initial demonstrator system which is able to process the speech of non-native speakers of French, English and Italian. The second phase of the project (P7153), now active, is aimed at developing the SPELL system as a marketable product. The main technical innovation behind SPELL is the departure from traditional practices which require exact whole utterance acoustic matching, usually involved when teaching pronunciation. Instead, speech processing techniques of normalization and segmentation are applied to achieve comparisons at a level of perceptual and ultimately phonological equivalence. In terms of speech technology, the SPELL research capitalizes as much as possible on the availability of existing basic algorithms and concentrates on the adaptation of this technology to the operative stage and on its extension to meet the application requirements.

## 1. Introduction

This paper presents an overview of the research work of the SPELL project. SPELL (Interactive System for Spoken European Language Training) is a four year ESPRIT initiative which has adapted many of the core speech technologies to the task of improving the pronunciation of foreign language students. The project which began in September 1990 has been split into two phases of two years each.

Before detailing these two phases, the main objectives of the project can be summarized as follows. The final aim of the project is the development of a workstation designed to improve the pronunciation of foreign languages by non native speakers. The SPELL workstation has been designed as a self-instructional device for computer-aided pronunciation teaching aimed at intermediate ability foreign language learners. This study is based primarily on the analysis of the speech characteristics of non-native speakers and on the development of tools to be used in the automated assessment and improvement of non-native language pronunciation. The target system will be able to analyze the phonetic characteristics of the speaker's mother tongue, to identify his/her pronunciation errors which are independent from his/her mother tongue, to help him/her to understand his/her errors, to display how he/she can correctly pronounce words or short phrases and finally to talk according to the pronunciation of a native speaker.

These global objectives have been kept in mind during all the first phase of the project, which is now completed and whose major aim was to conduct a feasibility study resulting in a demonstrator system involving three languages, namely French, English and Italian. This demonstrator is running on a IBM-PC compatible platform using the Microsoft Windows® graphical environment, the speech signal processing being executed on an extension board [1].

The analysis of these three languages naturally requires a high degree of international cooperation. Expertise in phonetic analysis, multilingual aspects, signal processing and computer-aided instruction is distributed across the project members. The partners in this collaborative project, their effort and their role are as follows :

- AGORA CONSEIL, a business office from France, acting as coordinator and apart from the general management of the project, mainly involved in marketing aspects and in activities related to the evaluation of the system,
- The Centre for Speech Technology Research from the University of Edinburgh engaged in the resolution of a large variety of problems including phonetics, courseware developments and evaluation,
- The research center from ALCATEL FACE in Italy with activities in signal processing and system development,
- Tecnopolis CSATA Novus Ortus also from Italy leading the user interface developments,
- OROS, a French SME involved in signal processing aspects,
- and finally the INFOCOM Department from the University of Rome "La Sapienza" bringing his experience in phonetic analysis.

## 2. The Feasibility Study (SPELL-I)

In terms of work, activities during the feasibility study involved major developments in three directions.

- First of all, development of methods for analyzing the characteristics of the speech of non-native speakers,
- Then development of metrics [2] for identifying differences between the user pronunciation and a so-called optimal one,
- And finally development of a significant interface able to provide the user with a variety of feedback modes including text, graphics and speech, so that he/she can improve his/her speaking skills.

Another aspect which was not clearly stated at the beginning of the project concerned the development of preliminary pieces of courseware.

In order to address all these technical problems, work was split into several tasks. In fact, the project workplan involved five activities.

Task 1 provided the project with a unique database involving both naive and native speakers. Such data were found particularly useful and formed the basic material for the analyses of the relevant features at the macro and micro levels.

Tasks 2 (on macro features) and 3 (on micro features) followed a quite similar strategy. In a first step, they involved the identification of distinctive features of interest which are able to characterize the pronunciation. Also, were proposed teaching exercises according to these features. Then signal processing implementations took place. These processings were needed to compute automatically the relevant parameters corresponding to the features. In parallel metrics were designed. They are needed to evaluate the similarity of the responses of the user when compared to a reference. Finally these developments were evaluated at component level, both from the point of view of performance, and from the point of view of computational complexity involving response time and memory requirements.

Task 4 was devoted to the development of the user interface. A set of elementary functions involving text, graphics and speech is now available. These functions can be easily combined together and when integrated with the signal processing and metrics computations, they form the basis of the courseware modules.

Finally task 5 was devoted to the evaluation of the existing SPELL demonstrator at system level.

## 3. Product Development (SPELL-II)

The aim of the second phase of the project, started about one year ago, is clearly to develop the demonstration system available from the feasibility study towards a marketable product.

To achieve these objectives, four distinct research areas have been identified.

- Research on phonetics mainly focused on consonants [6] and on nasals, two aspects which were not included in the first phase. In addition, the experimental validation of the chosen phonetic models will be done.

- System development involving development of additional courseware modules and refinement of hardware and software. Moreover two prospective activities are considered. On the one side hypermedia possibilities is under investigation, while on the other side prosody-controlled synthesis used as auditory feedback will be assessed.

- A full series of evaluation studies will be carried out starting with an exploratory phase involving language trainers and teachers up to a full size controlled field test experiment.

- Finally an objective of the work is to carry out a detailed market survey and to define and specify viable products deriving from the work.

Up to now, activities mainly focused on the first two points.

## 4. The SPELL Courseware

The main innovation behind SPELL is probably the departure from the traditional practice of whole utterance matching used when teaching pronunciation, here referred as practice courseware. By contrast, the use of a teaching courseware based on well founded phonetic and phonological principles provides directed instructions to the student allowing better predictions to be made about the student's performance.

Even if the system is designed in such a way to allow any possible instructional sequence, the present prototype is based on a paradigm called DELTA and involving four phases :

- **D**emonstrate : audio demonstrations by the system of various utterances (as well as visual representations) are used to highlight the pronunciation features of interest.

- **E**valuate **L**istening : small listening tests are completed by the student to evaluate his/her ability to perceive the pronunciation features of interest.

- **T**each : the actual teaching of the pronunciation features of interest takes place at this stage, with quantitative feedback for the student and directions for modifying inadequate performances.

- **A**ssess : this stage is the formal evaluation of the student's ability to pronounce the features of interest.

Following this strategy, four modules for teaching consonant production, vowel quality, rhythm and intonation are developed. Each module will be now briefly discussed.

## 4.1. Consonants

The analysis of consonants provides a useful illustration of the integration of linguistic knowledge and speech technology being achieved on the SPELL project. The first stage in the development of consonant teaching modules has been a survey of the likely errors in consonant production by non-native speakers of English, French and Italian. This has involved a comparison of the consonant systems of each language, to characterize the principal differences between each language pair and to predict the range of possible errors in consonant production by non-native speakers.

While there is a large number of possible errors in each source-target language combination, particularly at the level of acoustical realizations, not all such errors are equally important in terms of teaching priorities. The principal consideration is the effect of the error on the student's intelligibility. The errors identified in each language combination have therefore been ranked according to their expected effect on intelligibility.

Consonant teaching modules are now being developed for the high priority errors identified in each language pair. Errors are detected by using a Hidden Markov Model (HMM) segmenter [7], which labels the incoming speech using a sequence of acoustic phonetic units specified in an associated segment transition network. These teaching modules will use minimal pair examples to highlight the contrast between the target sound and the typical non-native speaker substitutions. The use of some basic articulatory information (the position of the lips, tongue and jaw, for example) will also be considered as part of the teaching strategy, using multimedia graphics where appropriate.

## 4.2. Vowels

A SPELL module has already been developed for teaching monophthong vowels in the three target languages. A similar phonetic approach to that of the consonants has being adopted, involving the identification of the most important errors in vowel production for each language pair. However, the analysis required to assess the quality of a student vowels is rather different.

A vowel similarity metric determines whether a given student's vowel token falls within a vowel space derived from multiple tokens spoken by a group of native speakers. Vowels tokens are represented in terms of two normalized formant parameters. The acoustic analysis which provides this representation first uses a HMM segmenter to isolate the vowel from surrounding speech sounds and silence. The first three formant frequencies are estimated using a modified McCandless algorithm, along with fundamental frequency (F0). The most stable region of the vowel is then chosen by a "steady-state" finder algorithm and the four acoustic parameters are then averaged across this stable vowel region [4]. The normalized formant parameters are then obtained by transforming measurements to a Bark scale and calculating the formant parameters are then obtained by transforming differences F1-F0 (corresponding approximately to the articulatory dimension of tongue height) and F2-F1 (corresponding approximately to tongue frontness-backness). Courseware for vowels, along the lines of that envisaged for consonants, is currently being implemented.

## 4.3. Rhythm

A major contributor to rhythm in English, French and Italian is the relationship between strong and weak syllables. In all three languages, syllable strength is marked acoustically by variations in one or more of the parameters of F0, intensity, duration and vowel quality (i.e. formants). However, the frequent occurrence of strong syllables in English and Italian, contrasting markedly with intervening weak syllables, produces a characteristic rhythmic alternation which does not occur in French. In addition, French minimizes the distinction between strong and weak syllables when compared with Italian and English.

The SPELL module for rhythm aims to improve the rhythmic quality achieved by learners by concentrating on a sub-set of the available parameters, namely duration and vowel quality [3]. Thus learners of English are taught to produce weak syllables with centralized vowel quality reduced duration; learners of French, conversely, must avoid any centralization of vowel quality or reduction in duration; while learners of Italian should aim for an intermediate position, contrasting duration but keeping vowel qualities uncentralized (the parameters of F0 and intensity have yet to be included in this analysis). Complete teaching modules or rhythm in English, French and Italian are now under development.

## 4.4. Intonation

The description and analysis of intonation adopted for the SPELL system has a practical phonetic basis which allows the major F0 movements associated with the contours of all three languages to be described using a common terminology and analyzed with a single similarity metric [2]. Central to this analysis is the relationship between the fundamental frequency contour of an utterance and its associated segmental sequence. A number of stylized contours in each language have been chosen for the initial implementation. Each contour is schematized using a set of *pitch anchors* -specifying the segmental locations of the major turning points and discontinuities within a stylized contour- and a corresponding set of *pitch tunnels* -describing the tolerances allowed for the path taken by an intonation contour between two pitch anchors.

Two analyses are performed on each input utterance : the derivation of a smoothed, normalized fundamental frequency contour and the extraction of the segmental sequence. The F0 contour is derived from the low-pass-filtered speech waveform by a modified super-resolution pitch determination algorithm [5]. The contour is heavily smoothed by a non-linear smoother, normalized by the mean and standard deviation of the speaker's F0, interpolated to fill in gaps and smoothed again. The segmentation is obtained using the Hidden Markov Model segmenter described above; the segment transition network which specifies the possible sequence of segment labels allows for a variety of alternative pronunciations, including errors predictable from the student's mother tongue, to ensure an accurate segmentation.

Complete courseware modules for English intonation have now been implemented and work on modules for French and Italian is currently under way.

## 4.5. User Interface

Figure 1 shows a typical example of the SPELL user interface. This figure is related to the intonation module, for a student studying English statement intonation.

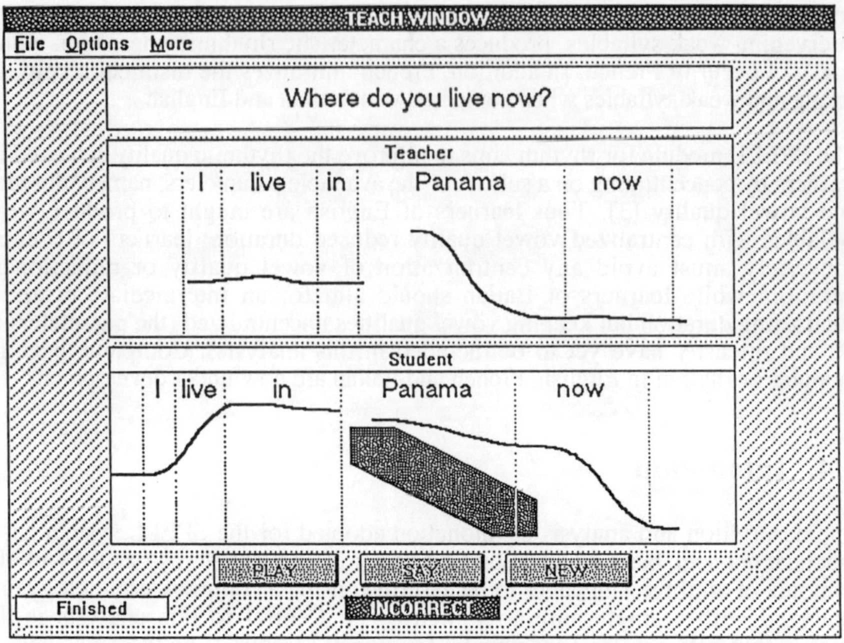


Figure 1 - An example of the user interface
for the SPELL intonation teaching module

The general interface conforms to the common user access conventions of the Microsoft Windows® graphical environment. The student controls the intonation teaching module using the PLAY, SAY and NEW buttons. PLAY allows the student to listen to either the teacher's model or his/her own production, SAY records and analyzes the student's own attempt, and NEW lets the student choose another sentence for practice. Statement intonation is taught using simulated dialogue, with the *question window* (top) providing a suitable context for the student's "reply". The *teacher window* (middle) displays the target intonation for the current phrase, with the teacher's smoothed F0 contour and a time-aligned orthographic representation to indicate the location of the intonational movements. The *student window* (bottom) displays the result of analyzing the student's utterance in a similar form, but with the facility to highlight errors in the student's production. In this example, the student has used the wrong intonation at the tonic ("Panama"), and the error is highlighted by the appearance of the correct pitch tunnel at this point. In addition a feedback window (bottom) displays a CORRECT or INCORRECT message, and a system voice announces "Well done" or "Try again" accordingly.

## 5. Conclusion

This paper has presented some aspects of the SPELL project on computer-aided pronunciation teaching. Modules have been implemented for teaching vowels, rhythm and intonation to learners of English, French and Italian. Each module has been built on a solid phonetic foundation and structured using sophisticated signal processing techniques on a PC. Work is now in progress to complete a module for teaching those consonants of each language which have the greatest effect on intelligibility when mispronounced. It is the aim of the present research to improve all the modules in order to bring the SPELL system to the market.

## References


[1] "Final Report", ESPRIT Project 5192, SPELL, ed. by J.P. Lefèvre, November 1992.

[2] Lefèvre J.P., Hiller S.M., Rooney E., Laver J., Di Benedetto M.G., "Macro and Micro Features for Automated Pronunciation Improvement in the SPELL System", Speech Communication, Vol. 11, N° 1, pp. 31-44, March 1992.

[3] Rooney E., Hiller S.M., Laver J., Jack M., "Prosodic Features for Automated Pronunciation Improvement in the SPELL System", Proc. ICSLP 92, Banff, Alberta, Canada, pp. 413-416, October 1992.

[4] Di Benedetto M.G., Carraro F., Hiller S.M., Rooney E., "Vowels Pronunciation Assessment in the SPELL System", Proc. ICSLP 92, Banff, Alberta, Canada, pp. 417-420, October 1992.

[5] Medan Y., Yair E., Chazan D., "Super Resolution Pitch Determination of Speech Signals", IEEE Trans. on Signal Processing, Vol. ASSP-39, N° 1, pp. 40-48, January 1991.

[6] Rooney E., Eckert M., Hiller S., Vaughan R., Laver J., "Training Consonants in a Computer-Aided System for Pronunciation Teaching", to appear in Proc. Eurospeech 93, Berlin, Germany, September 1993.

[7] McInnes F.R., Carraro F., Hiller S.M., Rooney E.J., "Evaluation and Optimisation of a Segmenter for a PC-based Pronunciation Teaching System", Proc. Institute of Acoustics, Vol. 14, pp. 109-116, 1992.

# A Multilingual Unlimited Vocabulary Stochastic Tagger

E. Dermatas and G. Kokkinakis
Wire Communications Laboratory
Department of Electrical Engineering
University of Patras, Patras, Greece

## Abstract

A multilingual probabilistic tagger is presented and tested in six languages (Dutch, English, French, German, Greek, Italian and Spanish) using two sets of grammatical tags and tagged corpora of 2.3 million words established in the framework of the ESPRIT I project 291/860 "Linguistic Analysis of the European Languages". The system is fully automatic both in the tagging and the learning process and is also able to tag unknown words using statistical information extracted from the last part of the words (word-endings). For each language the prediction quality of the tagger is compared with that of another recently presented stochastic tagger and is proved to be better.

## 1. Introduction

In the last years a great number of text taggers for natural language has been developed using one of the following three approaches to predict part-of-speech classes.

Rule based systems [6,7,10-13] use grammatical constraints which are dependent on the specific application tagset and are defined by experienced linguists. If a large set of grammatical categories is specified, the number of rules increases significantly. Thus the rule definition process becomes a highly costly and cumbersome method. Nevertheless several quality rule based systems have been already developed using an application dependent restricted set of grammatical categories [10-12].

On the other hand stochastic systems [1-4,14-16,18] use well formulated models, the parameters of which are estimated automatically from training texts. This gives a researcher the possibility to test various prediction models but requires a tagged text database to train the model parameters. In most cases these models are not dependent on the number and type of the tags and on the working text environment. For this reason they are preferred in applications with large tagsets and in multilingual tasks. Moreover this approach has the advantage to adapt successively the stochastic model parameters from new tagged texts.

Finally, a restricted number of connectionist models has been used for lexical acquisition [5-7]. These systems are trained on both morphological (word-endings) and contextual information (part-of-speech in the neighbourhood of the tagged word) extracted from a tagged text corpus. Correct classification rates up to 96.4% have been reported in experiments carried out for the Swedish language using the Teleman corpus [5].

Unlimited vocabulary stochastic taggers i.e. taggers handling also unknown words, have been presented in [4] and [15], and the tagging process is modelled as a Hidden Markov chain. The definition in [4] of the HMM parameters for the unknown word tags is achieved by assuming that the probability distribution of the unknown word tags is the same as the probability distribution of the tags of the less probable words in the training text [4]. In [15] the model parameters are estimated by taking into account the information of the last part of the unknown words. In this paper a multilingual unlimited vocabulary stochastic tagger is presented which uses the model described in [4] for the known words and a similar model to [15] for the unknown words employing word-endings morphological information.

The performance of the taggers has been measured in newspaper and EEC law texts for the English, Dutch, German, French, Greek, Italian and Spanish language using two alternative optimisation criteria and two tagsets differing in size. For each language the testing corpus consisted of approximately 300 000 words tagged with a more or less common set of grammatical categories established in the ESPRIT I project 291/860.

This paper is structured as follows. An introduction to stochastic tagger topics is given in this section. In section 2 the stochastic model for tagging known words and the optimisation criteria are briefly presented, followed by a detailed description of the unknown word prediction model in section 3. The environment of the carried out experiments, the size of the learning and the testing text, and also the type and the number of linguistic categories used in each language are presented in section 4 together with the system's performance. Finally, a discussion of the experimental results and a conclusion including further work are given in section 5 and 6 respectively.

## 2. Stochastic Tagging: Hidden Markov Model

The natural language text tagging problem can be solved using a stochastic model which defines the probabilistic dependencies between tags and words in a sentence environment, and the optimisation criterion for estimating the most probable solution. The tagging process is formulated as a Hidden Markov chain as follows. In the hidden level, the tag sequence is created by a first-order homogeneous Markov source, and each tag state produces a word event in the observation level. The best sequence of the hidden tags can be estimated using two apropriate criteria:

a. Choose the tag sequence that maximises the probability of occurrence given the model parameters and the word observations, as follows:

$$Tv = \arg\max P(t_1, \ldots, t_n, \ldots, t_N \mid w_1, \ldots, w_n, \ldots, w_N, M_m) \quad (1)$$

where,

$w_n$: is the $n^{th}$ word of the analysed sentence
$t_n$: is the tag for the $n^{th}$ word,
Tv: is the sequence of the N optimum tags and,
Mm: is the HMM parameters.

The solution of the above optimisation criterion is given by the well known Viterbi algorithm [9].

b. At each word event, the corresponding most probable tag is computed independently from the other word solutions, given the model parameters and the word observations:

$$Tv = \arg\max P(t_1, \ldots, t_n, \ldots, t_N \mid w_1, \ldots, w_n, \ldots, w_N, M_m) \quad (2)$$

In this optimisation criterion, the most probable tag is computed using the forward-backward probabilities [17].

## 3. Tagging Unknown Words Using Word-endings Morphology

When a new text is processed, several unknown words are spotted. The word-tag conditional probabilities for the unknown words are unidentified and for this reason the solutions of the optimisation criteria can't be computed. In order to complete the stochastic model three hypotheses have been employed:

a. The tag conditional probabilities distribution for the unknown words having the same word-ending is strongly non-uniform.
b. This distribution is approximated by the word-tag conditional probabilities of the words having the same word-ending in the training text.
c. The unknown words having a word-ending which has not appeared in the training text are assumed to follow the tag distribution of the most probable word-endings.

The validity of the above hypotheses has not been proved. Nevertheless the stochastic tagger prediction accuracy, measured in extensive experiments described in the last part of this paper, has confirmed their efficiency.

## 4. Experiments

The tagger performance has been tested in extensive experiments carried out on texts tagged in the framework of the ESPRIT project 291/860 for seven languages: English, Dutch, German, French, Greek, Italian and Spanish. In table 1, the total size of the natural language tagging text is given, derived from mixed sentences of newspapers and EEC-law tagged corpora. Each text has been divided into two parts; the training text which has a constant size of 250 kwords and the remaining part which is the testing text.

| English | Dutch | German | French | Greek | Italian | Spanish |
|---|---|---|---|---|---|---|
| 401097 | 333331 | 303496 | 298488 | 310301 | 356173 | 283378 |

**Table 1:** Size of the tagging text of each language (in words)

| English | Dutch | German | French | Greek | Italian | Spanish |
|---|---|---|---|---|---|---|
| 43 | 50 | 116 | 114 | 443 | 121 | 121 |

**Table 2:** Number of grammatical classes of the second set

| English | Dutch | German | French | Greek | Italian | Spanish |
|---|---|---|---|---|---|---|
| 1657 | 1223 | 1284 | 1298 | 2292 | 1885 | 1207 |

**Table 3:** Number of three character word-endings

Two subsets of grammatical categories were isolated from the detailed set using a common coding scheme for all languages [8]. In the first set the words of the text are classified into the following 11 main grammatical categories: Verb, Noun, Adjective, Adverb, Pronoun, Preposition, Article/Determine, Conjunction, Particle, Interjection, Miscella-neous (defined as the tag for every word entry not classified to the previous classes).

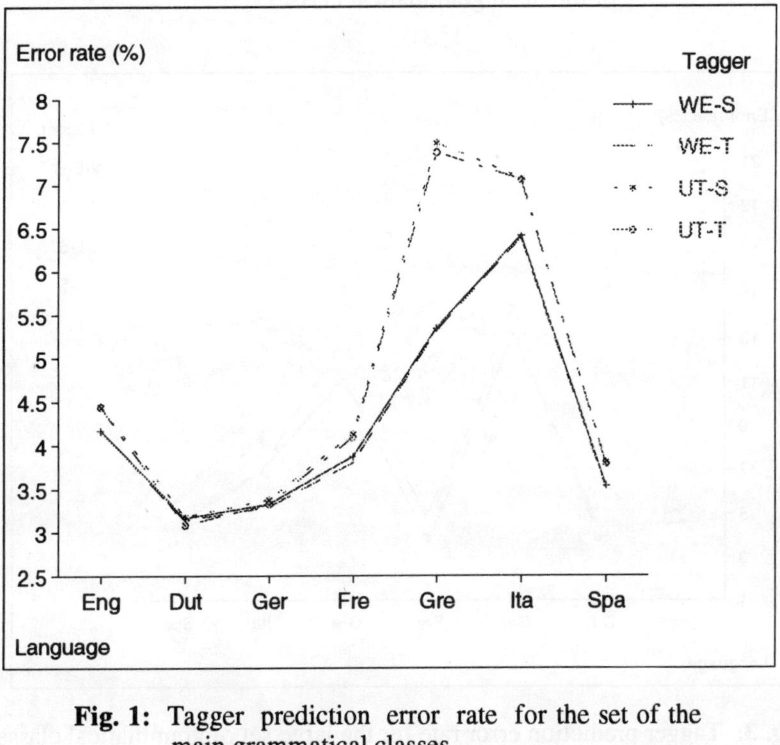


**Fig. 1:** Tagger prediction error rate for the set of the main grammatical classes

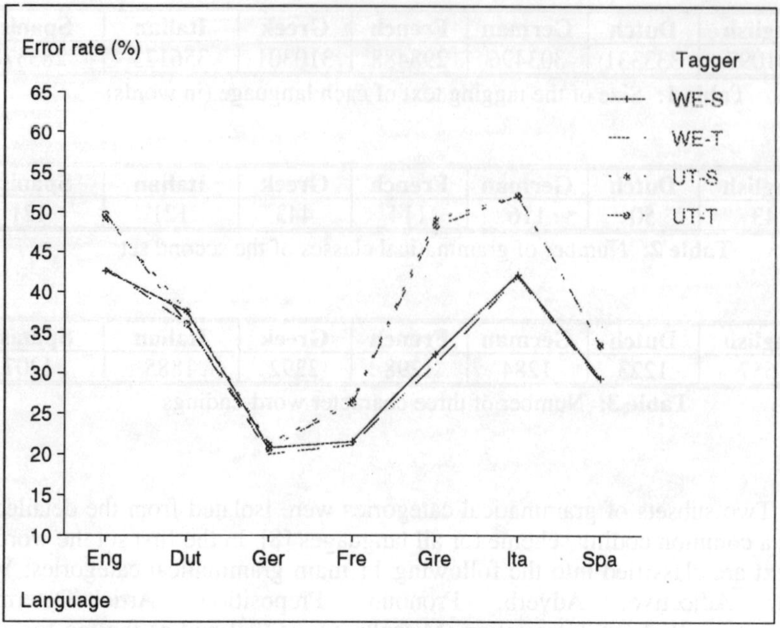


**Fig. 2:** Unknown word prediction error rate for the set of the main grammatical classes

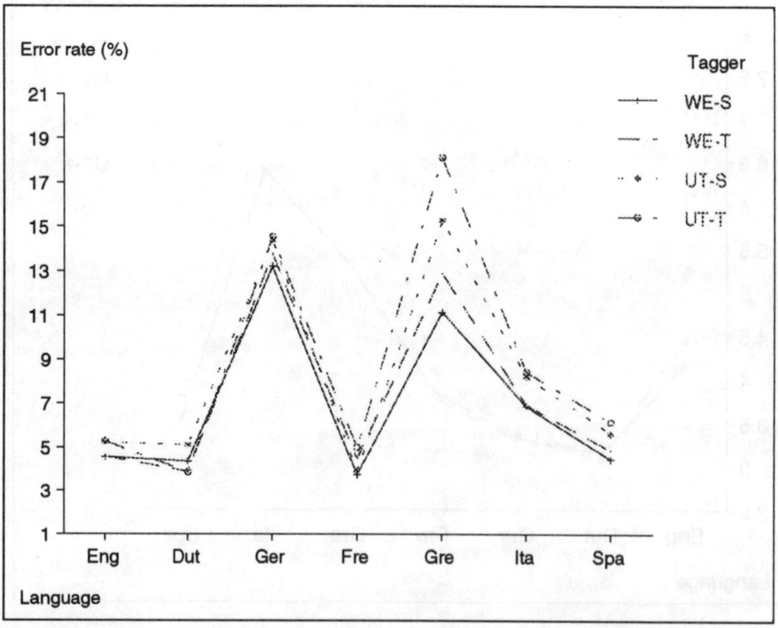


**Fig. 3:** Tagger prediction error rate for the large set of grammatical classes

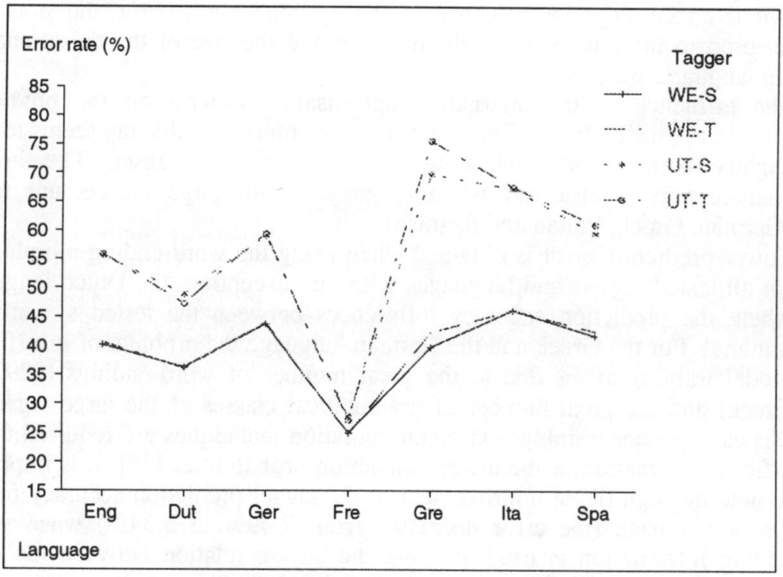


**Fig. 4:** Unknown word prediction error rate for the large set of grammatical classes

In the second set (large set) a detailed grammatical system, including sub-classes, is setup to describe each word entry. The structure has the main grammatical classes following by sub-classes such as tense, voice, mood, person, number, case, gender, regular, irregular, comparative, superlative, particular past, polite, interrogative etc. The number of grammatical classes for each language is given in table 2. For each language, the prediction accuracy of the proposed tagger and the previous reported tagger [4] was measured, for the two sets of grammatical classes and for the two optimisation criteria,. A total number of 2 (sets) x 7 (languages) x 2 (taggers) x 2 (optimisation criteria) = 56 experiments was carried out. The number of the different fixed-length word-endings [16] isolated in the training text is given in table 3.

The prediction accuracy of the taggers measured in the testing corpus and the unknown words for each language and tagset are given in the following figures. The two taggers have been designated as follows: The word-ending tagger using the optimisation criterion of the most probable tag sequence as WE-S, while when using the most probable tag as WE-T. The tagger presented in [4] using the optimisation criterion of the most probable tag sequence is designated as UT-S, while when using the most probable tag as UT-T.

## 5. Discussion

A detailed discussion of the experimental results for the tested languages is out of the scope of this paper. In the following general comments about the tagger behaviour concerning the influence of the optimisation criteria, the stochastic model used to tag unknown words, the type and the size of the tagset and the testing language are given:

a. The influence of the alternative optimisation criteria on the prediction accuracy is insignificant. The criterion of the most probable tag seems to give slightly better results when used on a restricted tagset. The inverse phenomenon is observed when languages with large tagsets are tested (German, Greek, Italian and Spanish).
b. Lower prediction error is obtained when using the word-ending morphology for all tested tagsets and languages with one exception: the Dutch language, where the prediction accuracy differences between the tested systems are minimal. For the Greek and the German language the problem of insufficient model training arises due to the great number of word-endings (2292 for Greek) and the great number of grammatical classes of the large tagset. In this case greater training text or interpolation techniques are required for an efficient estimation of the unseen transition probabilities [15]. It is important to note the significant improvement of the tagger prediction accuracy for the Greek language (the error decreases from 7.49% to 5.34%) when word-ending information is used, proving the strong relation between the word grammatical class and the type of the word ending.
c. Greater errors are generally observed when the large set of grammatical tags is used in comparison to the set of the main grammatical categories. The increase is insignificant in most languages but very substantial in German (the error rate increases approximately four times) and Greek (the error rate is 1.5 times).
d. Objective comparisons between languages can't be made when the large set of grammatical classes is used, due to the differences between the grammatical structures of the languages. For the experiments carried out with the set of main grammatical classes the language influence on the models' prediction accuracy is summarised as follows: German and Dutch are the most predictable languages by the first-order HMM approach. The most "difficult languages" are the Greek and the Italian due to their more free syntax.

## 6. Conclusion

An automatic stochastic tagger of natural language texts using word-endings morphology was presented, tested and compared with another stochastic tagger. Extensive experiments were carried out using two optimisation criteria for the definition of the optimum tag solution and two sets of grammatical tags.

The experiments have shown that the error rate depends strongly on the language, the type and the size of the tagset. A better prediction accuracy was achieved by the proposed stochastic model in exchange for greater memory requirements.

Improvement of the tagger model is in progress in two directions: An automatic method for a variable length word-endings set extracted from a training text is tested in order to approach the real "word-endings" of a language.

Various interpolation techniques are examined in order to predict the unseen transition probabilities when a small training set is available.

## References


[1] Church K., "A Stochastic parts program and noun phrase parser for unrestricted text", Second Conference on Applied Natural Language Processing., pp. 136-143, Austin, Texas,1988

[2] Dermatas E., Kokkinakis G., "Semi Automatic Labelling of Greek Texts", 7th FASE Symposium SPEECH'88, Book 1, pp. 239-245, Edinburgh 1988.

[3] Dermatas E., Kokkinakis G., "A System for Automatic Text Labelling", Eurospeech-90, pp. 382-385, Paris 1990.

[4] Dermatas E., Kokkinakis G., "A Fast Multilingual Probabilistic Tagger", Eurospeech-93, pp. 1323-1326, Berlin 1993.

[5] Eineborg M., Gamback B., "Back-propagation Based Lexical Acquisition Experiments", NeuroNimes: Neural Networks and their Industrial & Cognitive Applications, pp. 169-178, Nimes 1993.

[6] Elenius K., Carlson R., "Assigning parts-of-speech of words from their orthography using a connectionist model", European Conference on Speech Communication and Technology, vol. 1, pp. 534-537, Paris, Sep. 1989.

[7] Elenius K., Kjell, "Comparing a connectionist and rule based model for assignment parts-of-speech", ICASSP-90, pp. 597-600, Albuquerque, New Mexico, April 1990.

[8] ESPRIT 291/860, Unification of the word classes of the ESPRIT-I Project 860", Internal Report BU-WKL-0376, Oct. 1986.

[9] Forney G., "The Viterbi Algorithm", Proc. of the IEEE, vol. 61, n$^{o}$. 3, pp. 268-278, Mar. 1973.

[10] Garside R., Leech G., Sampson G., "The Computational Analysis of English. A Corpus-Based Approach" Logman eds. London, 1987.

[11] Karlsson F., "Constraint Grammar as a Framework for Parsing Running Text", XIII$^{th}$ Intern. Conference on Computational Linguistics, vol.3, ed. Hans Karlgren, pp.168-173, Helsinki, 1990.

[12] Karlsson F., Voutilainen A., Anttila A., Heikkila J., "Constraint Grammar: A Language-Independent System for Parsing Unrestricted Text, with an Application to English", Workshop Notes from the Ninth National Conference on Artificial Intelligence AAAI-91, Anaheim, California, July 1991.

[13] Krause W., Willee G., "Lemmatizing German newspaper texts with the aid of an algorithm", Computers and the Humanities, vol. 15, pp. 101-113, 1981.

[14] Kupiec J., "Robust part-of-speech tagging using a Hidden Markov Model", Computer Speech & Language, vol.6, n$^{o}$ 3, pp. 225-242, Jul. 1992.

[15] Maltese G., Mancini F., "A Technique to Automatically Assign Parts-of-Speech to Words Taking into Account Word-Ending Information through a Probabilistic Model", Eurospeech-91, pp. 753-756, Genoa 1991.

[16] Merialdo B., "Tagging text with a probabilistic model", ICASSP-91, pp. 809-812, 1991.

[17] Rabiner L.R., "A Tutorial on Hidden Markov Models and Selected Applications in Speech Recognition", Proc. of the IEEE, vol. 77, n° 2, pp. 257-25, Feb. 1989.

[18] Wothke K., Weck-Ulm I., Heinecke J., Mertineit O., Pachunke T., "Statistically Based Automatic Tagging of German Text Corpora with Parts-of-Speech - Some Experiments", IBM Germany, TR75.93.02, Heidelberg Scientific Center, Feb. 1993.

# SYMBOL : Multilingual and Multicode Lexical Learning System on CD-I Environment

Georges Rensonnet
Association Nationale des Parents d'Enfants Déficients Auditifs
10, Quai de la Charete, 75019 Paris, France

## Abstract

The project SYMBOL has been developed within the framework of the TIDE Programme of the European Community in order to support the technological initiatives for handicapped and elderly persons. It is positioned at the intersection of two areas: development of new technologies and application of pedagogic innovations for the purposes of rehabilitation.

## 1. Concept

SYMBOL involves the creation of a lexical learning system for all target groups experiencing communication distress due to an inability to link the signified (images) to their signifiers (words expressed or written in spoken or sign language). The two primary groups concerned are thus aphasics and the deaf. Although these persons control language with difficulty, they nonetheless possess a non-verbal representation of objects and actions which condition their world and their lives. By extension, the project will hold interest for all individuals learning a language, including young children, illiterate persons, and people learning a foreign language.

With the interactive procedure incorporating the signified (pictures of objects) and the signifier (words, gestures, pictograms), users are able to acquire new vocabulary or to extend their existing lexical base within a user-friendly database.

## 2. Prototype

The prototype consists of a CD-I disk including an image database of still pictures involving the home environment, here called "The Home". The user is able to access these images either through the set of paths of the system, or through itineraries which he or she can choose individually. For each object or selected action, which remains visually displayed in a window on the screen, the user finds a spoken and written representation, with a choice of 7 European languages : the pronunciation in audio, the common spelling, and the phonetic transcription (International Phonetic Alphabet). The complementary database offers other signifier choices. For the time being, these are limited to their equivalents in French Sign Language (FSL) and the visual form of French words in the Cued Speech (CS).

The technological innovation resides essentially in the creation of a universal system for navigation in a CD-I programme in order to establish the platform for a true "author system" through a network of European co-producers. A CD-I configuration has been preferred to a PC environment (DV-I, for example) in order to open the access to the widest public possible.

The psycho-pedagogical innovation lies primarily in the possibility of triple access to this "pictionary" : by logical choice, by cumulating or eliminating attributes, and by visual selection. For the user, this means a new independence and freedom which allow to create his own itineraries, thus further enriching the contents. Although research in vocal synthesis is very active, the development of non-verbal languages has so far been limited to the production of specific local and partial language dictionaries, which are available in printed form or, at best, on computer.

For the first prototype, an interactive compact disk for the learning of the signified (e.g. images) and their signifiers encountered in the microworld "Home" has now been designed and produced. It was developed in the following main stages :

- creation of modes of access to the signified contained in the "pictionary", built up from pictures of objects and actions organized in a tree structure,
- creation of the preliminary VO prototype from a model, and
- in-situ validation leading to the final prototype V1.

## 3. Extension

This extension of the product is aimed at the creation of a lexical generator of CD-I applications allowing users, via their institutions, to co-produce learning environments. The project will supply a learning kit including an applications *editor-generator*, "The Home" environment CD-I, and an accompanying guide for the use and the creation of applications. The extension will involve the following main steps, in consecutive order :

- creation of a linguistic, graphic and technical architecture, and an arborescent navigation path that can be modulated to all microworlds of real objects,
- technical development of the CD-I executor,
- technical development of the CD-I author system (applications editor-generator),
- pressing of a final version of "The Home" universe created on the first prototype,
- documentation in form of a User's Guide,

- development of the Teaching Kit to be distributed throughout the user-producer network, and
- longitudinal evaluation of the "socialization" of the CD-I "The Home".

*The user-producer network* will make it possible to pool and optimize experience and knowledge through a proximity tutoring device.

This lexical learning system offers two key advantages. On one site it takes into account specific particularities (individuals experiencing communication difficulties) while operating with a general public technology (CD-I environment). Secondly, it permits an enrichment of the contents by the users, who thus mutualize their knowledge and optimize their experience through auto-production.

## 4. The CD-I Author System

The CD-I Author System is composed of two clearly distinct entities : a common CD-I executor, and an associated multimedia database for each microworld This database includes informations on logical and visual links between multimedia objects, which are defined with an editor-generator.

The *CD-I executor* constitutes the driving force of the system. It contains the set logic for the different techniques of navigation. This logic is abstract and independent with respect to any particular microworld, since it is unattached to any concrete representation that it treats. The executor is written in C language.

To function, the CD-I executor must be supplied from a *multimedia database*. This database describes the particular microworld on which the executor is to work, in the nine Community languages. It includes photographs, animated pictures, video sequences, text, sound sequences, control pictograms and, for each type of navigation, a complete description of the logical or visual links between the different concepts of the microworld being examined.

The advantage of this architecture is that it allows complete detachment from the environment of development specific to the CD-I. It is indeed possible to build new databases, allowing the study of new microworlds, using an editor-generator operating in the PC environment, under Windows.

On the PC, this *editor-generator* generates the indexed database which will be used together with all media to produce the Symbol CD-I related to the given microworld. This database is constituted of a set of text files that can be displayed and printed using the editor. These files further describe all logical and visual links introduced into the editor. They constitute the reference documentation concerning each microworld being examined.

To a certain extent, *the generator* constitutes a CD-I author system making it possible to code all logical links (indexation related to the 5 techniques of navigation) and visual links (active interface zones) describing a microworld in the Symbol product line. This generator has the following main functions :

- creation, deletion, modification of a microworld,
- definition of the microworld concepts, text and phonetic transcription of concepts for each Community country,
- creation of logical and visual links for all 5 techniques of navigation,
- generation of the database,

- printing of the database, and
- configuration of the CD-I executor (active elements).

## 5. Valorisation

The industrialization of the product will benefit, on the one hand, from the marketing policy planned for the CD-I by Philips and Sony, and on the other hand, from the contacts that will be established with specific target groups in international networks to demonstrate the educational value of the system. The constitution of a "user network" for production and distribution will ensure an attractive market.

However, an effective strategy of marketing and distribution must also be applied, to ensure that the product may fully meet the aims for its intended use. It will thus certainly contribute to the creation of a single market in rehabilitation technology in Europe, which constitutes the final objective of the TIDE programme.

## 6. Consortium

The consortium is composed of an organisation of parents of deaf children developing and providing educational support for children, industrialists specialised in CD-I production, and research institutions with a strong background in linguistics and system development :

- *Computer Science Corporation (CSC Brussels/Belgium)* - in charge of technical development, together with Philips NV/SA,
- *Centre d'Etudes Pluridisciplinaires en Langue des Signes (CEPLUS Liège/Belgium)* - structuring of data from a linguistic viewpoint,
- *Facultés Universitaires Notre-Dame de la Paix (FUNDP Namur/Belgium)* - study covering the pedagogic aspects of the products, the exploitation of tracks and the evaluation of the learning system,
- *Système Expert Communication et Intelligence Artificielle (SECIA Paris/France)* - production of the media base (graphic chart, image base),
- *Association Nationale des Parents d'Enfants Déficients Auditifs (ANPEDA Paris/France)* - project leader in charge of coordination, management, and development of a marketing plan.

The product will be validated through the following user institutions :

- L'Institut Royal pour Handicapés de l'Ouïe et de la Vue (IRHOV Liège/Belgium),
- Die Gehörlosen Schule (Bremen/Germany),
- L'Association Régionale pour l'Intégration des Enfants Déficients Auditifs (ARIEDA Montpellier/France),
- L'Ecole J. Anspach (aphasic children) (Brussels/Belgium),
- Le Centre de Fraiture (aphasic adults) (Belgium), and
- The educational programme will be assessed by the Institut National de l'Audiovisuel (INA Paris/France).

## 7. Conclusions

We backed on CD-I technology which widely answers to our main preoccupation: to improve communication between hearing and hard of hearing persons. We hope that future developements will strengthen this choice.

# Speech Understanding and Dialogue over the Telephone

Jeremy Peckham
Vocalis Ltd,
Chaston House, Mill Court,
Great Shelford, Cambridge CB3 5LD, U.K.

## Abstract

The current generation of interactive dialogue systems for over-the-telephone applications in real environments is limited to speaker independent recognition of isolated words and phrases or limited continuous speech such as digit strings. The five year ESPRIT SUNDIAL project P2218, which concluded in August 1993, was aimed at developing a new generation of dialogue systems allowing spontaneous conversational interaction over the telephone. The project involved the development of four language prototypes for train timetable enquires in German and Italian and flight enquiries in English and French. A close integration of speech and language processing techniques has been achieved for understanding spoken input together with the use of AI techniques for intelligent dialogue management. Evaluation of prototypes in four languages has been completed with both naive and experienced users. A 96% transaction success rate has been achieved with the flight inquiry application in English over a local PBX connection using untrained speakers; lower performance was obtained for long distance PSTN connections with members of the public. A number of major lessons were learned from the project about the factors which are important in the design of spoken dialogue systems operating over the telephone. Some of these lessons are discussed in the paper.

## 1. Introduction

In the telephone network environment, speech recognition has now only just reached a threshold of acceptability, even for simple applications. Current applications for speech recognition over the telephone are driven either by the limitations of the telephone keypad, the need for hands-free operation in the car or the unavailability of a DTMF phone. Real world applications [8,9] deploying speech recognition are all menu based dialogues where users responses are restricted to single words and phrases or continuous digits. Generally speaking, these applications employ a small number of words such as control words and digits, although recent experiments with large vocabulary recognition [22] have shown great promise. Keyword spotting has also emerged as a viable technique for certain applications and is already being deployed in applications such as directory assistance.

This approach, whilst far from natural language understanding, has considerable potential for improving the robustness and usabilty of systems for naive users.

Ultimately, the acceptance by the public of automated telephone information services and other applications may be limited until more natural language dialogues are possible (see figure 1). Ideally, such systems should have the following capabilities:

- mixed initiative dialogue strategies
- understanding of a subset of natural language sufficient for the task domain
- robust handling of naive users who will not always speak after prompts or answer system questions simply
- robust handling of spontaneous speech phenomena such as 'uhm's and 'er's and pauses.

Achieving such a capability represents a formidable challenge requiring a number of technical issues to be addressed, including the following:

- speaker independence over the telephone, including the public network
- spontaneous speech recognition, including phenomena such as hesitations
- large vocabulary continuous speech recognition, sufficient to support natural language utterances
- integration of speech and natural language processing to achieve speech understanding
- intelligent, co-operative dialogue management to deal with recovery from user and system errors

In addition, systems will have to work in real time or very close to real time in order to provide meaningful evaluation results as well as future commercial products.

The SUNDIAL project began in September 1988 and was aimed at addressing these challenges in the development of a speech based co-operative dialogue system as an interface to computer applications in the information services domain. Partners from France, Gemany, Italy and Great Britain worked on the development of four 'national prototypes' with one partner per country taking specific responsiblity for the final integartion of the components for the prototype. A common architecture for the systems was developed at the start of the project which facilitated the exchange of components and provided a common basis for module evaluation.

Most of the participants had previous experience and existing technology in natural language processing and speech recognition and rather than start from scratch, partners built upon this experience and shared results with other partners. In the area of speech recognition for example several parallel experiments were conducted in order to refine the approach and determine which techniques gave the best performance. Towards the end of the project there was a convergence of these techniques into the final prototype.

In the area of natural language processing it became clear early in the project that significant pre-existing work would have to be discarded if a common approach to grammar representation were to be taken for each of the languages. It was decided instead to focus on developing a new and novel interface language (Semantic Interface Language - SIL) [13] to act as a common and language independent interface between linguistic processing and the dialogue manager. In addition partners experimented with different robust parsing strategies and the use of predictions.

A common dialogue manager was developed with contributions from several partners. A goal in the design of the dialogue manager was portability accross applications and languages, and this has been successfully demonstrated in the project with two applications and four languages.

Four separate language demonstrators were built with applications covering Intercity Train Timetable enquiries (Germany and Italy) and Flight Enquiries or Reservations (UK and France).

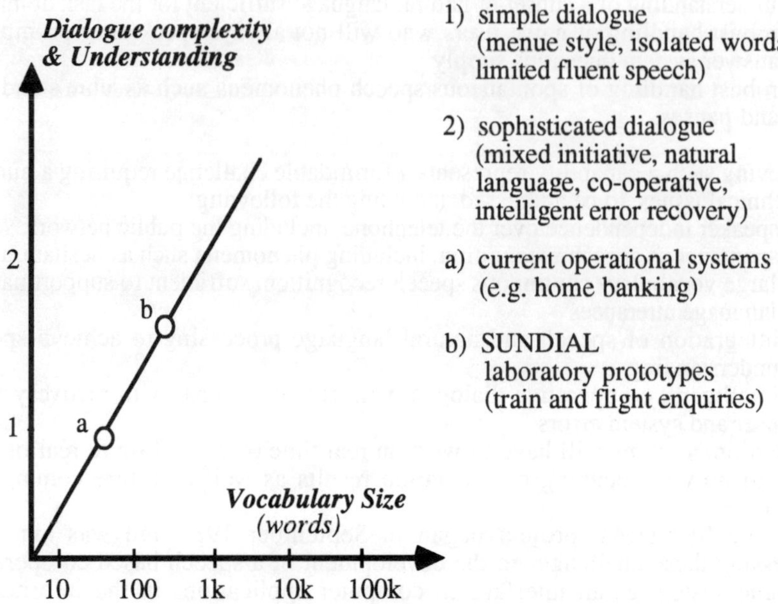


**Fig.1:** Towards natural dialogue systems

Although the original goal of the project was to develop speaker dependent technology first and then speaker adaptation, in fact all prototypes progressed very early on to speaker independent recognition.
The interactive dialogue component plays a crucial role in graceful error recovery and dialogue repair as well as eliciting further information, handling clarification and confirmation. The project chose to use text-to-speech synthesis for message output and it was decided to include work in the project on improving prosody by using dialogue knowledge. The capabilities of the prototypes are illustrated below with a dialogue taken from an English evaluation trial; the caller was a naive user using the system over a long distance telephone line (*S* = system, *U* = user).

Dialogue:

1 S: Welcome to British Airways Flight Information service.
How can I help you?
2 U: Can you tell me the departure time of flight BA seven three two?
3 S: Did you say British Airways flight seven three two?
4 U: Yes.
5 S: That flight departs at nineteen ten.
Do you have another inquiry?
6 U: No.
7 S: Thank you for calling. Good-bye.

## 1.1 Specifying System Requirements

In order to provide insight into the overall dialogue requirements for the system, the "Wizard of Oz" paradigm was used in a number of the chosen languages for the prototype applications [11,20]. A large corpus of human-human dialogues relating to flight enquiries and reservations was also collected. The corpora derived from these simulations was analysed to define more precisely the spoken language phenomena which occur, as well as the required lexicon, grammar, semantics and dialogue rules for the chosen applications [12,15,23].
It was concluded after analysis that many of the requirements in terms of dialogue strategies were common to the four languages studied and to the different applications. It is expected that these requirements will also prove to be generic to other information service domains. The typical vocabulary requirements for the four languages represented in SUNDIAL are around 1000 words including place names.

The WOZ paradigm was also used to evaluate parts of the system such as the Dialogue Manager and to investigate more closely the influence on users of particular dialogue management strategies, as well as specific prompts.

## 1.2 Architecture

The overall architecture developed is shown in figure 2; further details of this and the components have been reported elsewhere [19]. One of the objectives of the architecture was to provide a close coupling between each module with the aim of using appropriate knowledge and constraints in the process of understanding users utterances and recovering from errors.

An example of the interaction between the modules is the application of predictions to the recognition stage which are selected according to dialogue context [1,18]. As the dialogue progresses the Dialogue Manager is able to select appropriate modes of interaction (such as spelling when a place name is consistently mis-recognised), and prompt the user accordingly.

## 1.3 Recognising a large Vocabulary over the Telephone

The techniques developed for large vocabulary recognition were based on sub word models using CDHMM. Extensive experiments were carried out over the five year period of the project to identify the best set of techniques and algorithms for large vocabulary recognition over the telephone [7]. These experiments included investigation of techniques for dealing with the considerable level variation apparent over the Public Switched Telephone Network PSTN) as well as appropriate sub word units for each language.

At the speech recognition level spontaneous speech phenomena such as coughs, breath noise and hesitations (which include 'uhm's and 'er's) were dealt with by including special models. Other problems (such as ungrammaticality and words not present in the vocabulary) were approached through the interaction of acoustic evidence and linguistic knowledge at the parsing stage.

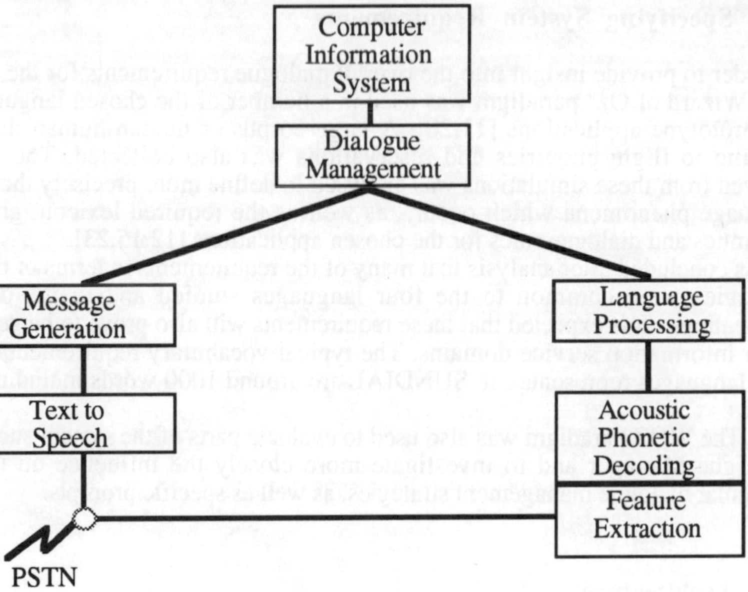


**Fig. 2:** SUNDIAL architecture

## 1.4 Understanding spoken Utterances

The Linguistic Processing component is based upon some well-known AI approaches to natural language parsing with modifications and extensions to handle speech as opposed to text input [2,3,5]. In particular the parser makes use of alternative word hypotheses represented in a lattice or graph in constructing a parse tree, and allowance is made for gaps and partially parsable strings. The parser makes use of both syntactic and semantic knowledge for the task domain and sends its results to the Dialogue Manager using a Semantic Interface Language (SIL) representation which was developed within the project and is language independent [13]. The lexicon size varies for each language but is of the order of 1000 entries including place names. Various iterations of evaluation together with the WOZ simulations have helped to refine the lexicon-grammars.

In the Italian system a feedback verification procedure has been developed where sentence hypotheses generated by the parser can be re-scored by the recogniser with forced recognition. This technique allows a resorting of the sentence hypotheses according to the new acoustic scores as well as the inclusion of hypothesised missing words in the re-matching process [4].

## 1.5 Intelligent Dialogue Management

It was a major goal of SUNDIAL to handle a number of the observed attributes of normal human-human dialogue such as: turn taking, anaphora and ellipsis (utterances which depend on their context for their meaning), hesitations, coughs, changing the subject, strategies for dealing with communication failure, implicit and explicit confirmation, and resolution of ambiguity via questioning. The Dialogue Manager (DM) was developed by several partners within SUNDIAL as a common component which would be substantially language and application independent [10,17]. The approach was based on a distributed database architecture in which various modules or agents (shown in figure 3) communicate with each other, maintaining their own histories or knowledge bases (the so called distributed database). Each module of the dialogue manager is responsible for dealing with various aspects of interpreting and managing the dialogue. These include a Belief Module, responsible for interpreting user utterances in the current dialogue context [13,14], and a Dialogue Module which contains rules for dialogue behaviour according to the progress of the interaction [6].

The Dialogue Manager (DM) provides for mixed initiative dialogue and acts as the source of predictions about the next utterance which are fed to other modules. A number of local variants of the Dialogue Manager were developed for the final prototypes, based on the same principals and techniques researched in the main Dialogue Manager component. These variants were designed to provide faster response times and improved robustness.

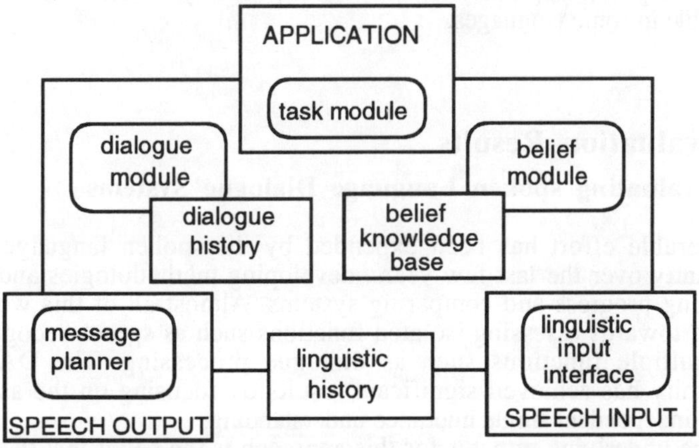


**Fig. 3:** Dialogue Manager Distributed Database Architecture

## 1.6 Generating Output to the User

Current dialogue systems generally make use of high quality digitally stored speech with words and phrases carefully spliced together to provide natural sounding output. As the number of messages to be output to the user grows, this method of speech output becomes less practicable. An alternative approach is to use a Text To Speech synthesiser (TTS) together with a language generator capable of deriving appropriate sentences from concept.

The particular requirements of spoken output in the course of a dialogue (intelligibility, reduced length, enumeration and requests for repetition etc) can be taken into account in the message generation component. Prosody (stress on words and melodic contour of an utterance) is affected by both linguistic and pragmatic constraints and these can be used to derive from a set of rules an appropriate intonation contour to be imposed on the synthesised output. A suitable symbolic description of the effects of these constraints on a particular utterance is passed, along with the text, to the synthesis module [24,25].

The message generation module contains a message planning and message generation component. The message planner is responsible for formulating the output according to context and overall prosodic contour planning, although not implemented in the project, it could also be extended to handle issues such as summarising. The linguistic generator makes use of the same grammar as the linguistic processing module for generating sentences. It handles ellipsis and refering expressions and also provides the final prosodically annotated output to the synthesiser.

The text to speech synthesisers (for each of the four languages) was based on existing systems (diphone synthesis from CNET and formant synthesis from Infovox).

Improvements were made in the segmental quality of both the diphone and formant synthesis approaches and a comparative evaluation of quality using preference tests was carried out for the four languages. Much of the work for British English was carried out by Infovox of Sweden who was a subcontractor to Logica. At the present time TTS is still some way from providing adequate quality for general public applications, although diphone synthesis is now very close to acceptable in some languages.

# 2. Evaluation Results

## 2.1 Evaluating spoken Language Dialogue Systems

Considerable effort has been expended by the spoken language technology community over the last few years, developing methodologies and metrics for evaluating progress and comparing systems. Almost all of this work has been directed towards assessing isolated functions such as speech recognition rather than multiple functions such as dialogue processing. The DARPA ATIS community has achieved significant results by focusing on the assessment of context-independent single utterance understanding.

The underlying impetus for this approach is the belief that the best way to proceed towards usable spoken language systems in the long term is to focus on optimising the component technologies now.

We were very sympathetic with this approach in the Sundial project. For this reason we developed a battery of 'glass-box' metrics for assessing the quality of the sub-components of our systems.

The results we gleaned played an important role in a development-and-test cycle which led to significant improvements in component functionalities over the lifetime of the project. However, the main goal of the project was not to produce a collection of effective components; rather, it was to design and build usable dialogue systems given the best technology available now.

In order to assess the extent to which we succeeded in satisfying this goal, it was necessary to develop a set of 'black box' metrics which measure aspects of the overall performance of complex multi-component spoken dialogue systems. Our evaluation methodology is described in more detail elsewhere [21] and more detailed analysis of results are also presented in project deliverables.

## 2.2 Dimensions of Variation in spoken Language Dialogue Systems

The large number of variables in spoken language dialogue systems can make interpretation of results and comparison of systems extremely difficult. Figure 4 shows three of the main axes along which variation may occur.

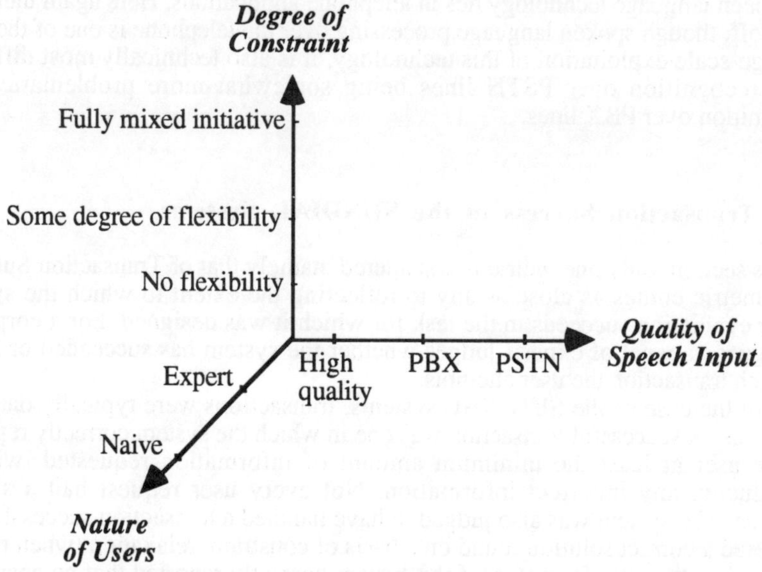


**Fig. 4:** Variables affecting SUNDIAL system performance

On the 'degree of constraint' axis, inflexible menu-style dialogue control can be unnatural and frustrating for users, but its benefit is that it reduces the complexity with which a dialogue system has to contend; systems with some degree of flexibility ask the user highly directed questions, but they are capable of dealing with reasonable deviations on the user's part from answering *exactly* the question which was asked; fully mixed initiative dialogues allow the user to redirect the dialogue at any point, but this greatly increases the perplexity at every point in the dialogue. Thus, selecting a point on this axis involves trading tractability off against usability.

Current commercial systems are located near the origin on this axis. The SUNDIAL DM is located somewhere on the upper half of the axis. Dialogue managers produced for the final prototypes in each language are located some way between the two.

The nature of the users also affects the complexity of the dialogue management task. Expert users learn - often subconsciously - how to get the most out of systems. This may constrain a wide range of behaviours, including the way a user speaks, their choice of words, the kinds of syntactic structures they use and the length of their utterances. If all users were experts, the problem of constructing a usable spoken language dialogue system would not be severe.

However, in the real world of applied spoken language systems, many users will be naive, and systems must be sensitive to their needs. The quality of the speech input is a very significant factor in any speech system. Most large vocabulary speech recognition research to date has concentrated on recognising high quality speech.

There are certainly some applications for which high quality speech input may be practical. However, we believe that a major part of the commercial future of spoken language technology lies in telephone applications. Here again there is a trade off: though spoken language processing over the telephone is one of the keys to large-scale exploitation of this technology, it is also technically most difficult, with recognition over PSTN lines being somewhat more problematic than recognition over PBX lines.

## 2.3 Transaction Success in the SUNDIAL Systems

In this section, only one metric is considered, namely that of Transaction Success. This metric comes as close as any to reflecting the extent to which the system under evaluation succeeds in the task for which it was designed. For a corpus of dialogues, a panel of experts judges whether the system has succeeded or failed for each transaction the user attempts.

In the case of the SUNDIAL systems, transactions were typically database retrievals. A successful transaction was one in which the system correctly reported to the user at least the minimum amount of information requested, without introducing any incorrect information. Not every user request had a simple solution. The system was also judged to have handled a transaction successfully if it offered a correct solution found on e basis of constraint relaxation (when part of the user's query was faulty), or if the system correctly reported that no answer to the user's query existed.

Original transaction success performance targets set earlier in the project are shown for comparison in table 1 and results of user trials for each of the prototypes are presented in table 2. Transaction success is shown versus a number of performance variables such as type of user, quality of speech (PBX, PSTN or microphone) and the characteristics of the dialogue manager.

In the final prototypes some customisation of the dialogue manager was carried out and this resulted in better performance over the generic dialogue manager (*DM*= dialogue manager). In all cases, analysis of the dialogues shows evidence of spontaneous speech phenomena such as hesitations, filler words, restarts, and self-corrections.

| ***Language*** | ***Target performance before evaluation began*** |
|---|---|
| ENGLISH | 80% |
| FRENCH | 80% |
| GERMAN | 80% |
| ITALIAN | 90% |

**Table 1:** Transaction success performance targets

| *Language* | *Transaction success* | *Conditions* |
|---|---|---|
| ENGLISH | 57% | PBX, naive callers, generic DM |
| | 70% | PSTN long distance, naive callers, customised DM |
| | 96% | PBX, staff callers, customised DM |
| FRENCH | 46.1% | PSTN local line, project staff, customised DM |
| | 62% | PBX, staff callers, customised DM |
| GERMAN | 65% | microphone, laboratory staff callers, generic DM |
| | 38% | microphone, naive callers, generic DM |
| ITALIAN | 51% | PBX, naive callers, generic DM |
| | 77.6% | PBX, naive callers, customised DM |
| | 83.3% | PBX, laboratory staff callers, generic DM |
| | 96.6% | PBX, laboratory staff callers, customised DM |

**Table 2:** Summary evaluation results

## 2.4 Discussion

Overall these results seem impressive but they do not, by themselves, allow any inferences to be drawn about the usability of the systems. This will be better understood when the transaction success rates are examined alongside the results of all the other evaluation metrics. Subjects in the Italian trials were however asked to score various aspects of the system. These results are shown in table 3.

| *Capability of the System* | *Subjective Rating (1-5)* |
|---|---|
| understanding | 3.60 |
| naturalness | 3.90 |
| speed | 3.37 |
| overall opinion | 4.00 |

**Table 3:** Subjective rating

A good sense of the character of the dialogues can be obtained by examining example dialogues, such as the one reproduced earlier in this paper. That example was entirely straightforward.

The following real example was collected using the English language system over a PBX line. It shows how the system behaves when things do not proceed quite so smoothly.

<u>Dialogue:</u>

1 S: Welcome to British Airways flight information service.
How can I help you?
2 U: Which terminal does BA five eight zero leave from?
3 S: Was that British Airways flight five eight zero?
4 U: Yes.
5 S: That flight departs from Heathrow Airport Terminal 1.
Do you have another inquiry?
6 U: Yes.
7 S: What would you like to know?
8 U: Can you tell me the arrival time of today's Madrid flight?
9 S: What is the number of the flight?
10 U: I don't know.
11 S: Where does the flight leave from?
12 U: Madrid.
13 S: Was that from Paris?
14 U: No, Madrid.
15 S: Did you say from Copenhagen?
16 U: Madrid.
17 S: Please answer 'yes' or 'no'. Did you say from Madrid?
18 U: Yes.
19 S: Please tell me the destination.
20 U: Heathrow.
21 S: Did you say to Heathrow Airport?
22 U: Yes.
23 S: Please tell me the departure time.
24 U: One o'clock in the afternoon.
25 S: Was that thirteen hundred hours?
26 U: Yes.
27 S: British Airways flight four six seven leaves from Madrid Barajas Airport at thirteen hundred hours. It arrives at London Heathrow Airport, Terminal 1, at fourteen fifteen.

The example shows how more than one query can be transacted in a single call to the service. The first transaction proceeds with considerable ease.

The availability of a flight number in some flight enquiries is very useful indeed since it serves as a unique identifier for the flight in question; once the flight number has been confirmed, it is not necessary to confirm anything else. Notice how the solution delivered in line 5 exactly answers the question posed in line 2. (The earlier dialogue example showed another kind of correctly focused solution; in that case the departure time was in focus). Experience has shown that the type of the query (arrival/departure time, arrival/departure terminal, etc) is hardly ever mis-recognised, so it is not explicitly confirmed. This is not to say that it is always recognised.

The request at the start of the user's second query is for an arrival time. However, the solution offered (line 27) is general enough to cover a range of different queries. This is indicative of the system's failure to discern the focus of the original query. This does not prove to be a serious problem since the system is opportunistic in its use of information. It tries to zero in on the most useful information by asking the user for the flight number (line 9). The fact that the user is unable to supply this information (line 10) does not cause the dialogue to fail; it just prompts the system to adopt a different line of questioning, thereby attacking the problem from a different angle. There follow two consecutive misrecognitions.

The utterances in lines 14 and 15 are worth noting because they show how users do not restrict themselves to answering exactly the question asked. In this case the user combines disconfirmation of 'Paris' with re-presentation of 'Madrid'. The system is capable of interpreting this correctly, though in this case it recognises 'Copenhagen' erroneously.

In line 17 the system recognises that there are problems and tightens the constraints on itself and on the user, effectively reducing itself to an explicit menu system. Fortunately, (line 16) it recognised 'Madrid' correctly (even though this is not a literally appropriate answer to a yes/no question), so the dialogue can proceed. Had this not been the case, the user would have been asked to spell the name of the place.

In our experience, spelling single words can be a very effective way of breaking recognition deadlocks, since it stretches the word in time, thereby giving the recogniser more data with which to discriminate. Although the system is capable of reducing dynamically to a highly constrained menu system, it always returns to a more flexible mode as soon as the local difficulty is resolved. Thus, in line 24, the user is able to answer the request for a departure time without any obvious constraints on how it may be expressed. The use of an alternative phraseology for the confirmation message never fails to impress users, though it is trivial to implement.

In this example we have seen how the system can use a flight number in the initial utterance, and how it can recover after it fails to extract anything useful from the first utterance. The next example demonstrates that the system is much more than a simple phrase spotter. Here the system succeeds in identifying several parameters of the request from the user's first utterance. The rest of the dialogue is taken up with confirming that this information has been correctly recognised:

Dialogue:

1. S: Welcome to British Airways flight information service. How can I help you?
2 U: I wonder whether you could tell me what time the next flight from Paris to Heathrow gets in.
3 S: Was that from Paris?
4 U: Yes.
5 S: Did you say to Heathrow Airport?
6 U: Yes.
7 S: That flight arrives at ten fifteen. Do you have another inquiry?
8 U: No thank you.
9 S: Thank you for calling. Good-bye.

## 3. Conclusions

Many conclusions can be drawn from a project as large and wide-ranging as SUNDIAL. Perhaps the most important of these is that *it really is possible* to deal successfully with spontaneous speech from naive users by using appropriate and closely integrated recognition and natural language processing strategies in the context of careful dialogue management. This is true even when the application requires PBX or PSTN quality speech and large-vocabulary speaker-independent recognition. The successes of the SUNDIAL project strongly suggest that there is a realistic possibility that commercial services based on this technology could be launched in the near future. A number of partners are now actively engaged in exploiting the results of the project in terms of new services and products. At least as far as task-oriented dialogue is concerned, the age of the conversational computer is about to dawn.

## References


1. Andry F. "Static and dynamic predictions: a method to improve speech understanding in co-operative dialogues", ICSLP'92, Banff, pp.639-642, October 1992.
2. Andry F. and S. Thornton "A parser for speech lattices using a UCG grammar", Eurospeech'91, Genoa, September, pp.219-222, 1991.
3. Baggia P., E. Gerbino, E. Giachin and C.Rullent "Real-time linguistic analysis for continuous speech understanding", Proceedings of the 3rd Conf. on Applied Natural Language Processing, Trento, pp.33-39, 1992.
4. Baggia P., L. Fissore, E. Gerbino, E. Giachin and C. Rullent: "Improving speech understanding performance through feedback verification", Speech Communication, 1992.
5. Baggia P. and C. Rullent "Partial Parsing as a Robust Parsing Strategy", ICASSP'93, Minneapolis, pp.123-126, April 1993.
6. Bilange E. and J-Y. Magadur "A robust approach for handling oral dialogue", COLING'92, Nantes, July 1992.
7. Charpentier F., G. Micca, E. Schukat-Talamazzini and T. Thomas "The recognition component of the SUNDIAL project", NATO Workshop, Biebiou, Spain, July 1993.
8. Clementino D. and L. Fissore "A man-machine dialogue for speech access to train time table information", *(in this volume)*.
9. Eckert W., T. Kuhn, H. Niemann, S. Riech, A Scheuer and E.G. Schukat-Talamazzini "A spoken dialogue system for German intercity train timetable enquiries", *(in this volume)*.
10. Eckert W. and S. McGlashan (1994) "Managing spoken dialogues for information services", *(in this volume)*.
11. Fraser N.M. and G.N. Gilbert "Simulating speech systems", Computer Speech and Language, 5, pp.81-99, 1991.
12. Fraser N.M. and G.N. Gilbert "Effects of system voice quality on user utterances in speech dialogue systems", Eurospeech'91, Genoa, pp.57-60, September 1991.
13. Heisterkamp P., S. McGlashan and N.J. Youd "Dialogue semantics for an oral dialogue system", ICLSP'92, Banff, October, pp.643-646, 1992.
14. Heisterkamp P. "Ambiguity and uncertainty in spoken dialogue", *(in this volume)*.
15. MacDermid C. "Features of naive callers' dialogues with a simulated speech understanding and dialogue system", *(in this volume)*.
16. Magadur J-Y., F. Gavignet, F. Andry and F. Charpentier "A French oral dialogue system for flight reservations over the telephone" *(in this volume)*.
17. McGlashan S., N.M. Fraser, G.N. Gilbert, E. Bilange, P. Heisterkamp and N.J. Youd "Dialogue management for telephone information systems", Proceedings of the 3rd Conference on Applied Natural Language Processing, Trento, April, pp.245-246, 1992.

18. Niedermair G.T. "Linguistic Modelling in the Context of Oral Dialogue", ICSLP'92, Banff, October, pp.635-638, 1992.
19. Peckham J. "Speech understanding and dialogue over the telephone: an overview of progress in the SUNDIAL project", Proceedings of the DARPA Speech and Natural Language Workshop, Pacific Grove, CA, pp.14-27, 1992.
20. Ponamalé M., E. Bilange and K. Choukri and S. Soudoplatoff "A computer-aided approach to the design of an oral dialogue system", Proceedings of the Eastern Multiconference, Nashville, Tenessee, April 1990.
21. Simpson A. and N.M. Fraser "Black box and glass box evaluation of the SUNDIAL system", *(in this volume)*.
22. Smith, G.W. and M. Bates "Voice activated automated telephone call routing", Proceedings of the Ninth IEEE Conference on Artificial Intelligence for Applications, Orlando, March 1993.
23. Wooffitt, R., N.M. Fraser, G.N. Fraser and S. McGlashan (forthcoming) "Designing Interaction: a conversation analytic study of human-(simulated) computer interaction", London, Routledge, *(forthcoming)* .
24. Youd, N.J. and J. House "Generating intonation in a voice dialogue system", Eurospeech'91, Genoa, pp.1287-1290, September 1991.
25. Youd, N.J. and S. McGlashan "Generating utterances in dialogue systems", In: R. Dale, E. Hovy, D. Rösner and O. Stock (eds) Proceedings of the 6th International Workshop On Natural Language Generation, Springer Verlag, Berlin, pp.135-149, 1992.

# Dialogue Development and Implementation in the Danish Dialogue Project

Hans Dybkjær, Niels Ole Bernsen and Laila Dybkjær
Centre for Cognitive Science, Roskilde University
PO Box 260, DK-4000 Roskilde, Denmark

## Abstract

This chapter presents results on dialogue development and implementation of the first prototype P1 in the Danish Dialogue project. The project as a whole is briefly presented in terms of system components and system architecture. The remainder of the chapter focuses on dialogue. Firstly, it is described how a dialogue model for the first prototype P1 was developed using Wizard of Oz (WOZ) experiments. The WOZ method is described and results from the WOZ experiments presented. Secondly, a description of the implementation of the dialogue model is provided. The conclusion presents a number of open questions to be answered during the test of the prototype.

## 1. Introduction

The Dialogue project is a Danish national project on spoken language dialogue systems. The project started in 1991 and is carried out with an effort of 30 man/years by the Center for PersonKommunikation (CPK, earlier the Speech Technology Centre - STC), Aalborg University, the Centre for Language Technology (CST), Copenhagen University, and the Centre for Cognitive Science (CCS), Roskilde University. The aim is to develop two application-oriented dialogue system prototypes called P1 and P2 in the domain of Danish domestic airline ticket reservation and flight information accessed through the telephone. The first prototype, P1, has been built and is currently being tested. The next step will be to develop P2 as a more advanced version of P1 based on the test results on P1.

The plan of the chapter is as follows. Section 2 briefly explains the main system components and the system architecture. Section 3 describes the dialogue design process including initial design specification, methodology and dialogue modelling results. Section 4 describes the implementation of the dialogue model. Section 5 concludes and discusses future work.

## 2. System Components and System Architecture

To provide the context for dialogue development and implementation an outline of the P1 prototype system is given in this section. P1 is outlined both in terms of logical system structure and physical system structure.

### 2.1 System Components

The logical system structure is presented in figure 1 which shows the main components of P1.

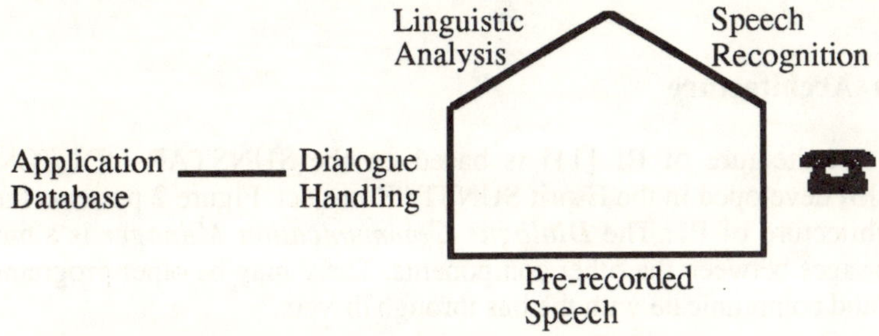


**Figure 1:** The main components of the P1 spoken language dialogue prototype system.

A user calls the system and provides input to the *Speech Recognition module* which processes the speech signal. The speech recogniser is a further developed version of the recogniser which was developed in the Esprit SUNSTAR project [13]. It is a speaker-independent continuous speech recogniser based on Hidden Markov Models (HMMs). In addition to user input, the speech recogniser needs predictions from the Dialogue Handling module on the sub-grammars to be used at any given point during the dialogue. The sub-grammars used in the Speech Recognition module are word pair grammars represented as finite state transition networks in which the transitions represent HMMs. Viterbi search is used to find a 1-best path through the network. This path represents a string of lexical references which constitutes the output of the Speech Recognition module.

The lexical string is input to the *Linguistic Analysis module*. The Dialogue Handling module indicates to the parser which sub-grammars to use and which semantic objects to fill in on the basis of the input string from the recogniser. The semantic objects are frame-like structures containing a number of slots for domain relevant information. The sub-grammars used for linguistic analysis are unification-based Augmented Phrase Structure Grammars (APSGs) implemented in a formalism which is a subset of the one used in the Eurotra project [6]. The Linguistic Analysis module analyses the input based on the active sub-grammars using a chart data structure and an object-oriented implementation of the Earley parsing algorithm. The parser uses semantic mapping rules for assigning semantic interpretations [14] which in turn are used for filling in the active semantic objects.

The *Dialogue Handling module* interprets the contents of the semantic objects received from the Linguistic Analysis module and decides on the next action to take which may be to send a query to the *Database* or send relevant output to the user. In the latter case, the Dialogue Handling module also sends predictions to the speech recogniser and the parser on the next sub-grammars to use, i.e. on which input now to expect from the user. The Dialogue Handling module, in particular the dialogue description, is discussed in detail in section 4 below.

The output module is based on *Pre-recorded Speech*. A number of words and (parts of) sentences have been recorded in advance and are selected, put together and replayed according to instructions from the Dialogue Handling module.

## 2.2 System Architecture

The system architecture of P1 [11] is based on the SUNSTAR DDL/ICM architecture [5] developed in the Esprit SUNSTAR project. Figure 2 presents the physical architecture of P1. The *Dialogue Communication Manager* is a bus carrying messages between the other components. These may be other programs or hardware and communicate with the bus through drivers.

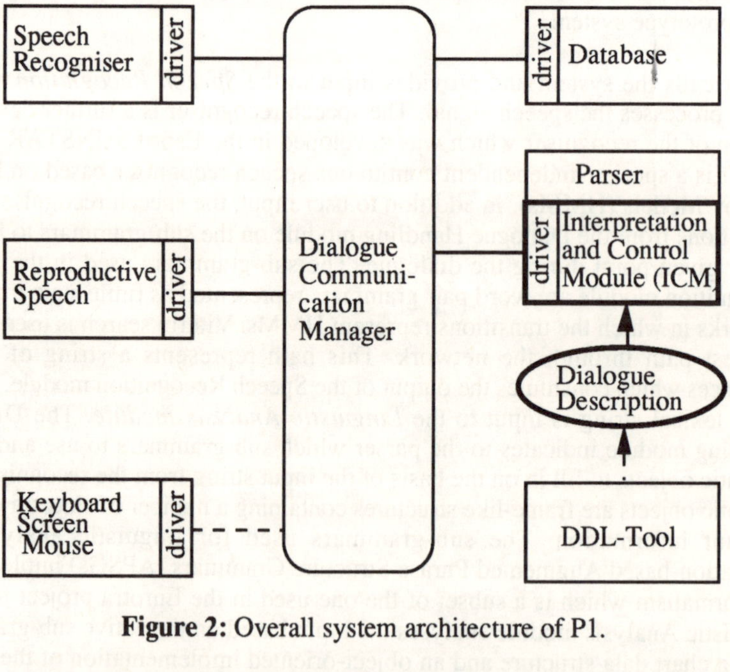


**Figure 2:** Overall system architecture of P1.

The core module is the *Interpretation and Control Module* (ICM). ICM interprets a *Dialogue Description* which is a program written in DDL (Dialogue Description

Language). DDL is an experimental language originally intended for primitive dialogues not involving natural language. DDL has been extended in the Dialogue Project to meet the particular needs of the P1 system. DDL has three layers: a graphical layer which specifies how the dialogue will be controlled in terms of event-driven recursive flow charts; a frame layer which declares data structures; and a textual layer which declares data structures and specifies actions. The DDL Dialogue Description has been created by using the *DDL-Tool* which is a graphical editor and debugger. The Dialogue Description and the ICM jointly form the Dialogue Handling module. The *Parser* has been implemented as a module external to the ICM.

When input from the *Speech Recogniser* is expected by the Dialogue Description, the ICM looks if there is a message. The message is passed through the Parser before the ICM continues its interpretation of the Dialogue Description. Queries to and answers from the *Database* are also exchanged as messages. Output information is sent as a message to the *Reproductive Speech module* and predictions are sent as messages from the ICM to the Speech Recogniser.

The *Keyboard, Screen, and Mouse modules* are not part of the running P1 system but support testing of the system. For instance, the speech recogniser may be simulated via keyboard input. The presence of the Keyboard, Screen and Mouse modules also enables later extension of the system into a multimodal system.

The P1 system's Speech Recogniser runs partly on a Digital Signal Processor (DSP) board and partly on a PC whereas the rest of the system runs on a Sun/Sparc station.

## 3. Dialogue Model Development

The goal of dialogue model development in the case of the spoken language dialogue system P1 was to enable the machine to conduct a dialogue with users which allowed them to solve their tasks in a way which was as natural as possible given the heavy technological and other constraints on the design process, many of which were imposed by the speech recogniser. This section describes, firstly, the initial design phase where knowledge is elicited for a first dialogue model and other design decisions are made which influence the rest of the design process. Secondly, the Wizard of Oz (WOZ) prototyping method used for iterative dialogue model design is described followed by a review of the main results obtained in attempting to meet the design process constraints.

### 3.1 The Initial Design Phase

A number of different information sources contributed to the design of the first dialogue model for P1. The research literature provided an update on the state of the art in spoken dialogue systems [12]. Field interviews provided information on the tasks done by human travel agents and how to define the domain of P1. Details on departures, fares, travel conditions, etc. were obtained from standard timetables. Due to practical difficulties, recordings of human-human dialogues in the selected domain of application were made too late to be used in defining the first dialogue model. The main issue which was identified was a set of conflicting constraints which had to be traded off against one another in order to build a usable and technologically feasible system.

*On the system side*, the dialogue model for P1 had to satisfy the following technological constraints which were mainly imposed by the speech recogniser:

- an average user utterance length of 3-4 words;
- a maximum user utterance length of 10 words;
- at most 100 words can be active in memory at a time for real time performance to be possible. Real time performance has high priority in usable systems in the chosen domain of application;
- project resources limit the vocabulary to about 500 words.

*On the user side*, the aim is to allow use of natural forms of dialogue and language. This will contribute to making the system easy to use by both novices and experts but obviously conflicts with the technological constraints just mentioned. Naturalness therefore has to be traded for system feasibility as naturalness is the only aspect of usability which reasonably may be thus traded. Other aspects of usability must be satisfied for the system to be at all usable. Basic system usability requires close-to-real-time performance, sufficient domain and task coverage, sufficiency of task-related vocabulary, natural grammar, robust handling of error, and that limitations on the naturalness of dialogue and language be principled and practicable by users [1]. So the trade-off process is further limited by these basic usability constraints.

No current theory is able to resolve this conflict. The best approach is to use an experimental and iterative design technique, such as WOZ.

### 3.2 The Wizard of Oz Method

WOZ [10] is a powerful empirical technique which is well suited to the iterative development and evaluation of intelligent interactive systems whether these be uni-modal, as in the current case where speech is being used for both input and output, or multi-modal. WOZ makes possible the testing of design ideas and the acquisition of detailed knowledge of the system, its users and user/system interaction prior to system implementation. Design goals and constraints may be simulated and adjusted until an acceptable trade-off has eventually been found.

WOZ involves one or more 'wizards', i.e. humans who simulate the performance of non-implemented or partially implemented computer systems in front of users who are preferably ignorant of the fact that they are interacting with a simulated system rather than a real one. Interactions are logged and recorded in various ways, often transcribed and indexed, and analysed for a variety of purposes. WOZ differs from other prototyping techniques, firstly in that it does not rely on reductions of the artifact and/or the task domain into presumed 'essential' or 'representative' features whose identification remains problematic. This means that, ideally, the end result of the WOZ specify-and-simulate test cycle will be a simulated system which can be implemented more or less directly on the assumption that the cycle has helped the designers to identify nearly all potential problems with the future system. Secondly, the presence of a human wizard allows simulation of a broad class of cognitively demanding tasks which humans are naturally good at, such as natural language understanding and generation, gesture recognition or visual scene understanding.

In developing a dialogue model for P1 seven generations of WOZ experiments were performed [9]. The simulation set-up is shown in figure 3.

The *graph structure* used by the wizard describes the dialogue structure including who has the initiative while the *predefined phrases* show the language to be used by the system. The graph structure and the phrases jointly constitute the dialogue model and are the crucial variables involved in finding an appropriate trade-off between technological constraints and naturalness. A *timetable* and a *calendar* acted as database.

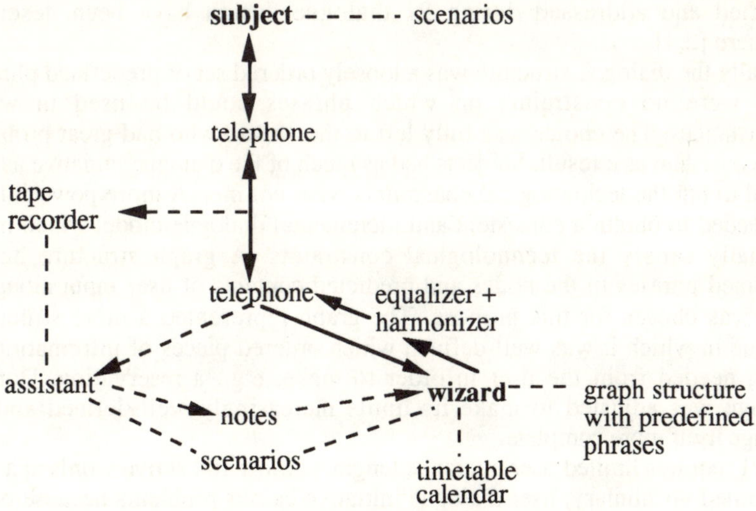


**Figure 3:** The set-up of the WOZ experiments.

In the later generations an *assistant* helped offload the wizard. The assistant operated the *tape recorder*, took *notes* on the information provided by subjects and gave other practical support.

To induce subjects into believing that they were speaking to a computer, an *equalizer* and a *harmonizer* were used to distort the wizard's voice during the last set of experiments [7].

The first five generations served training of the wizard and adjusting major shortcomings in the dialogue model. *Subjects* were exclusively system designers and colleagues. In each of the two last generations 12 subjects were used. The majority were external subjects and the rest were colleagues. External subjects were selected so that half of them had a background as secretaries (the expected end-user group) and the other half were computer scientists. The results obtained confirm that subjects' professional backgrounds influence the way they interact with the system [7]. Each subject received a letter which briefly introduced the system and informed on the subject's role. The letter also contained four *scenarios*, i.e. domain-relevant tasks which the subject was asked to perform, as well as a questionnaire to be filled in and returned after the experiments.

### 3.3 WOZ Results on the Dialogue Model for P1

Each WOZ generation produces large amounts of quantitative data which are used for measuring the extent to which quantitatively stated constraints are being met. This section describes the dialogue model development process focusing on the extent to which the mentioned (section 3.1) technological constraints were satisfied. A second, equally important, use of (quantitative, qualitative or structural) WOZ data during design is the use of data as evidence of user problems with the simulated system. The user problem types which were identified and addressed during P1 dialogue design have been described elsewhere [2,4].

Initially the dialogue structure was a loosely ordered set of predefined phrases. There were no constraints on which phrases could be used in which circumstances. The choice was fully left to the wizard who had great problems being consistent as a result. Subjects had as much of the dialogue initiative as they wanted to but the technological constraints were not met. A more powerful tool was needed to obtain a consistent and incremental dialogue model which might eventually satisfy the technological constraints. A graph structure having predefined phrases in the nodes and predicted contents of user input along the edges was chosen for this purpose. The graph represented a more structured dialogue in which it was well-defined which ordered pieces of information the system needed from the user in order to make, e.g., a reservation. Domain coverage was adjusted to make its limits increasingly well-defined and the coverage itself more complete.

As P1 requires limited user utterance length, at most 100 active words at a time and limited vocabulary, user dialogue initiative causes problems because of the length and unpredictability of users' utterances. To satisfy those constraints, the dialogue had to be made increasingly system-directed. This was done by converting user questions into system questions. Asking the questions allows the system to have well-defined expectations concerning user utterances (answers) in context.

As can be seen from figures 4 and 5, users' average utterance length and the average number of utterances exceeding ten tokens (words) decrease while more and more of the dialogue initiative is left to the system which asks nearly all the questions in the 7th generation (figure 6). Two other factors instrumental in reducing user utterance length were: (a) an introductory admonition to users to be brief when answering questions posed by the system, and (b) the fact that the system addressed users tersely rather than politely [15].

Interestingly, system-directed dialogue seems quite acceptable and natural in some tasks. Recordings of dialogues from a travel agency showed that once the customer has expressed a goal and a few constraints, the travel agent typically takes over and asks questions. This is particularly clear in the case of reservation tasks whereas customers typically ask more questions when performing information tasks. The difference between reservation and information tasks is that reservation tasks require the exchange, in some sequential order, of well-defined sets of information whereas information tasks have no such structure.

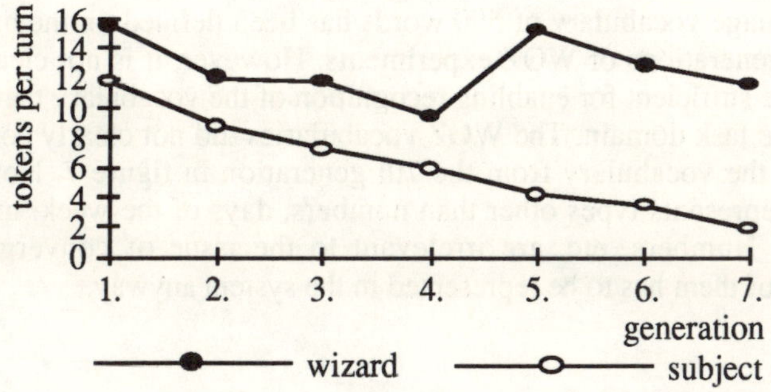


**Figure 4:** Average length of wizard and subject utterances in terms of tokens per turn. In the 5th generation, more information was included in the wizard's utterances, sparing users from having to ask for it.

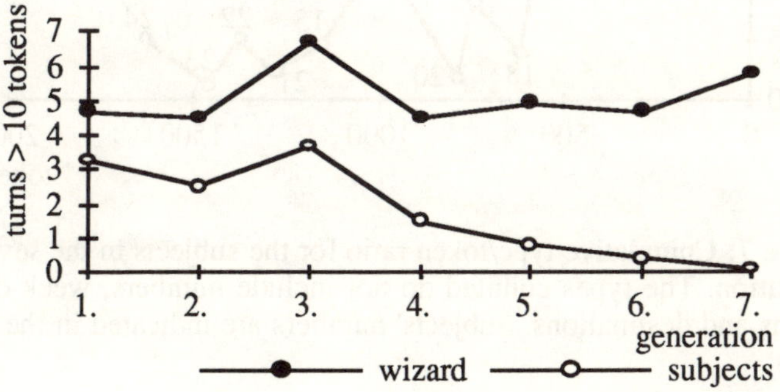


**Figure 5:** Average number of turns per dialogue exceeding 10 tokens.

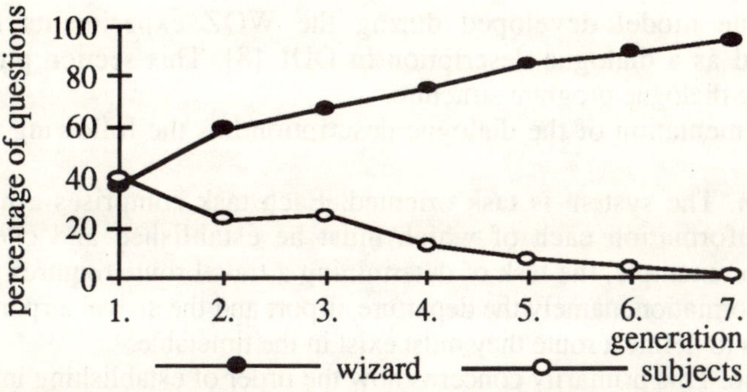


**Figure 6:** Number of questions in per cent of total number of turns.

Field recordings also showed that the average number of words per system/user exchange as well as per task were largely at the same level in the 7th WOZ generation as in similar human-human dialogues. This may be taken to indicate that a natural level of information exchange had been reached.

A sub-language vocabulary of 500 words has been defined on the basis of the 6th and 7th generations of WOZ experiments. However, it is not clear whether 500 words are sufficient for enabling recognition of the vocabulary that is natural to users in the task domain. The WOZ vocabularies did not clearly converge, as indicated by the vocabulary from the 7th generation in figure 7. Note that the figure only represents types other than numbers, days of the week, months and destinations. Numbers, etc. are irrelevant to the issue of convergence as a complete set of them has to be represented in the system anyway.

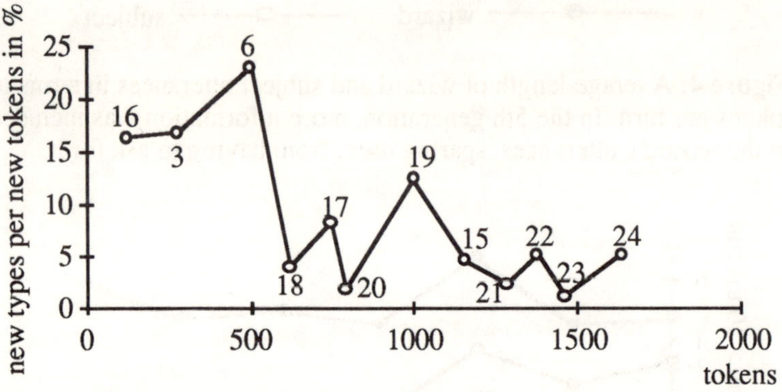


**Figure 7:** Cumulative type/token ratio for the subjects in the seventh generation. The types counted do not include numbers, week-days, months and destinations. Subjects' numbers are indicated in the data points.

## 4. Dialogue Implementation

The dialogue model developed during the WOZ experiments has been implemented as a dialogue description in DDL [8]. This section provides an outline of the dialogue program structure.

The implementation of the dialogue description has the following two main aspects:

1. Domain. The system is task oriented. Each task comprises a number of pieces of information each of which must be established and checked for bindings. For example, the task of determining a travel route requires in P1 two pieces of information, namely the departure airport and the arrival airport. For two such airports to define a route they must exist in the timetable.

2. Dialogue. This primarily concerns how the order of establishing information (i.e., the order of individual tasks) is defined, who has the initiative, and the built-

in facilities for supporting task-independent dialogue with the user such as the user commands *Repeat* and *Correct*.
The main flow of the implemented dialogue description is expressed by the DDL procedures (graphical level) shown in the figures below.

(a)

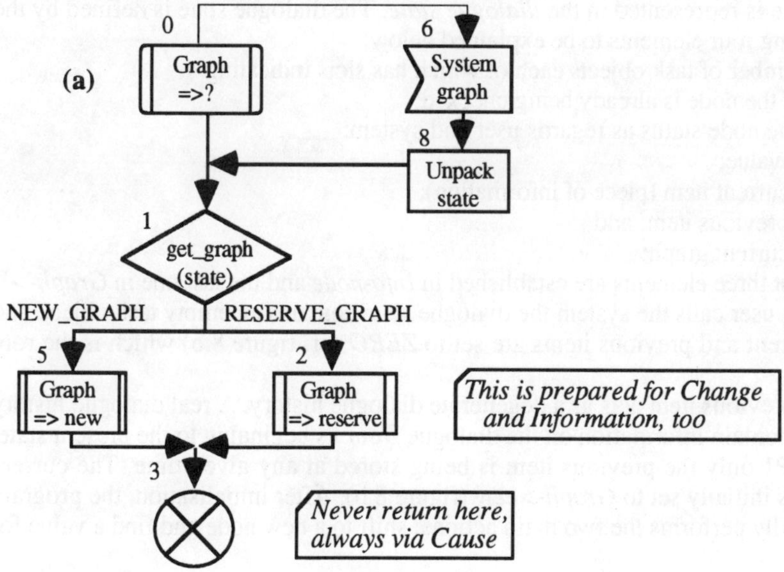


(b)

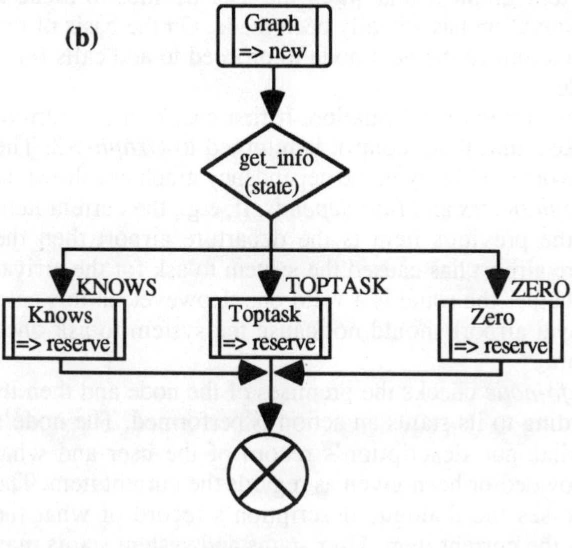


**Figure 8:** The graphical DDL representation of Graph => ? **(a)** and Graph => new **(b)**.

*Graph->?* (figure 8a) determines which node to proceed to, i.e. which piece of information to establish, and *Info-node* (figure 9) finds a value for that node. In broad terms, the entire dialogue is carried out by repeatedly performing these two main actions.

All information collected from the user as well as from the database during the dialogue is represented in the *dialogue state*. The dialogue state is defined by the following four elements to be explained below:

- a number of task objects each of which has slots indicating
  - if the node is already being checked;
  - the node status as regards user and system;
  - a value;
- the current item (piece of information);
- the previous item; and
- the current graph;

The first three elements are established in *Info-node* and the last one in *Graph->?*. When a user calls the system the dialogue state contains an empty task object, and the current and previous items are set to *ZERO* (cf. figure 8.b) which is the root node.

The previous item acts as a degenerate dialogue history. A real dialogue history would contain information on the dialogue from its beginning to the present state, but in P1 only the previous item is being stored at any given time. The current graph is initially set to *Graph->new* (figure 8.b). After initialisation, the program repeatedly performs the two main actions: shift to a new node and find a value for it.

*Graph->?* checks which graph is the current one. For instance, *Graph->new* (figure 8.b) is the current graph in the initial part of any dialogue, and *Graph->reserve* becomes the current graph if and when the user decides to make a reservation and until the reservation has actually been made. On the basis of the current graph, *Graph->?* determines the next node to proceed to and calls *Info-node* instantiated to this node.

*Info-node* controls the acquisition of information. It first checks if the current item is already being checked and, if so, control is returned to *Graph->?*. The purpose of this check is to avoid circularity in the dependency graph not shown in figure 9 but underlying *Info premises* and *Info depends*. If, e.g., the current item is the arrival airport and the previous item is the departure airport then the information on the departure airport has caused the system to ask for the arrival airport in order to check whether the route is a valid one. However, in this case the information on the arrival airport should not cause the system to ask once more for the departure airport.

If no circularity exists, *Info-node* checks the premises of the node and then its status is considered. According to its status an action is performed. The node's user status expresses the dialogue description's record of the user and what information the user has provided or been given as regards the current item. The node's system status expresses the dialogue description's record of what the system has done as regards the current item. User status and system status may each take one of the following values:

| | |
|---|---|
| *bottom* | the node has no value yet. |
| *no* | the value is marked as incorrect. |

| | |
|---|---|
| *check* | the value must be checked |
| *partial* | the value is only partially determined |
| *yes* | the value is determined and accepted |

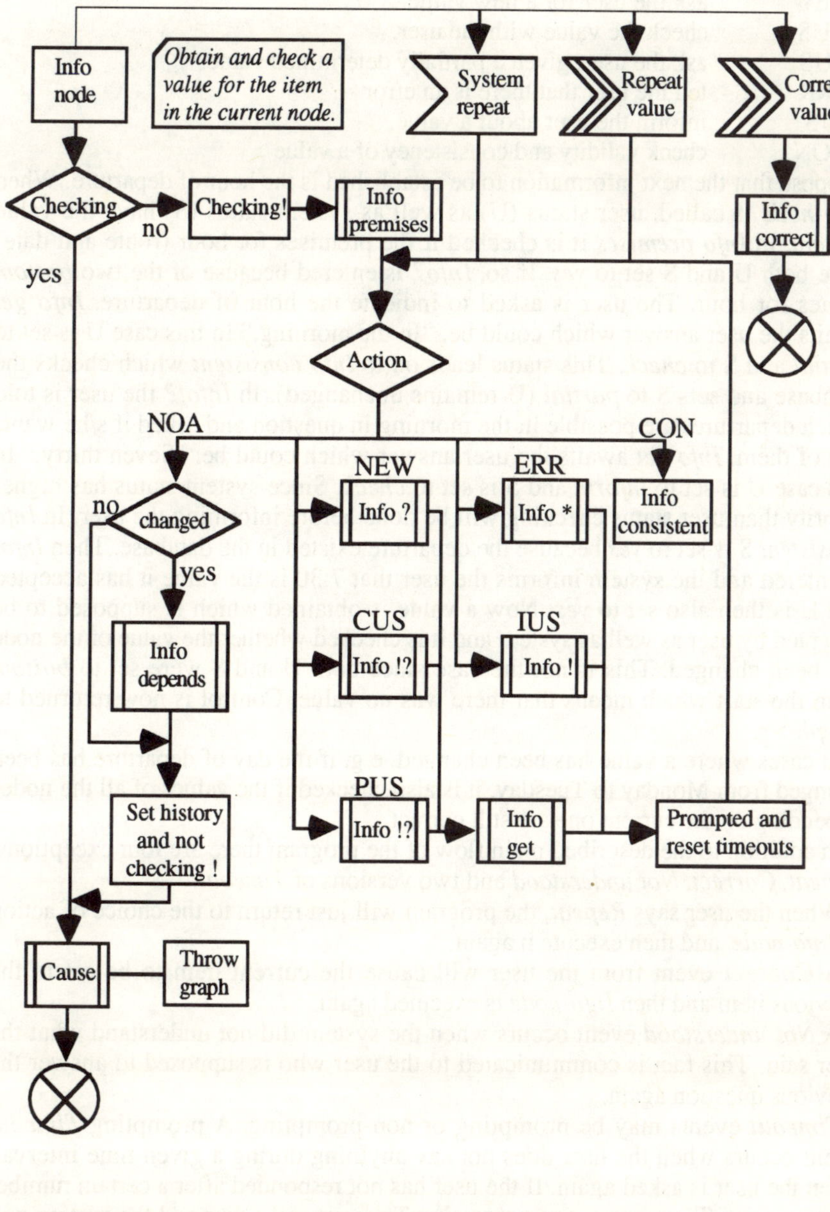


**Figure 9:** The graphical DDL representation of *Info-node*.

In addition, the user status may take the value:

*inform* tell the user the value.

The (user, system) status pair determines the action to be taken by the system in its next turn. Turn actions may be

NOA no action.
NEW ask the user for a new value.
CUS check the value with the user.
PUS ask the user, given a partially determined value.
ERR tell the user that there is an error.
IUS inform the user about a value.
CON check validity and consistency of a value

Suppose that the next information to be established is the hour of departure. When *Info-node* is called, user status (U) as well as system status (S) have the value *bottom*. In *Info premises* it is checked if the premises for hour (route and date) have both U and S set to *yes*. If so, *Info?* is entered because of the two *bottom* values for hour. The user is asked to indicate the hour of departure. *Info get* awaits the user answer which could be: "In the morning." In this case U is set to *partial* and S to *check*. This status leads on to *Info consistent* which checks the database and sets S to *partial* (U remains unchanged). In *Info!?* the user is told which departures are possible in the morning in question and asked if s/he wants one of them. *Info get* awaits the user answer which could be: "Seven thirty." In this case U is set to *inform* and S is set to *check*. Since system status has higher priority than user status checking will be done before informing the user. In *Info consistent* S is set to *yes* because the departure existed in the database. Then *Info!* is entered and the system informs the user that 7:30 is the value it has accepted and U is then also set to *yes*. Now a value is obtained which is supposed to be accepted by user as well as system and it is checked whether the value of the node has been changed. This is not the case since both U and S were set to *bottom* from the start which means that there was no value. Control is now returned to *Graph->?*.

In cases where a value has been changed, e.g. if the day of departure has been changed from Monday to Tuesday, it is also checked if the values of all the nodes depending on the current one are still correct.

In addition to the described main flow of the program there are four exceptions: *Repeat*, *Correct*, *Not understood* and two versions of *Timeout*.

When the user says *Repeat*, the program will just return to the choice of action in *Info-node* and then execute it again.

A *Correct* event from the user will cause the current item to be set to the previous item and then *Info-node* is executed again.

A *Not understood* event occurs when the system did not understand what the user said. This fact is communicated to the user who is supposed to answer the previous question again.

*Timeout* events may be prompting or non-prompting. A prompting *Timeout* event occurs when the user does not say anything during a given time interval. Then the user is asked again. If the user has not responded after a certain number of prompting *Timeouts*, a non-prompting *Timeout* will occur and the system will hang up.

## 5. Conclusion

Despite the unparalleled power of the WOZ prototyping method, WOZ does have a number of theoretical and practical limitations preventing it from delivering a system specification which is guaranteed to satisfy all design constraints [3]. Ongoing testing of P1 will help answering questions which were not fully resolved during the WOZ experiments. The main points are the following:

- Since no clear convergence of vocabulary could be observed in the WOZ data material it remains uncertain whether the defined and implemented 500 word vocabulary provides sufficient coverage of the task domain;

- sub-grammars and lexica have been defined and implemented for each node in the dialogue in order to cover the WOZ material from the two last generations. However, it remains uncertain whether no more than 100 active words are needed at any time during dialogue;

- user and system misrecognitions and their repair are difficult to simulate to any great quantitative detail with WOZ. In consequence, P1 may prove to be less robust than desirable. Furthermore, it is an open question whether the implemented task-independent support facilities *Correct* and *Repeat* are sufficient to ensure robustness. Additional error-handling mechanisms may be needed which exploit the power of error correction through dialogue with the user;

- the WOZ method does not in itself ensure a dialogue theory which is sufficiently formalised (for implementation) and abstract (for maintenance and portability of the application).

The P1 evaluation results will be used for developing the planned second prototype P2 which is intended to have improved naturalness, flexibility and robustness. The dialogue history and user model which in P1 are rather primitive will be augmented in P2. P2 should accept more complex user input including longer utterances. Experiments with a larger perplexity will be necessary and a new series of WOZ experiments will be performed to develop an improved dialogue model and determine to what extent the present sublanguage should be enlarged. DDL and the DDL-Tool will be extended to meet the more advanced requirements of P2. A computer-supported WOZ environment will be built in which revisions to the simulated dialogue structure are concurrently being implemented in DDL. On the output side, increased dialogue complexity will require the use of speech synthesis instead of pre-recorded speech.

## References

1. Bernsen, N.O. “The Structure of the Design Space”. In Byerley, P.F., Barnard, P.J. and May, J., (Eds.): Computers, Communication and Usability. Design Issues, Research and Methods for Integrated Services. Amsterdam, North-Holland, 221-244, 1993a.

2. Bernsen, N.O. “Types of User Problems in Design. A Study of Knowledge Acquisition Using the Wizard of Oz”. Esprit Basic Research project AMODEUS-2 Working Paper UM/WP 14. Included in Deliverable I.2, June 1993b.

3. Bernsen, N.O., Dybkjær, H. and Dybkjær, L. "Wizard of Oz prototyping: How and when?". Submitted to CHI'94, 1993.

4. Bernsen, N.O., Dybkjær, L. and Dybkjær H. "Task-Oriented Spoken Human-Computer Dialogue". Report 6a, Spoken Language Dialogue Systems, CPK Aalborg University, CCS Roskilde University, CST University of Copenhagen. To appear early 1994.

5. Bækgaard, A., Roman, A. and Wetzel, P. "Advanced Dialogue Design - DDL Tool and ICM". Esprit project 2094 SUNSTAR, Deliverable IV.6-2, August, 1992.

6. Copeland, C., Durand, J., Krauwer, S. and Maegaard, B. (Eds.) "The Eurotra Formal Specifications". Studies in Machine Translation and Natural Language Processing, vol. 2, 1991.

7. Dybkjær, H., Bernsen, N.O. and Dybkjær, L. "Wizard of Oz and the Trade-Off between Naturalness and Recogniser Constraints". Proceedings of EUROSPEECH '93, Berlin, September, 947-950, 1993.

8. Dybkjær, H. and Dybkjær, L. "Representation and Implementation of Spoken Dialogues". Report 6b, Spoken Language Dialogue Systems, CPK Aalborg University, CCS Roskilde University, CST University of Copenhagen. To appear early 1994.

9. Dybkjær, L. and Dybkjær, H. "Wizard of Oz Experiments in the Development of a Dialogue Model for P1". Report 3, Spoken Language Dialogue Systems, STC Aalborg University, CCS Roskilde University, CST University of Copenhagen. February 1993.

10. Fraser, N.M. and Gilbert, G.N. "Simulating Speech Systems". Computer Speech and Language 5, 81-99, 1991.

11. Larsen, L.B., Brøndsted, T., Dybkjær, H., Dybkjær, L. and Music, B. "Overall Specification and Architecture of P1". Report 2, Spoken Language Dialogue Systems, STC Aalborg University, CCS Roskilde University, CST University of Copenhagen, February 1993.

12. Larsen, L.B., Brøndsted, T., Dybkjær, H., Dybkjær, L., Music, B. and Povlsen, C. "State-of-the-art of Spoken Language Systems - A Survey". Report 1, Spoken Language Dialogue Systems, STC Aalborg University, CCS Roskilde University, CST University of Copenhagen, September 1992.

13. Lindberg, B., Kristiansen, J. and Andersen, B. "SUNCAR Functional Description". Esprit Project 2094 SUNSTAR, STC.WPIV.008, March 1992.

14. Povlsen, C. and Music, B. "Definition and Specification of the Sub-language for P1". Report 4, Spoken Language Dialogue Systems, CPK Aalborg University, CCS Roskilde University, CST University of Copenhagen. To appear early 1994.

15. Zoltan-Ford, E. "How to Get People to Say and Type what Computers can Understand". International Journal of Man-Machine Studies 34, 527-547 1991.

## Acknowledgements

The work described in this paper was carried out under a grant from the Danish Government's Informatics Research Programme whose support is gratefully acknowledged. Thanks are due to Tom Brøndsted, Anders Bækgaard, Paul Dalsgaard, Lars Bo Larsen, Børge Lindberg, Brad Music and Claus Povlsen for helpful comments.

# SUNSTAR

T. Balle
Jydsk Telefon
Sletvej 30, DK-8310 Aarhus-Tranbjerg, Denmark

## Abstract

The SUNSTAR project was an application oriented development project in which eight European companies, research institutes, and universities joined together to develop a very flexible speech processing system with integrated dialogue control. The goal was to build an open system based on a generalized architecture onto which the different applications with quite different requirements could be integrated. With this approach architectural aspects would be decoupled from latest technological developments, as for example in the fields of speech recognition or text-to-speech systems. Nevertheless, the architecture should allow the integration of technological achievements and advances into already running systems within a very short time frame. Thus, developments in enabling technologies were also part of the project as far as they were demanded by the applications. The project was launched in 1989 and lasted for three years. This paper presents the main results achieved during the project period.

## 1. SUNSTAR Applications

In the late 1980´s advances in speech technology made the realization of speech I/O applications in real life environment possible and economically feasible. Especially applications in the public, telephone network environment and the professional, office type environment looked commercially very attractive. However, it became also clear that no general architecture for speech systems was available to allow efficient application engineering, and to design application specific dialogues in an easy manner.

The most visible result of the SUNSTAR project is a realized set of five promising applications. The applications also demonstrate the usefulness of the modular and open system architecture. Below, the basic selection process for the applications is presented in figure 1 and a description of the main SUNSTAR applications is given in the next sections.

### 1.1 Public News Information Service

The News Service application is a service for all telephone users, which provides them with easy access to information of general interest. The user dials a special number and selects the desired information by speaking keywords. The information is accessible over a hierarchical tree menu structure. The user is guided through this menu. At each step the currently available options are transmitted to the user. Help information is always available. Daily updates are provided for the news information. The application will be made available nationwide for customers of Telefónica, the Spanish telecommunication operating company.

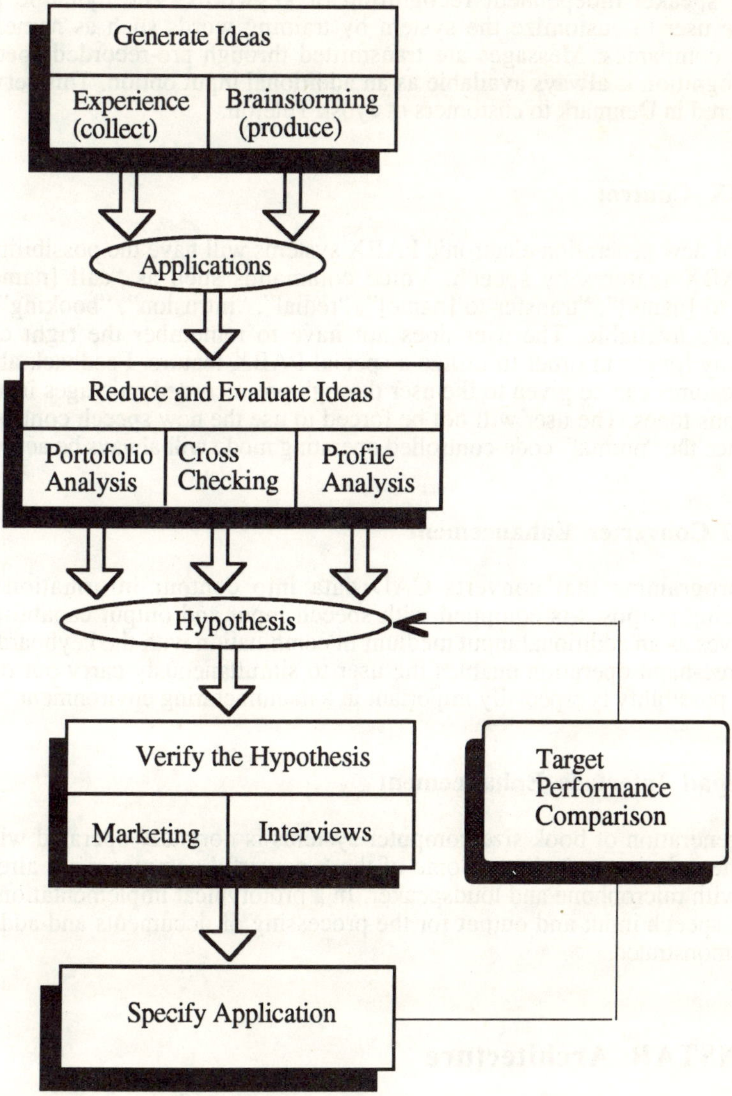


**Fig. 1:** Procedure of application analysis

### 1.2 Abbreviated Dialling and Alarm Call

This service offers speech-controlled abbreviated dialling and automated alarm call features to all subscribers, even if they do use a rotary dial telephone and are not connected to a digital exchange. The user is able to check, activate, or deactivate an alarm call. For abbreviated dialling the options edit, check, or the actual use are available after the user has trained his personal vocabulary. The vocabulary for speech recognition is split into a static and a dynamic part. The static vocabulary allows for speaker-independent recognition of keywords. The dynamic part enables the user to customize the system by training words such as names of persons or companies. Messages are transmitted through pre-recorded speech. DTMF recognition is always available as an additional input option. This service will be offered in Denmark to customers of Jydsk Telefon.

### 1.3 PABX Control

The users of new generation electronic PABX systems will have the possibility to control PABX features by speech. Voice commands such as "call [name]", "diversion to [name]", "transfer to [name]", "redial", "intrusion", "booking", or "resume" are available. The user does not have to remember the right code sequence any longer in order to utilize a special PABX feature. Feedback about activated features can be given to the user through pre-recorded messages instead of ambiguous tones. The user will not be forced to use the new speech controlled features since the "normal" code-controlled operating mode will always be active.

### 1.4 CAD Converter Enhancement

A CAD programme that converts CAD data into contour information for manufacturing purposes is equipped with speech input and output capabilities. Speech serves as an additional input medium in combination with the keyboard (or mouse). Free-hand operation enables the user to simultaneously carry out other tasks. This possibility is especially important in a manufacturing environment.

### 1.5 Notepad Interface Enhancement

The new generation of book size computer systems is normally operated with a stylus as the only input medium. Some of these powerful computers are already equipped with microphone and loudspeaker. In a prototypical implementation the benefits of speech input and output for the processing of documents and address data are demonstrated.

## 2. SUNSTAR Architecture

The major goal of the architectural design was to create a modular open system that can easily be extended. In this way new computer and operating systems, special purpose devices, or state of the art speech processing algorithms can be integrated very efficiently. An overview of the system architecture is shown in figure 2. Most modules are implemented by a separate UNIX process.

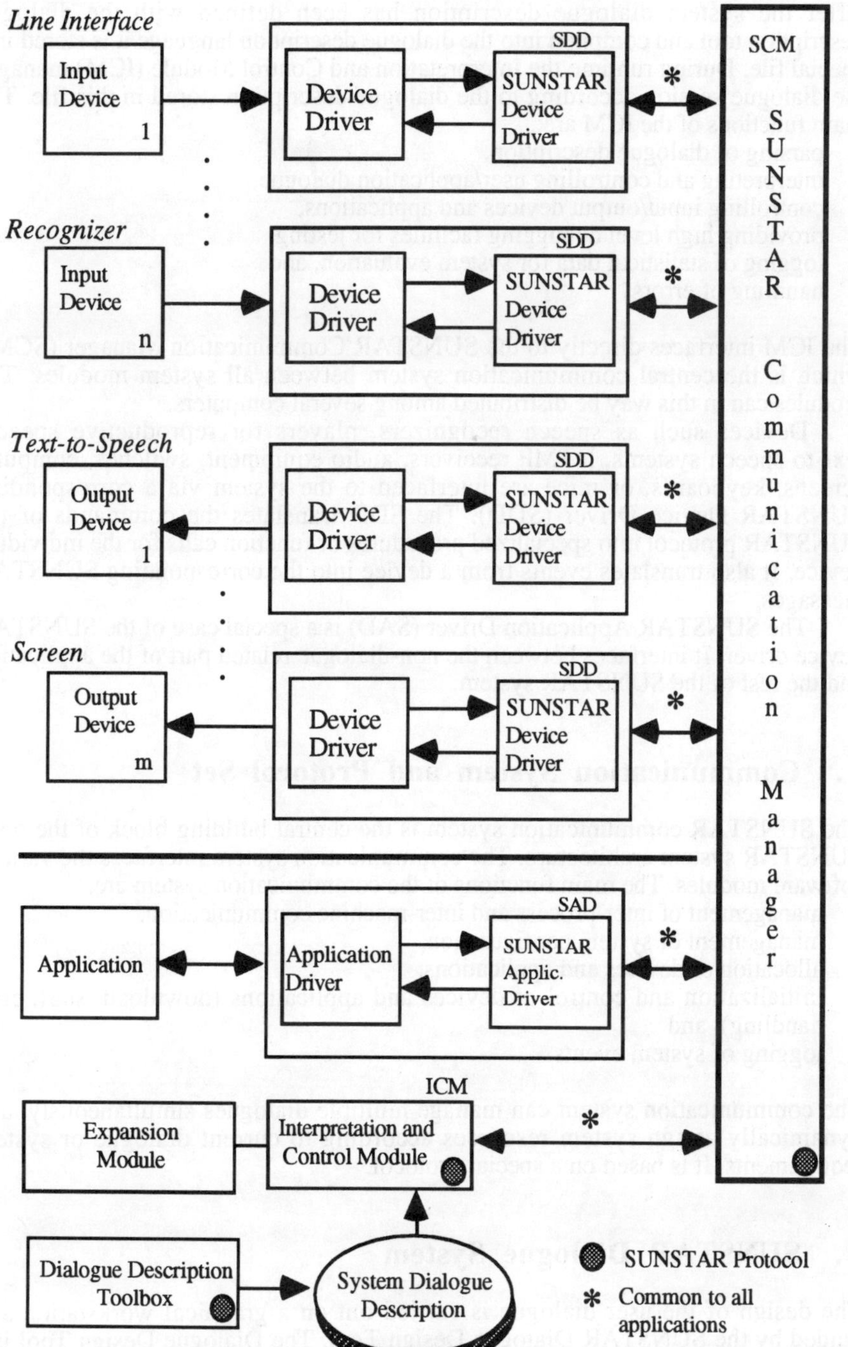


**Fig. 2:** System architecture

After the system dialogue description has been defined with the dialogue description tool and compiled into the dialogue description language it is stored in a special file. During runtime the Interpretation and Control Module (ICM) manages the dialogue session according to the dialogue description stored in this file. The main functions of the ICM are:

- parsing of dialogue description,
- interpreting and controlling user/application dialogue,
- controlling input/output devices and applications,
- providing high level debugging facilities for testing,
- logging of statistical data for system evaluation, and
- handling of errors

The ICM interfaces directly to the SUNSTAR Communication Manager (SCM), which is the central communication system between all system modules. The modules can in this way be distributed among several computers.

Devices such as speech recognizers, players for reproductive speech, text-to-speech systems, DTMF receivers, audio equipment, switches, computer screens, keyboards, or mice are interfaced to the system via a corresponding SUNSTAR Device Driver (SDD). The SDD translates the commands of the SUNSTAR protocol into specialized procedures or function calls for the individual device. It also translates events from a device into the corresponding SUNSTAR messages.

The SUNSTAR Application Driver (SAD) is a special case of the SUNSTAR device driver. It interfaces between the non-dialogue related part of the application and the rest of the SUNSTAR system.

## 3. Communication System and Protocol Set

The SUNSTAR communication system is the central building block of the open SUNSTAR system architecture. The communication system interfaces the various software modules. The main functions of the communication system are:

- management of inter-process and inter-machine communication,
- management of system configuration,
- allocation of devices and applications,
- initialization and control of devices and applications (download, start, error handling), and
- logging of system events.

The communication system can manage multiple dialogues simultaneously, and dynamically assign system resources according to current dialogue or system requirements. It is based on a special protocol.

## 4. SUNSTAR Dialogue System

The design of the user dialogue is carried out on a graphical workstation and guided by the SUNSTAR Dialogue Design Tool. The Dialogue Design Tool is a powerful graphical tool with multiple layers. The tool covers the full range from dialogue specification through dialogue implementation up to dialogue verification, and some system tests. It is based on a formal dialogue description language (DDL).

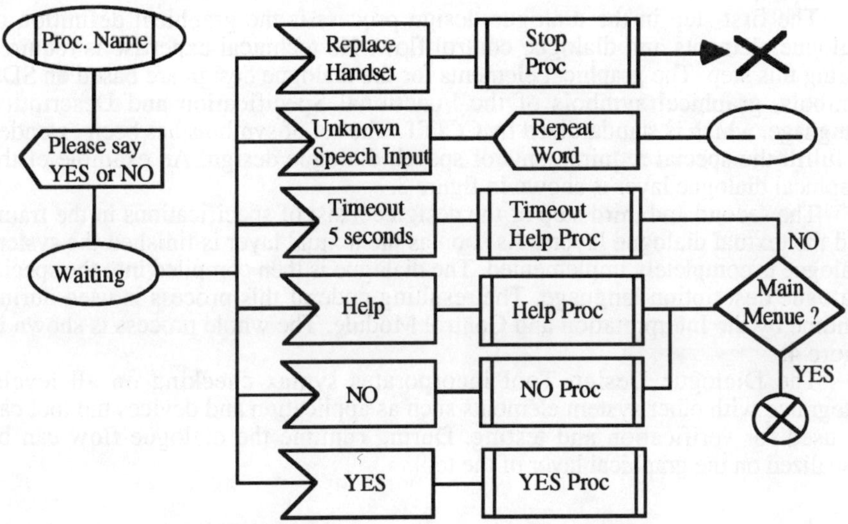


**Fig. 3:** Graphical layer of user dialogue

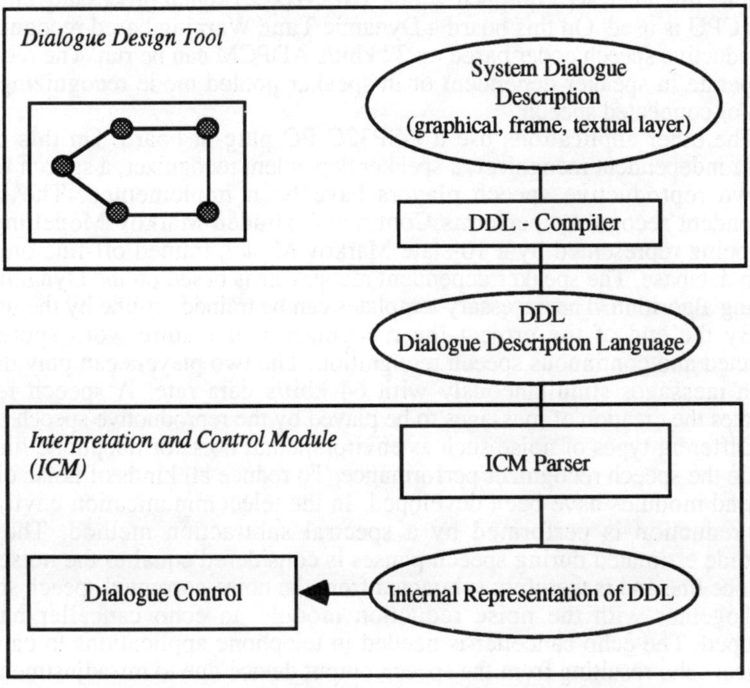


**Fig. 4:** From dialogue design to system control

The first step in the dialogue design process is the graphical definition of dialogue elements and dialogue control flow. No technical expertise is required during this step. The graphical elements for the dialogue design are based on SDL symbols, graphical symbols of the Functional Specification and Description Language, which is standardized by CCITT. The set of symbols has been extended to fulfill the special requirements of speech dialogue design. An example of the graphical dialogue layer is shown in figure 3.

The second and third step of the design consist of specifications in the frame and the textual dialogue layers. As soon as the textual layer is finished the system dialogue is completely implemented. The dialogue is then compiled into the special dialogue description language. The resulting code of this process is used during runtime by the Interpretation and Control Module. The whole process is shown in figure 4.

The Dialogue Design Tool incorporates syntax checking on all levels. Integrated with other system elements such as application and devices the tool can be used for verification and testing. During runtime the dialogue flow can be visualized on the graphical layer of the tool.

## 5. SUNSTAR Technology

Two different hardware platforms are available for speech recognition and reproductive speech within the project. In one application a PC plug-in board with telephone line interface equipped with a TMS320C25 signal processing chip and a 68000 CPU is used. On this board a Dynamic Time Warping based recognizer and a reproductive speech coder based on 32 kbit/s ADPCM can be run. The recognizer can operate in speaker dependent or in speaker pooled mode recognizing single words or connected speech.

The other applications use a DSP32C PC plug-in board. On this board a speaker independent recognizer, a speaker dependent recognizer, a speech recorder and two reproductive speech players have been implemented. The speaker independent recognizer performs Continuous Hidden Markov Modelling, each word being represented by a 10-state Markov Model, trained off-line on a large speech database. The speaker dependent recognizer is based on the Dynamic Time Warping algorithm. The necessary templates can be trained on-line by the user.

By the end of the project the recognizer will feature word spotting for connected and continuous speech recognition. The two players can play different speech messages simultaneously with 64 kbit/s data rate. A speech recorder facilitates the creation of messages to be played by the reproductive speech players.

Different types of noise such as environmental noise or telephone line noise degrade the speech recognizer performance. To reduce all kinds of noise different front-end modules have been developed. In the telecommunication environment noise reduction is performed by a spectral subtraction method. The signal amplitude estimated during speech pauses is considered equal to the noise on the telephone line and is therefore subtracted from the noise-corrupted speech signal.

Together with the noise reduction module an echo canceller has been developed. The echo canceller is needed in telephone applications to cancel the electrical echo resulting from the speech output device due to misadjustment of the telephone line interface at the system site. This module enables the user to break (or stop) a speech output message just by uttering a voice command (double talk operation). The echo signal is estimated by adaptive filtering of the speech output signal and subtracted from the echo-corrupted subscriber signal. To test the recognizer front-ends a large database with environmental noise and telephone line noise has been recorded. This database is called SUNROM-1 and is available on CD-ROM.

# 6. SUNSTAR Evaluation and Assessment

## 6.1 Method

Assessment and evaluation comprises three-level speech assessment, dialogue evaluation, and demonstrator evaluation.

Speech assessment focuses on the speech device level, i.e. the recognizers and reproductive speech players used in the applications are empirically analyzed. Speech recognition is tested with real users against the criteria accuracy, usability, learnability, robustness and user satisfaction. For assessment of speech output user satisfaction is the only criterion.

Dialogue evaluation consists of a formal part as well as an empirical part, using a single step and a multiple step procedure. In the formal part no real users are involved. Tests on the criteria completeness, flexibility, consistency and complexity are performed, based on the user dialogue descriptions of the applications. Special emphasis is put on an ergonomic dialogue design. The single-step analysis focuses on all available commands within a dialogue. In the multiple step analysis basic interaction sequences, i.e. paths in the dialogue structure from the start to a terminal user action, are examined. The empirical part of dialogue evaluation concentrates on the multiple step procedure. Real users of the system are asked to perform different basic interaction sequences, and their performance is evaluated.

For the demonstrator evaluation real users are observed in a realistic environment. This means that only the empirical part is relevant. The criteria that are evaluated are the same as for the dialogue evaluation. For the applications in the telecommunication environment real users access the services provided by the speech demonstrators, via the public telephone network. User response and behaviour is evaluated from log files, audio analysis, interviews and user questionnaires.

## 6.2 Field Trials

In order to evaluate the demonstrators in the real environment, field trials have been running where subscribers were invited to participate. The evaluation was based partly on analyzing tape recordings, partly on questionnaires filled out by the users. According to the test specification, the questionnaire included questions related to each of the test criterias: speed, accuracy, usability, learnability, robustness and satisfaction. Answers from the users were afterwards grouped into these fields. Additionally, some statistical information was achieved from log files created by the system during the field trial.

In order to get knowledge about any possible connection between errors/user-satisfaction and the "User profile", the field trial subscribers´ sex, age and profession were registered. The results from the tests were afterwards related to the different classes of users.

Before the field trials the subscribers received information about the facilities provided by the system. However, they did not get any detailed description related to the structure of the dialogue. In this way it was possible to examine how easy it was for the subscribers to be familiar with the dialogue structure.

Because of technical problems it was not possible to carry out the demonstrator evaluation for the professional application. However, the other demonstrators completed the evaluations where the analysis and feedback from the users gave a valuable picture of the performance of the running systems.
The "PABX" demonstrator test was performed with a user group of 20 people. Regarding the "NEWs Service" and "Abbreviated Dialling and Alarm Call", which were both public services 200 - 300 subscribers participated in each application. During the fields trial for "Abbreviated Dialling and Alarm Call" over 20.000 calls were handled by the system during the 4 months field trial period.

The results from the different evaluations reported some of the same error types. Most of the errors observed were caused by the fact that the recognizer was not immediately ready to accept input after a message had been played. It was obvious that an effective echo cancellation is necessary in order to handle this situation.

Despite that subscribers did not receive any information about the dialogue structure most people found it easy to get familiar with the system. Only few people chose a wrong command. Especially the field trial carried out in the public area showed that a randomly chosen group of subscribers was able to use a complex speech based application, even without being informed in any way about the complex hierarchical dialogue structure.

## 7. The SUNSTAR Speech Platform

Some of the SUNSTAR modules together constitute the basic software, here called the European Speech Platform, for the integration of dialogue controlled interactions between a user and a selected application. User-application interactions may be activated on the input side by a speech recognizer, keystrokes, mouse, other input media or combinations of these inputs, and may respond to the user via synthetic speech, reproduced live speech, screen text, and other selected output media or combinations of these. Examples of applications may be drawn from telecommunication services (e.g. public information service, alarm call, in-house PABX exchange), and from office services (e.g. workstations in connection with graphical oriented design systems, notebook computers, word processing tasks, ticket ordering system).

The following description concentrates on an application example the function of which is based on the integrated use of:

- the CHMM-based continuous speech recognizer (SUNCAR),
- the DDL-Tool, the DDL-Language and the ICM,
- the training and testing software SIRtrain, and
- commonly defined interfaces between these modules.

It has been an essential goal of the SUNSTAR project to define the interfaces between these modules in a structured and common way in order to allow for a flexible integration of new technological products like e.g. an alternative recognizer or application. On the other side it should be stressed that companies who want to establish new dialogue-controlled applications may merge their products (inputs, output and application) with the above given modules, as long as the commonly defined interface protocols are adhered to.

The central component of the SUNSTAR architecture is the DDL-Tool and the DDL-Language together with the ICM (Interpretation and Control Module). The DDL-Tool is used by the Dialogue Developer to describe the expressed user-application interactions by means of a graphical oriented state-diagramme layout system. The functionality of DDL-Tool is based on the same principles as used by the CCITT standard defined Specification and Design Language (SDL).

The dialogue description language is a language used by a dialogue developer to describe the various interactions between a user and an application. A tool which is called the DDL tool is available for the dialogue developer and it aids in the development and maintenance of dialogues.

The dialogue description language (DDL) is a compound language that consists of three levels:

- a frame graphical level - SDL (Specification and Description language),
- a frame level - FL, and
- a textual level - TL.

The three levels reflect three levels of abstraction: The most abstract level where the overall structure of a dialogue is described using DDL/SDL, the medium abstract level where details of the dialogue are described using the DDL/FL by filling slots of frame structures, and the least abstract level where the details of the dialogue are described using the DDL/TL.

The three levels may also be regarded as an explicit separation of the control structure, the declarative part and the computational part of a dialogue description, where the control structure is described using DDL/SDL, the declarative part is described using DDL/FL and the computational part is described using the DDL/FL or DDL/TL. DDL/SDL is a graphical language consisting of a number of DDL/SDL symbols which by means of connections may be combined to form DDL/SDL diagrammes. The three levels are combined by annotating DDL/FL and DDL/TL descriptions to DDL/SDL symbols. Hence, for each DDL/SDL symbol in a dialogue description, there is a DDL/FL or a DDL/TL annotation describing the semantics for that particular symbol in the given context. The DDL/SDL, DDL/FL and DDL/TL combined levels have a pure textual counterpart in the ICM language. This means that a DDL description may be translated into equivalent ICM language description.

Some of the language features are the same as those found in traditional programming languages (constants, types, variables, expressions etc.), but more novel features are included. The key design principles behind DDL/TL are simplicity and flexibility.

Facilities for defining and manipulating objects are available. It is the intention that the external world apparatus is modelled by objects. For example, the general concept of a device is one type of object, and specific devices are other types of objects, that inherit the attributes of the general device object types. Events are objects, and an object type hierarchy is formed, which is designed with a general event object type in the root, and specific events (depending on event type and event origin) are leaves of that hierarchy.

The DDL-tool will automatically ensure that the established graphical state-diagramme is complete. Furthermore, debugging facilities are available by which the Dialogue Developer is able to follow the control flow of the expected dialogue in a simulation mode, where user and application inputs are fed into the DDL-Tool by e.g. keystrokes.

The DDL-Tool output is compiled into the ICM-Language which is subsequently used during runtime by the Interpretation and Control Module (ICM). The ICM manages the user-application dialogue according to the dialogue description. The ICM is the core of the SUNSTAR architecture, and all communication is dealt with by the ICM, the main functions of which are:

- parsing of dialogue description,
- interpreting and controlling the user-application dialogue,
- controlling input and output devices and the application,
- logging of user interactions for assessment and errors, and
- support of high level debugging during system development phases.

The ICM interacts with other modules via a protocol-based interface. The ICM connects to e.g. the SUNCAR recognizer via this interface, and a specific device driver for the recognizer. The device driver for the recognizer has, on its turn to adhere to the common SUNSTAR protocol. This is the reason why any specifically manufactured input devices can be connected to the ICM. It is worth mentioning that e.g. for a recognition device, no real speech data will be involved in the communication between the recognizer and the ICM. In the SUNSTAR concept only "events" (e.g. the recognition of a certain word) are communicated in the SUNSTAR system between the ICM, the input/output devices and the application.

The SUNCAR recognizer uses a CHMM-based recognizer which can also handle word rejection (in this case its task is the recognition of isolated words) and word spotting (in connected spoken sentences). An alternative recognizer to use is another of the SUNSTAR products, the 3R-recognizer, which is a device, which can perform Recognition, Record user data and Replay these again. The 3R-recognizer, can perform speaker independent isolated word recognition on CHMM models, and speaker dependent isolated word recognition based on the DTW-algorithm using pertained models. Presently the SUNCAR recognizer is only implemented in software, but the SUNSTAR partners are willing to initiate collaborative work with new partners to e.g. establish a real-time implementation on a suitable and commonly available hardware platform.

The SUNCAR recognizer uses information in the ICM-Language file in its parsing of the incoming connected word sentence. The function of the SUNCAR recognizer is based on CHMM-models being trained by means of the SIRtrain software module (or other similar training software packages - the output of which can be converted into the CHMM-model structure used by SUNCAR). The SIRtrain package uses database - and configuration description files, which are in full compliance with the recommendations issued by the ESPRIT project 2589, SAM (Speech Assessment Methodology).

Apart from being a CHMM training software package, a speech recognizer testing module (called SIRtester) is included in the entire package. This module can perform a simulated recognition task of the models being trained. Furthermore, the module SIRsignal can perform speech signal analysis on the basis of a number of signal analysis procedures, which can be added together, and as such simulate alternative pre-processing analyses to be used in connection with the recognizer.

In conclusion, the above mentioned modules DDL-Tool, DDL-Language, ICM, SUNCAR or 3R recognizer, SIRtrain software package, and the interface protocol definition all together add up to the SUNSTAR product: the SUNSTAR Speech Platform.

## 8. SUNSTAR Publications

During the project a sizeable amount of publications have been presented to the public by the members of the SUNSTAR team. They formed the basis for a continuing information dissemination of results of SUNSTAR. Below the complete list of the SUNSTAR publications is given.

Anders Bækgaard and Paul Dalsgaard, "Tools for Designing Dialogues in Speech Understanding Interfaces", International Conference on Spoken Language Processing, Japan, November 1990.

Paulus H. Vossen, "Outline of a design-oriented evaluation framework for speech-driven applications", 2nd European Conference on Speech Communication and Technology, EUROSPEECH 91, Genoa, Italy, 24-26 September 1992.

Paulus H. Vossen, "Evaluating Speech Input and Output in a CAD System Using the Hidden-Operator Method", 2nd European Conference on Speech Communication and Technology, EUROSPEECH 91, Genoa, Italy, 24-26 September 1992.

A. Riccio, V. Lamanna, "Generation of telephone grade quality speech corpora: a proposal for a standard procedure", Workshop on International Co-operation and Standardisation of speech Databases and Speech I/O Assessment Methods, Chiavari, Italy, September 1991.

Carlos M. Ribeiro and Isabel M. Trancose, "Selection of Environmental and Telephone Line Noise Samples for SUNROM", Workshop on International Co-operation and Standardisation of speech Databases and Speech I/O Assessment Methods, Chiavari, Italy, September 1991.

Paulus H. Vossen, Brigitte Wandel, Peter Morlock, Barbara Federmann und Susan Thiermayer, "Spracheingabe an einem CAD-System: ein empirischer Versuch unter Verwendung der 'Wizard of Oz' Technik", Ergonomie & Informatik, ISSN 0940-1210, November 1991.

Paulus H. Vossen, "Outline of a comprehensive assessment methodology for speech-oriented applications", Human Aspects in Computing: Design and Use of Interactive Systems and Work with Terminals, Editor: H.-J- Bullinger, Elsevier Science Publishers, pp. 478-484, 1991.

Paulus H. Vossen, "The recognition coefficient: methodological and statistical issues concerning measurement of speech recognition accuracy", Human Aspects in Computing: Design and Use of Interactive Systems and Work with Terminals, Editor: H.-J- Bullinger, Elsevier Science Publishers, pp. 498-505, 1991.

A. Riccio, F. Ceglie, "Assessment of speech recognizers towards a European standardisation", Alcatel Technology Review, Stuttgart November 1991

Thomas Renner and Joachim Brettschneider, "Voice-Controlled Applications Based on a Common Architecture", Voice Systems World-wide '92, Hannover, Germany, 1992.

Per Raun Jensen & Georg Beck Kristensen, "Speech Systems Based on a Common European Platform", Speech Systems Worldwide '92, Japan July 1992.

Georg Beck Kristensen & Per Raun Jensen, "Experience with Speech Controlled Public Services", Voice Systems Worldwide '92, Japan, July 1992.

Palle Bach Nielsen & Anders Bækgaard, "Experience with a Dialogue Description Formalism for Realistic Applications", 1992 International Conference on Spoken Language Processing, ICSLP 92, Banff, Canada, October 1992.

B. Lindberg, B. Andersen, A. Bækgaard, T. Brøndsted, P. Dalsgaard, J. Kristensen, "An integrated Dialogue Design and continuous speech recognition system environment", 1992 International Conference on Spoken Language Processing, ICSLP 92, Banff, Canada, October 1992.

Palle Bach Nielsen and Georg Beck Kristensen, "Experience gained in a field trial of a speech recognition application over the public telephone network", IEEE Workshop on Interactive Voice Technology for Telecommunications Applications, Piscataway, N.J., October 1992.

Thomas Renner, "Dialogue Design and System Architecture for Voice-Controlled Telecommunication Applications", IEEE Workshop on Interactive Voice Technology for Telecommunications Applications, Piscataway, N.J., October 1992.

A. Riccio, F. Ceglie, "Standardized assessment of speech recognizers through telephone grade speech corpora", ESCA Workshop on Speech Processing in adverse conditions , Cannes-Mandelieu, France, 10-13 November 1992.

A. Brancaccio, F. Ceglie, G. D'Acunzo, C. Pelaez, A. Riccio, F. Rigosi, "A comparative study of the influence of parameter processing on two different approaches for speech recognition in adverse environment", ESCA Workshop on Speech Processing in adverse conditions, Cannes-Mandelieu, France, 10-13 November 1992.

Carlos J. Teixeira, Isabel M. Trancoso and António J. Serralheiro, "Single vs. Multiple Sink Models for Isolated and Connected Word Rejection", ESCA Workshop on Speech Processing in adverse conditions, Cannes-Mandelieu, France, 10-13 November 1992.

A. Riccio, F. Ceglie, G. D'Acuzo, F. Rigori, "Standardisation activities at Alcatel Italia for assessing speech recognizers in the Telephone environment", Alcatel Magazine 'Electrical Communication' December 1992.

A. Riccio, F. Ceglie, "Standardized assessment procedures for speech recognizer in telephone environment", 4th IEE Conference on Telecommunications Manchester, April 1993.

# The EAGLE Working Group on Spoken Language

Roger K. Moore
Speech Research Unit, DRA Malvern, Worcs, U.K.

## Abstract

This paper outlines the initial activities of an EC part–sponsored Working Group, who's objective is to create a 'handbook' of recommended working practices in the spoken language research and technology area. The handbook is intended to be used as an everyday reference in European speech research and development laboratories. The Group is one of five in the language engineering area known under the collective heading of 'EAGLES'.

## 1. Background

In January 1993, DG XIII launched a new initiative, under the auspices of the Linguistic Research and Engineering (LRE) Programme, aimed at accelerating the provision of common functional specifications for the development of large–scale language resources, such as electronic text collections (corpora), lexicons, grammars and *speech*. The initiative, known as 'EAGLES' (Expert Advisory Group on Language Engineering Standards), has arisen from consultations with primary industrial and academic actors, and from recommendations stemming from the Language Engineering strategy committees. EAGLES is founded on the active participation of more than thirty research centres, industrial organisations, associations and research networks from most EC countries. The Group is co–ordinated by the Consorzio Pisa Ricerche (Italy), and is to present its findings in the form of a set of guide-lines in spring 1995. The Community contribution allocated to this initiative amounts to 1.25 MECU.

The EAGLES Group has the following objectives:

- to produce publicly defined and commonly agreed specifications and guide-lines for specific areas of language engineering, by capitalising on the knowledge accumulated in the participants' organisations and consortia, and thus making recommendations for a more uniform approach;
- to bring together industry and academia in an attempt to reconcile the often heterogeneous interests and approaches pursued by the two groups, and foster collaborative arrangements between the member organisations;
- to create focal points of expertise in Europe, by concentrating highly reputed language scientists and engineers at prominent centres of European R&D; the participating associations and research networks, such as ESCA and ELSNET, serve as a primary source of expertise, while providing the mechanisms for bringing together the Natural Language and *Speech* communities;
- to complement European R&D projects, falling under LRE, ESPRIT and EUREKA, by providing consensus based scientific advice and orientation; at a later stage, make adherence to the guide-lines resulting from EAGLES compulsory in further R&D ventures, in order to enhance usability, portability and comparability of projects results and thus maximize return on investment in the development of language products and services;
- to contribute to consensus building on an international scale by interacting with national and international standardization initiatives, while safeguarding the multilingual dimension of Europe.

The actual definition of specifications and guide-lines is carried out in five working groups set up in response to the most urgently felt requirements in advanced language engineering: common methodologies for the creation and interchange of electronic language resources such as text corpora, computational lexicons, grammars and speech databases and the evaluation and quality assessment of language processing systems and components. Those working on written language–based data and software are assisted by speech experts, in a first attempt to reconcile the needs and practices of the two R&D communities.

The activities of the EAGLES Group are therefore distributed over:

- the five specialist technical working groups,
- five centres designated to 'host' these groups,
- a Management Board and
- a central support facility provided by the co–ordinator

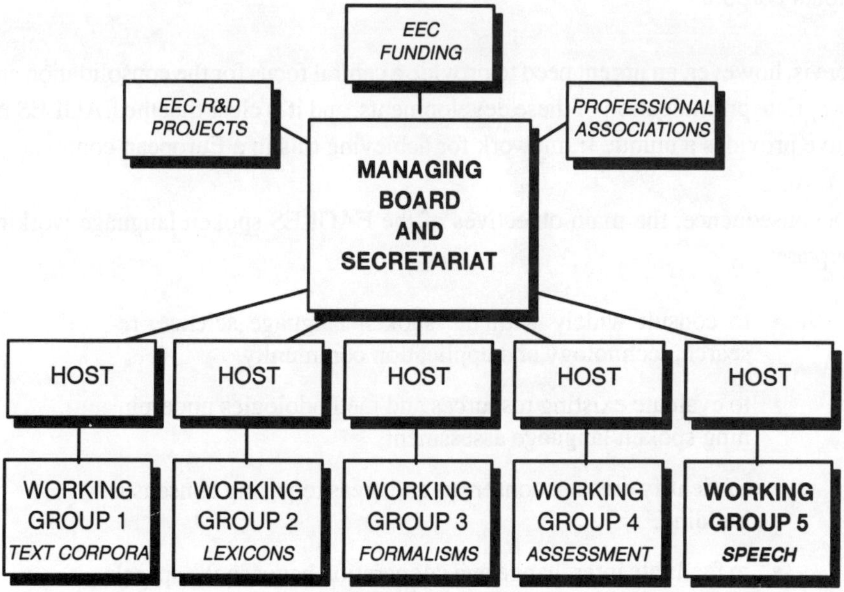


Figure 1: The main structure of the EAGLES Group.

The EAGLES Management Board is chaired by Prof. Rohrer of Stuttgart University (Jeremy Peckham of Vocalis, Cambridge, UK is vice–chairman). Currently the board consists of thirteen ordinary member organisations representing:

- European projects in Natural Language and Speech, established under the ESPRIT, LRE and EUREKA programmes: MULTILEX, PLUS, ACQUILEX, NERC, GENELEX, SAM–A, SUNDIAL, EUROLANG, TWB, ONOMASTICA and DELIS
- Several European associations and co–ordinating bodies such as ELSNET, ESCA, FOLLI and the European Chapter of the ACL

## 2. The Spoken Language Working Group (WG5)

Clearly, within the speech field, very substantial resources already exist in regard to established spoken language corpora and widely accepted systems of data description. Also available are integrated systems of assessment and, in some areas, detailed methods of evaluation. In particular, the prior work of the ESPRIT SAM project has made a substantial contribution to both ESPRIT project activities and also to several national corpora.

There is, however, an urgent need to provide a central focus for the consolidation and appropriate promulgation of these developments, and it is clear that the EAGLES initiative provides a unique framework for achieving this in a European context.

As a consequence, the main objectives of the EAGLES spoken language working group are:

- to consult widely with the spoken language science, research, technology and application community,
- to evaluate existing resources and methodologies underpinning spoken language assessment,
- to identify areas of consensus and areas requiring consensus building,
- to facilitate interchange and cooperation between the speech and natural language communities in a multilingual environment,
- to provide a focus for liaison with other national and international bodies in the field,
- to communicate results to the spoken language community, and
- to identify research areas requiring further funding.

Work towards these objectives is already under way in accordance with two phases of activity, each of fifteen months duration (see figure 2). At the present time, work is concentrated on surveying existing resources and standards and the production of a set of initial recommendations.

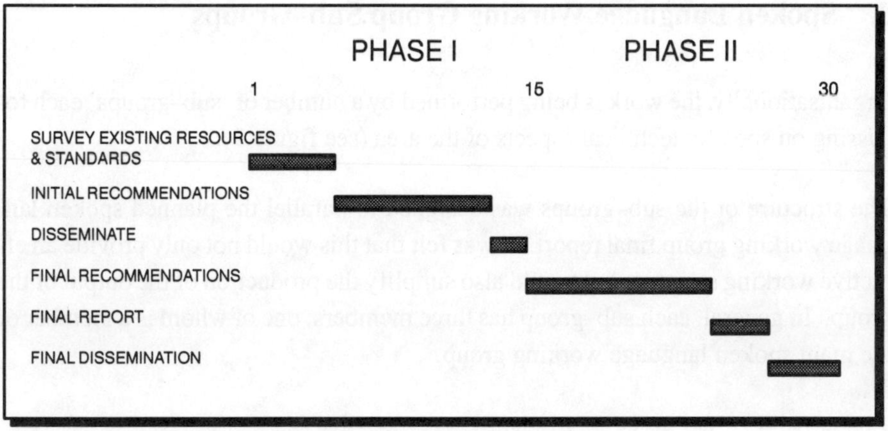


Figure 2: Workplan for the spoken language working group.

The main topics of study by the spoken language working group are (i) spoken language corpora, (ii) spoken language assessment, (iii) spoken language system design and specification, and (iv) spoken language terminology.

Within these four technical areas, the following actions are currently in progress:–

- contact people working in the field,
- identify priority requirements,
- assemble working papers/reports/material,
- identify relationships with other activities,
- identify scope of EAGLES activities,
- produce initial survey report,
- disseminate within group and externally,
- produce initial working terminology document,
- critically evaluate existing resources/methods,
- extend scope of existing recommendations, and
- disseminate to 'community' for comment.

## 3. Spoken Language Working Group Sub–Groups

Organisationally, the work is being performed by a number of 'sub–groups' each focussing on specific technical aspects of the area (see figure 3).

The structure of the sub–groups was designed to parallel the planned spoken language working group final report. It was felt that this would not only provide an effective working structure but would also simplify the production of the output of the group. In general, each sub–group has three members, one of whom is a member of the main spoken language working group.

## 4. Relationships with Other Working Groups – 'Cross–Groups'

Within the EAGLES activity, there are obvious connections between all the working groups and, specifically, between the spoken language working group and the four other groups (see figure 1). Therefore, the exchange of information between groups is encouraged and is taking place in various ways.

In the first instance, some members of the spoken language group are also taking part in other groups. Also, in view of the very specific commonalities that exist between some activities in the spoken language working group and the Lexicon and Corpus working groups, common 'cross–groups' have been set up.

## 5. International Collaboration

Finally, the spoken language working group is seeking to ensure that its activities are conducted in the context of international initiatives such as the International Committee for Collaboration in Speech Assessment and Databases (COCOSDA).

## Acknowledgement

The author wishes to thank all of the working group and sub–group members who have contributed to this paper.

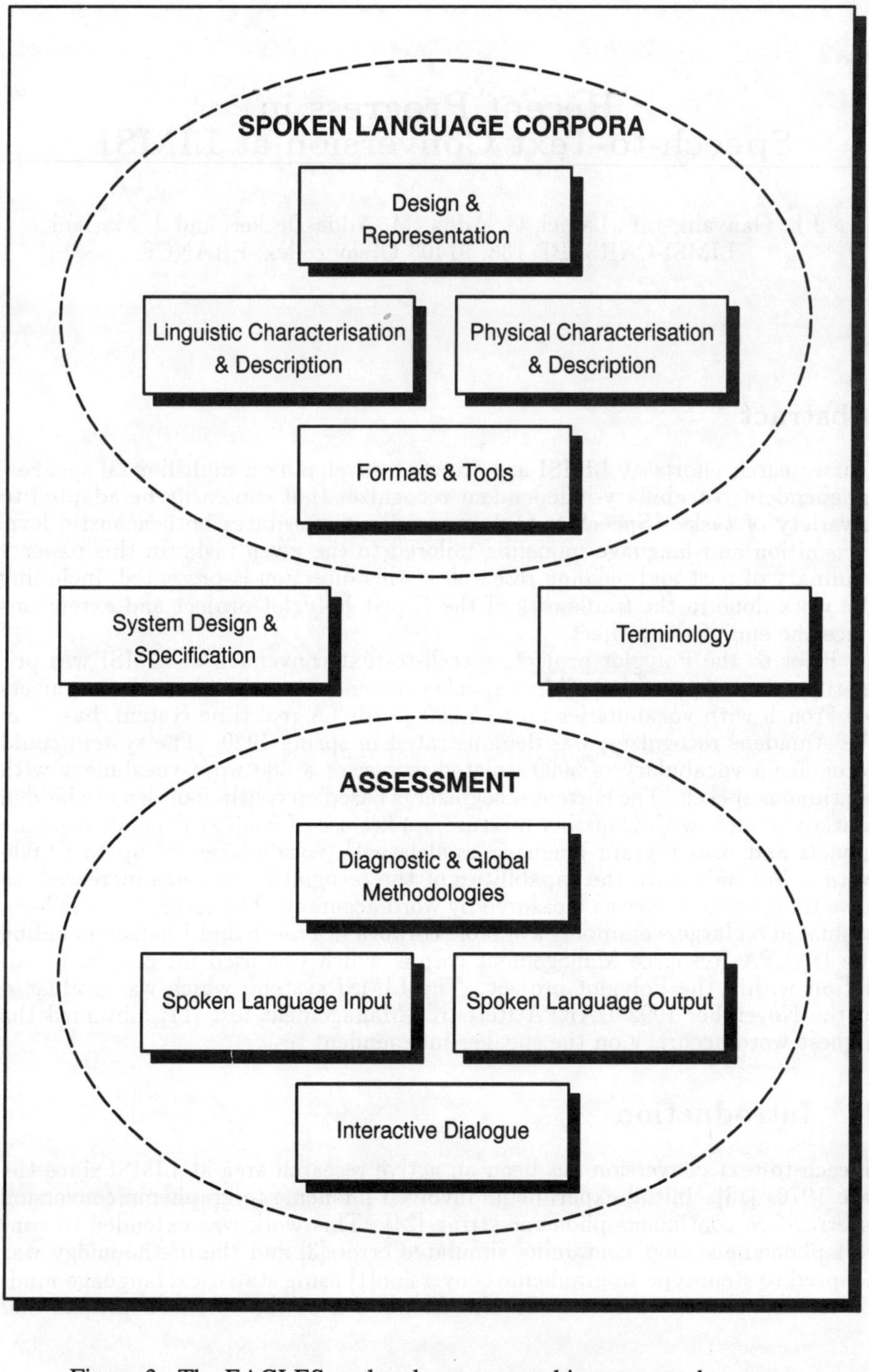


Figure 3: The EAGLES spoken language working group sub–groups.

# Recent Progress in Speech-to-Text Conversion at LIMSI

J.L. Gauvain, L.F. Lamel, G. Adda, M. Adda-Decker, and J. Mariani
LIMSI-CNRS, BP 133, 91403 Orsay cedex, FRANCE

## Abstract

Our research efforts at LIMSI are directed developing a multilingual speaker-independent, vocabulary-independent recognizer that can easily be adapted to a variety of tasks. Speech-to-text conversion necessitates both acoustic level recognition and language modeling tailored to the given task. In this paper a summary of past and ongoing research in this direction is presented, including the work done in the framework of the Esprit Polyglot project and extensions since the end of the project.

Prior to the Polyglot project, speech-to-text conversion at LIMSI was primarily oriented towards building speaker-dependent, isolated word recognizers for French with vocabularies up to 5,000 words. A real-time system, based on the Amadeus recognizer, was demonstrated in spring 1989. The system could recognize a vocabulary of 5000 isolated words, or a 300 word vocabulary with continuous speech. The current recognizer is based on continuous density hidden Markov models with Gaussian mixture, makes use of context-dependent phone models and uses n-gram language models with vocabularies of up to 64,000 words. Not only have the capabilities of the recognition systems increased, so have their performance as measured by word accuracy. The recognizer has been evaluated on large, commonly available corpora in French and English including the DARPA Resource Management corpus which was used for common evaluation within the Polyglot project. The LIMSI system, which was evaluated in the November 1992 DARPA Resource Management test [11], obtained the highest word accuracy on the speaker-independent test.

## 1. Introduction

Speech-to-text conversion has been an active research area at LIMSI since the late 1970s [13]. Initial experiments involved phoneme-to-grapheme conversion of error-free continuous phoneme strings[24]. This work was extended to convert phoneme strings containing simulated errors[3] and the methodology was adapted to stenotype-to-grapheme conversion[1] using statistical language models trained on text corpora. In the framework of the ESPRIT project 860

"Linguistic Analysis of the European Languages," LIMSI's approach to language modeling was compared with other closely related approaches, on 7 different European languages (English, Italian, French, Dutch, Spanish, Greek, and German)[5]. This 4-year project was followed by the ESPRIT Polyglot project, which had the goal of designing speech-to-text and text-to-speech systems for each of the same 7 languages.

LIMSI has also been active in developing real-time speech recognizers including the first French single-board isolated-word speech recognizer, *Moise*, and the first single-board connected-word recognizer, *Mozart* [16, 10] which was able to recognize a vocabulary of about 100 words. A specialized DTW chip for pattern recognition ($\mu$PCD)[34, 35] was designed at LIMSI, in collaboration with the Bull and the Vecsys companies. Acoustic recognition was first demonstrated with a chip emulator in March 1987, and a complete dictation system using the chip was demonstrated in spring 1989.

Presently, the primary research efforts in speech recognition are directed at the speech dictation and spoken language understanding. For both applications, a multilingual, speaker-independent (SI), vocabulary-independent (VI), phone-based recognizer is being developed, so as to be easily adaptable to various tasks. For the dictation effort three corpora have been used to assess the performance of the recognizer: The DARPA Resource Management corpus (RM)[32, 19] and ARPA Continuous Speech Recognition Wall Street Journal corpus (WSJ)[29, 12] for English, and the BREF corpus [14, 23] for French. The immediate goal is to work with read speech material from a large number of speakers, so as to be able to build base acoustic models which can be augmented and adapted to specific speakers or tasks.

An ongoing dialog project is oriented toward Air-Traffic Controller training, in collaboration with the Centre d'Etudes de la Navigation Aérienne. Currently, the student training sessions are limited by the availability of the human instructor who plays the role of a pilot. The goal is to replace the instructor by a spoken dialog system. This allows for more availability of the system, and may force the student to adhere to the pre-defined phraseology, the learning of which is part of training. The dialog system is built around the *Amadeus* speech recognizer[9] and an associated synthesis module. Another project, undertaken in collaboration with colleagues in the Spoken Language Systems Group at MIT, is to develop a French version of the MIT ATIS system[4].

The remainder of this paper is as follows. Section 2 presents some distributional properties of French gathered from the study of a large text corpus. In Section 3 some of the problems encountered in speech-to-text conversion are addressed, highlighting those problems specific to French. Section 4 summarizes previous research on speaker-dependent isolated word dictation and in Section 5 speaker-independent continuous speech recognition is addressed. Finally, issues related to porting the recognizer to specific applications, and its incorporation in a spoken language system are discussed.

## 2. Distributional properties of French

In order to be effective in speech-to-text conversion, it is necessary to determine and account for the distributional properties of the language. In this section, a brief analysis of text material taken from the French newspaper *Le Monde* is presented. The source texts consisted of three months of *Le Monde*, representing about 5 million words of text (4.2 million after cleaning up the text).

The distributional properties of the texts were determined by counting the occurrences of sentence, word, and subword units. Table 1 shows the distribution of sentences in *Le Monde* according to sentence type, and shows for each type the minimum, average, and maximum sentence lengths. Sentences were classified as declarative, interrogative and exclamative types, or as more complex formulations which included ellipses, parenthetic expressions, and/or quotations. Simple sentences contain no internal punctuation markers other than comma, and no embedded parenthetic expressions or quotations. Conversely, complex sentences contain at least one of these. It can be seen that the vast majority of sentences are declarative, and that a substantial portion contain numbers or quotations.

| *Sentence Type* | *Percent* | *Number of Words* | | |
|---|---|---|---|---|
| | | *Ave* | *Min* | *Max* |
| Declarative | 95 | 23 | 1 | 222 |
| Interrogative | 3.8 | 15 | 1 | 191 |
| Exclamatory | 1.2 | 13 | 1 | 104 |
| Simple Sentences | 57 | 19 | 1 | 191 |
| Complex Sentences | 43 | 33 | 3 | 222 |
| Numbers | 22 | 30 | 1 | 165 |
| Acronyms | 11 | - | - | - |
| Quotations | 22 | 34 | 2 | >400 |
| Parenthetic | 11 | 35 | 2 | >100 |

**Table 1**: Sentence types and lengths in the text corpus of the newpaper *Le Monde.*

Each sentence was phoneticized using grapheme-to-phoneme rules[33, 30], and erroneous pronunciations were hand-located and the most frequent errors were corrected using an exceptions dictionary. The most common mispronunciations occurred on foreign words and names, and acronyms. The set of 35 phone labels used in grapheme-to-phoneme rules is given in Table 2. Word and subword units were counted in the phonemicized, syllabified text. Punctuation markers were considered to be non-verbalized, and therefore were not counted as words but were replaced by a silence "phone". Table 3 summarizes the counts for the different units for the complete text of *Le Monde.* In the 167,359 sentences there were 4.2 million words, of which over 90,000 are orthographically distinct. These words correspond to about 64,000 phonemically distinct words, indicating that there are about 30% homophones in this corpus. For comparison, there are roughly 3% homophones in the 1000-word DARPA Resource Managment lexicon[32], less than 2% for the DARPA TIMIT lexicon[8], and 6% for the ARPA Wall Street Journal 20,000 word lexicon.

| *Phone* | *Example* | *Phone* | *Example* |
|---|---|---|---|
| Vowels | | Consonants | |
| i | lit | s | sot |
| e | blé | z | zèbre |
| E | sel | S | chat |
| y | suc | Z | jour |
| X | leur | f | fou |
| x | petit | v | vin |
| @ | feu | m | motte |
| a | patte, pâte | n | note |
| c | sol | N | digne |
| o | saule | l | la |
| u | fou | r | rond |
| Nasal Vowels | | p | pont |
| I | brin, brun | b | bon |
| A | chant | t | ton |
| O | bon | d | don |
| Semivowels | | k | cou |
| h | lui | g | gond |
| w | oui | . | silence |
| j | yole | | |

**Table 2**: The 35 phone symbol set.

| *Unit* | *Le Monde* | *Senat* |
|---|---|---|
| #sentences | 167,359 | 64,613 |
| #words (total) | 4,244,810 | 1,137,928 |
| #orthographically distinct | 92,185 | 26,807 |
| #phonemically distinct | 63,981 | |
| #syllables (total) | 6,903,017 | 1,956,423 |
| #distinct syllables | 9,571 | |
| #distinct dissyllables | 37,636 | |
| #phones (total) | 16,416,738 | 4,737,578 |
| #distinct phones | 35 | 35 |
| #distinct diphones | 1,160 | 1,105 |
| #distinct triphones | 25,999 | 17,079 |

**Table 3**: Distributional properties of word and subword units.

On the average, there were 2.3 phones/syllable, 3.2 phones/dissyllable[1] (in-

[1]The dissyllable is defined from the midpoint of one vowel to the midpoint of the next

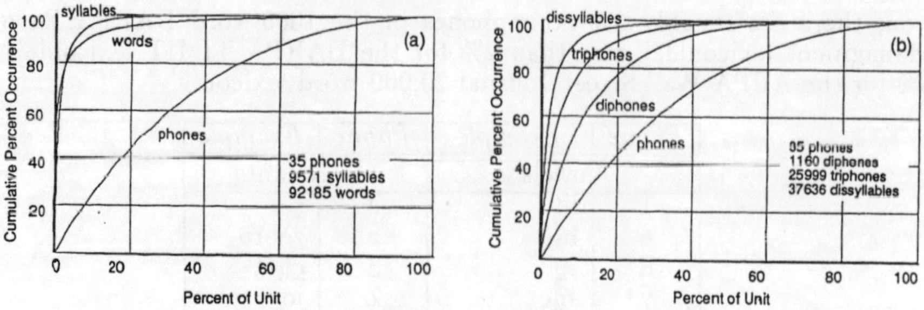


**Fig. 1**: Frequency of occurrence for word and subword units.

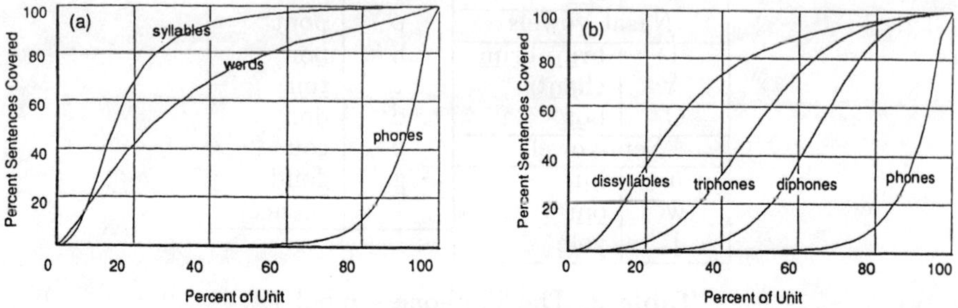


**Fig. 2**: Percentage of sentences covered as a function of the percentage of units.

cluding both vowels), and 3.7 phones/word. Most of the possible diphones were found to exist (1160 out of 1225, taking into account the silence "phone"), as were 60% of the possible triphones.

Figure 1 shows plots of the frequency of occurrence for the word and subword units in percentages. Part (a) has curves for words, syllables, and phones, and part (b) has curves for dissyllables, triphones, diphones, and phones. The units have been separated as such since words, syllables, and phones have no constraints internal to the unit itself restricting which units may follow, whereas the units in part (b) have internal constraints limiting the possible following units. Phones are shown in both for comparison as the basic unit.

Less than 20% of the distinct words account for over 95% of all word oc-

vowel, and therefore contains all the intervening consonants. This unit has been successfully used for speech recognition and speech synthesis in French[36], in part because French vowels are acoustically relatively stable over time.

currences. In fact, 40% (about 35,000 words) occurred only once in the text, and 60% of the words appeared at most 3 times. This effect is even more pronounced for syllables, where the roughly 20% most common syllables account for 98% of all syllable occurrences. Almost 80% of the text is covered by only the most frequent 232 (20%) diphones. 20% of the triphones and dissyllables cover over 90% and 95% of the text, respectively.

But perhaps more interesting is the opposite question: given that 40% of the words only occurred once in the text, how many sentences can be pronounced if these words are eliminated? The curves shown in Figure 2 illustrate the percentage of sentences covered as a function of the percentage of word or subword units. The curve for phones is very gradual - with 80% of the phones, only 10% of the sentences can be covered. For words, however, over 80% of the sentences are covered using only 60% of the distinct words, effectively eliminating all of the single occurrence words. The effect is even stronger for syllables: roughly 40% of the syllables cover over 90% of the sentences. Curves are shown for phones, diphones, triphones, and dissyllables in Figure 2b.

## 3. Problems specific to French speech-to-text conversion

Phoneme-to-grapheme conversion of French seems to be more difficult than in other languages such as Spanish or Italian[30], due to the large number of homophones, as well as liaison and apostrophe, and mute-e. Expanding a source dictionary of 22,000 baseforms results in a full-form lexicon of about 162,900 graphemic words, as shown in Table 4. Grapheme-to-phoneme translation of those words produces about 90,000 distinct phonemic forms, indicating that for such a large full-form lexicon, a phonemic word corresponds to, on the average, 1.8 different graphemic words.

As can be seen in the table, the main problem arises from verb conjugation. A single verb has on average 40 graphemic forms. Among these, there are as many as three different spellings for each pronunciation. Another source of homophones is that the mark of plurals (an -s at the end of the word) for most substantives, most adjectives, and all the past participles, is never pronounced in isolation, and only sometimes pronounced in fluent speech. Similarly, the mark of the feminine form (-e at the end of the word) for some substantives, most of the adjectives and the past participles, is never pronounced.

In addition, there are the more typical "word" homophones, such as the demonstrative adjective *ces (those)* and the possessive adjective *ses (his)*, which have the same pronunciation /se/. Some examples of the different types of homophones are given in Figure 3.

For continuous speech, the problem of segmenting the continuous phoneme string into words seems to be especially difficult in French. In experiments on a simple sentence containing 9 phonemes, "J'ai mal au pied." (My foot hurts.), with a 162,900 word full-form lexicon, more than 32,000 possible transcriptions (segmentations and orthographic translations) were obtained at the lexical level. Even after applying phonological rules, syntactic and semantic constraints there are still two acceptable sentences (the original and its plural form "J'ai mal aux pieds." (My feet hurt.)) that require a pragmatic analysis in order to get the

| | % *Words* | # *Words* | # *Forms/Word* | # *Forms* |
|---|---|---|---|---|
| Verbs | 14% | 3,100 | 40 | 124,000 |
| Substantives | 56% | 12,300 | 2 | 24,600 |
| Adjectives | 23% | 5,100 | 2.5 | 12,800 |
| Adverbs and others | 7% | 1,500 | 1 | 1,500 |
| Total | 100% | 22,000 | (avg.) 7.3 | 162,900 |

**Table 4**: Full-forms derived from a dictionary with 22,000 baseforms.

**Verbs:**
/kas/ casse, casses, cassent (break)
**Substantives (Masculine/Feminine):**
/ami/ ami (friend (he)), amie (friend (she))
**Substantives (Singular/Plural):**
/tas/ tasse, tasses (cup, cups)
**Adjectives (Masculine/feminine):**
/ene/ aîné (older masc.), aînée (older fem.)
**Adjectives (Singular/plural):**
/grAd/ grande, grandes (big)
**Past Participles:**
/kase/ cassé, cassés, cassée, cassées (broken)

**Fig. 3**: Examples of common homophones.

right graphemic transcription.

In French one must also deal with "liaison", the links made between words. These are phonemes that are pronounced at the junctions between two words, but would not be pronounced at the end of the first word, or at the beginning of the second one, if the words were pronounced in isolation. For example, the word sequence "les amis" (the friends) is pronounced /lezami/, where the word pronunciations in isolation would be /le/ and /ami/. Some examples of liaison are given in Figure 4. Another more complicated form of liaison is the insertion of /t/, in certain inverted verb forms. Instead of forming the question "A il ...", the written and spoken form is "A-t-il ...". In certain cases this liaison is the only indication to distinguish between the singular and plural forms of a word as in the sentences "Il aime le pain." (He likes bread.) and "Ils aiment le pain." (They like bread).

Another problem is the optional pronunciation of mute-e. For example, the word *devenu* can be produced with 2 or 3 syllables: /dxvnu/ or /dxvxnu/. The same phenomena can also occur across words: *beaucoup de gens* may be pronounced as /bokudxZA/ or as /bokudZA/. This problem of schwa-deletion is also found in English, however the phonemic environments are somewhat

**Liaison:**

| *Word string* | *Phoneme string* | |
|---|---|---|
| **des** | /de/ | (some) |
| **amis** | /ami/ | (friends) |
| **des amis** | /dezami/ | (some friends) |
| **bon** | /bO/ | (good) |
| **bon ami** | /bcnami/ | (good friend) |
| **petit ami** | /pxtitami/ | (boy friend) |
| **petits amis** | /pxtizami/ | (boy friends) |

**Apostrophe:**

| *Word string* | *Written form* | *Phoneme string* | |
|---|---|---|---|
| **le ami** | l'ami | /lami/ | (the friend) |
| **de ami** | d'ami | /dami/ | (from a friend) |

**Fig. 4**: Examples of liaison and apostrophe in French.

different. Additionally, there are situations where the word-final mute-e is pronounced. This effect is to some extent context and dialect dependent. Speakers from the south of France typically pronounce the mute-e, whereas speakers from the Parisian area will usually omit it.

A final problem which is mentioned only briefly here is with apostrophe, where the final vowel of certain words can be deleted when the next word begins with a vowel. In the written form, this results in word sequences like *l'enfant, c'est, n'a, s'amuser* as shown in Figure 4. From a lexical point of view, apostrophe results in either a relatively large number of frequent monophone words (if the consonant is represented as a word) or in a large expansion of the lexicon (if the two words are treated as a single lexical item). When representing the consonant preceding the apostrophe as a distinct lexical entry almost 20% of the words in the running text of *Le Monde* are monophone words.

## 4. Speaker-dependent isolated-word speech dictation

The goal of the isolated-word speech-to-text conversion at LIMSI was to integrate the necessary components for a speaker-dependent Voice Activated Typewriter (VAT) on a stand-alone personal computer[25, 9] with a vocabulary of several thousand words. The language model was given by bigrams of grammatical categories[2, 7], where the probabilities were computed by counting the occurrences in the training text material. For general French dictation task a set of 59 grammatical classes were used[25], whereas for a research report dictation an extended set of 160 grammatical classes were defined. Recognition was a two step process consisting of a fast match to select a small subset of the lexicon, followed by a more detailed, DTW-based word match giving an ordered list of word-candidates with their recognition score. On average, the fast match returned about 2% of the lexical entries.

The system was tested on the vocabulary of the textbook in French for foreigners. It has 5,127 phonemic words, corresponding to 6,700 graphemic words. All punctuation markers were pronounced as words, numbers were spoken as digit strings, and liaisons between words were not spoken. On a 1000-word text dictated by one speaker, a phonemic word recognition rate of 91% was obtained. This increased to 99% correct phonemic word recognition using the language model. Recognition of the graphemic words was 92.5%, with 75 errors. All tests were made on text data that were used for building the language model. The average recognition time for a word was 480 ms.

Although isolated-word dictation helps to constrain the recognition task by removing the problem of finding the word boundaries, other problems are introduced, particularly with respect to ease of use for the speaker. For example, it is not evident what to do about the liaisons made at word junctures. While one possibility is to never pronounce the liaison, the resulting speech sounds very unnatural. Another option is to pronounce the liaison at the beginning of the following word. This has the undesired side effect of increasing the size of the vocabulary, as all the possible liaisons at the beginning of the word must be allowed. A third possibility is to pronounce the liaison as a separate word, thus saying three words instead of two. But pronounciation of the liaison in isolation is very difficult for the speaker as it is so unnatural. Another approach is dictating isolated syllables instead of isolated words[26] however while this provides a more natural way to pronounce the liaison at the start of a syllable, the resulting task is still unnatural for the speaker.

A similar problem arises with the apostrophe as discussed in Section 3 (see Figure 4). In pronouncing these words there are several options: The first one is to say the first word as if it had not been modified, followed by the second word. The second option, which is to pronounce the words together as one word, has the unfortunate effect of greatly enlarging the size of the vocabulary. A third option is to say a sequence of three words, verbalizing the word "apostrophe" in the middle of the two other words.

The problems associated with how to pronounce the liaisons and apostrophes in isolated word dictation emphasize the need for continuous dictation in French. While continuous dictation avoids these problems on the part of the speaker, they still remain for the recognizer, and increase its complexity.

## 5. Speaker-independent continuous speech recognition

Our current efforts focus on speech-to-text conversion of continuously spoken sentences, from any speaker, for very large, eventually, unlimited, vocabularies. Because of the ambitiousness of the task, the system should be both independent of the speaker and the vocabulary or task. To this extent, a phone-based approach is being used, where phone-like units are trained with data from a large number of speakers and covering a large number of phone contexts. In this section we briefly summarize studies in phoneme-to-grapheme conversion of text materials. This is followed by a description of the recognizer, and an evaluation of the recognizer on three corpora: the DARPA Resource Management corpus (RM)[32] used for common evaluation in the Polyglot project, the ARPA

Wall Street Journal-based CSR corpus (WSJ0)[29], and the BREF-*Le Monde* corpus[23]. All three corpora contain large amounts of read speech material from a large number of speakers, recorded under similar conditions (8kHz bandwidth, close-talking microphone, read-speech). WSJ and BREF also have associated text materials which are used for statistical language modeling. For these two corpora, experiments with comparable size lexicons and test perplexities have been carried out in order to allow for cross-language performance ccomparisons. The recognizer was evaluated in the September 1992 DARPA continuous speech recognition evaluation on the 1000-word Resource Managment task[27] and also in the ARPA Wall Street Journal evaluation in November 1992[28].

## 5.1 Phoneme-to-grapheme conversion of text

Work in phoneme-to-grapheme conversion was carried out as part of the ESPRIT project 291/860 on the Linguistic Analysis of the European Languages. An important part of the project was the building of a language model for 7 different languages (English, Italian, French, Dutch, Spanish, Greek, and German). A statistical approach was taken using bigram and trigram models based on grammatical categories.

The main results of this project were to provide statistics on phoneme clusters, grapheme-to-phoneme and phoneme-to-grapheme conversion software, language models and syntactic parsers. These elements were integrated using a blackboard structure and an attempt was made to assess the "quality" or "difficulty" of each language[5, 37]. One measure was the number of context-dependent rewrite rules necessary for phoneme-to-grapheme conversion for a lexicon of about 10,000 entries. Table 5 shows that for Italian, a set of 67 rules is able to transcribe the phonemic form into the graphemic form with only 0.5% of the generated graphemic words not existing in the language, and 0.5% graphemic words unable to be transcribed. In contrast, for French, 98% of the words generated by a set of 586 rules do not exist in the vocabulary, and 30% of the vocabulary words are missing in the resulting graphemic cohorts. While this result is clearly highly dependent on the quality of both the rules and the system which handles these rules, it seems obvious that the Italian language will require less linguistic processing than the French language in order to translate a phonemic string. Concerning the phoneme-to-grapheme conversion software, since the same system had to be used for all 7 languages the constraints imposed by this system, limiting the maximum number of rules and the type of possible rule contexts, contribute to explain the very high figures of overgeneration for some languages. Nevertheless these figures give an idea of the difficulty of the phoneme-to-grapheme conversion task for the different languages involved.

## 5.2 Recognizer Overview

In speech recognition systems, the problem of phoneme-to-grapheme conversion is more difficult, as the recognizer cannot be expected to produce error-free phone strings. Being aware of this, many researchers and system designers have adopted a top-down solution in a sense that only phone strings corresponding to actual lexical items are hypothesized at the acoustic level. Adopting this

| *Language* | *# Rules* | *# Graphemic words/ phonemic words* | *% Over generation* | *% Under generation* |
|---|---|---|---|---|
| Dutch | 289 | 6 | 90 | 20 |
| English | 530 | 10 | 90 | 6 |
| French | 586 | 250 | 98 | 30 |
| German | 551 | 400 | 99 | 10 |
| Greek | 394 | 100 | 100 | 2.5 |
| Italian | 67 | 1 | 0.5 | 0.5 |
| Spanish | 845 | 1 | 7 | 6 |

**Table 5**: Phoneme-to-grapheme translation for 7 European languages.

approach, our recognizer uses a time-synchronous graph-search strategy which is shown to be viable with vocabularies of up to 20K words, when used with bigram back-off language models (LMs). This one level implementation includes intra- and inter-word context-dependent (CD) phone models, intra- and inter-word phonological rules, phone duration models, gender-dependent models, and a bigram language model[19, 11]. When a trigram language model is used, a second pass is run making use of a word graph generated using the bigram. The HMM-based word recognizer graph is built by putting together word models according to the grammar in one large HMM. Each word model is obtained by concatenation of the phone models for each word, according to its phone transcription as found in the lexicon. Decoding consists of Viterbi search, a one pass beam search. The male and female models are run in parallel, and the output with the highest likelihood is chosen.

The acoustic models are sets of context-dependent (CD) phone models, which include both intra-word and cross-word contexts, but are position independent. Each phone model is a 3-state left-to-right HMM with Gaussian mixture observation densities. The covariance matrices of all the Gaussians components are diagonal. Duration is modeled with a gamma distribution per phone model. The HMM and duration parameters are estimated separately and combined in the recognition process for the Viterbi search. Maximum a posteriori (MAP) estimators are used for the HMM parameters[15] and moment estimators for the gamma distributions. Separate male and female models are used to more accurately model the speech data.

The lexicon is represented phonemically and has alternate pronunciations for some of the words. A pronunciation graph is generated for each word from the baseform transcription to which word internal phonological rules are optionally applied during training and recognition to account for some of the phonological variations observed in fluent speech. In addition some phonological rules are used to modify the phone network to take into account such variations at word boundaries. Using optional phonological rules during training results in better acoustic models, as they are less "polluted" by wrong transcriptions. Their use during recognition reduces the number of mismatches. The mechanism for the phonological rules initially developed for English allows the potential for generalization and extension, and has been used to handle liaisons, mute-e, and final consonant cluster reduction for French.

For BREF and WSJ bigram and trigram backoff[18] language models were estimated on the training text material. The backoff mechanism has been efficiently implemented using a tree. The LM size can be arbitrarily reduced by relying more on the backoff. For RM, the standard deterministic word-pair grammar was used.

### 5.3 Experiments using RM

The DARPA RM speech corpus[32] is a corpus of read speech designed to provide speech data for evaluation of continuous speech recognizers with medium size vocabulary (1000 words) and has been used in comparative evaluations in Polyglot and worldwide. The standard set of 3990 sentences (SI-109) has been used to train two sets of 2300 CD phone models, from the male and female speakers data. The standard word-pair grammar (perplexity 60) was used.

The RM lexicon is represented with a reduced set of 36 phones so as to eliminate infrequent phones for which there was insufficient training data, and to provide a means of better sharing of phone contexts. In doing so, more data is available to train the remaining models, and the number of potential triphone contexts is reduced. Reducing the phone set gave an improvement of about 10% on the 3 development tests.

The lexicon was also expanded to provide alternate pronunciations for about 10% of the words, and to allow some phones to be optional. For example, the word MONTICELLO has the pronunciations /mantxsElo/ and /mantxtSElo/, and the /t/ in COUNTED (/kawn{t}xd/) is optional. Intra- and inter-word phonological rules are optionally applied during training and recognition. The use of phonological rules for the RM task has been previously reported by SRI[6] and AT&T[17]. In the case of AT&T, phonological rules were used only with CI phone models. A single speaker may mark phonetic distinctions in different ways even in similar phonetic environments. This means that the use of CD phones as they are typically defined, combines allophones which can be acoustically very different. The use of phonological rules during training should result in purer acoustic models, and thus improve the system performance.

Some examples of the phonological rules used for the RM task can be found in [19]. These include general rules for well known variants such as palatalization, glide insertion and gemination, as well as rules to handle allophonic variation, using only the reduced phone set. Since the CD models are position independent, instead of having syllable- or word-final allophones for the voiceless stops, they are optionally allowed to be replaced with their voiced counterparts. Some more specific rules allow the deletion of the offglide /w/ in the phone sequence /aw/, in certain contexts. While this is a fairly general phenomenon, in the context of RM this rule becomes very specific for the word sequences "how much" and "how many."

Results on the last 5 DARPA tests are reported in Table 6. The JUN88, FEB89, and OCT89 test sets were used as development data to evaluate various alternatives for the front end, the representation of the lexicon, phonological rules, and to estimate some parameter values such as the word insertion penalty.

| *DARPA test* | *Corr.* | *Subs.* | *Del.* | *Ins.* | *WErr.* |
|---|---|---|---|---|---|
| JUN88 | 97.1 | 2.5 | 0.4 | 0.4 | 3.3 |
| FEB89 | 97.7 | 1.7 | 0.5 | 0.2 | 2.5 |
| OCT89 | 97.0 | 2.2 | 0.9 | 0.3 | 3.3 |
| FEB91 | 97.7 | 1.9 | 0.4 | 0.3 | 2.6 |
| SEP92* | 96.0 | 2.9 | 1.2 | 0.4 | 4.4 |

**Table 6**: Word recognition results on the DARPA-RM-SI corpus with a WP grammar of perplexity 60. (*official DARPA SEP92 evaluation results)

Error analysis took into account the output of a phone recognizer in addition to the output of the word recognizer[19, 21]. The FEB91 test data was reserved for evaluation at the end of each development cycle. This system achieved the highest word accuracy on the Sep92 DARPA test. After the Sep92 DARPA evaluation, the contribution of the system components to the performance on the Sep92 test data was assessed and indicated that the interword phonological rules and the sex-dependent models had the largest influence in reducing the word error[19].

### 5.4 Experiments using WSJ

The ARPA WSJ corpus[29] was designed to provide general-purpose speech data with large vocabularies. Text materials were selected to provide training and test data for 5K and 20K word, closed and open vocabularies, and with both verbalized (VP) and non-verbalized (NVP) punctuation. The standard WSJ0 SI-84 training data include 7240 sentences from 84 speakers. The language model is a bigram-backoff estimated on the 33 million word standardized WSJ text provided by Lincoln Labs[29]. The lexicon is represented using a set of 46 phones. The pronunciations were obtained from various existing lexicons (TIMIT, Pocket and Moby), missing forms were generated by rule when possible, or added by hand with some of the missing proper names transcribed by the ORATOR system of Bellcore.

Phonological rules are optionally applied during training and test. For the present, only well known phonological rules have been incorporated in the system. These rules include word-internal rules for glide insertion, stop deletion, and homorganic stop insertion. The interword rules include palatalization, stop reduction, and voicing assimilation.

This system was evaluated in the Nov92 DARPA evaluation test for the 5k-closed vocabulary using the standard bigram language models[29]. The official reported results are given in the first line of Table 7 using 493 CD models for the NVP condition, and a 32 component feature vector. Increasing the number of CD models and the number of features (line 2), reduced the error rate by about 20% over the system used for the Nov92 evaluation. Results are also given in Table 7 for the Nov92 NVP 64k test data using both open and closed 20k vocabularies. (The 20k closed vocabulary includes all the words in the test data whereas the 20k open vocabulary contains only the 20k most common

| *WSJ - Conditions* | *Corr.* | *Subs.* | *Del.* | *Ins.* | *Err.* |
|---|---|---|---|---|---|
| 493m, 32f, 5k* | 91.8 | 6.9 | 1.3 | 1.5 | 9.7 |
| 884m, 48f, 5k | 94.1 | 5.2 | 0.7 | 1.0 | 6.9 |
| 884m, 48f, 20k | 88.3 | 10.1 | 1.5 | 2.0 | 13.6 |
| 884m, 48f, 20k+ | 86.8 | 11.7 | 1.5 | 2.7 | 15.9 |

**Table 7**: Word recognition results on the WSJ0 Nov92 SI NVP test data with a probabilistic grammar (2-grams) estimated on WSJ text data. (5k: 5000 word lexicon, 20k: 20,000 word lexicon, 20k+: 20,000 word lexicon with open test, *official DARPA NOV92 evaluation results).

words in the WSJ texts[29]). It can be seen that the error rate is doubled when the vocabulary size goes from 5k to 20k with corresponding test perplexities of 111 and 244, respectively. The higher error rate with the 20k+ open lexicon can be contributed to the out-of-vocabulary words, which account for almost 2% of the words in the test sentences.

One problem using the bigram-backoff LM is that the number of connections is very large. We investigated the effects of reducing the size of the bigram model by relying more on the backoff. Using a count threshold of 4 occurrences, reduces the bigram size by 53% and gives a word error of 7.2% on the 5k-NVP test. This is only a slight increase in the error compared to the 6.9% obtained with a threshold of 1 (baseline bigram[29]). Use of a trigram language model in a second pass results in an error reduction of 37% (to a word error of 4.3%) on the same test data.

### 5.5 Experiments with BREF

BREF is a large read-speech corpus, containing over 100 hours of speech material, from 120 speakers (55m/65f)[23]. Six of the speakers were recorded for the Polyglot project. The text materials were selected verbatim from the French newspaper *Le Monde*, so as to provide a large vocabulary (over 20,000 words) and a wide range of phonetic environments[14]. The text material was read without verbalized punctuation. All the data used for the experiements reported in this paper comes from the BREF80 sub-corpus (2 CDs). 2770 sentences from 57 speakers were used for training. A bigram-backoff language model was estimated on about 4 million words of normalized text material from *Le Monde*. Normalization of the text material entailed a processing rather different from the pre-treatment of the WSJ texts[29], primarily in the treatment of case and or compound words and abbreviations[12]. In BREF the distinction between the cases is kept when the upper case designates a distinctive graphemic feature, but not when the upper case is simply due to the fact that the word occurs at the beginning of the sentence. The base lexicon, represented with 35 phones, was obtained using text-to-phoneme rules[33], and was extended to annotate potential liaisons and pronunciation variants.

As for the WSJ task, two vocabularies have been used for the recognition

| *BREF - Conditions* | *Corr.* | *Subs.* | *Del.* | *Ins.* | *Err.* |
|---|---|---|---|---|---|
| 500m, 48p, 5k | 87.1 | 10.3 | 2.6 | 1.7 | 14.5 |
| 500m, 48p, 20k | 84.6 | 12.8 | 2.6 | 2.9 | 18.3 |
| 500m, 48p, 5k-H | 90.7 | 7.2 | 2.6 | 1.7 | 11.5 |
| 500m, 48p, 20k-H | 89.4 | 8.0 | 2.6 | 3.0 | 13.5 |

**Table 8**: Word recognition results on the BREF80 corpus with a probabilistic grammar (2-grams) estimated on *Le Monde* text data. (5k: 5000 word lexicon, 20k: 20,000 word lexicon, 5k-H: 5k word lexicon with homophone errors not counted).

experiments, corresponding to the 5k and 20k most common words in the *Le Monde* texts. It should be noted that the word coverage for French: 5k (86%), 20k (95%) is significantly smaller than for the same size lexicons for WSJ: 5k (92%), 20k (98%). For French, the lexicon size must be doubled to obtain the same coverage as in English. The test data consist of 100 sentences for each vocabulary size, with perplexities of 122 for the 5k sentences and 205 for the 20k sentences.

Word recognition results using 500 CD models and the bigram-backoff language model estimated on the normalized text material from *Le Monde* are shown in Table 8. The word error is 14.5% for the 5k lexicon and 18.3% for the 20k lexicon. The last two entries give the results when the recognizer output is scored without counting homophone errors. These results are provided because French has more homophones than English (as discussed in Section 3). The difference in the results scored with and without homophones points out the need for better language modeling.

## 6. Summary of progress in speech recognition

The research summaries presented in Sections 4 and 5 enable the following observations to be made about progress in speech recognition. There have been major changes in the capabilities of speech recognizers, in part due to algorithm development concerning the training of more accurate speech models and their subsequent use during decoding, but also due to technological advances - the availability of faster computers, more memory, and cheaper mass storage (hard disk and CDROM). However, arguably the most important factor contributing to these advances is the availability of large corpora for recognizer development and systematic evaluation.

The advances have been along the following axes. Speech-to-text systems have moved from speaker-dependent to speaker-independent systems. While given enough training data better performance can be obtained with a speaker-dependent system, acquiring the necessary data is prohibitive for even medium-size vocabularies. Recent work in speaker-adaptation has shown that with relatively small amounts of speaker-specific training, speaker-independent systems can be adapted to the speaker, and obtain performances comparable to speaker-dependent systems.

State of the art research systems are able to handle continuous speech and larger vocabularies. Not so many years ago a vocabulary containing 1000 words was considered large. Now systems can handle vocabularies on the order of 5,000 to 20,000 words, and are heading towards 100,000 words. Recognizer preformance, as measured by word accuracy, is also improving. At the same time, due to the availability of speech and text corpora, recognizers have been developed in several languages. Multilinguality allows us to compare the performance of algorithms across languages, and to assess language-dependent issues in speech recognition. While these advances have been demonstrated for laboratory recognition systems, we believe that such technology is ready to be integrated in smaller, more constrained applications.

## 7. Future Directions

As mentioned earlier, our aim is to develop a phone-based speech recognizer that is task, speaker and vocabulary independent so as to be easily adaptable to particular tasks or applications. In particular we are extending our research to the realm of spoken language systems, where the goal of the system is to help a user complete a task, through simple and natural dialogues. As computers are becoming faster and more economical, and there is a rapid explosion of information services becoming available over networks and phone lines, (French MINITEL is a prime example), such that a large number of potential applications for speech are reaching the point of marketability. It is possible to foresee applications, for example, information centers in public places such as train stations and airports, where the spoken query is to be recognized without even prior knowledge of the language being spoken. Our recent research in French/English language identification indicates that it is possible to automatically identify the language being spoken, and to respond appropriately in the user's language[22].

Spoken language systems introduce new challenges that are not present, or are at least less frequent in dictation. The problem becomes one of understanding the meaning of a query or a dialog, as often the query can not be understood without reference to the context. Research in the ARPA Air Travel Information Service (ATIS)[31] domain has demonstrated that for vocabularies on the order of 1000 words, the system performance is not limited by the recognition component, but rather the natural language component is the bottleneck[28]. The system performance with spoken input is approaching that of typed input.

Spoken language systems necessitate the development of task-specific vocabularies and language models, as well as an interpretation mechanism and a dialog manager to enable the use of the dialog history or context. One must be able to deal with spontaneous speech phenomena, such as hesitations, false starts, repetitions and reparations, incomplete sentences and other grammatical formulations. Such systems will need to be able to be easily extended to handle new words or constructions. While ideally it will not be necessary to supply task-specific acoustic data to train the acoustic models, in practice, at least in the near term, use of such task-specific data will enhance the performance of the system.

A step in this direction is the development of L'ATIS[4], a French version of the MIT Air Travel Information Service (ATIS) system[38] used to interrogate a database derived from the Official Airline Guide (OAG). We have chosen to access the English-based system at the level of the semantic frame, so as to produce a language-independent meaning representation. The same core back-end component is used for the two languages, with only the input and output modules replaced by French versions. In addition, the input module uses the same mechanism to convert an input sentence to a semantic frame, with the English grammar rules and constraints being replaced by corresponding French versions, and a common approach for language generation is used for both systems. Once a core system in French was operational, data were collected in the form of typed queries so as to expand the rules and vocabulary, as well as spoken queries using a wizard-of-Oz (WOZ) setup. This speech material can be used to adapt the task-independent acoustic models (generated using BREF) and to evaluate the degree of task-independence of our recognizer.

## 8. Summary

In this paper an overview of the research at LIMSI in the area of speech-to-text conversion has been given. Research projects in this domain have been pursued since the 1970's. The projects include phoneme-to-grapheme conversion of ideal strings and strings containing simulated errors, isolated-word speech recognition, and continuous speech recognition. Prior to the Polyglot project the main research directions were oriented towards building speaker-dependent, isolated word recognizers for French with vocabularies up to 5,000 words, and on developing real-time systems. Current research in speech recognition at LIMSI is directed at developing phone-based speech recognizers that are task-, speaker- and vocabulary-independent so as to be easily adapted to various applications. The recognizer uses a time-synchronous graph-search strategy which includes intra- and inter-word context-dependent phone models, intra- and inter-word phonological rules, phone duration models, gender-dependent models, and n-gram language models. The recognizers has been applied to dictation tasks and evaluated on the DARPA RM and WSJ corpora in English, and the BREF corpus in French with vocabularies containing up to 20K words. The same recognizer is used in spoken language systems with more limited, task-dependent vocabularies. We now work on recognition in multiple languages and aim to develop multilingual spoken language systems which automatically detect the language being spoken so as to avoid having to ask the user to select the language before beginning to interrogate the system.

Multilinguality also allows us to compare the performance of algorithms across languages, and to assess language-dependent issues in recognition and understanding. For example, speech-to-text conversion of French presents difficulties different from those found in English primarily due to the large number of homophones and monophones in French. In fact, even though better phone recognition accuracies are obtained for BREF than for WSJ[20, 21], word recognition in English is better due to the higher lexical ambiguity for French.

Progress in speech recognition has been made due to technological advances, as well as the availability of large corpora for recognizer development and systematic evaluation. Research speech-to-text systems, have moved from speaker-dependent to speaker-independent, and can handle continuous speech with vocabularies of over 20,000 words. The capabilities of these systems become sufficient to envision their use in real-world applications.

## References


1. G. Adda (1987), *Reconnaissance de Grands Vocabulaires: Une étude Syntaxique et Lexicale*, Thèse de Docteur-Ingénieur, Université Paris XI, December, 1987.
2. L.R. Bahl, R. Bakis, P.S. Cohen, F. Jelinek, B.L. Lewis, and R.L. Mercer (1978), "Recognition of a Continuously Read Natural Corpus," *Proc. IEEE ICASSP-78*, Tulsa, AZ, April 1978, pp. 422-425.
3. D. Bellilty, A. Lund (1984), "Conversion phonèmes-graphèmes de suites phonétiques entachées d'erreurs," LIMSI internal report, July, 1984.
4. H. Bonneau-Maynard, J.L. Gauvain, D. Goodine, L.F. Lamel, J. Polifroni, and S. Seneff (1993), "A French Version of the MIT-ATIS System: Portability Issues," *Proc. EUROSPEECH-93*, Berlin, Germany, September 1993, pp. 2059-2062.
5. L. Boves, M. Refice *et al.* (1987), "The Linguistic Processor in a Multi-Lingual Text-to-Speech and Speech-to-Text System," *European Conference on Speech Technology*, Edinburgh, September 1987, pp. 385-388.
6. M. Cohen (1989), *Phonological Structures for Speech Recognition*, PhD Thesis, U. Ca. Berkeley, 1989.
7. A.M. Derouault (1985), *Modélisation d'une langue naturelle pour la désambiguation des chaînes phonétiques*, Thèse de Doctorat d'Etat, Univ. Paris VII, April 1985.
8. J.S. Garofolo, L.F. Lamel, W.M. Fisher, J.G. Fiscus, D.S. Pallett, and N.L. Dahlgren (1993), "The DARPA TIMIT Acoustic-Phonetic Continuous Speech Corpus CDROM" (printed documentation for NIST Speech Disc 1-1.1), NTIS order number PB91-100354.
9. J.L. Gauvain (1990), "Le système de reconnaisance *AMADEUS*: Principe et algorithmes," LIMSI internal report, June 1990.
10. J.L. Gauvain and J.J. Gangolf (1983), "Terminal integrates speech recognition and text-to-speech synthesis", *Speech Technology*, Sept-Oct 1983.
11. J.L. Gauvain, L.F. Lamel, G. Adda (1993), "LIMSI Nov92 WSJ Evaluation," presented at the *DARPA Spoken Language Systems Technology Workshop*, Cambridge, MA, January 1993.
12. J.L. Gauvain, L.F. Lamel, G. Adda, M. Adda-Decker (1993), " Speaker-Independent Continuous Speech Dictation," *Proc. EUROSPEECH-93*, Berlin, Germany, September 1993, pp. 125-128.
13. J.L. Gauvain, L.F. Lamel, G. Adda, and J. Mariani (1994), "Speech-to-Text Conversion in French," to appear in *Int. J. Pattern Recognition & Artificial Inelligence.*

14. J.-L. Gauvain, L.F. Lamel, and M. Eskénazi (1990), "Design Considerations and Text Selection for BREF, a large French read-speech corpus," *Proc. ICSLP-90*, Kobe, Japan, Nov. 1990, pp. 1097-2000.
15. J.L. Gauvain and C.H. Lee (1992), "Bayesian Learning for Hidden Markov Model with Gaussian Mixture State Observation Densities," *Speech Communication*, **11**(2-3), 1992.
16. J.L. Gauvain and J. Mariani (1982), "A Method for Connected Word Recognition and Word Spotting on a Microprocessor", *Proc. IEEE ICASSP-82*, Paris, France, May 1982, pp. 891-894.
17. E. Giachin, A.E. Rosenberg, and C.H. Lee (1991), "Word Juncture Modeling using Phonological Rules for HMM-based Continuous Speech Recognition," *Computer Speech & Language*, **5**, 1991, pp. 155-168 .
18. S.M. Katz (1987), "Estimation of Probabilities from Sparse Data for the Language Model Component of a Speech Recognizer," *IEEE Trans. Acoustics Speech & Signal Processing*, **ASSP-35**(3), March 1987, pp. 400-401.
19. L.F. Lamel and J.L. Gauvain (1992), "Continuous Speech Recognition at LIMSI," *Proc. DARPA Continuous Speech Recognition Workshop*, Stanford, CA, Sept. 1992, pp. 77-82.
20. L.F. Lamel, J.L. Gauvain (1993), "Cross-lingual Experiments with Phone Recognition," *Proc. IEEE ICASSP-93*, Minneapolis, MN, April 1993, pp. 507-510.
21. L.F. Lamel, J.L. Gauvain (1993), "High Performance Speaker-Independent Phone Recognition Using CDHMM," *Proc. EUROSPEECH-93*, Berlin, Germany, September 1993, pp. 21-24.
22. L. Lamel, J.L. Gauvain, "Identifying Non-Linguistic Speech Features," *Proc. EUROSPEECH-93*, Berlin, Germany, September 1993, pp. 23-30.
23. L.F. Lamel, J.-L. Gauvain, M. Eskénazi (1991), "BREF, a Large Vocabulary Spoken Corpus for French," *Proc. EUROSPEECH-91*, Genoa, Italy, September 1991, pp. 505-508.
24. J. Mariani (1977), *Contribution à la Reconnaissance de la Parole Continue utilisant la notion de Spectre Différentiel*, Thèse de Docteur-Ingénieur, Université Paris VI.
25. J. Mariani (1987), "HAMLET: A Prototype of a Voice-Activated Typewriter," *Proc. European Conference on Speech Technology*, Edinburgh, September, 1987, pp. 222-225.
26. B. Merialdo (1987), "Speech Recognition with Very Large Vocabulary," *Proc. IEEE ICASSP-87*, Dallas, TX, pp. 364-367.
27. D.S. Pallett, J.G. Fiscus, and J. Garofolo (1992) "Resource Management Corpus - September 1992 Test Set Benchmark Results," *Proc. DARPA Continuous Speech Recognition Workshop*, Stanford, CA, September 1992, pp. 1-18.
28. D.S. Pallett, J.G. Fiscus, W.M. Fisher and J. Garofolo (1993), "Benchmark Tests for the DARPA Spoken Language Program," *ARPA Workshop on Human Language Technology*, March 1993.

29. D. Paul and J. Baker (1992), "The Design for the Wall Street Journal-based CSR Corpus," *Proc. DARPA Speech and Natural Language Workshop*, Harriman, NY, February 1992, pp. 357-362.
30. Polyglot Consortium, "A Multilingual System for Text to Speech and Speech to Text", *Final Report POLYGLOT, ESPRIT Project 2104*.
31. P. Price (1990), "Evaluation of Spoken Language Systems: The ATIS Domain," *Proc. DARPA Speech and Natural Language Workshop*, Hidden Valley, PA, June, 1990, pp. 91-95.
32. P. Price, W.M. Fisher, J. Bernstein, and D.S. Pallett (1988), "The DARPA 1000-word Resource Management Database for Continuous Speech Recognition," *Proc. IEEE ICASSP-88*, New York, NY, April 1988, pp. 651-654.
33. B. Prouts (1980),*Contribution à la synthèse de la parole à partir du texte: Transcription graphème-phonème en temps réel sur microprocesseur*, Thèse de docteur-ingénieur, Université Paris XI, November, 1980.
34. G. Quénot, J.L. Gauvain, J.J. Gangolf, and J. Mariani (1986), "A dynamic time warp VLSI processor for continuous speech recognition", *Proc. IEEE ICASSP-86*, Tokyo, Japan, April 1986, pp. 1549-1552.
35. G.M. Quénot, J.L. Gauvain, J.J. Gangolf, and J. Mariani (1989), "A Dynamic Programming Processor for Speech Recognition", *IEEE J. of Solid-State Circuits*, **24**(2), April 1989, pp. 349-357.
36. H. Singer and J.L. Gauvain, (1988) "Connected speech recognition using dissyllable segmentation,"*Fall meeting of the Acoust. Soc. of Japan.*
37. V. Vittorelli (1987), "Linguistic Analysis of the European Languages," ESPRIT'87 Achievements and Impact, North-Holland, 1987, pp. 1358-1366.
38. V. Zue, J. Glass, D. Goddeau, D. Goodine, l. Hirschman, M. Phillips, J. Polifroni, and S. Seneff (1992), "The MIT ATIS System: February 1992 Progress Report," *Proc. DARPA Speech and Natural Language Workshop*, Harriman, NY, February 1992, pp. 84-89.

# Sound-to-Gesture Inversion in Speech: The *Speech Maps* Approach

**Christian Abry*, Pierre Badin*, Celia Scully**, et al.**[1]
* Institut de la Communication Parlée
URA CNRS N°368 – INPG – Université Stendhal, France
** Department of Psychology
The University of Leeds, United Kingdom

## Abstract

The aim of this project is to answer – theoretically and technologically – the question: *Can an articulatory robot learn to produce articulatory gestures from sounds?*

Such modelling requires the most advanced knowledge in *inverse mapping* from speech sounds to articulatory gestures. Inversion is of course a difficult problem, namely an *ill-posed problem*, primarily because of the non-linear, many-to-one, relationship of articulation to acoustics. Due to recent outstanding progress in other fields, particularly that of vision in robotics, a new interest in the problem of inverse mapping in speech has arisen.

One can conceive of two complementary approaches to the speech inversion problem. The first uses all the knowledge in *signal processing* to identify the characteristics of the *sources* and *filters* corresponding to the vocal tract which produced the speech signal. The second is borrowed from *control theory*, and aims at determining inverse kinematics and/or dynamics for an articulatory robot with excess degrees of freedom. Following basic schemes in robotics, the speech production model is represented by a realistic articulatory model, the *plant*, driven by a *controller*, in our case a sequential network capable of synthesising motor sequences from sound prototypes. This ensemble – called *Articulotron* – displays fundamental spatio-temporal properties of *serial ordering* in speech (*coarticulation* phenomena) and adaptive behaviour to *compensate* for perturbations. In both approaches, there is a clear need of knowledge of *direct mapping* (from articulation to acoustics, through sources and vocal tract modelling), to find *constraints* in order to regularise the solution. Moreover, in a general framework for inversion, one needs not only to use regularities but also to look for *low level specific processing*.

---

[1] "Abry, Badin & Scully", as first authors, only means that this text has been signed by the three members of the steering committee of the project. "et al." means that all the names to be found in the detailed list of contributions have been omitted in the title due to mere space constraints.

The robotic approach for speech inversion allows the unification of *Action* and *Perception.* Speech communication being conceived as a trade-off between the cost of production and the benefit of understanding, the *constraints* are borrowed from the articulatory level, and the *specific low level processing* from auditory, and visual, perception. Using an *Audiovisual Perceptron* to incorporate vision – whose importance in speech is easily shown (e.g., for the deaf or in noisy background) – will lead to a more comprehensive formulation of the inversion problem, to wit: *How can articulatory gestures be learned from hearing and seeing speech?*

## 1. Main objectives and structure of the project

This project, dedicated to inversion in speech, summons up the competence of researchers in different domains in order to meet the technological challenge of making an articulatory robot – the *Articulotron* (see Fig. 1) – learn to synthesise motor sequences from speech sounds.

The pivot strategy is to elaborate sound prototypes, from the speech acoustic and optic signals, through an *Audiovisual Perceptron,* in order to feed the *Articulotron.*

The design of such an *Articulotron* and *Perceptron* calls in the most advanced knowledge, covering the different steps of inverse mapping, from speech sound perception to inverse dynamics through inverse acoustics. In a complementary way, this project naturally requires advanced knowledge also in the direct mapping, i.e. speech production, including speech motor control, dynamics, aerodynamics and acoustics. Knowledge in the auditory and visual domains for bimodal speech integration processing has to be increased in order to be able to connect *Audiovisual Perceptron* as a front end of the *Articulotron.*

Hence, the project falls naturally into four main actions referred to as Working Programmes.

WP1 – *From speech signal to acoustic sources* – aims at improving the modelling of acoustic sources in the vocal tract, and at building tools to recover the commands of these models from the signal.

WP2 – *From speech signal to vocal tract geometry* – aims at improving the knowledge of the mapping between vocal tract shapes and speech sound relevant characteristics, and at discovering the constraints imposed on the vocal tract configurations by the reduced number of degrees of freedom involved in a speech production model.

WP3 – *Dynamic constraints and motor controls* – aims at increasing the knowledge of the constraints on speech "skilled" gestures, in order to propose a solution to the problem of quantitatively controlling an articulatory model to learn motor sequences.

WP4 – *Perceptual processing for gesture recovery* – aims at developing specific processings for speech, using advanced knowledge of auditory and visual perception, to elaborate an integration model.

There are obvious links between WP1 and WP2, as they approach inverse acoustics through the improvement of the knowledge of direct mapping, using composite models. Close interactions do also exist between WP3 and WP4, since they aim at building the *Articulotron* and the *Audiovisual Perceptron*, the latter providing the former with inputs. The complementarity of speech control (WP3) and biophysics handled by the different composite models (WP1 and WP2) is ensured by the use of the *Articulotron* as a pivot model. This model should integrate the advances achieved by WP1 and WP2 in defining the plant to be controlled in order to learn successfully articulatory gestures from sounds.

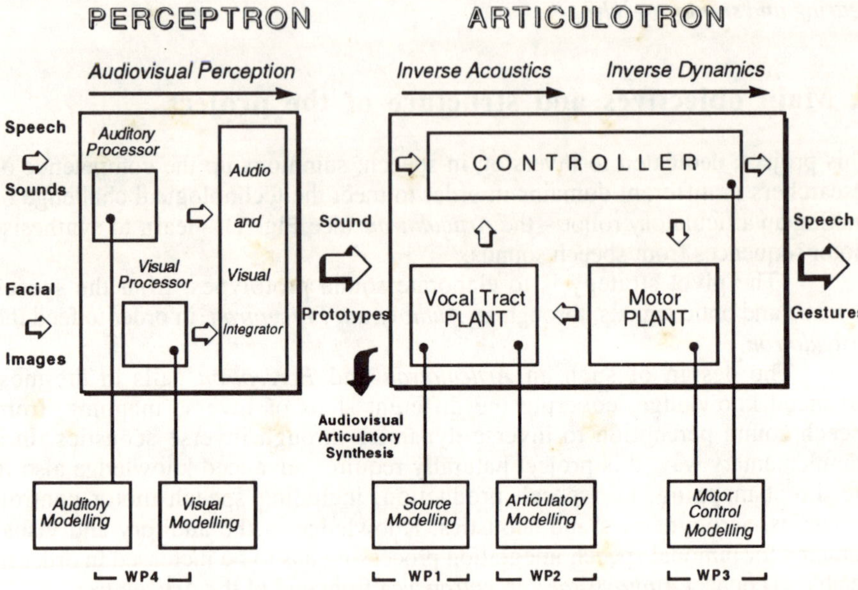


**Fig. 1 – The structure of the *SPEECH MAPS* robot.**
The connection lines indicate the flow of modelling knowledge developed around the pivot model by the different partners, and feeding the *Perceptron* and the *Articulotron*. Audiovisual articulatory synthesis is indicated as a major spin-off.

## 2. Rationale

The aim of this project is clearly to answer the question: *Can an articulatory robot learn to produce articulatory gestures from sounds?* In other words, given an acoustic, auditory or audiovisual input as target, can a *mouth plant* (a phonatory and articulatory system) driven by a *controller* (a mental analogue of the Central Nervous System), *play back* the proper speech gestures through learning, and henceforth become capable of generalisation to synthesise other speech motor sequences ?

### 2.1 Speech gestures recovery and inverse problems

Inversion has remained a very difficult general problem. So far, it has been in many domains an *ill-posed problem*, in the mathematical sense – i.e., it is not certain that the solution exists, is unique, and continuously dependent on the initial conditions. This has been restated in the mid eighties, for vision, by Poggio (1984) – using the above Hadamard's (1923) definition of "illness" for physical problems – and this had already been perfectly captured in the acoustic domain a few decades before by the mathematician Kac (1966), in his famous paper: *"Can one hear the shape of a drum ?"* It took about 25 years – and a lot of cooperation between American, Japanese, Swiss and French mathematicians – to answer this question, leading to the recent summary paper by Cipra (1992): *"You can't hear the shape of a drum."*

Since the problem in acoustics is actually ill-posed, one has to look for an appropriate strategy. Currently, in inverse optics, one has to regularise the solution in order to solve the problem. Regularisation methods typically call for identification of *constraints* (e.g., rigidity/elasticity of objects) and *variational principles* (e.g., shape from shading or motion). Moreover, theoreticians of visual processing (following Marr, 1982) have strongly emphasised the fact that, in a general framework for inversion, one needs not only to use regularities but also to look for *specific processing*. Their claim is that the study of the organisation of processing and representations, as revealed by physiology and psychology, can lead to the selection of a possible algorithm rather than another one, and more generally greatly help understand the mechanisms of *low level* perception (e.g., *retinal* vision).

It must be emphasised that such an inversion, contrary to the top-down approach often used in pattern and speech recognition, relies on the feasibility of a low level, *bottom up* processing.

This approach has led to outstanding progress in computer vision and robotics. In speech, the need for recovering *gestures* in the perception of speech has been a constant claim coming both from *Motor Theory of Speech Perception* (Liberman *et al.*, 1967, Liberman & Mattingly, 1985, Mattingly & Studdert-Kennedy, 1991), and from the Gibsonian *Direct-realist* perspective (Fowler, 1986). In fact, at least in the last version of Motor Theory, *gestures* are indeed very abstract since they are no longer actual vocal-tract shapes, but commands. The only *computational* approach which attempted actually to recover vocal-tract shapes from speech waves has come from *signal processing* (e.g., Atal *et al.*, 1978).

For years, the latter approach, in spite of eminent students in the field, has experienced limited success, primarily because of the complexity of the relationship between articulation and acoustics. Recently, interest in inverse mapping has risen anew (e.g. Hogden, 1991; Jospa, 1991; McGowan, 1991; Sorokin, 1992; Yehia & Itakura, 1993; etc.), reinvigorated in part by the conjunction of articulatory models and neural nets (Bailly *et al.*, 1991; Shirai & Kobayashi, 1991; Soquet *et al.*, 1991; Honda & Kaburagi, 1993; Rahim et al., 1993; etc.).

Thus one can ask why the use of inversion methods has progressed so slowly in speech.

### 2.2 The ill-posed nature of inverse acoustics in speech

Inversion in speech is classically conceptualised as the identification of the characteristics of the *source* (glottal or supraglottal) and of the *filter* (determined by vocal tract shape or area function) corresponding to a given speech signal.

The main difficulties of this approach are at least three-fold.

(1) *Non-linearities* are crucial, in the sense that large *local* changes in the vocal-tract may have no acoustic consequences, and conversely, small changes may have major ones. These non-linearities inspired Kenneth Stevens' *quantal theory* (1972, 1989), which claims that natural language sound systems are structured by articulatory-to-acoustic stabilities and boundaries. Obviously such non-linearities do not help recover the various possible tract shapes from the signal, until some constraints are used, which could be inferred from principles of continuity and economy underlying trajectories of coordinated articulators.

(2) In fact, *many-to-one mapping* is the usual case. This is particularly clear when *overall* changes in the vocal tract can lead to the same output. This is the case in some kinds of *compensation*, where, for instance, a tract with a small area at the lips and no marked oral constriction gives the same acoustic resonances as a tract open at the lips and fairly constricted orally. In such cases, it seems that only the extra constraint of (e.g., visual) information regarding the lips can help solve the inversion problem.

(3) *Undershoot* is a very common phenomenon in speech, where planned targets may or may not be reached, depending on rate, effort, etc. However, the kinematic information conveyed by the acoustic signal is generally sufficient for human subjects to recover the intended target. But only a step upstream from acoustic inversion, i.e., *dynamic* inversion, could lead to the recovery of intended target commands.

Absent any solutions to these difficulties (with constraints of the type identified above), an apparent dead end has led, until recently, to pessimism and/or scepticism about inversion from some speech scientists, including proponents of auditory (Diehl *et al.*, 1991), auditory-motor (Nearey, 1990), and even motor theory of perception (Liberman & Mattingly, 1985).

## 2.3 Speech robotics as an alternative approach for inversion

Leaving aside, for the moment, these seemingly insurmountable difficulties of inverse acoustics in recovering articulatory gestures from the speech signal without proper constraints, one can look the other way round and conceive of an alternative purpose for inversion in speech.

Inversion is being extensively used in robotics. In this field, inversing currently consists of computing inverse kinematics and/or dynamics for a robot with degrees of freedom in excess, and to make it reach the planned targets via proper trajectories. Here too, there is a need for constraints to regularise the solution of ill-posed problems, precisely because of the excess of degrees of freedom.

Following basic schemes in robotics, the speech production system is represented in the project by a realistic articulatory model (Maeda, 1979, 1988), the *plant*, driven by a *controller*. The latter consists in our case of a sequential multilayer network capable of learning and generalising in order to produce motor sequences, starting from sound prototypes (see Fig. 1). This ensemble – called *Articulotron* – aims at displaying certain fundamental spatio-temporal properties of *serial ordering* in speech (*coarticulation* phenomena), and adaptive behaviour to *compensate* for perturbations, thus behaving as *dextrously* (not to say *intelligently*) as possible in the present state of the art in *anthropomorphic speech robotics*[2].

The research strategy of the project in the field of speech robotics involves different steps: (1) Assessing the articulatory model with adapted degrees of freedom and using it to generate a proper acoustic space, and an articulatory-acoustic code-book; (2) Adapting the sequential network to the specific speech problem of timing control (Laboissière et al., 1990, Vatikiotis-Bateson et al., 1992); (3) Designing another network, that implements control signals, and is used to perform inverse dynamics from the kinematics of the articulatory model. Later on, this network will be integrated into the general controller.

In this perspective, both approaches – speech inverse acoustics and speech robotics – can be considered as complementary, since in both cases, there is a clear need for knowledge of *direct mapping*, to identify *constraints* in order to regularise a solution.

## 2.4 Complementarity of speech control and biophysics

It is not underestimated in this project that knowledge of biophysical mechanisms involved in the direct mapping is still limited. This is true for speech dynamics, aerodynamics and even acoustics (especially for consonant production, i.e., plosives and fricatives), in spite of Kenneth Stevens' and Gunnar Fant's pioneering work. It is precisely one of the project goals to bring together the most advanced competence in model-making within this field.

One of the basic problems in the robotics conception is to determine what should be assigned to the *controller* or the *plant* (Perkell, 1991; Scully, 1991). For instance, it would be premature to incorporate too much of the dynamics into the controller. Future research may show that biomechanical and aerodynamic properties of the plant account for a large proportion of speech movement characteristics, and critical aerodynamic and acoustic properties may influence the pattern of control itself.

Moreover, from this knowledge of speech biophysics, constraints for inversion can be inferred. The anthropomorphism of the plant offers anatomical constraints for shaping the vocal tube, and the experimental determination of its degrees of freedom and of its working space again narrows the number of possible solutions to inversion. Direct mapping through extensive simulation to build a code-book leads to the emergence of control parameters, and of task descriptions and target representations used for planning (Boë et al., 1992). Also, biological control principles can be inferred from the knowledge of human skilled behaviour including speech (Nelson, 1983)[3]. Thus, these two fields of knowledge, biophysics and movement control, offer regularisation principles to the ill-posed problems currently encountered in inverse acoustics.

---

[2] For the concept of anthropomorphic robotics, see Benati et al. (1980a, b). As concerns speech, see Laboissière (1992) for a comparison with studies carried out in the US – at Haskins Laboratories (Saltzman and Munhall, 1989; Smith et al., 1993; McGowan, submitted) and MIT (Jordan, 1990; for speech in collaboration with Bailly et al., 1990) – and Japan (Hirayama et al., 1992).

[3] For recent developments in the field of arm trajectory formation, cf. Jordan et al. (in press).

Through this complementarity, the strategy for achieving our objectives in speech inversion is to maintain a continuous flow between production data and composite models of sources and vocal tract behaviour available in the project, the *Articulotron* being used as a global model to test major issues and design new experiments in speech learning by a robot.

**2.5 Integration of Action and Perception in speech**

The robotics approach is particularly appropriate for the unification of *Action* and *Perception*. Speech communication being conceived as a trade-off between the cost of production and the benefit of understanding, the *constraints* are clearly inspired from the articulatory field, and the *specific processing* from *auditory* and *visual* perception.

One of our main objectives, grounded on physiological and/or psychological knowledge, is to build a multilayer *Audiovisual Perceptron* in order to integrate vision and audition (see Fig. 1). Indeed, since the famous work by McGurk & MacDonald (1976) on audiovisual conflicts ("hearing lips and seeing voices"), it is known that the visual information is not just a secondary help for speech perception in the cases of difficult audition, i.e. hearing impairments, and speech in noise (from Sumby & Pollack, 1954, to Yuhas & Goldstein, 1991, and Robert-Ribes, 1991), but rather a systematic input to the speech perception system. Moreover, it has to be integrated with the more classical – and probably primary – auditory input (since Massaro, 1987, cf. for recent support to this idea: Campbell, 1992; Summerfield, 1992; Vroomen, 1992).

Visual processing is used in order to recover lip parameters and 3-D mouth shapes through a structured light based system. From the point of view of inversion, this provides extra constraints on the vocal tract shape, delivers continuous information in spite of speech sound interruptions (e.g., during silent plosives, pauses, etc.) and allows the enhancement of speech in noise.

Auditory processing, in the frame of sound-to-gesture inversion, will help recover important articulatory manoeuvres through two possible "smart" integration processes (Schwartz et al., in press): (1) coincidence of neural discharges enable detection of acoustic *events* (see continuing interest in *landmarks* at MIT, Stevens et al., 1992) which are particularly important to anchor further dynamic processing; (2) auditory trajectory analysis (inspired by Bregman's *Auditory Scene Analysis*) can perform a continuous estimation of the underlying target – whether it is actually reached or not – from estimation of perceived acoustic parameters positions and velocities.

Integrating both types of information, the *Audiovisual Perceptron* should be able to deliver elaborated sound prototypes (for this concept, cf. Kuhl, 1992) to the *Articulotron* for learning. In fact, the *Perceptron* is more than simply the ear and the eye of the robot (for sensing and fusion), since it incorporates a categoriser that must achieve speech sound identification. In this case again, the *Articulotron* plays the role of a pivot model fed by one of the different composite models involved in the project.

This ensemble, *Articulotron* plus *Perceptron*, will cover all the different steps of inverse mapping, from speech sound perception to inverse dynamics through inverse acoustics, thus achieving a major realisation in the *Mapping of Action and Perception in Speech*.

## 3. Work in progress

Working parts of the project carried out during the first year cover the main four areas of research, i.e. Sources and Vocal Tract modelling (WP1 & WP2), Motor control (WP3), and Audio & Visual Processing (WP4).

- In WP1, aerodynamic, acoustic and laryngographic data have been recorded in order to study excitation sources generation (voice and noise sources). These data will be used, in conjunction with vocal tract data (coming from WP2), to develop direct modelling.
- A voice source model (Liljencrants-Fant) has been assessed by comparison with inverse filtered natural speech. This model will later be used for inversion.
- Dynamics of voice and noise sources has been studied, especially glottis-constriction coordination for fricatives, and variations of the voice source in vowel-consonant sequences. This will constitute one of the main source of knowledge to perform source inversion.
- As concerns vocal tract geometric and acoustic data (WP2), scanner and video measurements of the vocal tract have been carried out, and a software for digitising labial and X-ray films has been developed. Vocal tract bioacoustic measurements have been performed, and compared with a database of reference transfer functions. As mentioned above, these vocal tract data are used in the development of articulatory/acoustic modelling.
- Articulatory-to-acoustic modelling has resulted in an acoustic vocal tract simulation software, including several new features (sources, subglottal coupling). An articulatory-acoustic codebook has been generated with a first version of the Speech Maps Interactive Plant "SMIP". All this will be used next year to elaborate in WP3 the *forward model* of the *Articulotron*.
- In WP3, a first set of data on articulatory timing has been recorded for the study of vocalic and consonantal coarticulation. These data will be used to update knowledge gained in the same WP on motor encoding-programming.
- A speech timing model has been developed as a first step towards modelling motor encoding-programming.
- Methods for the recovery of articulatory trajectories of vowel-vowel (VV) gestures have been tested, together with inverse dynamics for selected articulators. Self-organised motor relaxation nets have been used to study trajectory formation. Learning of coarticulation and compensation phenomena has been experimented for selected VV with a control model. This constitutes the basis of the *controller* module in the first state of the *Articulotron*, planned for next year.
- In WP4, methods for the recovery of undershoot vocalic targets, from acoustic parameters relevant for perception, have been tested using principles of dynamics. These methods will be developed in conjunction with progress on the topic in WP3.
- To obtain visual input data for audiovisual integration, a set of labial gestures in vowels and consonants has been recorded and processed. The main body of these data will be incorporated in the visual processor of the *Audiovisual*

*Perceptron*. Part of these data will also contribute to vocal tract articulatory modelling development (WP2).
– Visual perception of labial anticipation has been tested, and audiovisual integration models have been implemented and assessed, in order to build the first version of the *Audiovisual Perceptron* next.

Here is the up-to-date detailed list of contributions of the partners in the consortium[4]. The results of several of these studies are published in the Proceedings of the *EUROSPEECH'93* conference.

**WP1 - From speech signal to acoustic sources**
• *Aerodynamic and acoustic data for sources*: Aerodynamic and acoustic data (C. Scully, K. Stromberg, S. Mair, SLL), Anechoic recordings with laryngograph channel (C.H. Shadle, DECS)
• *Voice source model assessment* (I. Karlsson, KTH)
• *Voice and noise sources dynamics*: Glottis-constriction coordination for fricatives (E. Castelli, ICP), Dynamic variation of the voice source in VCV & CVC (A. Ní Chasaide, C. Gobl, P. Monahan, TCD)

**WP2 - From Speech Signal to Vocal Tract Geometry**
• *Vocal tract geometric and acoustic data*: Scanner and video measurements of the vocal tract (L.J. Boë, P. Perrier, T.M. Lallouache, ICP), Software for digitising labial and X-ray film data (S. Maeda, ENST, J.P. Zerling, P. Simon, A. Bothorel, F. Wioland, IPS), Vocal tract sweep tone data and interpretation (M. Båvegård, G. Fant, J. Gauffin, J. Liljencrants, KTH), Acoustic transfer functions for vowels and consonants (P. Badin, E. Castelli, Y. Pham Thi Ngoc, ICP)
• *Articulatory-to-Acoustic models and codebooks*: Codebook and sound prototypes with the first state plant (P. Perrier, L.J. Boë, Y. Payan, C. Savariaux, N. Vallée, ICP), Time and frequency domain acoustic models of the vocal tract (E. Castelli, P. Badin, ICP), Impedance measurements for the vocal tract (R. Scaife, A. Kreitmeyr, W. Hohan, DCU), Vocal tract computation: how to make it more robust and faster (Q. Lin, KTH), A new three-parameter model of VT area functions (G. Fant, KTH), Some problems in voice source analysis (G. Fant, KTH)
• *Speech Maps Interactive Plant "SMIP"* (L.J. Boë, ICP)

---

[4] The fourteen institutions involved in the project are referred to as follows: *CEDI* = Institut d'Estudis Catalans, Barcelona, E; *DCU* = School of Electronic Engineering, Dublin, IRL; *DECS* = Department of Electronics & Computer Science, Southampton, UK; *DIST* = Dipartimento di Informatica, Sistemistica, Telematica, Genova, I; *DLGS* = Département de Linguistique Générale, Strasbourg, F; *DLPL* = Department of Logopedics and Phoniatrics, Lund, S; *ENST* = Département Signal, Paris, F; *ICP* = Institut de la Communication Parlée, Grenoble, F; *IPK* = Intitut für Phonetik in Köln, G; *IPS* = Institut de Phonétique de Strasbourg, Strasbourg, F; *KTH* = Department of Speech Communication and Music Acoustics, KTH, Stockholm, S; *LAIP* = Laboratoire d'analyse informatique de la parole, Lausanne, CH; *SLL* = Speech Laboratory at Leeds, UK; *TCD* = Centre for Language and Communication Studies, Trinity College, Dublin, IRL.

**WP3 - Dynamic constraints and motor controls**

- *Data on Articulatory timing*. Data on vocalic anticipation (C. Abry, T.M. Lallouache, ICP), Anticipatory coarticulation in consonant production (D. Recasens, J. Fontdevila, M.D. Pallarès, CEDI)
- *Models of motor encoding and programming*: A speech timing model (B. Gabioud, E. Keller, B. Zellner, LAIP)
- *Methods for recovery of articulatory trajectories*: Inverse dynamics for selected articulators (P. Perrier, ICP), Self-organised motor relaxation nets (P. Morasso, V. Sanguineti, DIST), Trajectory formation in neural networks (P. Morasso, V. Sanguineti, DIST), Learning coarticulation and compensation for selected VV with a control model (G. Bailly, R. Laboissière, ICP)

**WP4 - Perceptual processing for gesture recovery**

- *Recovery of undershoot targets from acoustic parameters*: Recovery of VV reached vs. non-reached targets (D. Beautemps, J.L. Schwartz, ICP), Resonances and affiliations for VVs (G. Bailly, ICP)
- *Lip geometry data for audiovisual integration*: Input data for the audiovisual integration models (J. Robert-Ribes, T.M. Lallouache, ICP), Labial gestures of VCV sequences (R. Greisbach, IPK)
- *Perception results and audiovisual modelling*: Audiovisual integration models for vowel perception (J. Robert-Ribes, P. Escudier, J.L. Schwartz, ICP), Visual perception of labial anticipation (M.A. Cathiard, C. Abry, ICP)

## 4. Perspectives

Working parts of the project to be carried out during the next year, are planned as follows.

- In WP1, 3-D data (obtained by enhanced electropalatography) are required for frication sources. These data will be used to improve direct source modelling, and ultimately to elaborate tools for source inversion.
- Voice and noise source models will be delivered to WP2 in order to develop improved integrated versions of the VT plant.
- Updated methods for the recovery of sources (WP1), together with specific constraints in vocal tract geometry (WP2), will be delivered to WP3 in order to teach the first version of the articulotron (*Articulotron I*) to learn speech gestures.
- Improved versions of the articulatory-to-acoustic models and code-books developed in WP2 will be delivered to WP3 in order to elaborate the *forward model* for the *Articulotron I*.
- In WP3, data on articulatory timing and models of motor encoding-programming will be integrated into the controller of the *Articulotron I*.
- From WP4, specific lip geometry data will be delivered to WP2 in order to provide additional constraints for articulatory-to-acoustic inversion.
- Articulatory oriented auditory processing and visual data will be incorporated into the *Audiovisual Perceptron I*.
- The *Audiovisual Perceptron I* will be tested as a front end to the *Articulotron I*.

This coupling of the first versions of *Articulotron* and of *Audiovisual Perceptron* will be the big challenge for next year.

It is clear that *Speech Maps* deals with basic problems in speech production and perception. One can, however, envision scientific and technological advances. The integrated approach propounded here can be expected to deliver major "spinoffs" in R&D, beyond the *Articulotron,* the *Audiovisual Perceptron,* and other tools for speech processing, including Multi Layer Perceptrons.

Low bit-rate transmission of speech, using articulatory code-books, is currently being developed at *Bell Laboratories* (cf. e.g. Rahim et al., 1993). The access to the code-book in such a system could greatly benefit from the inversion approach advocated in this project.

Speech recognition would also benefit from this low level inverse mapping (cf. Bailly et al., 1992; Iso, 1993), including the enhancement by vision of the acoustic signal in noise (cf. Petajan, 1984; Finn, 1986; Goldschen, 1993).

Speech synthesis could greatly benefit from the learning ability of a robot which takes advantage of adaptive biological principles. Articulatory kinematics generated by the articulotron could be used as input to high quality terminal analogues currently used in text-to-speech synthesis. In this vein, following Stevens' suggestions (Stevens, 1991), constraints among its command parameters could simplify the control of Klatt's formant synthesiser (Stevens suggests that this could be achieved through an appropriate mapping from 10 higher level control parameters to the 48 lower-level command parameters of KLSYN88).

In addition, articulatory kinematics coming from the articulotron could drive a *face synthesiser* (such as those developed by Parke, 1974, Platt, 1985, Waters, 1987, the latter with a solution to inverse dynamics, cf. Terzopoulos & Waters, 1991), thus leading to the development of audiovisual synthesis.

At present, the integration of both acoustic and optic information in the design of an ensemble *Audiovisual Perceptron* plus *Articulotron* seems unique. But beyond speech, this trend is more generally developing in the frame of European projects in the field of multimedia R&D.

## Acknowledgements

We are specially indebted for this text to people who participated intensively in the writing up of the project, namely Pascal Perrier & Jean-Luc Schwartz. Tom Sawallis helped us a lot in hunting French idiomatic expressions in a first version of this text, as well as Rudolph Sock. All errors are of the first authors' responsibility. Finally, among all those that have been forgotten, we have a special thought for those who helped us in endless discussion on the main topics of the project.

## References


Atal, B.S., Chang J.J., Mathews M.V. & Tukey J.W. (1978). Inversion of articulatory-to-acoustic transformation in the vocal tract by a computer sorting technique. *J. Acoust. Soc. of Am.*, 63, 1535-1555.

Bailly G., Jordan M., Mantakas M., Schwartz J.L., Bach M., & Olesen M. (1990). Simulation of vocalic gestures using an articulatory model driven by a sequential neural network. *J. Acoust. Soc. of Am.*, 87, S1, 105.

Bailly G., Laboissière R. & Schwartz J.L. (1991). Formant trajectories as audible gestures: an alternative for speech synthesis. *J. of Phonetics*, 19, 9-23.

Bailly G., Abry C., Boë L.J., Laboissière R. & Schwartz L.J. (1992). Inversion and speech recognition. In *Signal processing VI: theories and applications.* (J. Vandewalle R., Boite M., Moonen A. & Oosterlinck eds), Proceedings of EUSIPCO 92. Sixth European Signal Processing Conference. Bruxelles, Belgium, August 24-27, 1992. Vol.1, pp. 159-164. Elsevier Science Publishers.

Benati M., Morasso P., Tagliasco V., & Zaccaria R. (1980a). Anthropomorphic robotics. I: representing mechanical complexity. *Biological Cybernetics*, 38, 125-140.

Benati M., Morasso P., Tagliasco V., & Zaccaria R. (1980b). Anthropomorphic robotics. II: analysis of manipulator dynamics and the output motor impedance. *Biological Cybernetics*, 38, 141-150.

Boë L.J. Perrier P. & Bailly G. (1992). The geometric vocal tract variables controlled for vowel production: proposals for constraining acoustic-to-articulatory inversion. *J. of Phonetics* 20, 27-38.

Campbell R. (1992). The neuropsychology of lipreading. In *Processing the facial image*(V. Bruce, A. Cowey, A.W. Ellis, & D.I. Perrett, eds), pp. 39-45. Oxford: Clarendon Press.

Cipra B. (1992). You can't hear the shape of a drum. *Science*, 255, 1642-1643.

Diehl R.L., Walsh M.A., & Kluender K. R. (1991). On the interpretability of speech/nonspeech comparisons: a reply to Fowler. *J. Acoust. Soc. of Am.*, 89, 2905-2909.

Finn E.K. (1986). An investigation of visible lip information to be used in automated speech recognition. Doctoral dissertation, Georgetown University, Washington DC.

Fowler C.A. (1986). An event approach to the study of speech perception from a direct-realist perspective. *J. of Phonetics*, 14, 3-28.

Goldschen A.J. (1993). Continuous automatic speech recognition by lipreading. Doctoral dissertation, George Washington University.

Hadamard J. (1923). *Lectures on the Cauchy problem in linear partial differential equations*. New Haven: Yale University Press.

Hirayama M., Vatikiotis-Bateson E., Kawato M., & Honda K. (1992). Neural network modeling of speech motor control. In *Proceedings of the 1992 International Conference on Spoken Language Processing*, Banff, Canada, Vol.1, paper Fr.sAM.3.3, 883-886.

Hogden J.E. (1991). Low-dimensional phoneme mapping using a continuity constraints. Unpublished Ph. D. dissertation, Stanford.

Honda M. & Kaburagi T. (1993). Estimation of articulatory-to-acoustic mapping using input and output measurements. *J. Acoust. Soc. Am.*, 93, (N°4, Pt. 2), 2353.

Iso K. (1993). Speech recognition using dynamical models of speech production. Technical report of IEICE, SP92-126, 25-32.

Jordan M.I. (1990). Motor learning and the degrees of freedom problem. In *Attention & Performance XIII* (M. Jeannerod, ed.), pp. 796-836. Hillsdale: Lawrence Erlbaum Associates.

Jordan M.I., Flash T., & Arnon Y. (1993). A model of the learning of arm trajectories from spatial targets. *The J. of Cognitive Neuroscience*, in press.

Jospa P. (1991). Des paramètres formantiques au profil articulatoire. In *Proceedings of the XIIth International Congress of Phonetic Sciences*, Vol. 2, 378-381.

Kac M. (1966). Can one hear the shape of a drum ? *Am. Math. Monthly*, 73 (4), II, 1-23.

Kuhl P.K. (1992). Speech prototypes: Studies on the nature, function, ontogeny and phylogeny of the "centers" of speech categories. In *Speech perception, production and linnguistic structure* (Y. Tohkura, E. Vatikiotis-Bateson, & Y. Sagisaka, eds), pp. 239-264. Tokyo: Ohmsha.

Laboissière R. (1992). Préliminaires pour une robotique de la communication parlée: inversion et contrôle d'un modèle articulatoire du conduit vocal. Thèse de Docteur Ingénieur de l'INP, Grenoble.

Laboissière R., Schwartz J.L., & Bailly G. (1990). Motor control for speech skills: a connectionist approach. In *Connectionist models* (D.S.Touretzki, J.L. Elman, T.L. Seinowski & G.E. Hinton, Eds), Proceedings of the 1990 Summer School, pp.319-327. Morgan Kaufmann Publishers.

Liberman A.M., Cooper, F.S. Shankweiler D., & Studdert-Kennedy M. (1967). Perception of the speech code. *Psychological Rev.*, *74*, 431-461.

Liberman, A.M. & Mattingly I.G. (1985). The motor theory of speech perception revised. *Cognition*, 21, 1-36.

Maeda S. (1979). An Articulatory Model of the Tongue Based on a Statistical Analysis. *J. Acoust. Soc. Am.* 65, S22.

Maeda S. (1988). Improved articulatory models. *J. Acoust. Soc. Am.* 84, S146.

Marr D. (1982). *Vision. A computational investigation into the human representation and processing of visual information*. San Francisco: W.H. Freeman and Company.

Massaro D.W. (1987). *Speech perception by ear and eye: a paradigm for psychological inquiry.* London: Laurence Erlbaum Associates.

Mattingly I.G. & Studdert-Kennedy M. (eds) (1991). *Modularity and the Motor Theory of Speech Perception* (Proc. of a conf. to honor A.M. Liberman, 1988). Hillsdale: Lawrence Erlbaum Associates.

McGowan R.S. (1991). Recovering tube kinematics using time-varying acoustic information. In *Proceedings of the XIIth International Congress of Phonetic Sciences*, Vol. 4, 486-489.

McGowan R.S. (Submitted). Recovering articulatory movement from formant frequency trajectories using task dynamics and a genetic algorithm.

McGurk H. & MacDonald J. (1976). Hearing lips and seing voices. *Nature*, *264*, 746-748.

Nearey T.M. (1990). The segment as a unit of speech perception. *J. of Phonetics*, 18, 347-373.

Nelson W.L. (1983). Physical principles for economies of skilled movements. *Biological Cybernetics* 46, 135-147.

Parke F.I. (1974). A parametric model for human faces. Doctoral Dissertation, University of Utah.

Perkell J.S. (1991). Models, theory and data in speech production. In *Proceedings of the XIIth International Congress of Phonetic Sciences*, Vol. 1, 182-191.

Petajan E.D. (1984). Automatic lipreading to enhance speech recognition. Doctoral Thesis, University of Illinois.

Platt S.M. (1985). A structural model of the human face. Ph D. dissertation of the University of Pennsylvania.

Poggio T. (1984). Low-level vision as inverse optics. In *Computational models of hearing and vision* (M. Rauk, ed.) pp. 123-127. Tallinn: Acad. of Sc. of the Estonian S.S.R.

Rahim M.G., Goodyear C.C., Klejin W.B., Schroeter J., & Sonhi M.M. (1993). On the use of neural networks in articulatory speech synthesis. *J. Acoust. Soc. Am.* 93, 1109-1121.

Robert-Ribes J. (1991). Intégration audition-vision par réseaux de neurones. Une étude comparative des modèles d'intégration appliqués à la perception des voyelles. Mémoire de D.E.A. Signal-Image-Parole, INP, Grenoble.

Saltzman, E.L. & Munhall K.G. (1989). A dynamical approach to gestural patterning in speech production. *Ecological Psychology*, 1 (4), 1615-1623.

Schwartz J.L., Beautemps D., Arrouas Y., & Escudier P. (1993). Auditory analysis of speech gestures. In *The Psychophysics of speech perception II*(Schouten M.E.H., ed.) (in press).

Scully C. (1991). The representation in models of what speakers know. In *Proceedings of the XIIth International Congress of Phonetic Sciences*, Vol. 1, 192-197.

Shirai K. & Kobayashi T. (1991). Estimation of articulatory motion using neural networks. *J. of Phonetics* 19, 379-385.

Smith C.L., Browman C.P., McGowan R.S., & Kay B. (1993). Extracting dynamic parameters from speech movement data, *J. Acoust. Soc. Am.* 93, 1580-1588.

Soquet A., Saerens M., & Jospa P. (1991). Trying to determine place of articulation of plosives with a vocal tract model. In *Proceedings of the XIIth International Congress of Phonetic Sciences*, Vol. 2, 66-69.

Sorokin V.N. (1992). Determination of vocal-tract shape for vowels. *Speech Communication*, 11, 71-85.

Stevens K.N. (1972). The the quantal nature of speech: Evidence from articulatory-acoustic data. In *Human Communication: a Unified View* (E.E. David & P.B. Denes, eds), pp. 51-66. New York: Macgrow-Hill.

Stevens K.N. (1989). On the quantal nature of speech. *J. of Phonetics*, 17, 3-45.

Stevens K.N. (1991). The contribution of speech synthesis to phonetics: Dennis Klatt's legacy. In *Proceedings of the XIIth International Congress of Phonetic Sciences*, Vol. 1, 28-37.

Stevens K.N., Manuel S.Y., Shattuck-Hufnagel S., & Liu S. (1992). Implementation of a model for lexical access based on features. In *Proceedings of the 1992 International Conference on Spoken Language Processing*, Banff, Canada, Vol.1, paper Th.fAM.3.2, 499-502.

Sumby W.H. & Pollack I. (1954). Visual contribution to speech intelligibility in noise, *J. Acoust. Soc. Am.* 26(2), 212-215.

Summerfield Q. (1992). Lipreading and audio-visual speech perception. In *Processing the facial image* (V. Bruce, A. Cowey, A.W. Ellis, & D.I. Perrett, eds), pp. 71-78. Oxford: Clarendon Press.

Terzopoulos D. & Waters K. (1991). Techniques for realistic facial modelling and animation. In *Computer Animation '91* (N. Magnenat-Thalmann & D. Thalmann, eds), pp. 59-74. Berlin: Springer Verlag.

Vatikiotis-Bateson E., Hirayama M., Honda K., & Kawato M. (1992). The articulatory dynamics of running speech: gestures from phonemes ? In *Proceedings of the 1992 International Conference on Spoken Language Processing*, Banff, Canada, Vol.1, paper Fr.sAM.3.4, 887-890.

Vroomen J.H.M. (1992). Hearing voices and seeing lips: Investigations in the psychology of lipreading. Doctoral dissertation, Katolieke Univ. Brabant.

Waters K. (1987). A muscle model for animating three-dimensional facial expression. In *Proceedings of Computer Graphics*, 21, 17-24.

Yehia H. & Itakura F. (1993). Dynamic vocal tract shape determination from formant frequencies using two-dimensional Fourier analysis. Technical report of the Institute of Electronics, Information and Communication Engineers of Japan, SP92-143, 49-56.

Yuhas B.P. & Goldstein M.H. Jr. (1991). Comparing Human and Neural Network Lipreaders. *J. Acoust. Soc. Am.* 90 (1), 598-600.

# Esprit II Project 5516 ROARS
# Robust Analytic Speech Recognition System

Pierre Alinat
Thomson Sintra ASM, 525 Dolines,
F-06903 Sophia Antipolis, France

Jean-Marie Pierrel
CRIN / CNRS, BP 239,
F-54506 Vandoeuvre, France

## Abstract

The overal objective of the ROARS[1] project is to implement a feature based speech recognition system, that is to say using knowledge about phonetic features (and the corresponding acoustic cues), phonemes, syllables and words. More precisely the ROARS project aims firstly to improve the robustness of the feature-based approach against inter and intra speaker changes in articulation and against ambient noise, including changes in articulation due to ambient noise (Lombart effect), secondly to adapt knowledge for two languages: French and Spanish and thirdly to take the speech understanding and dialogue aspect into account in the context of a demonstration relative to an Air Traffic Control console using a connected word language.

Up to now the recognition system has been implemented for the French language: the recognized phones are localized according to their mode of articulation and, for each phone, parameters are estimated according to manner and place of articulation. A 96% recognition rate has been obtained in a two digit number recognition tasks (speaker independent). The Spanish version will soon been tried.

The main advantage of this feature-based approach is to allow the manipulation of the coarticulation and word junction rules, the dialect differences and lax pronunciation in a natural way. Each of these problems, indeed, has an effect on one (or sometimes two) phonetic feature and the statistics relative to this feature can be easily modified accordingly.

The main difficulty with this approach is to determine effective acoustic cues corresponding to each phonetic feature. A study of the noise impact on the various steps of the recognition system was completed and modifications are in progress in order to be able to take into account more or less stationary ambient noise.

[1] The ROARS consortium comprises: THOMSON SINTRA ASM, France; ENA Telecomunicaciones, Spain; Centre de Recherche en Informatique de Nancy, France; Universidad Politecnica de Valencia, Spain.

# 1. Introduction

The goal of the ROARS project is to implement a robust voice input, for finite state grammar language, continuously uttered connected words, two languages: French and Spanish. Robustness concerns intra and inter speaker changes in articulation and various disturbing ambient noises (Telephone speech is not considered in this project). In the last few years, reported accuracy rates of speech recognition systems have improved steadily [15]. Despite that, obviously much more effort will be needed for bridging the gap between current speech technology and the market of real spoken language in real conditions. In fact only a small part of the potential market can be satisfied by the currently commercially available recognition systems because people want to converse with a computer as they would with another person (at least in the very limited domain subject of the dialogue). Efficient solutions are still to be found for many problems concerning the various levels of speech communication (or concerning the links between the levels):

- Phonological level: variability due to dialects, word junctions, coarticulations, varying speech production rates, pauses, allophones, lax pronunciation, possible aperiodic glottal excitation ..., disturbance due to steady or transient ambient noise, but also speaker generated non speech events (such as breathing noise, caughing, laughter, throat clearing, lip smacking) and other people's speech overlapping.
- Language level (syntax, semantic, contextual information): non lexical or grammatical speech, repetition, correction, indetermination, use of prosody.

In the ROARS project, in order to begin to obtain robustness against some of these problems or to be able in the future to deal efficiently with others, the work has mainly been focused on two points:

- Phonetic feature-based (that is to say analytic) recognition (rather than HMM at word or phoneme level).
- Understanding and dialogue, because even for the very simple language we are dealing with in this project, voice input must include such a component, especially dialogue that is to say feedback [24].

The work for these two points started from a previous system implemented for the French language[2]. In this paper we first explain why a feature-based approach has been chosen for ROARS. Then Chapter 3 gives an overview of the ROARS recognition system. The Man Machine Dialogue component is described in Chapter 4. Finally some preliminary recognition results and comments about these results are given in the last section.

# 2. Why Feature-based Speech Recognition?

## 2.1 The Hidden Markov Model Approach

The HMM (Hidden Markov Model) approach using word or phoneme as the modeling units is the most widely used today and has been applied so successfully

[2] Work supported by "Direction des Recherches, Etudes et Techniques", Paris France.

that some people actually think present HMM modeling is more or less the right solution for speech recognition. In this approach speech is modelled by a hidden (from the observer) stochastic process which is observed through another stochastic process. The hidden process is assumed to be discrete Markovian [12]. The main advantage of this model is that the stochastic nature of speech is taken into account in such a way that the various parameters of the model can be estimated by rigorous (and tractable) mathematical methods.

But the HMM model is not fully appropriate because of several limitations (due to its simplicity):

- In this model the probability distribution related to duration of each state does not match correctly the speech phoneme on subphoneme duration [20].
- Obviously speech is not really a string of stationnary states: acoustic realization of a phoneme can be dynamically modified by the adjacent phonemes. In other words the different parts of the vocal tract can move more or less continuously, not necessarily simultaneously.
- Because there is often relatively small change in the vocal tract shape from one acoustic vector to the next, the assumed independence between these observations is not always verified.
- Classical HMM based speech recognition system use words or phonemes as basic units of speech. In word-based HMM all the intra word coarticulatory effects are automatically incorporated into the model but coarticulatory effects between adjacent words are very difficult to take into account. Moreover, because each word has to be trained individually, training becomes a time consuming task for large vocabulary. In phoneme-based HMM the coarticulatory effects are a problem not only at the junction between words as in the previous case but also within words. In order to capture the acoustic variability associated with the two adjacent phonemes a popular solution is to use triphone model, that is to say model of a phoneme in a particular phonetic context (for example the SPHINX system [11]. However, the adjacent phonemes are only one among the various roots of acoustic variability: stressed or unstressed phonemes, function words, minimum articulatory effort necessary for providing a correct transmission of information in a given pragmatic context, various dialects. For all these reasons the number of elementary models would have to be vastly increased and problems would arise with the size of the training set. Some other basic units have been proposed: subphonemic segment syllable or part of syllable [19], but the problem of training set size remains essentially the same.
- The used training algorithm maximizes likelihoods (MLE criterion) instead of a posteriori probabilities (MAP criterion) [2].

In order to overcome some of the limitations of the classical HMM systems it seems natural to try to incorporate into the recognition system more knowledge derived from phonetics, both from the perceptive and the articulatory point of view. Some attempts in this direction have been made inside the general HMM framework. A first example is provided in the SPHINX system [11] by the reduction of the number of triphones from about 7000 to 1000 by grouping the phonetic contexts with the same articulation place (for instance the triphones [tVX] and [dVX] are fused because normally the stops [t] and [d] in this case induce the same distortion). A second example consists in using multivalued phonetic-features as the components of the observation vector used in the HMM framework [3]. A third example [5] consists of using parameters for representing each member of the phone set that are phone class specific combined with dynamic model of speech parameters.

In all these examples the basic HMM model is retained with its advantages and disadvantages. Considering that the HMM approach corresponds perhaps to a local minimum of the recognition error rate surface, it is interesting to try to escape from this local minimum by using a different speech model [4].

## 2.2 The Phonetic Feature-based Approach

Although the first attempts at Automatic Speech Recognition only date back to the 1950's, mankind has always been studying speech. The result is a science called Phonetics which has enabled us to discover such notions as phonetic features, phonemes, syllables and words. Phonetics has also enabled us to establish a classification [13] of phonemes based on phonetic features (mode, manner, and place of articulation), thanks to careful observation of speech articulation but also due to the auditory capacities of certain researchers. For example the phoneme [p] is described phonetically as stop (mode), unvoiced (manner) and labial (place).

The advent in 1947 of the sonagraph improved the results obtained in phonetics by means of a more quantitative study of phonetic features (and the corresponding acoustic cues) in time and frequency (in particular the works of the Haskins Laboratories [9]).

The sonagraph also confirmed that phonemes are not simply juxtaposed but more or less overlapping. That is to say that the different features do not change their value simultaneously and are influenced by the neighbouring features. Such results have been used for implementing speech recognizer in the so-called knowledge-based approach. This name seems badly chosen because every recognition system is based on a model, in other words, knowledge. The only difference is the structure of the model in particular the speech levels taken into account. In triphone HMM for example, the knowledge embedded into the model is relative to the phoneme level. In contrast in knowledge-based systems the embedded knowledge is relative to phoneme and phonetic feature levels. For that reason we prefer to name them feature-based rather than knowledge-based.

The drawback to this approach is the need to improve the acoustic cues, that is to say the relationship between the various phonetic features and the observed acoustic signal. Despite all the work of gathering the knowledge used to read spectrograms [25], our knowledge of acoustic cues has still to be improved and work is in progress for that [16]. At the beginning, in order to be simple, the feature-based recognizers dealt with more or less deterministic acoustic cues and deterministic use of these cues. It was a major limitation because statistical models seem to be the only means to overcome the great variability of speech. In fact a feature-based model can be stochastic as a phoneme-based model.

An important part of feature-based systems is the temporal matching between the series of basic units of speech (e.g. phonemes) and the acoustic signal. A classical solution is to segment the acoustic signal, that is to say to partition the acoustic signal in a sequence of adjacent segments. In some cases the segmentation is multilevel in order to capture the various strengh of changes in the acoustic signal (as in SUMMIT, [26]). In such a segmentation, problems arise because of the overlap between adjacent phonemes (for example the frequent overlap between [R] and the vowel in some [RV] syllable). For that reason in the ROARS project the classical segmentation was discarded. The phonemes are divided into broad classes according to their mode of articulation. For example in French there are five classes: Vowels - Semivowels - Fricatives -Plosives and Liquids. Phonemes of each class are searched, independently of phonemes of other classes, by using the acoustic cues corresponding to the mode of articulation of its class.

Finally the speech model used in ROARS is a phoneme string, each phoneme being described by a set of phonetic features. The segments of acoustic signal corresponding to the phonemes can more or less overlap. The relations between the observed acoustic signal and the phonetic features are stochastic. Moreover the corresponding statistics can be modified accordingly to context (coarticulation, stress ....). Several advantages can be expected from such a feature-based model:

a. The reduction of dimensionality. The dimensionality of the observed vectors is a problem when applying statistical techniques to a classification problem. According to results of the ESPRIT BRA project 6891 ELENA (Enhanced Learning for Evolutive Neural Architecture) for estimating a Gaussian underlying density in dimension d with a 10% precision, N samples are needed with $\log_{10}$ N _ 0,6 (d - 1/4): for example, we need N _ 800 000 samples for d = 10 and N _ 800 samples for d = 5. When dealing with HMM, dimensions are currently d = 25 or above and if the components are independent it seems difficult to use a sufficiently large training set size ($10^{15}$ samples for d = 25 !). Fortunately there is probably some dependence between the components and the real dimension is lower. For instance Linear Discriminant Analysis has been used in order to take into account this possible reduction of the dimension of observed vector [6]. But the real dimension still remains large and the above formula clearly shows that in stochastic modelling it is important to deal with as low dimensionality as possible: the feature-based approach reduces the dimensionality by splitting the obervation space in several independent (or approximately independent) subspaces. In other words each acoustic cue is supposed to be independent of others and depending only on a small part of the whole observation: typically the dimension of the observation restricted to what is necessary for an acoustic cue is between 1 and 5, that is to say quite tractable. Such a reduction of the needed size of the training sets results from the used of a more exact knowledge of the inner structure of speech.

b. The coarticulatory effects can be taken into account in a more elegant and concise way than just considering as many triphones as necessary. In the feature-based approach the conditional probabilities corresponding to individual phonetic features can be modified by the coarticulation rules concerning this feature. If the probabilities are parametrized, each rule can be expressed simply (and approximately) by a modification of the parameters of the pdf. Instead of 1000 triphones, only about 40 phonetic features (in fact distinct distributions), and 40 coarticulation rules (in the actual ROARS system) have to be considered. So the effort necessary for obtaining the corresponding statistics may be reduced.

c. It is worth noting that the coarticulation between adjacent phoneme is not the only cause of speech variability. Usually, in order to minimize his effort, a speaker can relax his articulation of some of the phonetic features insofar as he knows that it does not endanger the understanding of his speech by the person he is speaking to [10]. For example, in French, the first formant of the [u] vowel in the number "douze" is statistically higher than normal probably because "doze" is still sufficiently different from other numbers and easier to pronounce. That is a very important aspect of the relationship between speech recognition and speech understanding. In a feature-based recognizer such effects can be taken into account in the same manner as the real coarticulatory effects by using specific rules relative to the statistical description of the concerned feature.

d. Lexical access based on features. Several authors [7] [23] have underlined that the feature-based approach could decrease the computation load needed for lexical access by using broad phonetic features in a first step and the remaining features only when necessary. In other words, the analytic recognition can be organized in a hierarchical fashion, such that for each word only the necessary features are extracted, when considering all the contextual information. The ROARS recognizer does not include such a refinement but it is a potentiality of a feature-based recognizer.

## 3. Overview of the ROARS Recognition System

The ROARS recognition system contains three parts: signal analysis, phone extraction, and sentence recognition. Each of these parts is described in the following pages.

### 3.1 Signal Analysis

The human ear is the normal receiver for speech and therefore some matching between speech and ear is likely. For this reason the analyzer employed here is a coarse cochlear model comprising a bank of 45 linear bandpass filters with center frequencies and transfer functions based on human characteristics (known by direct and psychoacoustic measurements). The analyser frequency band is 70 Hz - 8500 Hz. Each filter is followed by detection-integration and a "spectrum" is obtained every 8 ms. Moreover, in addition to this spectrum, the analysed bandwidth is divided in three subbands and the percentage of voice energy and friction energy are estimated in each of these subbands.

### 3.2 Phone Extraction

For the sake of brevity, in the following, "phone" means recognized phoneme opposed to phoneme for phonemes composing the vocabulary words.

The localization of phones is achieved in parallel, independently by broad class: vowels, semi vowels, fricatives, plosives. The acoustic cue used for detecting the phone of a class corresponds normally to the mode of articulation defining this class. For example, for vowels it is more or less the presence of a maximum of voiced energy, and for plosives it is more or less the presence of a quick energy increase (or in some cases decrease). The phone detection is not binary but rather, a score is estimated for each detected phone in order to provide information about the quality of this detection. In fact this score constitutes the part of the observation useful for the detection. Generally the dimension of this score is 1 (and for that reason we named it score) but when necessary the dimension may be higher.

For each detected phone a zone is determined corresponding to a rough estimate of its extent. Being obtained independently the zone of the various phone may widely overlap. It must be emphasized that such a localization process is very different from the traditional segmentation process: here the concept of a frontier between adjacent phonemes simply does not exist. For each detected phone, the values of parameters associated with the phonetic features normally attributed to its class are estimated (manner and place of articulation). These parameters are related to the classification of the phone inside its class.

For instance: for fricatives: voicing score<br>compactness score<br>formant position and movement

Some other estimated parameters are relative to supraphonemic information (stress ...): position, duration, amplitude, pitch (for vowels).

When useful, in particular for the formant position, several values can be given for some of these parameters with an estimated probability associated with each value. In this way, about five phone strings are obtained with each phone described through the name of its class and the value of its parameters. So one does not try to obtain a string of labelled phonemes because without syntactic and semantic knowledge it is not possible to decide firmly about phonemes and words as soon as input speech is fluent and natural. Up to this point the process is strictly bottom up: a more top down process would reduce the computation load but would also increase the overall complexity of the system.

## 3.3 Sentence Recognition

The ROARS system deals with connected word sentences. No specific a priori probability is attached to the words and sentences that is to say all the possible words at a given place are supposed to have the same a priori probability.

The goal of the recognition system is to decide which sentence $S_i$ has been uttered among the sentences possible from a given connected word lexicon and syntax. According to the classical Bayesian detection theory if:

- costs assigned to right decision = 0
- cost assigned to wrong decision = 1 (that is to say any error of equal importance), the risk is minimized if the chosen sentence $S_i$ is that with the largest a posteriori probability p ($S_i$ / observation).

The sentence is a string of phonemes $S_i$ = ph1 ph2 ... phn. Under the assumption of independence of the successive phonemes we can write:

$$p(Si/obs) = \prod_{j=1}^{n} p(phj/obs) \times ( p(\text{nothing else}/obs)$$

(This assumption is clearly an approximation: the a priori probability of a phoneme depends on the neighbouring phonemes).

In a similar way each phoneme is decomposed in phonetic features. For example in the case of the vowel [i]

p(i / obs) = p (vowel exists/obs) p(oral/obs) p (F1 from [i]/obs) p(F2 from [i]/obs)

Again this assumption is only an approximation because the phonetic features are not fully independent: some combinations of features are not used. For example formant position is not to be taken into account for diffuse fricatives and for oral vowels all combination of F1 and F2 value are not allowed.

When comparing a phoneme X with a phone x (generally of the same class) the phone x or more precisely the various parameters of phone x are taken as observation.

In the previous example, observation used in p(vowel exists / obs) is the score of the vowel phone. From processing a speech database the conditional probabilities p(score/vowel exists) and p(score / vowel does not exist) and the a priori probability p(vowel exists) and p(vowel does not exist) can be estimated by considering all the detected vowel phones. Finally using the Bayes formula the a posteriori probability p(vowel exists / score) is obtained. Again in the previous example for the term p(F1 from [i] / obs), observation is the observed value of F1. From processing a speech database the conditional probabilities p(observed F1 / vowel [i]) and p(observed F1 / vowel other than [i]) and the a priori probabilities p(vowel [i]) and p(vowel other than [i]) can be estimated, and finally using the Bayes formula the a posteriori probability p(F1 from [i] / observed F1) is obtained. When several values f have been retained for the formant position, then:

$$p(F1[i]/obs)= \sum_{f} p(F1[i]/\text{observed } F1=f)\ p(F1=f/obs)$$

In fact the estimation of p(phoneme j / obs) is not so simple because coarticulatory effects must be taken into account. Here, for brevity , coarticulatory effect means, the more or less probable modifications of acoustic characteristics of phonemes in various phonetic environments inside a word or at the junction between adjacent words, but is also extented to all contextual effects as lax pronunciation of unstressed phonemes or possible particular pronunciation of a word. In the ROARS system about 40 rules are used for coarticulation, for example:

– *"Vus"* (unstressed vowel): the formants of an unstressed vowel can be more or less moved toward the formants of [Schwa].
– *"Unvoiced, voiced"*: [unvoiced consonant] + [voiced consonant] _ the first consonant can become more or less voiced.
– *"V"*: [pause] + [vowel] _ an extra glottal pulse may precede the vowel.

It must be noticed that some coarticulation rules can be particular to a word or a few words. Generally, coarticulation rules act by modifying the probalities:

- either the conditional probabilities corresponding to the phonetic features such as vowel nazalisation, formant position, etc.,

- or the probability p(phoneme X invisible) (that is to say not pronounced or so badly pronounced that it cannot be detected),
- or the probability p (phone x explained) (that is to say not directly associated to a phoneme but explained by the coarticulation rule).

In some cases coarticulation rules can also act on the choice of phone class that can be associated with a phoneme or on the choice of the formant value to be taken into account for vowels and fricatives. When a phoneme X is not associated with a corresponding phone x in the comparison process, then the corresponding phone x is supposed to have been undetected.

Such a miss may be due to two different causes: either phoneme X was so badly pronounced that it cannot be detected or phoneme X was pronounced but has not be detected (that is to say score = 0).

In the comparison process we take the most probable of the two probabilities:

max [p(phoneme X invisible), p(phoneme X exists / score = 0)]

When a phone x is not associated with a corresponding phoneme X in the comparison process, then the phone x is supposed to be due to an extra detection caused by either a real extra detection or a coarticulation rule explaining the phone x. In the comparison process we take:

p(phone x to be jumped/obs) =

p(phoneme X does not exist/score)+p(phone x explained).

In the vocabulary each word is described as a phoneme string. Each phoneme X is described by: identity X -stress level (for vowel) - p(phoneme X invisible) -list of coarticulation rules -for the phonemes that can be at the junction with adjacent words, list of possible coarticulations rules (only active for same junction with adjacent words). The phoneme string describing a word is complemented with possible junction phoneme, that is to say vowel @ or consonant that can be added at the junction between two successive words. Finally it can happen that the last phoneme of a word can be deleted in some context.

Concerning the matching of the recognized phone strings and the vocabulary phoneme string, a dynamic programming algorithm cannot be used directly, because it is not always clear which is the first one and which is the second one for each couple of phones from two different classes. However it is worth noting that among the 5 phone classes the vowel class is the most reliable: less missing phones, less extra phones than for the other classes. Consequently the vowel phones can be used in different and more fundamental manner and the matching of the strings is implemented in two steps. The first step concerns the comparison between the vowel phones string and the vowel phonemes string. A dynamic programming algorithm can be used here because the order of the vowel phones is clearly defined. The second step concerns the consonants between the vowels. In this case all the possible associations between the two strings are tried. This second step remains tractable because the phones are classified by categories and in each category the number of phones between two successive vowels is low. In this way the notion of syllables is more or less taken into consideration.

As explained previously the goal of the system is to find the phoneme string [ph1 ... phn] that maximizes p(ph1 ... phn/ obs), the phoneme string ph1 ... phn corresponding to one of the possible utterances of a sentence $S_i$ allowed by the language. The number of different possible sentences (word strings) can be very high and the number of corresponding phonemes strings still higher. Then the

major problem is to limit the computation load without significant degradation of the result. Finally in ROARS the computational cost of the dynamic programming algorithm is reduced by a "time synchronous beam search technique" in a manner similar to HARPY [8].
It has been shown that such a strategy is efficient in terms of complexity of the Control structure, memory requirement and recognition error rate [14].

## 4. Understanding and Dialogue in ROARS System

### 4.1 Importance of an efficient Dialogue Management

As indicated in section 1, the main purpose of the ROARS project is to design a voice-activated man-machine interface which is at the same time robust and user-friendly, and which will be based on an analytical front-end. In fact, designing such an interface cannot be based on the sole recognition of the user's utterances [17, 18] but has to exploit the recognition results in the more general context of the dialogue and the application under consideration. This urges the interface designer to:

- Validate the results coming from the recognition process. Indeed, several errors or ambiguities can occur during the recognition phase such as wrong global or local recognitions, lexical ambiguities, syntactic/semantic ones, weak overall recognition scores, etc.
- Realise a contextual interpretation of the message, a step which is of the utmost importance as soon as we allow the user to formulate his requests/commands in a natural way - i.e. by using the full scope of referring expressions (anaphoras, ellipses) and by integrating several elementary commands within a single utterance (expression of a general goal, distribution of a command over different objects or a series of commands on a same object).
- Generate the retro-actions or answers corresponding to the user's requests.
- Determine the actual goal of the user as expressed in his initial statement and consequently to be able to design a sequence of possible actions which may fulfil it more generally, this consists in managing the general evolution of the dialogue.

If our purpose is - in the short-term perspective - to fully integrate voice-activated front-ends within operational systems we believe that we must at the same time operate towards the definition of a robust recognition step and design an advanced dialogue interface dedicated to an application or a class of applications. Considering the relative failure of the present use of vocal front-ends in industrial applications, we have come to the conclusion that it is not possible to blindly integrate a black-box recognition process - whatever its robustness - without a strong interaction with a dialogue system. If this aspect is neglected, it can only lead to the expression of simple oral commands for a given interface, thus loosing the main advantages that speech may provide to man-machine communication.

## 4.2 Man-machine Dialogue in ROARS System.

a) *Dialogue Situations*

The dialogue in ROARS corresponds to a series of exchanges between the user and the system. An elementary dialogue unfolds in three steps. The user gives an initial order followed by an adjustment phase aiming at making the interpretation of the system coincide with the user's request, and finaly the order is executed. At that point, the system is ready for a new input.
There are two categories of sentences - we will call them orders - in the ROARS system:

- The dialogue management sentences, which are independent of the application under control. These have a specific goal confirmation of an order (ok), cancelling the recognition (cancel), cancelling the execution (negative), repeating the execution (again).
- The control sentences, which may act upon the objects of the application or give values to the components of the objects. The orders, each of which is given a specific name, are made of different sub-parts. They have a main element called 'command' and other elements called parameters. In the following example the parentheses mark these different elements, the bold characters show the command part.

Example: (*paint*) (square) (in red).

The adjustment phase makes the interpretation of the system coincides with the user's request. Since the speech recognition rate never reaches 100%, the system may misinterpret the sentence. Similarly, we can admit that the user may be wrong. When adjusting an order, we suppose that, in any case, an initial order was given. The system analyses the request and answers with a message. In the best case, it is the right interpretation which is produced and the system moves on to the execution phase.

Example:
User: *Paint square in red*
System: Paint square in red
# execution of "paint square in red" #

The system may propose a wrong order (bad recognition or misinterpretation). This is why it always allows the user to correct one of the elements. The operation is done by using the word "negative" followed by the right element.

Example:
User: Paint square in red
System: Paint square in blue
User: *Negative, in red*
System: Paint square in red

The message sent by the dialogue system is not always the proper interpretation of the command. The system may send an error message which points out the nature of the problem.

| | | |
|---|---|---|
| Example: | User: | Paint square in red |
| | System: | The square is already red |

A third kind of message that the dialogue system may send is an additional information request. This happens when the system has not been provided with all the elements which are necessary to execute an order: it thus asks a question to the user.

| | | |
|---|---|---|
| Example: | User: | Paint square |
| | System: | *Paint square in which color ?* |
| | User: | In red |
| | System: | Paint square in red |

The user may cancel the order proposed by the system. Two kinds of cancellation are possible. First cancelling the recognition. In this case, the system will work as if it had never recognized the corresponding command.

| | | |
|---|---|---|
| Example: | User: | Paint square in red |
| | System: | Select the square |
| | User: | *Negative* |
| | System: | What am I to do ? |
| | User: | Paint |
| | System: | Paint what ? |

Cancelling the interpretation is done by means of the word "cancel". It indicates to the system that the order must not be taken into account (e.g. the user changed his mind). Still, the sentence will be kept in the dialogue history.

| | | |
|---|---|---|
| Example: | User: | Paint square in red |
| | System: | Paint square in red |
| | User: | *Cancel* |
| | System: | Cancel |
| | User: | Paint |
| | System: | Paint square in red |

From now on, we will suppose that the command and its parameters have been correctly analyzed. To execute the order, the system asks the user to confirm its interpretation. Three kinds of confirmation have been considered: explicit confirmation, implicit confirmation, absence of confirmation. Each type of order must be associated with a type of confirmation. This labelling depends on the consequences of the execution of the order in the task. If the order is expected to erase data which cannot be recovered, the confirmation should be explicit. If the user can easily recover the previous state, the confirmation may be an absence of confirmation.

One of the strong points of the ROARS dialogue system is to be able to use elements of the previous orders to execute the new one. The interpretation is realized on the basis of the current input together with the general context of the

dialogue. The speaker can make an ellipsis of the command or of one of the parameters. The system will then be entrusted with the recovering of the missing parts. The ellipsis of the command is used to repeat an action on different objects and the ellipsis of the parameter is used to do several actions on the same object.
A cancellation or a correction may be done after an execution. Some predicates are designed to accept it, others are not. The feasibility is linked to the possibilities of the application.

| | | |
|---|---|---|
| Example: | User: | Size 2 |
| | System: | Size 2 |
| | User: | Cancel |
| | | # restauring the initial size # |

| | | |
|---|---|---|
| Example: | User: | Delete file x |
| | System: | Delete file x |
| | User: | Cancel |
| | System: | This order can't be cancelled |

*b) Good Parameterization*

A dialogue system, such as the one described above may be based on two kinds of knowledge sources: static-knowledge source and dynamic-knowledge source.

The static-knowledge source memorizes the models of the different constituents occurring in the dialogue system. We can distinguish:

- The *language model*, that is, the lexical and syntactic description of the sentences expressed by the speaker. It is used at the speech recognition level (syntax and phonetic representation), at the sentence interpretation level and when generating answers to the user.
- The *task model*, which defines the objects which are manipulated by the application, the feasible operations on these objects, the conditions of validity of these operations (coherence management). It also includes all the possible default values which may be suggested to the dialogue system.
- The *dialogue model*, which presents the strategy in use for the sentence interpretation, the knowledge sources which may be referred to (dialogue memory, default values, questions to the user) the order of their interrogation, the possible speaker's interventions (affirmation, confirmation, cancellation, correction) and the system's (request for further information, confirmation request).
- The *user's model* which describes the speakers' specifics regarding the acoustic-phonetic decoding, the lexical and syntactic choices, as well as his knowledge concerning the system capabilities and the task characteristics (not included in ROARS).

The dynamic-knowledge source includes:

- The *state of the task* which influences the interpretation of a sentence in a given direction rather than in another, in order to limit the speaker's words at a given time and to suggest default values.
- The *dialogue history* which allows a contextual interpretation of the sentences, in order to resolve ellipses and anaphoras. It may be divided into two

components the short term memory which keeps the partial interventions of the speaker affirmations, answers, corrections ... and the long term memory which keeps the sentence interpretation.

The general guidelines of the ROARS project are to design a fully integrated system and to validate it upon a realistic application but in no case is it to build an ad hoc system upon a given application. As a consequence, if we wish to have such a system maintained and let it evolve, while at the same time allowing a possible parameterisation of the task and of the language, it is necessary to have a clear idea of the specific knowledge general procedures of the application. This leads us to the definition of a parameterisable system together with specific procedures to help the interface designer towards this parameterisation.

*c) Diapason Development Environment*

The dialogue tools allow the designer to introduce the specific knowledge (which is necessary to the lexical, syntaxic and semantic levels) of the application into the components of the DIAPASON environment.

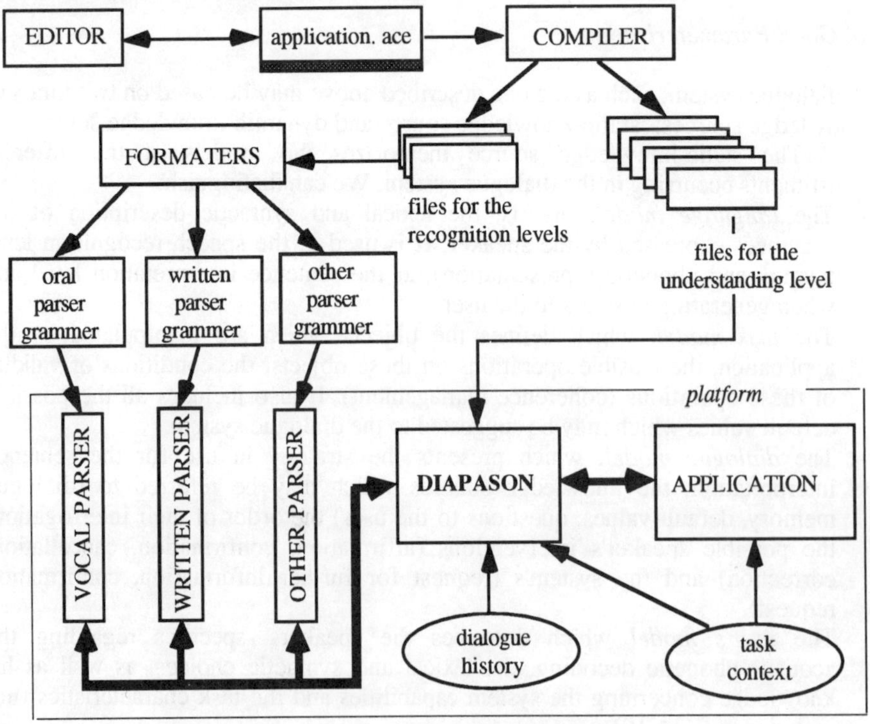


**Fig. 1** : The Diapason environment

- The *development platform* allows a system designer to create and to test a new application without writing a new dialogue manager. The designer has to create the application together with its visualization, and has to define the content of the exchanges between the dialogue system and the application.

- The *syntactic-semantic editor* is the tool which will allow the dialogue system designer to capture the orders of the application to implement. The visual aspect of the order is close to the syntactic-semantic representation defined for DIAPASON. An order is made up of an arrangement of elements (next and alternation), an element is made of words. Information is given at three levels.

At the order level the following global information must be given:

- The axioms from which the order may be derived. Axioms allow the designer to gather orders into groups. At a given time, one or several axioms will be available to the parsers depending on the dialogue and the application context.
- The kind of confirmation associated with the order (explicit, implicit or no confirmation).
- The syntactic order of the elements when it is different from the corresponding semantic order.At the element level the following information must be given:

At the element level the following information must be given:

- the definition of the element in term of words;
- the default value for the element;
- the question to ask when the next element is missing;
- the semantic characteristic of the element (the element has a syntactic occurence or not);
- the generic characteristic of an element (shared by different order or not).

Finally, for a specific arrangement of elements, the designer may give a particular confirmation (different from the global one given at the order level).

The result file contains any information concerning the orders of the application. This file will be analysed by the syntactic-semantic compiler.

- *The syntactic-semantic compiler* provides the whole specific knowledge of the application to the dialogue system as introduced by the editor. From the editor file, the compiler builds two kinds of files those dedicated to the recognition systems and those to the understanding system.
- *The formatters* have to translate the general vocabulary/syntax files from the compiler into files describing the same vocabulary/syntax given in the specific format expected by the parser they are intended for.
  The formatter for the oral parser only generates the description of the syntax of the sentences. The phonetic structure of the lexicon has to be done by the designer of the recognition system.
- *The task context* is very useful for a correct interpretation of the sentences. It eliminates hypotheses which would lead to incoherent interpretations. Furthermore, the task context proposes default values to the dialogue system.
  At the present time, the task context is implemented by a classical data structure and the modifications are made by functions. It thus has to be re-written for each new application. We should study a representation of the task which is more independent of the application.
- *For the development of this environment*, we have defined a small test application which consists of the selection of an object (square, circles, triangle or bottom) in order to change its color and its size [21, 22]. In the case of the ROARS project we have effectively chosen an Air Traffic Control application [1]. This application does not aim at solving the real ATC problem but rather provides a simplified ATC problem. This ROARS demonstration will not be connected to a real ATC environment but only to a simulated input supplied by

the Thomson SDC division. This simplified ATC demonstration is representative of the operator interaction style with the workstation.

## 5. Experimental Results

The work about the ROARS system is still in progress and only some preliminary experimental results have been obtained for a simple (but difficult) task domain: the recognition of two digits numbers (considered as two connected words sentences). The recognizer must be evaluated at two different levels: phonetic feature and sentence.

Evaluation of the phonetic feature results is important for deciding what must be improved in a feature-based recognizer. But it is a rather complex task: because of the coarticulations and lax pronunciation influence there is no clear reference at this level. As a matter of fact in a way the reference itself must be considered as probabilistic. On the other side the phone presence and the values of parameters are also probabilistic. Consequently the comparison between the obtained phones and the reference is uneasy. Here for brevity we only give a summary of the phone detection results.

| | Vowels | Fricatives | Plosives |
|---|---|---|---|
| Undetected Uttered phoneme | 0,5 % | 15 % (mainly [v]) | 8 % |
| Explained Detected phone | 3 % | 42 % | 19 % |
| Extra Detected phone | 3 % | 15 % | 30 % |

It is worth nothing that the extra phone percentages given here correspond to all the extra phone detected in the system. In fact a large part of these extra phones has a low probability of presence. For example when applying a threshold on the scores, these extra phone percentage are reduced down to 7 and 11 % respectively for fricatives and plosive without perceptable change of undetected phoneme percentage.

At the number level a 96% recognition accuracy has been obtained for a test set of 200 numbers ((4 male + 4 female speakers) x 25 number in French). Across the speakers this accuracy varies between 100 % and 85 %. Tests in Spanish are in progress.

Concerning robustness against noise, these results take into account speaker generated non speech events (breathing noise, lip smacking ...) but have been obtained in laboratory conditions. Some modification of the system are in progress for adapting some of the used statistics to the stationnary ambient noise level in order to minimize the noise action an the results. In parallel the modification of speech due to noise (Lombard effect) was also studied in both French and Spanish and some of the statistics will also be modified accordingly.

The understanding and dialogue module has been completed but it is not yet connected to the recognizer. So results are not yet available at this level.

## References


[1] Alinat B. and G. Souvay, "Specification and design of the French Air Trafic Control Demonstration", ROARS Esprit Project, Deliverable 36, 1993.

[2] Bourlard C., "Neural Nets and Hidden Markov Models: review and generalization", Eurospeech 91, pp. 363-368, 1991.

[3] Deng K. Erler K., "Structural design af Hidden Markov Model speech recognizer using multivalued phonetic features: Comparison with segmental speech units", J. Acoust. Soc. Am. 92 (6), pp. 3058-3067, Dec 1992.

[4] Fant C., "Speech research in perspective", Speech Communication 9, pp. 171-176, 1990.

[5] Frimpong-Ansah D., B. Pearce, W.J. Holmes, N.G. Dixon, "A stochastic/feature based recognizer and its training algorithm", Proc. ICASSP-89, pp. 401-404, 1989.

[6] Haeb-Umbach H., H. Ney, "Linear discriminant analysis for improved large vocabulary continuous speech recognition", ICASSP - 92, pp. I-13, I-16, 1992.

[7] Huttenlocher V., W. Zue, "A model of lexical access from partial phonetic information", Proc. ICASSP-84, paper 26.4, 1984.

[8] Klatt P., "Review of the ARPA speech understanding project", Acoust. Soc. Am. 62 (6), December 1977, pp. 1345-1366, 1977.

[9] Liberman A.M et al., "Perception of the speech code", Psychol. review, vol. 74, n°6, pp. 431-461, Nov. 1967.

[10] Lindblom D., "On the teleological nature of speech processes", Speech Communication 2, pp. 155-158, 1983.

[11] Lee, H.W. Hon, R. Reddy, "An overview of the SPHINX speech recognition system", IEEE Trans. ASSP vol. 38, n°1, pp. 35-45, Jan 1990.

[12] Levinson S.E., "Structural methods in automatic speech recognition", Proc. IEEE, vol. 73, n°11, pp. 1625-1650, Nov 1985.

[13] Meng V., W. Zue, "Signal representation comparison for phonetic classification", Proc. ICASSP-91, pp. 285-288, 1991.

[14] Ney G., "A comparative study of two search strategies for connected word recognition: dynamic programming and heuristic search" IEEE Trans. Pattern Analysis and Machine Intelligence, vol 14, n°5, pp. 586-595, May 1992.

[15] Pallett J., G. Fiscus, W.M. Fisher, J.J. Garofolo, "Benchmark tests for the DARPA spoken language program", ARPA Human language technology workshop, March 1993

[16] Phillips W., V. Zue, "Automatic discovery of acoustic measurements for phonetic classification", Proc. ICSLP-92, pp. 795-798, 1992.

[17] Pierrel S., "Dialogue oral homme-machine", (ed.) Hermes, 240 pages, Paris, 1987.

[18] Pierrel S., "Aspects of Man-Machine voice dialogue", in Fundamentals in Computer Understanding, J.P. Haton (ed.), Cambridge University Press, pp. 249-274, 1987.

[19] Ruske A., B. Plannerer, T. Schultz, "Stockastic modeling of syllable based units for continuous speech recognition", Proc. ICS-LP-92, pp. 1503-1506, 1992.

[20] Russel J., K. Moore, "Explicit modelling of state occupancy in Hidden Markov models for automatic speech recognition", Proc. ICASSP-85, pp. 5-9, 1985.

[21] Souvay J., M. Pierrel, P. Druart, "Technical report on understanding and language tools", ROARS Esprit Project, Deliverable 35, 1992.

[22] Souvay J., and P. Druart, "ACE : Applications Creation Editor", ROARS Esprit Project, Deliverable 36, 1993.

[23] Stevens K.N,, S.Y. Manuel, S. Shattuck-Hufnagel, S. Lin, Proc. ICSLP-92, pp. 49-502, 1992.

[24] Taylor M., D.A. Wangh, "Principles for integrating voice I/O in a complex interface", AGARD conference, May 1992

[25] Zue W., L.F. Lamel,"An expert spectrogram reader: a knowledge-based approach to speech recognition", Proc. ICASSP-86, paper 23.2, 1986.

[26] Zue W., J. Glass, D. Goodine, M. Philipps, S. Seneff, "The SUMMIT speech recognition system: Phonological modelling and lexical access", ICASSP-90, pp. 49-52, 1990.

# POLYGLOT Project: Hybrid System NN/HMM for continuous Speech Recognition

Laurence Devillers and Christian Dugast *
LIMSI-CNRS, BP133, 91403 Orsay Cedex, France
* Philips Research Laboratories, Postfach 1980, 5100 Aachen, Germany

## Abstract

This paper concerns the research on hybrid systems carried out by the LIMSI and Philips laboratories during ESPRIT Project 2104 - Polyglot "A multilingual system for text to speech and speech to text" and pursued after the end of this project. Hybrid systems, using Hidden Markov Models (HMMs) and Neural Networks (NNs) are designed to combine the qualities of each model. We present an experimental study of hybrid systems combining Time Delay Neural Networks (TDNNs) developed by LIMSI and Continuous mixture densities HMMs (CHMMs) developed by Philips. The aim of this study was to assess the discriminative power of NNs in improving the performance of temporal decoders like state-of-the-art CHMMs.

The innovation of the hybrid TDNN/CHMM system proposed here lies in the connectionnist device in form of a hierarchical tree of TDNNs and in the way the two constituents, TDNN and CHMM, interact with each other. The outputs of the TDNNs are combined with the probabilities issued of the CHMMs during the recognition phase. The recognition rates obtained on a part of DARPA Resource Management speaker dependent database, show the complementarity of these approaches since we notably improved (from 15% to 20%) performances of the state-of-the-art CHMM systems. The work done during this contract has furnished good performance results with hybrid systems and showed real potential for neural networks used in cooperation with HMMs.

## 1. Introduction

Neural Networks (NNs) are now widely used in speech recognition. If state-of-the-art speech recognition systems are based on Hidden Markov Models (HMMs), NNs possess some qualities such as a segmental discriminative power that most HMM based systems do not possess.

The principal interest of NNs stems from the use of different training criteria together with highly connected structures that do not require any statistical assumption related to the underlying process. As opposed to the conventional Maximum Likelihood Estimation (MLE) applied in most Hidden Markov Model (HMM) based systems, NNs are generally trained under some discriminative criterion such as the Mean Squared Error (MSE). Nevertheless, most neural networks possess some major drawbacks, such as their immense need for computation time during the learning phase, their lack of capability to cope with temporal distorsions, as well as their incapacity to integrate different levels of knowledge (lexical, syntactical...) with the same formalism.

Hybrid systems are designed to try to combine the advantages of each system. In our case, these advantages are the static classification ability of NNs and the temporal alignment ability and the power to deal with low and high-level sentence decoding of HMMs. An experimental study is reported that investigates the contribution of a modular architecture of NNs from the class of the Time Delay Neural Network (TDNN) trained under MSE [1] to Continuous mixture density HMM (CHMM) trained under MLE [2]. The aim of this work is to present a hybrid connectionist/Markov model recognizer with a simple design, running on a mono-processor computer, which improves the performances of a state-of-the-art CHMM system for large vocabulary continuous speech recognition.

Recently several papers have been published describing attempts at using Neural Networks (NNs) in conjunction with Dynamic Programming (DP) or with the Hidden Markov Models (HMMs) time-alignment framework. Most of them propose theoretical issues [3] but until now, on large databases, few results have been obtained showing better performance compared to state-of-the-art HMMs.

Two principal classes of hybrid systems can be distinguished, based on how the NNs are integrated in the HMM system. NNs can be used as pre-processors of HMMs with or without global optimization of both systems, i.e. embedded models [4][5] or sequential learning of the two systems [6][7]. NNs can also be used as post-processors of HMMs [8][9]. The first hybrid system proposed corresponds to the first class described above and combines HMMs and NNs in a sequential way. A second system has been developed to prove the complementarity of the training criteria of both TDNN and HMM. This approach, which we have called "combined system", consists of a linear combination of HMM and NN probabilities during the recognition phase. The proposed system is closely related to the one presented by Renals in [10]. The most noticeable difference concerns the NN architecture used.

An obvious bottleneck in NN systems is the huge computing power required for training. Therefore, hybrid systems applied to large databases are usually implemented on multi-processor computers (for example, 5-Ring Array Processors or 64 transputers in [6][10][11]). To cope with this CPU requirement, we proposed a modular architecture of hierarchically ordered TDNNs running on a 20-MIPS workstation. This allows the training process to be divided into sub-tasks corresponding to sub-sets of phonemes.

TDNNs, by definition, do not rely on a time-alignement concept. This can be solved by integrating the TDNN in a Viterbi framework [12][13]. The TDNN output scores are identified after appropriate normalization as posterior probabilities of the output labels [14]. Accordingly, after being divided by the a priori probabilities, the normalized output scores can be interpreted as emission probabilities from an equivalent HMM state [10][12]. This system will be called "integrated TDNN system". In this way, a consistent framework is achieved that permits direct comparison of the TDNN/MSE pair with the HMM/MLE pair.

Furthermore, it becomes easy to combine the scores resulting from each system, the normalized output scores of an integrated TDNN with the CHMM emission probabilities. This combined system has led to improve recognition performance observed with respect to a state-of-the-art HMM system on the DARPA Resource Management speaker-dependent database [15].

Three recognition systems will be presented in the next sections: the first hybrid system called "integrated hierarchical TDNN", the second hybrid system called "combined system" and a CHMM-based system. All three systems share a common acoustic analysis and decoding procedure, based on the same HMM topology. This permits comparison of the three systems solely on the training methods discussed.

The organization of the paper is as follows. In Section 2 we propose a hierarchical structure of TDNNs which is trainable on a workstation. We discuss its integration in a Viterbi-framework in Section 3. In Section 4 we briefly describe the CHMM. Section 5 will be devoted to the combination of TDNN and CHMM. Finally, Section 6 and 7 presents experiments and conclusion.

## 2. TDNN

Use of TDNNs for speech recognition were introduced by Waibel [16]. Compared to a Multi-Layer Perceptron (MLP) [17], the TDNN architecture offers the advantage of reducing the number of weighted connections and has the interesting property of time translation invariance. In contrast to Recurrent Networks (RN) which employ internal feedback to model context dependency, TDNNs use a fixed length contextual input window to model dynamics of speech patterns. This simplifies the implementation of the gradient descent algorithm.

The design of the TDNN used is quite similar to the basic one proposed by Waibel. However, in our case, the TDNN is only composed of three layers without a last fully-connected layer. The dimension of the last layer also corresponds to the number of labels to discriminate. But, the input window was 10ms time-shifted on the frame sequence, so the network produced an output vector every 10ms. The input patterns are sequences of spectral vectors and the output vectors correspond to the phonetic label scores.

In our design, the width of the input window has been set to 70ms of speech for the generation of an output vector, i.e. the width of the contextual window is 30ms for the TDNN first layer and 50ms for the second one. This 70ms window corresponds to the average phone length in the DARPA RM database. The segmentation of the training set that provides the TDNN with initial targets has been generated by the continuous HMM system presented in this paper (with context-independent models).

The training of TDNNs was done with an error back-propagation algorithm with the Mean Squared Error criterion. The TANH sigmoid function is applied after linear combination of the weights. A stochastic gradient descent method was used. This method has been shown to be faster than a deterministic gradient [18]; After one cycle, i.e. one presentation of a pattern for each label, the parameters were updated. Futhermore, in order to avoid overtraining, we used cross-validation during training [12].

## 2.1 Hierarchical architecture of TDNNs

The performance of a training method is given by its generalization power when dealing with unknown data (or test set). The larger the database, the more complex the training. Training has to deal with a compromise between reliability and cost. In the case of large databases, a global network is hardly trainable on a standard computer without parallel processors. Modular architectures are a solution to train large databases. Instead of having a large network that captures all the regions of the feature space, we have built a modular architecture of TDNNs [19].

The modularity has been obtained by dividing the phoneme set into broad-classes of phonemes. For each broadclass, a network (hereafter called sub-network) is trained to discriminate the phonemes of the broadclass, as such, amongst one another. The organization into sub-networks can be seen as bringing in a priori knowledge or constraints about likely phone confusions. In addition to these sub-networks, a network is trained to discriminate the broad-classes between broadclasses.

9 broadclasses of phonemes were defined [7][13]. The different consonant classes have been determined by articulation mode: voiced plosives, unvoiced plosives, voiced fricatives, unvoiced fricatives, glides and nasals. The position of the formants, F1, F2, has been used to distinguish among three different vowel classes corresponding to the extremes of the vocalic triangle. All sub-nets are composed of three layers where the dimension of the last one corresponds to the number of labels to discriminate.

The modular architecture described can be compared to a tree [1], the root being the broadclass network, the leaves being the specialized sub-networks. The broadclass network has the labels of each sub-net of phones as outputs. This network has the role of connecting the sub-networks together. We now have a two-step classifier, first deciding among broadclasses, then deciding within a broadclass.

The network output scores are identified after appropriate normalization as posterior probabilities of the output labels [14]. Once the different networks have been trained, integration of the output scores is straightforward: the phoneme posterior probabilities within a broadclass have to be multiplied by their corresponding broadclass posterior probabilities:

$$P(\phi|x_t) = P_B(K|x_t) \times P_K(\phi|K, x_t) \tag{1}$$

where $P_B(K|x_t)$ denotes the a posteriori probability of broadclass $K$ given the observed $x_t$ in the broadclass network $B$ and $P_K(\phi|K, x_t)$ the a posteriori probability of phoneme $\phi$ given the observed $x_t$ in the sub-network, $K$.

# 3. Integrated TDNN: I_TDNN

TDNN is a powerful classifier for static patterns. But as such it does not rely on a time-alignment concept. This can be solved by integrating the TDNN in a

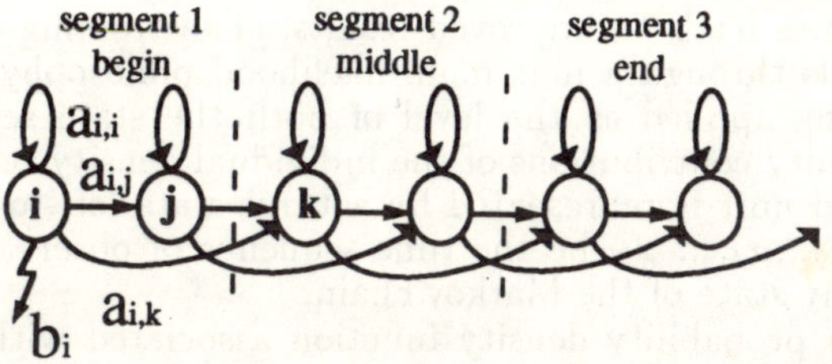


Figure 1: Topology of a Hidden Markov Model: *The emission probability* $b_i$ *of state i is tied over the 2 states of the segment.*

Viterbi framework [13]. The TDNN network is trained to generate phoneme-like labels. Suppose we must discriminate n phonemes. Every 10 ms, we present the HMM with an n-dimensional vector whose elements are activation values of the n TDNN output units.

The network output scores are identified after appropriate normalization as posterior probabilities of the output labels, $P(\phi|x_t)$. Accordingly, after dividing by the a priori probabilities, $P(\phi)$ , the normalized output scores can be interpreted as emission probabilities from an equivalent HMM state [10][12].

In the case of the TDNN architecture, a phoneme is modeled with a unique network output. But it is obvious that the network acts differently at the beginning of a phonetic segment than at the end. A temporal model differentiating between beginning, middle and end of a phoneme would be helpful, see Fig. 1. A confusion matrix is evaluated during a Viterbi-forced time-alignment procedure. Thus, the probability of each state results in the multiplication of the TDNN emission probability by the confusion probability $C(\phi_{best}|s,\phi)$ of being in state $s$ (begin, middle or end) of the phonetic model of $\phi$ for the phoneme $\phi_{best}$ corresponding of the best score to the TDNN outputs. This hybrid system will be called $I\_TDNN$.

$$P(x_t|s) = \frac{P(\phi|x_t)}{P(\phi)} \times C(\phi_{best}|s,\phi) \qquad (2)$$

The same topology, see Fig. 1 will be used in the CHMM system in order to allow easy combination of the integrated TDNN and the CHMM.

## 4. Continuous Density HMM: CHMM

This section gives a brief description of the baseline system that relies on continuous mixture density HMM's of triphones. Linear Discriminant Analysis (LDA) is used as a pre-processing step. The basic idea of linear discriminant analysis is to find a linear transformation such that the class separability is increased [14]. According to a previous study [20], classes are defined at the level of context-dependent phoneme states and the affiliation of each training pattern is automatically obtained as a by-product of standard HMM training done in the original acoustic space.

Concerning the acoustic features, the inclusion of time differences appears very important prior to the transformation and moreover, adjoining several centi-second frames leads to improved results. The training of the HMM parameters proceeds through a maximum likelihood philosophy, the Viterbi approximation being applied at the level of both the state sequences and the emission probability contributions of the individual density components.

Each subword unit is represented by a three-state left-to-right HMM (see Fig. 1). Let $x_1, ..., x_t, ..., x_N$ be the time sequence of observation vectors and $s = 1, ..., S$ be any state of the Markov chain.

The emission probability density function associated with each state $s$ is assumed to be of the form [21]:

$$Q(x_t|s, \Theta_s) = \sum_{k=1}^{K(s)} w_{k,s}\ b_k(x_t|s, \theta_{k,s}) \ , \qquad (3)$$

where each mixture component $b_k(.|.)$ is a unimodal density with parameter vector $\theta_{k,s}$ (e.g. mean and covariance), $w_{k,s}$ are the mixture weights subjected to stochastic constraints and $K(s)$ is the number of component densities. In the present case, Laplacian-type densities have been implemented. The vector of absolute deviations has been pooled over all mixtures and states while the location vector has been treated specifically for each mixture component.

Triphones have been selected on the basis of their number of occurrences in the training script: 134 short function word triphones and 635 triphones were selected in addition to the 46 phoneme-like units, making a total of 815 models [2].

## 5. Combined System: I_TDNN + CHMM

This section describes a hybrid system which linearly combines the output scores of I_TDNN system with the probabilities of CHMM system.

By "combined system", we mean that a TDNN and a continuous HMM are trained separately: in our case the TDNN hierarchical structure is integrated in an HMM formalism (as in Section 3) and the emission probabilities of the integrated TDNN are linearly combined with those of the CHMM from Section 4.

The combination rule for a state $s$ is as follows:

$$\log P_{comb}(x_t|s) = \alpha \times \log P(x_t|s) + (1-\alpha) \times \log Q(x_t|s) \qquad (4)$$

where $P(x_t|s)$ corresponds to the emission probability given by the I_TDNN (equation 2) and $Q(x_t|s)$ corresponds to the CHMM (equation 3) emission probability. The parameter $\alpha$ is chosen to be positive and less than one after appropriate scaling.

## 6. Experiments

Experiments were run on the speaker-dependent part of the DARPA Naval Resource Management (RM1) task [22]. The vocabulary size is 991 words. The training set is composed of 600 sentences making a total of 20 minutes of speech. The linguistic content of the test sentences is different from speaker to speaker. Three speakers were selected for the tests: JWS0, BEF0 and CMR0, two men and one woman. Exactly the same testing conditions were followed during the different experiments presented in this paper so that the results can be compared. The same recognition system has been used for all trained models presented here. Acoustic analysis and decoding are common to all experiments, only the evaluation of the parameters has been carried out according to the training criteria and structures discussed here.

## 6.1 Acoustic Analysis

The acoustic signal is low-pass filtered and digitized with a sampling frequency of 16 kHz. A 512-point FFT is performed every 10 ms and 30 cepstrally smoothed logarithmic intensities are sampled in the frequency range from 200 Hz to 6400 Hz, roughly corresponding to a Mel-frequency scale. Each acoustic vector $y(t)$ is further augmented by slope and curvature information over the time axis, following:

$$x_t = \begin{bmatrix} y(t) \\ y'(t) \\ y''(t) \end{bmatrix} \approx \begin{bmatrix} y(t) \\ y(t) - y(t-T) \\ y(t+T) - 2y(t) + y(t-T) \end{bmatrix} \quad (5)$$

The time delay $T$ for computing the differences is 30 ms. For the slope and curvature of the 30 spectral intensities, pairs of adjacent channels are averaged so that the total number of components is 63. This will be referred to as "slope-curvature" vector. A "short vector" has been obtained by taking only every other point along the frequency axis. These 15 spectral intensities are then in turn appended with their respective slope values together with the average energy value and its first and second derivatives, leading to 33 components in all.

## 6.2 Time Synchronous Decoding

The recognition procedure progresses by searching for the most likely state sequence, this sequence being given by Fig. 1 for a phoneme-like unit. These units are concatenated to build words. With a 1,000-word lexicon, the potential search space is relatively manageable without having to resort to particular techniques like lexical tree-organization and phoneme look-ahead [23]. Therefore, the recognition has been accomplished with a data-driven organization of the Viterbi beam search algorithm [24], all lexical and syntactical constraints being dynamically expanded. The emission probability values are computed on demand according to the estimation criterion being tested (See equation 3 for CHMM, equation 1 for integrated-TDNN and equation 4 for the combined system).

## 6.3 Results

After having briefly described the database on which experiments were run, we will report on key-features which lead to improvements of a TDNN (without any time alignment concept). Next, results for the integrated TDNN system and the combination of integrated TDNNs with HMMs will be presented.

Experiments with TDNNS were made on different feature space vectors: the spectral values alone without derivatives, the reduced form of the vector (33 coefficients, see Section 6.1) and the complete form (63 coefficients). It appeared that derivatives are of importance for TDNNs. The reduced form of the vector which gave good results with CHMM is not satisfying here. Furthermore, to avoid "freezing" the connection weights when output reaches maximal activity of $-1$ or $+1$, the target outputs were chosen at 0.9 and $-0.9$. It has been observed that the frame error rates are greatly improved, around 30% better, at expense of CPU time now two to three times longer with this training.

Results of the CHMM system are discussed in detail in [2]. The main improvements achieved with CHMM on the three speakers selected are summarized in Table 1. Table 2 gives detailed results of the best CHMM system configuration for the three selected speakers.

Table 1 gives the average results obtained on three speakers with the combined I_TDNN + CHMM system. First, appropriate scaling of the log probabilities had to be ensured in order to combine the systems. The value of $\alpha$ (equation 4) has been empirically varied between 0.05 and 0.50 and an optimal value of 0.20 has been computed. More tests will be necessary in order to find a better fit between both probabilities. For example a deleted interpolation technique can be used to automatically define them.

Table 1: *Average word error rate (WER) in the Word-Pair grammar case when combining three different CHMM systems with the same Integrated HMM which gives 6% WER, over the three speakers on 100 development test set sentences.*

| CHMM | | CHMM + I_TDNN |
|---|---|---|
| **Variant** | **WER** | **WER** |
| 47 CI Phones | 3.2% | 2.5% |
| + 769 CD Phones | 2.2% | 1.8% |
| + LDA | 2.0% | 1.7% |

The I_TDNN system is combined with different configurations of the CHMM system: a base-line system with only 47 context independent models (CI), then with an addition of 769 context dependent (CD) phones and the last one including a linear discriminant analysis (LDA) before modeling the 769 + 47 phones. The latter configuration gives state-of-the-art results. Despite its rather low accuracy, the I_TDNN hybrid system improves recognition results systematically when combining it with a CHMM. Relative improvement ranging from 20% to 15% with respect to the CHMM is observed. Table 2 gives detailed results per speaker.

For each of the speakers a similar improvement has been observed. Recovered errors have been mainly observed on word substitutions such as (from/for), (the/all), (their/the), (of/two)... Furthermore, small words which were previously deleted are recovered, such as the word "the" (recovered four times).

Table 2: *Error rates per speaker for the Integrated TDNN, Continuous HMM and combination of both, in the Word-Pair grammar case.*

| Speaker | I_TDNN | CHMM | I_TDNN + CHMM |
|---|---|---|---|
| JWS0 | 4.7% | 2.1% | 1.8% |
| CMR0 | 4.5% | 2.7% | 2.3% |
| BEF0 | 8.9% | 1.1% | 1.0% |
| **Average** | **6.0%** | **2.0%** | **1.7%** |

These examples show that the neural networks have coded information that is complementary to CHMMs. The combination of both systems allows recovery of many errors with the discriminative information given by the NNs. To conclude, the word error rate of a state-of-the-art system could be relatively reduced by 15% to 20%. These results are encouraging for cooperation of both systems. The critical problem is still the training time of the NNs on a monoprocessor computer. On a 20 MIPS computer, the training time of the global structure TDNN is around one month instead of one night for CHMMs. On the contrary, for recognition, on a 20 MIPS machine, the NN probabilities are computed in real-time whereas the CHMM emissions are evaluated in four times real-time. The combination of both probabilities takes five times real-time.

## 7. Conclusion

We have investigated hybrid systems composed of TDNNs and HMMs and conducted experiments on a large database with two different types of cooperation for these techniques, an "integrated TDNN system" and a "combined system". A consistent framework has been achieved that allows to compare directly the integrated TDNN system to the CHMM system. Futhermore, it allows a straightforward combination of the probabilities resulting from each system.

The combined system gave impressively good results compared to the results from the integrated TDNN system. What is decisive here is the use of a different training scheme, allowing extraction of other classification characteristics that are complementary to the first ones. In theory, whatever training criterion may be used, MLE or MSE, the same word error rate should be reached if enough training data is available. For large vocabulary continuous speech recognition, this is never reached. The idea of combining two different criteria, each of them extracting different characteristics of the feature space, is a way to cope with the insufficient training data problem for smoothing the emission probabilities obtained during training.

The problem inherent to the training of large databases with NNs has been partly solved by using a modular architure of sub-networks. The architecture of hierarchically ordered TDNNs developed in our hybrid systems is very simple and has been trained without a parallel processing computer contrary to most of the known results [6][11][10] in this field. Despite of the sub-optimality of this neural architecture, we have improved the results obtained with state-of-the-art HMMs by combining probabilities issued from HMMs and TDNNs during recognition. The work done during this contract has furnished good performance results with hybrid systems and showed real potential for neural networks used in cooperation with HMMs.

## References


1. L. Devillers, "Continuous Speech Recognition using a Hybrid System combining Neural Networks and Hidden Markov Models", Ph.D. thesis (in french), Paris-South University, Orsay France, 1992.
2. X. Aubert, R. Haeb-Umbach, H. Ney, "Continuous Mixture Densities and Linear Discriminant Analysis for Improved Context-Dependent Acoustic Models", *Proc. ICASSP'93*, Vol II-648, Mineapolis, 1993.
3. J.S. Bridle, "Training Stochastic Model Recognition Algorithms as Networks can Lead to Maximum Mutual Information Estimation of Parameters", Advances in Neural Information, 1990.
4. P. Haffner, "Connectionist Word-Level Classification in Speech Recognition", *Proc. ICASSP'92*, Vol. I-621, San Francisco, CA, 1992.
5. M. Franzini, K.F. Lee, A. Waibel, "Connectionist Viterbi Training: a New Hybrid Method for Continuous-Speech Recognition", *Proc. ICASSP'90*, pp. 425-428, Albuquerque, NM, 1990.
6. H. Bourlard, N. Morgan, Ch. Wooters, S. Renals, "CDNN: a Context Dependent Neural Network for Continuous-Speech Recognition", *Proc. ICASSP'92*, Vol. II-349, San Francisco, CA, 1992.
7. Ch. Dugast, L. Devillers, "Incorporating Acoustic-Phonetic Knowledge in Hybrid TDNN/HMM Frameworks", *Proc. ICASSP'92*, Vol. I-421, San Francisco, CA, 1992.
8. S. Austin, G. Zavaliagkos, J. Makhoul, R. Schwartz, "Speech Recognition using Segmental Neural Nets", *Proc. ICASSP'92*, Vol. I-625, San Francisco, CA, 1992.
9. D. Boiteau, P. Haffner, "Connectionist Segmental Post-processing of the N-best Solutions in Isolated and Connected Word Recognition Task", *Proc. Eurospeech'93*, Vol. III-1933, Berlin, Germany, 1993.
10. S. Renals, N. Morgan, M. Cohen, H. Franco, "Connectionist Probability Estimation in the Decipher Speech Recognition System", *Proc. ICASSP'92*, Vol. I-601, San Francisco, CA, 1992.
11. A. Robinson, "A Real-Time Recurrent Error Propagation Network Word Recognition System", *Proc. ICASSP'92*, Vol. I-617, San Francisco, CA, 1992.
12. H. Bourlard, N. Morgan, Ch. Wooters, "Connectionist Approaches to the Use of Markov Models for Speech Recognition", Advances in Neural Information Processing Systems 3, Morgan Kaufman, 1991.
13. L. Devillers, Ch. Dugast, "Comparison of Continuous Mixture Densities and TDNN in a Viterbi-Framework: Experiment on Speaker Dependent DARPA RM1", *Proc. Eurospeech'91*, pp. 991-994, Genova, Italy, 1991.

14. R.O. Duda, P.E. Hart, "Pattern Classification and Scene Analysis", Wiley-Interscience Publication, p. 155, 1973.
15. L. Devillers, Ch. Dugast, "Combination of Training Criteria to Improve Continuous Speech Recognition", *Proc. Eurospeech'93*, Vol. III-2211, Berlin, Germany, 1993.
16. A. Waibel, T. Hanazawa, G. Hinton, K. Shikano, K. Lang, "Phoneme Recognition using Time Delay Neural Networks", IEEE Trans ASSP, 1989.
17. D.R. Hush, B.G. Horne, "Progress in Supervised Neural Networks: What's New Since Lippmann?", IEEE signal processing magazine, january 1993.
18. A. Benveniste, M. Metivier, P. Priouret, "Algorithmes adaptatifs et approximations stochastiques", édition Masson, France, 1987.
19. A. Waibel, "Connectionist Glue: Modular Design of Neural Speech Systems". Proceedings of the 1988 Connectionist Models Summer School, Carnegie Mellon University, pp. 417-421, 1988.
20. R. Haeb-Umbach, H. Ney, "Linear Discriminant Analysis for Improved Large-Vocabulary Continuous-Speech Recognition", *Proc. ICASSP'92*, Vol. I-13, San Francisco, CA, 1992.
21. L.R. Rabiner, B.H. Juang, S.E. Levinson, M.M. Sondhi, "Recognition of Isolated Digits Using HMMs with Continuous Mixture Densities", AT&T Tech. J, Vol.64, No.6, pp 1211-1234, 1985.
22. P.J. Price, W. Fisher, J. Bernstein, D. Pallett, "A Database for Continuous-Speech Recognition in a 1000-word Domain", *Proc. ICASSP'88*, pp. 651-654, New-York, NY, 1988.
23. H. Ney, R. Haeb-Umbach, B.-H. Tran, M. Oerder, "Improvements in Beam Search for 10000-Word Continuous-Speech Recognition", *Proc. ICASSP'92*, Vol. I-9, San Francisco, CA, 1992.
24. H. Ney, D. Mergel, A. Noll, A. Paeseler, "A Data Driven Organization of the Dynamic Programming Beam Search for Continuous-Speech Recognition", *Proc. ICASSP'87*, Vol II-833, Dallas, TX, 1987.

# Principles and Applications of the VINICS Continuous-Speech Recognition System

Yifan Gong and Jean-Paul Haton
RIFA Group
CRIN / CNRS, INRIA Lorraine
BP 239, F-54506 Vandoeuvre, France

**Abstract**

VINICS system is based on a new approach to phoneme-based continuous speech recognition, in which a time function of the plausibility of observing each phoneme (*spotting result*) is given. We introduce a criterion for best sentence, related to the sum of plausibilities of individual symbols composing the sentence. This sum is maximized in terms of the transition between successive symbols and of the duration probability of each symbol. The phoneme plausibilities are estimated using either an artificial neural network vectorial interpolation technique or a stochastic trajectory model. Validation experiments are reported and several applications of the system are described. On-going works to enhance the system performance are also outlined.

# 1 Introduction

Recently, recognition techniques which *spot* symbols in continuous speech have received increasing attention. We mean by symbols the elementary recognition units of a recognition system, e.g. phonemes or words. These techniques give at each time slot the plausibility of each phoneme with respect to the speech input, without specifying the beginning and ending points. This approach provides new potentiality for the integration of context information in the recognition process.

The plausibility is also called the likelihood of a symbol, or the similarity between the input speech and the acoustic image of a reference symbol. Typically, techniques for instantaneous symbol plausibility estimation are based either on reference comparison [12, 29, 8], and more recently artificial neural networks [28, 7, 5, 32], or some other theories such as hidden Markov models.

Although the estimation of plausibility can be very powerful, the lack of methods to make use of them efficiently limits their application. Traditionally, a time-alignment procedure is used for computing most plausible utterances, based either on Viterbi algorithm [1, 2] or on dynamic time warping [24] to determine the best time-warped symbol sequence.

In this paper, we formulate the continuous speech recognition problem as the maximization of the plausibility of observing component phoneme symbols. This maximization is performed over all possible transition times between symbols, taking into account the duration probability of each symbol. *VINICS*, our experimental system based on this principle, has achieved an average sentence recognition rate of 95% on a speaker-dependent, continuous speech recognition application, and a word recognition rate of 99.9% for French alphabet recognition.

In section 2 we give a formulation of the recognition technique. Section 3 presents the *VINICS* system. A description of several application of the system is given in section 4. In section 5 some on-going works are outlined.

# 2 Recognition techniques

## 2.1 Introduction

We first formulate in subsection 2.2 the sentence recognition based on the plausibilities of individual phonemes and then in subsection 2.3 we describe two methods to compute the phoneme plausibilities.

## 2.2 Sentence recognition

### 2.2.1 Plausibility of a sentence

The recognition of a sentence consists in evaluating a sum of plausibilities, with explicit duration constraints. From a recognition point of view, a sentence is a sequence of phoneme symbols. Let

$$\mathbb{P} \triangleq \{s_1, s_2, \ldots, s_H\}$$

be a set of $H$ symbols representing phonemes. Let $\mathbb{F}$ be the set of all grammatical sentences defined as concatenation of symbols in $\mathbb{P}$. A particular sentence $\omega \in \mathbb{F}$ is composed of $L(\omega)$ symbols:

$$\omega \triangleq a_0, a_1, ...a_h, ...a_{L(\omega)-1}, \ \forall h, \ a_h \in \mathbb{P}$$

Notice that for different $h$, $a_h$ may be the same, e.g. the same phoneme may appear several times in a sentence. Let $N$ be the number of analysis frames of an utterance. We suppose that, using a suitable model, the plausibility of the symbols $a_h$ at time slot $n$ is available:

$$\mu_{n,a_h}, \ 0 \leq n < N, 0 \leq h < L.$$

The duration of a symbol is considered as a random variable $\tau$, and the probability of symbol $a_h$ with duration $\tau = d$ is noted as $p_h(d)$. Let $t_h$ be a time slot index of the vector sequence corresponding to the symbol $a_h$. We introduce the cumulated plausibility for $a_h$, which is the sum of plausibilities cumulated for $a_h$ from $t_h$ to $t_{h+1} - 1$, weighted by the corresponding duration probability:

$$q(h) = p_h(t_{h+1} - t_h) \sum_{t_h \leq n < t_{h+1}} \mu_{n,a_h} \tag{1}$$

Given a test utterance of $N$ vectors, $t_h$'s are unknown quantities except $t_0 = 0$ and $t_{L(\omega)} = N$.

The plausibility of the sentence is defined as the normalized non-overlapping sum of cumulated plausibility of its composing symbols:

$$\theta(\omega | t_0, t_1, ...t_{L(\omega)-1}) = \frac{1}{N} \sum_{0 \leq h < L(\omega)} q(h) =$$

$$\frac{1}{N} \sum_{0 \leq h < L(\omega)} \left[ p_h(t_{h+1} - t_h) \sum_{t_h \leq n < t_{h+1}} \mu_{n,a_h} \right] \tag{2}$$

The value range of $\theta$ is between 0 and 1. The plausibility of the sentence is therefore a function of $t_h, \forall h$. We optimize $t_h$'s so that $\theta(\omega)$ is maximized:

$$\Theta(\omega) = \max_{t_0, t_1, ...t_{L(\omega)-1}} \theta(\omega | t_0, t_1, ...t_{L(\omega)-1}) \tag{3}$$

Sentence recognition consists in evaluating the maximized cumulated plausibility for all possible sentences, and in assigning the most plausible sentence as the recognized sentence $\hat{\omega}$:

$$\hat{\omega} = \operatorname*{argmax}_{\omega \in \mathbb{F}} \Theta(\omega) \tag{4}$$

For simplicity, we will intentionally omit $(\omega)$ in $L(\omega)$, $\theta(\omega)$ and $\Theta(\omega)$ whenever such a use does not introduce an ambiguity.

### 2.2.2 Computation of sentence plausibility

We develop the algorithm for solving Eq-3 efficiently. We can compute the plausibility cumulated until the $j^{th}$ symbol $\Xi(j)$, as:

$$\Xi(j) = \sum_{0 \leq h < j-1} \left[ p_h(t_{h+1} - t_h) \sum_{t_h \leq n < t_{h+1}} \mu_{n,a_h} \right] + p_j(t_{j+1} - t_j) \sum_{t_j \leq n < t_{j+1}} \mu_{n,a_j} \tag{5}$$

Or, recursively:

$$\Xi(j) = \Xi(j-1) + p_j(t_{j+1} - t_j) \sum_{t_j \leq n < t_{j+1}} \mu_{n,a_j}, \quad 0 \leq j < L \tag{6}$$

We have

$$\theta = \frac{\Xi(L-1)}{N}.$$

In Eq-6 $t_h, t_{h+1}$ are unknown, denoted respectively by $k$ and $l$. To determine $t_h, \forall h$, a search is performed over $k$. We introduce a function of $l$ and $j$:

$$\Pi(l,j) = \max_{0 \leq k < l} \{\Pi(k, j-1) + p_j(l-k) \sum_{k \leq n < l} \mu_{n,a_j}\} \quad 0 \leq l \leq N, 0 \leq j < L \tag{7}$$

We have

$$\max_{t_0, t_1, \ldots t_j} \Xi(j) = \Pi(N, j).$$

In [8, 13] another efficient algorithm for Eq-3 was proposed, based on the high plausibility region of the plausibility functions and capable of varying the search density according to input speech variation.

## 2.3 Plausibility estimation

### 2.3.1 Introduction

An important factor for accurate speech recognition based on the just presented formulation is the design of an accurate system for computing the phoneme plausibility function $\mu$. We will now present two different methods, respectively based on non-linear vectorial interpolation [7] and on stochastic trajectory models [11].

### 2.3.2 Non-linear vectorial interpolation

We assume that the vectors of the input speech as well as the components of a vector are correlated and that the correlation is specific to a phoneme.

Therefore, if the input data are appropriately divided into two parts, then the information carried by one part can be used to interpolate the other part. We use non-linear vector interpolators to model the correlation of each phoneme, which are trained to give minimum interpolation error with respect to that specific phoneme. The trained interpolators contain therefore information about phonemes and, during recognition, the interpolation error of a specific phoneme can serve as indication of the plausibility of that phoneme.

A spoken utterance is made up of a sequence of phoneme symbols, each of which $s \in \mathbb{P}$ is observed as an acoustic image $I_s$, represented by a sequence of $L_s$ parametric vectors $I_s = v_0^s, v_1^s, v_2^s, ...v_{L_s}^s$. For simplicity, in the following we will drop the subscript $s$. Parametric vectors can be spectrum, cepstrum, etc.

We decompose $I$ into two sets of vectors, $I_a$ and $I_b$, which are not necessarily equal in size. We suppose that the two sets of vectors are redundant, so that an approximation of $I_b$, $\hat{I}_b$, can be restored from information in $I_a$, $\hat{I}_b = f_s(I_a)$. Function $f_s$ is called the interpolation function. If the correlation between $I_b$ and $I_a$ is specific to symbol $s$, then $f_s$ is specific to $s$ and can be used to recognize $s$.

We denote the interpolation error by:

$$e_s = ||\hat{I}_b - I_b|| = ||f_s(I_a) - I_b|| \tag{8}$$

Once an observation of phoneme $s$ is given, $f_s$ can be adjusted so that $e_s$ be minimized. If $N_s$ realizations of phoneme $s$ are available, the average error of interpolation $E_s$ can be defined as:

$$E_s = \frac{1}{N_s}\sum_{k=1}^{N_s} e_s^k = \frac{1}{N_s}\sum_{k=1}^{N_s} ||(f_s(I_a) - I_b)_k|| \tag{9}$$

where $(\cdot)_k$ means that expression $\cdot$ is evaluated for the $k^{th}$ realization. $\frac{1}{N_s}$ is a normalization factor and will be dropped in the following for simplicity. The interpolation model of symbol $s$ can be estimated by minimizing $E_s$ over all realizations, i.e.:

$$M_s = \underset{f_s}{\operatorname{argmin}}\, E_s \; \forall s \in \mathbb{P}$$

The major problem in designing an interpolation system is to decide which quantities to be interpolated. The decomposition of $I_s$ into two vector sets can result in different types of models. We have given particular interest to three families of models in which the vector decomposition is just division. We introduced *vector-pair*, *vector-center* and *component-pair* models [7], depending on how $I$ is divided into $I_a$ and $I_b$. In the following $v_m^i$ denotes the

$i^{th}$ component of vector $v_m$. $\mathcal{P}$ is the parameter vector space of dimension $D$, i.e. $\mathcal{P} = I\!R^D$.

*Vector-pair* model is based on the assumption that consecutive vectors in the vector sequence of a symbol are closely correlated. In such models, the even-numbered parameter vectors are used to interpolate the odd-numbered ones. A model is obtained by minimization of a weighted average interpolation error. $I$ is decomposed into: $I_a = [v^i_{2m}]$ and $I_b = [v^i_{2m+1}]$ where $i = [0, D-1], m = [0, [\frac{L_s}{2}]]$. Eq-9 becomes

$$E^v_s = \sum_{k=1}^{N_s} \sum_{m=0}^{[\frac{L_s}{2}]-1} \sum_{i=0}^{D-1} |(f^{m,i}_{s,v}(I_a) - v^i_{2m+1})_k|^2 w^m_v \quad (10)$$

where: $f_{s,v} : \mathcal{P}^{[\frac{L_s}{2}]} \rightarrow \mathcal{P}^{[\frac{L_s}{2}]}$. $w^m_v$ weights the error as a function of frame index $m$ so that the center of the acoustic image plays a more important role than the sides of the image. Under our experimental conditions, vector-pair model gave the best recognition result among the three models.

*Vector-center* model explicitly exploits the fact that the realization of a speech vector is conditioned by both its past and future. If only past is considered, then the system is reduced to a traditional predictor. In these models, a selected parameter vector is interpolated by the remaining parameter vectors in the acoustic image. If the selected vector is at the center of the acoustic image, i.e. $q = [\frac{L_s}{2}]$, the model interpolates the central parameter vector $v_q$ using its left and right neighboring vectors. *Component-pair* model assumes that consecutive components of a vector in a suitable parametric space are dependent. In these models, the even-numbered components of parameter vector are used to interpolate the odd-numbered ones. More information about the two models can be found in [7, 6].

When the structure of the interpolation functions is specified, several multivariable optimization techniques are available to obtain these functions. We implemented them using multi-layer feed-forward neural networks trained by error-back propagation, since the error minimization process as defined by Eq-9 is a typical least-mean-square error problem and the error-back propagation training procedure can find an optimum solution to this least-mean-square problem [21, 16].

Recognition consists in sliding all phoneme models over the test speech frame sequence and computing the interpolation error Eq-8 frame by frame. We thus obtain interpolation error sequences for each phoneme at each time instant, which is then converted into plausibility values.

The non-linear vectorial interpolator models generalize the idea of linear scalar prediction [23] to non-linear vectorial interpolation. Recent artificial neural network predictors for speech recognition such as Linked Predictive Neural Networks [32], Neural Prediction Models [17] and Hidden Control Neural Architecture [20], which use only past speech frames to predict current frame, can be considered as special cases of non-linear vectorial interpolators.

### 2.3.3 Trajectory models

Represented in a parametric space, for example cepstral space, a speech signal is a point, which moves as articulatory configuration changes. The sequence of moving points is called the trajectory of speech. Within different utterances, the trajectory of a phoneme can vary significantly, due to speaker variability and context influence. Speech recognition should rely on the trajectory of speech rather than on the absolute position in the parameter space, since a given point can be part of different trajectories.

The trajectories of phoneme-based speech units can be modeled by random trajectory sources. For each phoneme, we model clusters of trajectories by mixtures of sequence of states with Gaussian observation probability density. Duration of trajectories are integrated in the modeling. We call the resulting modeling stochastic trajectory model [11], or STM for short.

Let us consider a sequence of parameter vectors:

$$\mathbf{x}_0, \mathbf{x}_1, \ldots \mathbf{x}_n, \ldots$$

Each point $\mathbf{x}_n \in \mathbb{R}^D$ is a $D$-dimensional vector of some parameter space. Let $\mathbf{X}_n$ be a sequence of $Q$ vectors centered at time slot $n$:

$$\mathbf{X}_n \triangleq \mathbf{x}_{n-\frac{Q}{2}}, \mathbf{x}_{n-\frac{Q}{2}+1}, \ldots \mathbf{x}_n, \ldots \mathbf{x}_{n-\frac{Q}{2}+Q-1} \tag{11}$$

In our formulation each phoneme symbol is associated with a stochastic model of trajectories. Let $p(\mathbf{X}_n, T_k, d, s)$ be the joint pdf of vector sequence $\mathbf{X}_n$, $k$-th component trajectory source $T_k$, duration $d$ and phoneme symbol $s \in \mathbb{P}$. According to the chain rule of conditional densities [26]:

$$p(\mathbf{X}_n, T_k, d, s) = p(\mathbf{X}_n|T_k, d, s)Pr(T_k|d, s)Pr(d|s)Pr(s) \tag{12}$$

where $p(\mathbf{X}_n|T_k, d, s)$ the pdf of $\mathbf{X}_n$ given $T_k$, $d$, and $s$, $Pr(T_k|d, s)$ the probability of $T_k$ given $d$, and $s$, $Pr(d|s)$ the probability of $d$ given $s$, and $Pr(s)$ the *a priori* probability of $s$. Probabilities rather than pdfs are used for $T_k$, $d$, and $s$, since these variables only have discrete values.

The marginal pdf of $p(\mathbf{X}_n, s)$ can be obtained by summing up $p(\mathbf{X}_n, T_k, d, s)$ over all trajectories $T_k$ and all durations $d$:

$$p(\mathbf{X}_n, s) = Pr(s)\sum_d \sum_k p(\mathbf{X}_n|T_k, d, s)Pr(T_k|d, s)Pr(d|s) \tag{13}$$

The probability of phoneme $s$, given observation $\mathbf{X}_n$ is therefore:

$$Pr(s|\mathbf{X}_n) = \frac{p(\mathbf{X}_n, s)}{p(\mathbf{X}_n)}. \tag{14}$$

The critical part in our formulation of the probability of a phoneme is the modeling of $p(\mathbf{X}_n|T_k, d, s)$. $T_k$ is the $k$-th component trajectory in a mixture of pdf of component trajectories. The mixture allows the approximation of complex continuous density functions by a sum of density functions [31]. In order to characterize $\mathbf{X}_n$ completely in a statistic sense, we now specify the parametric model of its pdf.

Assuming that each of the $Q$ points on the component trajectory $T_k$ is produced by an independent distribution, the pdf of $\mathbf{X}_n$ given $T_k$, $d$, and $s$ is modeled as:

$$p(\mathbf{X}_n|T_k, d, s) = \prod_{i=0}^{Q-1} \mathcal{N}(\mathbf{x}_{n-\frac{d}{2}+i\frac{d}{Q}}; \mathbf{m}^s_{k,i}, \mathbf{\Sigma}^s_{k,i}) \tag{15}$$

where superscript $\cdot^s$ indicates that the parameter $\cdot$ is specific to phoneme $s$. In Eq-15, the distribution assigned to each of the $Q$ sample points on a trajectory is characterized by a multivariate Gaussian distribution with a mean vector $\mathbf{m}_{k,i}$ and a covariance matrix $\mathbf{\Sigma}_{k,i}$:

$$\mathcal{N}(\mathbf{x}; \mathbf{m}_{k,i}, \mathbf{\Sigma}_{k,i}), \ \ (0 < k \leq K, 0 \leq i < q)$$

where

$$\mathcal{N}(\mathbf{x}; \mathbf{m}, \mathbf{\Sigma}) \triangleq \frac{1}{\sqrt{(2\pi)^D \det \mathbf{\Sigma}}} \exp^{-\frac{1}{2}(\mathbf{x}-\mathbf{m})^T \mathbf{\Sigma}^{-1} (\mathbf{x}-\mathbf{m})} \tag{16}$$

and $K$ is the number of components for the mixture.

The plausibility of phoneme used in this paper is defined after Eq-14. Since $p(\mathbf{X}_n)$ in this equation does not depend on $s$, for our propose of phoneme recognition, i.e. finding the best $s$, it is a constant and will be discarded in subsequent treatment.

Based on Eq-14 we define the plausibility of the symbol $s$ at time slot $n$, $\mu_{n,s}$, as the logarithmic pdf of $s$ given observation sequence $\mathbf{X}_n$:

$$\mu_{n,s} \triangleq \log p(s|\mathbf{X}_n) \tag{17}$$

A model of speech trajectory was proposed in [12], in which trajectories of phonemes were represented by vector-quantified trajectory templates.

# 3 Description of the *VINICS* system

Based on the principle described above, we designed the *VINICS* system. Independent of language and of application, *VINICS* can be used to develop a variety of speech recognizers. Three components of the system allows the user to build specific speech recognition applications: language model, duration probability model of phonemes, acoustic models of phoneme.

The language model describes the sentence set $\mathbb{F}$ to be recognized by the system. The model can be specified by two techniques. The first one consists in using context-free language grammar, mostly used to define well structured application tasks. The second consists in using a set of training texts and generating automatically a corresponding grammar, based on an extension of [18]. The resulting grammar is guaranteed to generate training texts as a subset of all the texts it defines. From either of the two forms, *VINICS* compiles the specification and produces the language model. The model is a non-deterministic transition network where nodes correspond to phoneme labels.

The duration probability model of phonemes contains, for each phoneme, the probabilities of duration measured in number of parameter frames. We use $\Gamma$-functions to model the duration distributions, which have been shown to be efficient [22].

The acoustic models of phonemes specify the acoustic realization of each phoneme in term of parameter models. The models can be either non-linear vectorial interpolators (2.2) or stochastic trajectory models (2.3). The parameters are obtained using labeled speech utterances. We developed an automatic labeling system [10] for large databases of spoken sentences. The system uses a different, already labeled utterance of each sentence to be labeled. When labeling an utterance, a time alignment between this utterance and a reference utterance is performed. Cross-speaker mismatch is reduced by iterating two steps: alignment against the labeled speech and transformation of parameter vectors from test to reference. The transformation is based on a linear scalar transform for each component of a parameter vector. To improve accuracy, the duration of phoneme segments is also integrated in the alignment [9].

# 4 Applications

## 4.1 Introduction

We have developed two types of applications with *VINICS*. The first application was used for tuning the parameters in the algorithms to maximize the performance and establish a recognition rate reference, using separate training and testing speech databases. The other type is for speech recognition demonstration systems, which require no formal evaluation of the recognition accuracy. The plausibility estimation is based on the non-linear interpolation technique for the first application and on the stochastic trajectory models for others.

## 4.2 Applications for performance evaluation

We report four applications designed to evaluate the recognition accuracy of the *VINICS* system. The first two are task-dependent and the others are task independent. For all tests, the acoustic model of phonemes are context-independent.

The first deals with continuous speech. The application task is described by a French semantic grammar of 1500 rules with a vocabulary of 700 words generating over $10^{13}$ different sentences of 1 to 30 word length, covering city name, number, railway reservation, robot control and library information request. The transition network compiled from the grammar consists of 15000 states. The evaluation is based on 17 sentences. Each speaker uttered 3-5 times these sentences, in a random order. The first set of the 17 sentences were used to train the system and the remaining were used for tests. In speaker-dependent test [14] for five speakers, the sentence recognition rates range between 100% and 91.2%, with an average rate better than 95%.

The second consists in recognizing the French alphabet. The database consists of 51 repetitions of the French alphabet (a-z) augmented with the letter *é*, spoken by one male speaker. The recording was done in an office and performed over a period of several weeks. Randomly, 26 utterances of the alphabet were selected for training and 25 utterances for evaluation. One utterance was manually labeled and the remaining utterances for training were automatically labeled. The total number of tokens in the test is thus $27 \times 25$. Results show that the recognition accuracy increases as training data quantity increase, with 99.9% accuracy for 26 repetitions. On a similar task, using whole word continuous density mixture HMM models with state duration control, an average speaker dependent recognition accuracy of 96.9% (best 98.2%) has been reported [19].

The third and fourth applications are word recognition tasks, one for American English and one for French. Training texts consist of about 100 sentences. Utterances of continuous speech were recorded following auditory presentation of recordings. Utterances of test speech were recorded while reading words individually presented on the computer terminal screen. For English, 206 words were randomly selected from the TIMIT [3] database vocabulary. For French 302, words were randomly selected from the BDLEX [27] database vocabulary. No effort was made to select a test word belonging to the training text. We obtained 95.2% (196/206) for English and 94.7% (286/302) for French.

### 4.3 Other applications

Several more application-oriented recognizers have been developed using *VINICS*:

- Database access in noisy environment by continuous speech for the maintenance of complex installations, i.e. nuclear power plant. This work is done in collaboration with CEA France.
- Dialogue by continuous speech with information retrieval system, for instance AIDS information. The work is in collaboration with the Communications Research Centre of Canada.
- large vocabulary, isolated word recognition with a vocabulary of 33000 French words.

Other applications such as telephone banking services are in study.

## 5 On-going works

### 5.1 Recognition in various noisy environments

When a speech recognition system trained under clean conditions is tested under noisy conditions, recognition rates degrade severely, due to the mismatch between clean and noisy environments. Maintaining speech recognition accuracy under noisy conditions is of great interest for practical purposes.

We have developed an adaptive template-based technique, called base-transformation, which converts an environmental difference into a difference of representation bases and reduces the difference by a base transformation. On a 206 word recognition task, for speech corrupted by additive Gaussian noise at SNRs better than 10 dB, the adaptive technique maintained the recognition accuracy to 95% of that for clean speech [4]. However, performance was dependent on the relative noise levels of the reference and test environments.

We extended this work by addressing the problem of sensitivity to different noise types and levels. We assume that noise is stationary during an utterance. A reference environment that is most similar to the test environment is first recognized from a set of preclassified reference environments. Then, the transformation parameters associated with the selected reference environment are used to transform the noisy utterance. In recognition tests, we obtained a noise-independent 90% recognition rate for different types of noises with SNRs from 10-40 dB. Noise types include car, bus, aircraft as well as Gaussian noises [33].

## 5.2 Lombard speech recognition

Most of the techniques for noisy speech recognition deal with reducing mismatches in the spectral domain between clean and noisy speech. In presence of noise, speech is modified according to the Lombard effect. This causes a modification of the duration distribution of each phone, as well as other changes in the short term spectrum of the speech signal.

Since earlier work has shown that the recognition accuracy of a speech recognition system can be significantly improved with an adequate representation of the temporal structure of speech, we worked on the reduction of the mismatch between the phone duration in Lombard and clean speech. We choose the Bayesian estimation as a framework for performing the parameter adaptation of phone duration models. We observed that phone duration adaptation brings a discriminative information to a speech recognition system trained with normal speech, and tested with Lombard speech. When testing on a 49 alphanumeric vocabulary in isolated mode, we found that the adaptation of phone duration models leads to an improvement in the recognition rate, especially for female speakers [30]. This experiment indicates that the re-estimation of the acoustic models will also increase the robustness for Lombard speech recognition.

## 5.3 Symbolic modeling of phonetic context

Phonetic content of speech is specified in *VINICS* using a symbolic description called phonetic transcription. This transcription does not contain contextual influence of articulation or possible liaisons between words, neither the effects of speaking rate. Such contextual deformations are one of the main sources of error for continuous speech recognition systems that use phoneme as basic recognition unit. It has been shown that modeling phonetic context improves speech recognition accuracy. In our view, speech is materialized as acoustic images which are the representation of phonemic symbols in a parameter space. Contextual deformations can therefore be modeled at two levels: parametric or symbolic level. We propose to model the contextual variation at a symbolic level to enhance the performance of continuous speech recognition. Our objective is to compile the transition network of phonemes in the recognition system, together with a dictionary of phonetic transcriptions and with context models, to produce a new transition network in which context deformations are taken into account by an explicit context-dependent model. Preliminary tests show that our model leads to improvement in the recognition rate, especially for speaker independent mode [25].

## 5.4 Joint compensation of channel and noise

The degradation in recognition accuracy caused by noise background and transmission channel can be jointly compensated by modeling an environment as additive noise and unknown linear filtering. We are currently studying the integration of this approach into the stochastic trajectory models of the *VINICS* system.

## 5.5 Compensation of duration

In *VINICS*, models of phoneme duration are created from continuous utterances of sentences in a training database. Therefore, recognition tokens obtained from shorter utterances may not be well represented by models trained from longer utterances. We designed an experiment to compute observed average phoneme duration as a function of the number of phonemes per utterance. We observed that, for short utterances, the average duration consistently increases as the number of phonemes per utterance increases. The experiment showed that the average duration of phonemes in words spoken in isolation may be as much as 50% longer than the average duration of phonemes in continuously spoken sentences. The variation of phoneme duration as a function of utterance duration is modeled in both the phoneme probability estimation stage and the utterance search stage of a recognition system. As a result, a 47% reduction in word recognition error was obtained [15].

# References

[1] G. D. FornyJr. The Viterbi algorithm. In *Proc. IEEE*, volume 61, pages 268–278, Mar 1973.

[2] M. Franzini, K. F. Lee, and A. Waibel. Connectionist Viterbi Training: A New Hybrid Method for Continuous speech Recognition. In *Proc. IEEE Int. Conf. on Acoustics, Speech and Signal Processing 1990*, volume 1, pages 425–428, Albuquerque, New Mexico, USA, April 1990.

[3] J. S. Garofolo. *The structure and format of the DARPA TIMIT CD-ROM prototype.* National Institute of Standards and Technology, Gaithersburg, MD, 1988.

[4] Y. Gong. Base transformation for environment adaptation in continuous speech recognition. In *Proceedings of European Conference on Speech Communication and Technology*, volume 3, pages 2227–2230, Berlin, Germany, September 1993.

[5] Y. Gong, Y. Cheng, and J.-P. Haton. Neural Network Coupled with IIR Sequential Adapter for Phoneme Recognition in Continuous Speech. In *Proc. IEEE Int. Conf. on Acoustics, Speech and Signal Processing 1991*, volume 1, pages 153–156, Toronto, Canada, May 1991.

[6] Y. Gong and J.-P. Haton. Comparing two phoneme identification methods using continuous speech recognizer. In *Proceedings of European Conference on Speech Communication and Technology*, volume II, pages 417–420, Genova, Italy, Sept. 1991.

[7] Y. Gong and J.-P. Haton. Non-linear vector interpolation by neural network for phoneme identification in continuous speech. In *Proc. IEEE Int. Conf. on Acoustics, Speech and Signal Processing 1991*, volume 1, pages 121–124, Toronto, Canada, May 1991.

[8] Y. Gong and J.-P. Haton. Signal-to-string conversion based on high likelihood regions using embedded dynamic programming. *IEEE Trans. on Pattern Analysis and Machine Intelligence*, 13(3):297–302, March 1991.

[9] Y. Gong and J.-P. Haton. DTW-based phonetic labeling using explicit phoneme duration constraints. In *Proc. of Int. Conf. on Spoken Language Processing 1992*, volume II, pages 863–866, Banff, Alberta, Canada, October 1992.

[10] Y. Gong and J.-P. Haton. Iterative transformation and alignment for speech labeling. In *Proceedings of European Conference on Speech Communication and Technology*, volume 3, pages 1759–1762, Berlin, Germany, September 1993.

[11] Y. Gong and J.-P. Haton. Stochastic trajectory modeling for speech recognition. In *IEEE International Conference on Acoustics, Speech and Signal Processing*, Adelaide, Australia, April 1994.

[12] Y. Gong and J.-P. Haton. Phoneme based continuous speech recognition without pre-segmentation. In *Proceedings of European Conference on Speech Technology*, volume 1, pages 121–124, Edinburgh, September, 1987.

[13] Y. Gong, J.-P. Haton, and F. Mouria. Continuous speech recognition based on high plausibility regions. In *Proc. IEEE Int. Conf. on Acoustics, Speech and Signal Processing 1991*, volume 1, pages 725–728, Toronto, Canada, May 1991.

[14] Y. Gong, F. Mouria, and J.-P. Haton. Un système de reconnaissance de la parole continue sans segmentation. In *Actes du* $7^{ème}$ *congrès Reconnaissance des Formes et Intelligence Artificielle*, volume 3, pages 1191–1203, Paris, France, Nov. 1989. AFCET, INRIA.

[15] Y. Gong and W. C. Treurniet. Duration of phones as function of utterance length and its use in automatic speech recognition. In *Proceedings of European Conference on Speech Communication and Technology*, volume 1, pages 315–318, Berlin, Germany, September 1993.

[16] G. E. Hinton. Connectionist learning procedures. *Artificial Intelligence*, 40(1-3), September 1989.

[17] K. Iso and T. Watanabe. Speaker-independent word recognition using a neural prediction model. In *Proc. IEEE Int. Conf. on Acoustics, Speech and Signal Processing 1990*, volume 1, pages 441–444, Albuquerque, New Mexico, USA, April 1990.

[18] William Katke. Learning language using a pattern recognition approach. *The AI Magazine*, pages 64–73, spring 1985.

[19] C. H. Lee, C. H. Lin, and B. H. Juang. A study on speaker adaptation of the parameters of continuous density hidden Markov models. *IEEE Trans. on Signal Processing*, 39(4):806–814, April 1991.

[20] E. Levin. Word recognition using hidden control neural architecture. In *Proc. IEEE Int. Conf. on Acoustics, Speech and Signal Processing 1990*, volume 1, pages 433–436, Albuquerque, New Mexico, USA, April 1990.

[21] R. P. Lippmann. An introduction to computing with neural nets. *IEEE ASSP Magazine*, 3:422, April 1987.

[22] A. Ljolje and S. E. Levison. Development of an Acoustic-Phonetic Hidden Markov Model for Continuous Speech Recognition. *IEEE Trans. on Signal Processing*, 39(1):29–39, Jan. 1991.

[23] J. D. Markel and A. H. Gray Jr. *Linear Prediction of Speech*. Springer-Verlag, New York, 1976.

[24] N. Morgan and H. Bourlard. Continuous speech recognition using multilayer perceptrons with hidden Markov models. In *Proc. IEEE Int. Conf. on Acoustics, Speech and Signal Processing 1990*, volume 1, pages 413–426, Albuquerque, New Mexico, USA, April 1990.

[25] F. Mouria, Y. Gong, and J.-P. Haton. Use of explicit context-dependent phonemic models in continuous speech recognition. In *Proceedings of European Conference on Speech Communication and Technology*, volume 3, pages 2223–2226, Berlin, Germany, September 1993.

[26] A. Papoulis. *Probability, Random Variables, and Stochastic Processes*. McGraw-Hill Book Company, second edition, 1984.

[27] G. Pérennou and M. de Calmes. BDLEX volume 1: Le lexique general. Technical report, GRECO CNRS de la communication parlee, July 1987.

[28] H. Sawai, A. Waibel, M. Miyatake, and K. Shikano. Spotting Japanese CV-syllables and phonemes using time-delay neural networks. In *Proc. IEEE Int. Conf. on Acoustics, Speech and Signal Processing 1989*, volume 1, pages 25–28, Glasgow, Scotland, May 1989.

[29] D. Sciarra and C. Scagliola. Two step recognition of large vocabulary isolated words based on diphone spotting. In *Proceedings of European Conference on Speech Technology*, volume 2, pages 164–167, Paris, September, 1989.

[30] O. Siohan, Y. Gong, and J.-P. Haton. A Bayesian approach to phone duration adaptation for Lombard speech recognition. In *Proceedings of European Conference on Speech Communication and Technology*, volume 3, pages 1639–1642, Berlin, Germany, September 1993.

[31] H. W. Sorenson and D. L. Alspach. Recursive Bayesian estimation using Gaussian sums. *Automatica*, 7:465–497, 1971.

[32] J. Tebelskis and A. Waibel. Large vocabulary recognition using linked predictive neural networks. In *Proc. IEEE Int. Conf. on Acoustics, Speech and Signal Processing 1990*, volume 1, pages 437–440, Albuquerque, New Mexico, USA, April 1990.

[33] W. C. Treurniet and Y. Gong. Noise independent speech recognition for a variety of noise types. In *IEEE International Conference on Acoustics, Speech and Signal Processing*, Adelaide, Australia, April 1994.

# The Philips Research System for Large-Vocabulary and Continuous-Speech Recognition

V. Steinbiss, H. Ney, R. Haeb-Umbach, B.-H. Tran, U. Essen,
R. Kneser, M. Oerder, H.-G. Meier, X. Aubert, C. Dugast, D. Geller
Philips GmbH Forschungslaboratorien, D-52066 Aachen, Germany

W. Höllerbauer, H. Bartosik
Philips Dictation Systems, A-1102 Wien, Austria

## Abstract

This paper gives a status report on the Philips research system for phenome-based and large-vocabulary continuous-speech recognition. Like that of many other systems, the recognition architecture is here based on an integrated statistical approach. We describe the characteristic features of the system as opposed to other systems as follows: The Viterbi criterion is consistently applied both in training and testing. Continuous mixture densities are used without tying or smoothing. A time-synchronous beam search is used in connection with a phoneme look-ahead facility, and is applied to a tree-organized lexicon.

This system has been successfully applied to the American English DARPA RM task. Here, we report experimental results for a German 13 000-word Philips internal dictation task. In addition to the scientific prototype, a PC version has been set up which is described here for the first time.

## 1. Introduction

There are a number of operational prototype systems in research for large-vocabulary and continuous-speech recognition. The aim of this work is to design a system similar to these systems, and the IBM system for 20 000-word recognition of isolated-word input,. The prototype system described in this paper is based on techniques of statistical pattern recognition and stochastic modelling, where training data are heavily exploited and local decisions are avoided as much as possible. See [12, 16] for references.

The characteristic features of the approach to be presented are:

- A large-sized acoustic vector capturing first and second-order derivatives is used. There is no splitting into separate streams as in most other systems that use tied-mixtures.
- The Viterbi criterion is used both in training and recognition. Continuous mixture densities are used in a way that amounts to what can be called 'statistical template matching'.
- Linear discriminant analysis improves the acoustic analysis.
- For bigram language modelling, a non-linear interpolation has been developed that gives consistently lower perplexities than linear interpolation.
- The concept of time-synchronous beam search has been extended towards a tree organization of the pronunciation lexicon so that the search effort is significantly reduced. A phenome look-ahead technique results in an additional improvement. A PC based implementation (see section 8) underlines the efficiency of this search strategy.

The organization of the paper is as follows. We first summarize the statistical approach to speech recognition and then describe the four main entities of our system: acoustic analysis, acoustic-phonetic modelling, language modelling and search. A section with experiments on our internal dictation task follows. The final section describes a PC based implementation of our system.

## 2. System Architecture

Figure 1 presents a block diagram of the system architecture.

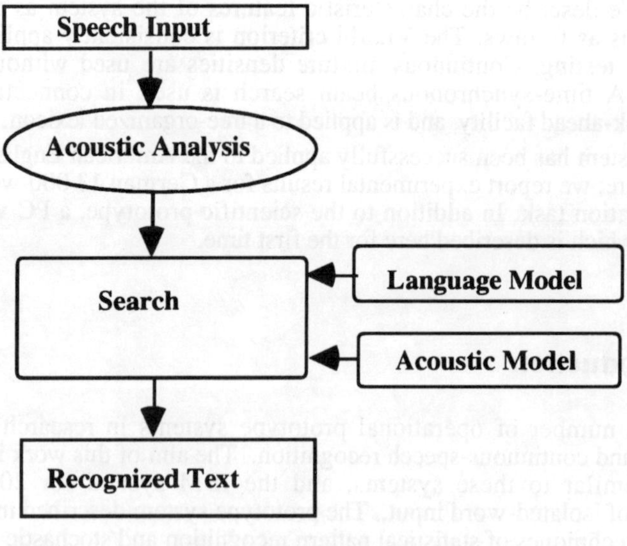


**Fig. 1:** System Architecture

In the preprocessing step of *acoustic analysis*, the speech signal is transformed into a sequence of acoustic vectors $x_1,...,x_T$ (over time t=1,...,T). Since the speech signal, and thus this sequence of observations is not exactly reproducible, a statistical approach is used to model its generation.

Statistical decision theory tells that in order to minimize the probability of recognition errors, one should decide for the word sequence $W=w_1,...,w_N$ (of unknown length N) that maximizes [8]:

$$Pr(w_1,...,w_N) \ Pr(x_1,...,x_T|w_1,...,w_N) \ . \qquad (1)$$

The first term, the a priori probability of word sequences $Pr(w_1,...,w_N)$, is independent of the acoustic observations and is completely specified by the *language model*.. It reflects the system's knowledge of how to concatenate words of the vocabulary to form whole sentences and thus captures syntactic and semantic restrictions.

The *acoustic-phonetic modelling* is reflected by the second term. $Pr(x_1,...,x_T|w_1,...,w_N)$ is the conditional probability of observing the acoustic vectors $x_1,...,x_T$ when the words $w_1,...,w_N$ were uttered. These probabilities are estimated during the training phase of the recognition system. A large-vocabulary system typically is based on subword units like phonemes, which are concatenated according to the *pronunciation dictionary* to form word models.

The decision on the spoken words must be taken by an optimization procedure which combines information of the language model and of the acoustic model, the latter being based on the phoneme models and the pronunciation dictionary. The optimization procedure is usually referred to as *search* in a state space defined by the knowledge sources.

# 3. Acoustic Analysis

## 3.1 Spectral Analysis

The acoustic signal is low-pass-filtered and digitized with a sampling frequency of 16 kHz. The following steps are performed for every frame, i.e. every 10 ms:

- Application of a Hamming window to a 25-ms segment.
- 512-point FFT after padding with zero-valued samples.
- Cepstral smoothing of the logarithmic FFT intensities using a *sin(x)/x* kernel function.
- In the range from 200 Hz to 6400 Hz, sampling at 30 frequency points that roughly correspond to a Mel-frequency scale.
- Normalization of the 30 spectral intensities with respect to their mean value. Together with this "energy" value, they form the 31-dimensional acoustic vector y(t).

To account for varying recording conditions in the dictation task, each acoustic vector is normalized with respect to the long-term spectrum as obtained by averaging over a part of the sentence.

In order to capture the temporal structure of the speech signal, each acoustic vector y(t) is then augmented by slope and curvature information over the time axis. Thus, the original sequence of y(t) of acoustic vectors is replaced by:

$$x(t) := \begin{bmatrix} y(t) \\ y'(t) \\ y''(t) \end{bmatrix} = \begin{bmatrix} y(t) \\ y(t) - y(t - \Delta t) \\ y(t + \Delta t) - 2y(t) + y(t - \Delta t) \end{bmatrix}, \quad (2)$$

where the first- and second-order differences were chosen to cover the time intervals [t-$\Delta$t, t] and [t-$\Delta$t, t+$\Delta$t], respectively. The time delay $\Delta$t is typically 30 ms. The new sequence of acoustic vectors $x_1,...,x_T$ in a higher-dimensional vector space serves as input to the subsequent processing steps. For the first and second differences of the 30 spectral intensities, pairs of adjacent spectral intensities are averaged so that the final vector consists of 63 components: 30 spectral intensities, 15 first- and 15 second-order differences, and 3 components representing energy and its differences.

### 3.2 Linear Discriminant Analysis

Linear discriminant analysis (LDA) is a well-known technique in statistical pattern classification for improving the discrimination between classes in a high-dimensional vector space ([3] on page 114). The basic idea is to find a linear transformation such that a suitable criterion of class separability is maximized. The transformation is obtained as the eigenvector decomposition of the product of two scatter or covariance matrices, the total-scatter matrix and the inverse of the average within-class scatter matrix. Recently, this technique has been successfully applied to speech recognition, for both small [4, 7] and large-vocabulary tasks [6].

When applying LDA to speech recognition, the choice of the proper classes to be discriminated is not obvious - are they whole phonemes, phoneme states or the mixture components of a state? Our experiments indicated that the states are a good choice. The computation of the LDA transform is further complicated by the time alignment problem. Therefore, we use a three-step training. With our standard iterative training we obtain a segmentation of the training data, which provides the class labels for the subsequent estimation of the LDA transform. The third step is a new iterative training using LDA-transformed acoustic vectors.

Note that since a *single* class-*in*dependent transformation matrix is employed, the matrix multiplication is done in the acoustic front end once per frame rather than for each log-likelihood calculation.

## 4. Acoustic-Phonetic Modelling

The acoustic conditional probabilities $Pr(x_1,...,x_T|w_1,...,w_N)$ are obtained by concatenating the corresponding word models, which again are obtained by concatenating phoneme models according to the pronunciation lexicon. We use inventories of 40-50 phoneme symbols including symbols for silence and maybe glottal stop. As in many other systems, these subword units are modelled by stochastic finite-state automata, the so-called Hidden Markov Models (HMMs) [2, 8, 11].

For each state s of the HMM, there is an emission probability density $q(x_t|s)$ of generating the vector $x_t$. The phoneme unit shown in figure 2 has a tripartite structure in order to take account of left and right acoustic dependences.

Each of the three parts consists of two states with identical emission distributions. The transition probabilities, which allow loop, jump and skip, are tied over all states. Unlike most other HMM structures, this structure has a simple durational model whose most likely duration of 60 ms is close to the average phoneme duration.

**Fig. 2:** Topology of phoneme HMM

No pronunciation variants are used in the pronunciation lexicon, such that the emission distributions have to model deviations from the standard pronunciation as well as coarticulatory effects. The best results were obtained for continuous mixture densities:

$$q(x_t|s) = \sum_k c_k(s)\, b_k(x_t|s) \quad \text{with } 0 \le c_k \le 1 \text{ and } \sum_k c_k(s) = 1 \tag{3}$$

where the so-called component densities $b_k(.|.)$ are unimodal densities such as Gaussians or (as in our system) Laplacians:

$$b_k(x_t|s) = \prod_n \left(\frac{1}{2v_n}\right) \cdot \exp\left(-\sum_n \frac{|x_t(n) - r_{k,s}(n)|}{v_n}\right) \quad . \tag{4}$$

(n) is the index of the vector components. Each density is completely specified by its location vector $r_{k,s}$. The vector of absolute deviations, $(v_1,\dots,v_N)^t$, is assumed to be independent of both the component densities and the states and thus serves as an overall scaling for the acoustic vectors.

In contrast to other systems, the Viterbi criterion is used both in training and recognition. This applies even to the level of mixture components, such that the sum over the component densities in equation (3) is replaced by their maximum [12].

While we typically develop our system on a speaker-dependent German task (cf. sect. 7), we also successfully benchmarked our system on both the speaker-dependent and the speaker-independent part of the well-known American English DARPA (Defense Advanced Projects Agency) RM (resource management) task [1] [12].

The major modifications of our system were the usage of context-dependent phoneme models and a large number of densities. In contrast to other systems, the system does not use across-word models, and there is typically no smoothing of emission probabilities.

## 5. Language Modelling

The language model provides, for each word sequence, an estimate of the probabilities $Pr(w_1,...,w_n)$ or, equivalently, of the conditional probabilities $Pr(w_n|w_1,...,w_{n-1})$. *m*-gram models [9] have established themselves as both a good way to reliably estimate the parameters and to keep them limited so they can be stored and retrieved. In view of the size of corpora available, we typically use a word bigram model $P(w_n \mid w_{n-1})$ or a category-based bigram model (bigram class model) with automatically generated classes [10].

While maximum-likelihood estimation would suggest to take relative frequencies of bigram counts, it is common knowledge that these are particularly bad as estimates and that smoothing is important. The smoothing method that we use is different from those used in other systems. The non-linear interpolation scheme that we use essentially amounts to substracting a constant *d* from the counts and distributing the gained probability mass on less detailed distributions [13]. With this method, we achieve better results than with backing-off or linear interpolation.

## 6. The Search Procedure

Time-synchronous beam search has successfully been used in the Philips continuous-speech recognizer for several years [15]. We found that it is efficient also for 10 000 or more words [14]. First, all knowledge sources are available at the same level in the integrated search. Second, all hypotheses refer to the same acoustic vector sequence in time-synchronous search. These two key points allow a drastic reduction of the actual search space by pruning less promising hypotheses.

### 6.1 Tree Lexicon

A straight-forward approach of constructing the search space is to synthetically build up word models from concatenating the appropriate phoneme models as given by the pronunciation lexicon. In this space, different copies of the same phoneme occur due to the lexical constraints. For similar reasons, the language model restrictions make it necessary to introduce several copies of the same word, representing contexts that allow for different continuations. This organization, where each state belongs to exactly one word, will be called *linear lexicon*.

When the lexicon grows larger, e.g. from 1000 to 10 000 words, it is more efficient to arrange the pronunciation lexicon as a tree of phonemes (*tree lexicon*). The compression factor for the tree lexicon as compared to the linear lexicon is even surpassed by the reduction in the number of active states, because most of the active states are located in the word beginnings (near the tree's root). The tree organization of the lexicon also has an undesired consequence for the organization of the search space. In contrast to a linear lexicon, the word identities are unknown at the word beginnings. Particularly for a bigram language model, this means that separate tree copies have to be held, depending on the predecessor word. While the potential search space is blown up by a factor of the vocabulary size, e.g. 10 000, the actual search space grows much more moderately, typically by only a factor of 2. The tree organization is thus very beneficial for large-vocabulary tasks. A detailed discussion with experiments is given in [14].

### 6.2 Phoneme Look-Ahead

The phoneme look-ahead additionally reduces the number of active states by estimating whether a started phoneme will or will not survive the next few time frames (in our system typically 60 ms). In a first step, the likelihood of each phoneme ahead of the current time frame is estimated by carrying out a time-alignment. Then, each time a state hypothesis crosses a phoneme boundary, these figures are utilized for probability estimates for the best path extensions both of this and of any other state, which in turn are used to perform an additional pruning [5].

For the phoneme look-ahead, the original phoneme models are used without any simplification. Note that, in particular for the case of monophones, the number of generic states is much smaller than the number of state hypotheses. The likelihood scores are stored for later use in the detailed match. Like the conventional search, the look-ahead is sped up by beam pruning; in addition, there is no need for book-keeping as in the detailed match. To further reduce computation, the look-ahead is carried out only every other time frame. For the omitted time frame, the look-ahead scores of the previous time frame are used.

## 7. Experimental Tests

We give a very brief look on experiments conducted in connection with our speaker-dependent dictation task. Additional experiments on other, public available databases, that allow a comparison with other systems, are described elsewhere [12, 16].

The data in these experiments are real-life field data from professional text producers. Speakers M-60 and M-61 are lawyers, M-72 and M-73 are radiologists. All speakers are male and work in Vienna, Austria. The speakers were asked to dictate as usual; this includes verbalized punctuation.

| *Speaker* | *Vocabulary* | *Test-set perplexity* | *Active states* in seconds | *Word-error rate in %* | | |
|---|---|---|---|---|---|---|
| | | | | Deleted | Inserted | Total |
| M-60 | 12 073 | 113 | 87 | 3.1 | 1.0 | 10.2 |
| M-61 | 15 188 | 176 | 93 | 1.9 | 1.5 | 12.1 |
| M-72 | 13 095 | 267 | 116 | 2.4 | 1.9 | 11.2 |
| M-73 | 13 095 | 42 | 140 | 0.6 | 1.7 | 5.7 |

**Table 1:** Baseline system on 4 field test speakers. Bigram LM, look-ahead, no LDA, 9 h training, 16 000 mixture components.

The dictations were recorded with hand-held microphones on desktop dictation equipment. We processed exactly the same recordings that were also given to the secretaries for transcription. Although the speakers are very experienced with dictation, we found that recognition was harder on this material than on read texts.

Table 1 shows the performance of our system with high acoustic resolution (16 000 mixture components) and about 9 hours of training material, but without LDA. The test material comprised 2000 - 3000 spoken words. The number of active states per second before pruning refers to the search effort.

| Training / density | 0.7 h | 1.2 h | 2.0 h | 3.2 h | 9.5 h |
|---|---|---|---|---|---|
| 4000 | 16.1% | 14.4% | 13.1% | 12.3% | 11.4% |
| 8000 | - | 13.4% | 12.9% | 11.7% | 10.8% |
| 16000 | - | - | - | 11.6% | 10.1% |

**Table 2:** Error-rate as a function of training set size and number of densities. Speaker M-60, vocabulary size 12 073 words, test-set perplexity 113.

Table 2 shows how the error-rate depends on the training-set size and the acoustic resolution. Monophones were used here; we expect improvements with context-dependent phonemes.

The improvement by LDA is substantial. For speaker type M-60 the decrease by LDA of the word-error rate is from 12.3% to 10.4%, and for speaker type M-61 the decrease by LDA of the word-error rate is from 15% to 12.3% (with about 3 hours of training, and 4 000 densities).

## 8. A PC-based and Continuous-Speech Recognition System for Dictation

Real-world dictation, which is typically connected with large and open vocabulary, is a difficult task that pushes today's technology to its limits. Despite the considerable progress made in recent years, even for co-operative speakers and restricted domains like free-text medical reporting, error-free speech recognition so far cannot be achieved.

Up to now, large-vocabulary systems for dictation have required isolated word input. While this reduces both the word-error rate and computational costs as compared to continuous-speech input, it burdens the user with an unnatural speaking style. In addition, dictating with pauses between words takes more time.

For people who professionally generate large amounts of texts, e.g. physicians and lawyers, text generation is characterized by a two-step process: The phase of dictation, where speech is recorded either digitally or on tape, and a subsequent separate transcription phase where secretaries transcribe the dictations. (We ignore the proof-reading in this discussion.)

The system developed at Philips Dictation Systems, Vienna, and described here adopts this non-interactive approach and thus allows the person to dictate with a natural speaking style. After the speech is processed by the speech recognizer, the secretary has only to correct the recognition errors, which is both faster and a more interesting job to do.

This three-step approach naturally results in the system architecture as summarized in figure 3:

- The dictation is recorded using a microphone; the usual record/replay/fast-forward/rewind functionality is available. So, no change of work methodology is required. Punctuation should be verbalised. The recorded speech is stored on a fileserver in a PC network.
- Speech recognition runs remotely on a PC which is connected to the network. An acoustic front-end performs the acoustic analysis. Recognition is sped up by a dedicated co-processor board containing application-specific ICs. Depending on the speaker and the specific boundary conditions, recognition with a 10 - 20 000-word vocabulary runs in 1 - 3 times real-time.
- In contrast to typing the whole text, the secretary only corrects the errors that occurred in the recognition process. With a special speech-synchronous editor that uses the link between the recording and the text as given by the hypothesized word boundaries, it is possible to listen to parts of the recording while moving through the text.

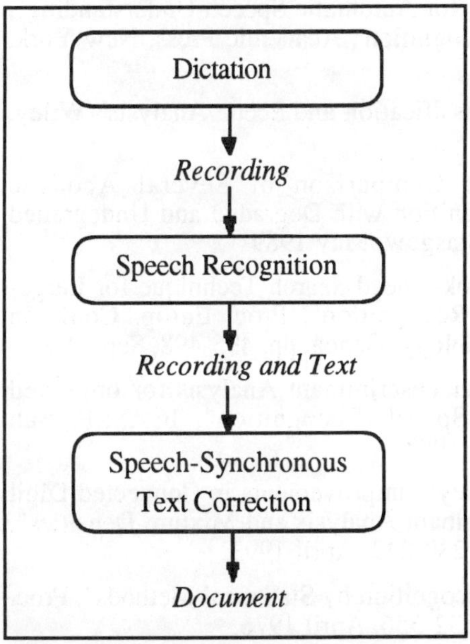


**Fig. 3:** System architecture of the PC based continuous-speech recognition system for dictation.

Three measures have been taken to achieve the lowest possible error-rates without hindering the person who dictates:

- The system has been set-up in speaker-dependent mode such that each of the speakers gets optimal performance.
- Training is done with the dictations that are being produced anyway, together with their proper transcriptions. After several hours of dictations, the system reaches optimal performance.
- A high-quality acoustic analysis together with a large number of mixture components guarantee a high acoustic resolution.

The first release of this system is a German version. Field trials are being carried out in several hospitals in Austria and Germany.

## References

*Abbreviation:* ICASSP stands for Proc. IEEE Int. Conf. on Acoustics, Speech and Signal Processing.

[1] X. Aubert, R. Haeb-Umbach, H. Ney: "Continuous Mixture Densities and Linear Discriminant Analysis for Improved Context-Dependent Acoustic Models", ICASSP, Minneapolis, MN, pp. II 648-651, April 1993.

[2] J. K. Baker: "Stochastic Modeling for Automatic Speech Understanding", in D. R. Reddy (ed.): 'Speech Recognition', Academic Press, New York, pp. 512-542, 1975.

[3] R.O. Duda, P.E. Hart: 'Pattern Classification and Scene Analysis', Wiley, New York, 1973.

[4] M. J. Hunt, C. Lefebvre: "A Comparison of Several Acoustic Representations for Speech Recognition with Degraded and Undegraded Speech", ICASSP, pp. 262-265, Glasgow, May 1989.

[5] R. Haeb-Umbach, H. Ney: "A Look-Ahead Search Technique for Large-Vocabulary Continuous-Speech Recognition", Proc. Europ. Conf. on Speech Communication and Technology, Genoa, pp. 495-498, Sep. 1991.

[6] R. Haeb-Umbach, H. Ney: "Linear Discriminant Analysis for Improved Large Vocabulary Continuous Speech Recognition", ICASSP, San Francisco, CA, pp. I 13-16, March 1992.

[7] R. Haeb-Umbach, D. Geller, H. Ney: "Improvements in Connected Digit Recognition Using Linear Discriminant Analysis and Mixture Densities", ICASSP, Minneapolis, MN, pp. II 239-242, April 1993.

[8] F. Jelinek: "Continuous Speech Recognition by Statistical Methods", Proc. of the IEEE, Vol. 64, No. 10, pp. 532-556, April 1976.

[9] F. Jelinek, R. L. Mercer, S. Roukos: "Principles of Lexical Language Modeling for Speech Recognition", *in* S. Furui, M. M. Sondhi (eds.): 'Advances in Speech Signal Processing', Marcel Dekker, New York, pp. 651-699, 1992.

[10] R. Kneser, H. Ney: "Improved Clustering Techniques for Class-Based Statistical Language Modelling", *elsewhere in these* Proc. Europ. Conf. on Speech Communication and Technology, Berlin, Sep. 1993.

[11] S. E. Levinson, L. R. Rabiner, M. M. Sondhi: "An Introduction to the Application of the Theory of Probabilistic Functions of a Markov Process to Automatic Speech Recognition", The Bell System Technical Journal, Vol. 62, No. 4, pp. 1035- 1074, April 1983.

[12] H. Ney: "Modeling and Search in Continuous-Speech Recognition", *elsewhere in these* Proc. Europ. Conf. on Speech Communication and Technology, Berlin, Sep. 1993.

[13] H. Ney, U. Essen: "On Smoothing Techniques for Bigram-Based Natural Language Modelling", ICASSP, Toronto, pp. 825-828, May 1991.

[14] H. Ney, R. Haeb-Umbach, B.-H. Tran, M. Oerder: "Improvements in Beam Search for 10000-Word Continuous Speech Recognition", ICASSP, San Francisco, CA, pp. I-9 - I-12, March 1992.

[15] H. Ney, D. Mergel, A. Noll, A. Paeseler: "Data Driven Organization of the Dynamic Programming Beam Search for Continuous Speech Recognition", IEEE Trans. on Signal Processing, Vol. SP-40, No. 2, pp. 272-281, Feb. 1992.

[16] H. Ney, V. Steinbiss, R. Haeb-Umbach, B.-H. Tran, U. Essen, "An Overview of the Philips Research System for Large-Vocabulary Continuous-Speech Recognition", *to appear in* Int. Journal of Pattern Recognition and Artificial Intelligence, 1994.

**Acknowledgement**

The work on the speaker dependent RM task and on language modelling was partly carried out in the ESPRIT-funded POLYGLOT project (No. 2104).

# DANDELION: Variations of Discourse Functions and Representations According to Context

J.A. Bateman
Gesellschaft für Mathematik und Datenverarbeitung
Dolivostr. 15, D-64293 Darmstadt, Germany

## Abstract

This paper summarizes the goals, methods, and some current results of the Dandelion project—a basic research action that is developing an empirically and psychologically motivated theory of written discourse that is valid cross-linguistically. Central to the project is the tenet that it is vital to consider the discourse/text functioning of particular lexical and grammatical phenomena in *concrete contexts of use in particular text types.* This basic property of discourse restricts the effectiveness of studies that take the formal description of the sentence as basic and try to extend it to accommodate the properties of text. The project accordingly adopts a particular view of context which should render our results equally relevant to work on spoken language.

## 1 Introduction

### 1.1 General Goals

The general goals of the Dandelion project (ESPRIT Basic Research Project 6665) are to develop an empirically and psychologically motivated theory of discourse that is valid cross-linguistically—the initial languages of the project are English, German and Dutch. The theory and accompanying descriptions are intended both to provide further input for the large-scale linguistic knowledge bases that are currently being planned within Europe and to support discourse workbenches for further use in discourse research, in the training of

[1]Much of the material in this paper is drawn from the Dandelion project description and individual deliverables as cited in the text. Although the work described represents the general Dandelion approach and interim results, particular statements of theoretical position and the emphases given to particular aspects of the project may not be shared by all members of the project equally. Responsibility for the opinions expressed and any errors therefore lies solely with the author. The members of the Dandelion consortium are: the Center for Language Studies (Tilburg, Holland), GMD-IPSI (Darmstadt, Germany), Universidad Complutense (Madrid, Spain), University of Edinburgh (Edinburgh, Scotland), and Universität des Saarlandes (Saarbrücken, Germany). The project is coordinated by Dr. Gisela Redeker (currently Vrije Universiteit, Amsterdam). The author's email address is: '`bateman@gmd.de`'.

students working on text and discourse, and in the support of linguistic software that needs functionalities in the area of text and discourse processing, generation and translation.

Linguistic analysis within the project is directed at providing accounts for linguistic expressions and constructions whose interpretations are propositionally equivalent, but pragmatically different. On the basis of linguistic analysis and psycholinguistic experimentation, the project is defining mappings of pragmatic discourse functions and contextual conditions onto linguistic expressions and constructions for each of the languages under consideration. Examples of these will be given below. A complete mapping of contextual conditions would require the study of a wide range of text types and contexts. Within the limits of this project, we are mostly concentrating our efforts on newspaper reports, editorials, and magazine articles, which vary along several contextual dimensions. This variation is reflected in the global and local organisation of the texts as well as in the use of linguistic expressions and constructions. The patterning of discourse functions, discourse structures, and lexico-grammatical phenomena is yielding hypotheses about form-function mappings and interactions, which can then be experimentally tested. Moreover, since a main objective of the project is to show how lexico-grammatical phenomena usually pattern *together* to realise particular discourse effects, the range of lexico-grammatical phenomena addressed must be broad enough to demonstrate that text is, in fact, structured by deploying linguistic resources in symphony and not individually. Our selection of a number of core phenomena reflects the compromise between broad coverage and manageability. For each phenomenon we expect our work significantly to further our understanding of that phenomenon's discourse functioning and lexico-grammatical description — both individually and in interaction with other phenomena.

One of the longer-term goals of the endeavour is to make a substantial contribution to the creation of a discourse-researcher's workbench geared towards the systematic investigation of discourse phenomena and their interactions. We will employ a proof-of-concept generation system being developed in the project to investigate desirable functionalities of such a workbench such as, for example, showing the concrete textual consequences of modelling decisions that the discourse theorist makes.

The project began in October 1992 and is scheduled to end in September 1995.

## 1.2 Particular methodological approach of the project

The basic tenet that shapes the project is the observation that it is vital to consider the discourse/text functioning of particular lexical and grammatical phenomena in *concrete contexts of use in particular text types.* This basic property of discourse restricts the effectiveness of studies that take the formal description of the sentence as basic and try to extend it to accommodate the properties of text. Many properties will be reached in this way, and our approach is explicitly compatible with the results of such work—indeed, some members of the project are even following this strategy—but, crucially, many vital properties *will not be revealed* in this way. And it is to address this lack that we adopt the methodology here described. Only by *combining* the results of sentence-based research and text-based research will a reasonably complete account of the properties of text and discourse functions be achieved. Our approach to uncovering the theoretical constructs required of the discourse level(s) is to examine the discourse contexts of a range of lexical and grammatical phenomena to uncover regular patterns of occurrence of those phenomena with respect to the discourse functions. This is an iterative process of hypothesis, experiment and refinement since existing descriptions of discourse contexts are still not sufficiently well developed. The range of approaches to text organisation being explored at the partner sites prior to the project is serving as a set of initial heuristics by which we can segment naturally occurring texts in order to seek evidence for or against the existence of the boundaries and units hypothesised. The organisation of the discourse level that we are constructing will be modelled as a declarative executable specification whose function is to provide conditional constraints on the deployment of resources drawn from all previously existing levels of description, i.e., the levels of grammar (paradigmatic and syntagmatic), lexis, semantics, and concepts/ontologies. The conditions must be expressed in terms of the theoretical units and their functions proposed for the discourse representation level.

This concern with the various levels of analysis being proposed within the project leads to one of our fundamental methodological decisions. In general, we attempt an analysis of linguistic phenomena that is **vertically organized**. That is, as opposed to describing, for example, how a wide range of syntactic properties relates to other syntactic properties (horizontal relations), we are concerned with how any particular syntactic property relates 'vertically' to a semantic level of description, which in turn is related to a situational level of description, which in turn is related to a text type level of description. This guarantees that phenomena are always being related back to text type and to their functional motivations. Examples of the deployment of the 'vertical methodology' follow below.

Finally, it should be noted that there are already rather prominent beneficial synergies arising between research groups in the project. Many of these are attributable to the contribution of the general view of text and of the relation between text type and linguistic realization found in systemic-functional linguistics [Halliday, 1978]. This theoretical position was adopted prior to the project by GMD-IPSI, Saarbrücken, and Madrid but appears now to be offering a convenient framework for incorporating and synthesizing disparate empirical results from other project partners within a single unified account that is then more easily convertible to formal computational representation. Some examples of this will also be given below.

### 1.3 Project starting points

All of the participants in the project have had a prior concern with discourse and so a variety of theoretical approaches to discourse phenomena are represented within the project. These approaches range from experimentally based studies (cf. [Vonk and Noordman, 1987, Vonk and Noordman, 1990, Sanders *et al.*, 1992]), through analyses of texts and of grammatical phenomena that function textually (cf. [Redeker, 1990, Caenepeel, 1989, Maes, 1990, Maes, 1991, Oversteegen, 1989]), through computational proposals for text planning and discourse organization (cf. [Bunt, 1987, Bateman *et al.*, 1991a, Hovy *et al.*, 1992, Rothkegel, 1993]) and for translation and multilinguality (cf. [Steiner *et al.*, 1988, Bateman *et al.*, 1991b]).

In addition, a number of the participants have access to, or experience with, large-scale linguistic resources at the lexicogrammatical levels of description and, to a lesser extent, to semantic levels of description also. Thus, Edinburgh has had considerable experience with the Alvey Natural Language Tools [Grover *et al.*, 1993] and the project as a whole is considering adopting the development environment PLEUK developed originally at Edinburgh [Calder and Humphreys, 1991]. Similarly, the GMD-IPSI internal project KOMET [Bateman *et al.*, 1991a, Bateman *et al.*, 1993] is developing large-scale grammar and semantics resources for multilingual text generation for German and Dutch, building on the English resources of the Penman project [Penman Project, 1989] developed at USC/Information Sciences Institute (Los Angeles). Here the multilingual resource development environment reported in [Bateman *et al.*, in preparation] is available to the project. Finally, CLS has already made use of some of the results of the ESPRIT Project PLUS (EP 5254) for constructing the outlines of an HPSG-style analysis of Dutch including an event-based semantics and interpreted level of quasi-logical form and Saarbrücken is developing further the German grammatical resources available from GMD-IPSI. In short, the project has available both very extensive computational lexicogrammatical resources offering the kind of wide coverage that is necessary for supporting more detailed discourse work and some more formally detailed accounts necessary for contact with sentence-based approaches. An overview of these inputs and their role in the projected architecture overall is included in figure 1 below.

### 1.4 General phenomena addressed

A good indication of the range of discourse phenomena being addressed by the project is given by the set of deliverables that marked the end of the first year of the project. These included:

- A study of the global organization of texts, showing how particular text types (e.g., recipes, news reports, medical reports, etc.) have particular symptomatic constituent-like structures (cf. [Lavid, 1993]). Each component of such structures has in turn particular symptomatic patterns of lexicogrammatical and discourse structure realizations. We see this in more detail in Section 2.3 below.

- A study of text connectivity, concerning how text parts are chained together sequentially and how this serves to express more hierarchically organized underlying text structures (cf. [Rothkegel and Villiger, 1993]).

- A study of discourse 'coherence relations', i.e., the relations between components of a text by which the text hangs together as a coherent entity rather than a collection of unrelated parts (cf. [Degand and Bateman, 1993]).

- A study of nominal anaphors in discourse (cf. [Hustinx *et al.*, 1993]), in which it is argued that nominal anaphors not only play a part in the management of reference in discourse, but also in a number of semantic as well as pragmatic mechanisms in discourse, on both local and global levels: they express interactive relations between writer and reader, they contribute to the semantic representation of discourse and they express structural thematic relationships in discourse.

- A study of the selection of grammatically realized 'thematic elements' in German, which we will see in more detail in Section 2.1 below (cf. [Steiner and Ramm, 1993]).

- A study of the selection criteria for connectives typically expressing temporal relations in Dutch, which we will see in more detail in Section 2.2 below (cf. [Oversteegen, 1993]).

- A study of the effect that distinct text types have on the aspectual constructions in discourse, particularly of the discourse function of aspectual information in narrative fictional texts and in newspaper reports in English (cf. [Caenepeel, 1993]).

For the purposes of this paper, rather than going into all of these at a necessarily too superficial level of detail, I will instead present three selected examples illustrating the vertical methodology. Two of these will be drawn from areas closer to linguistic surface forms and the third will briefly introduce the essential link to context with which all accounts in the project attempt to make contact. The view of context adopted within the project makes project results potentially very valuable for research in other areas of natural language processing—including approaches to spoken language.

Figure 1 summarizes in overview the contributions of the above mentioned areas of investigation to the project as a whole. The figure also shows the levels of description playing a role in the project and positions the above phenomena accordingly. Here we see the vertical methodology represented both at the scale of the entire project and again within individual work areas. The reoccurring paradigmatic/syntagmatic distinction is clarified in the next section.

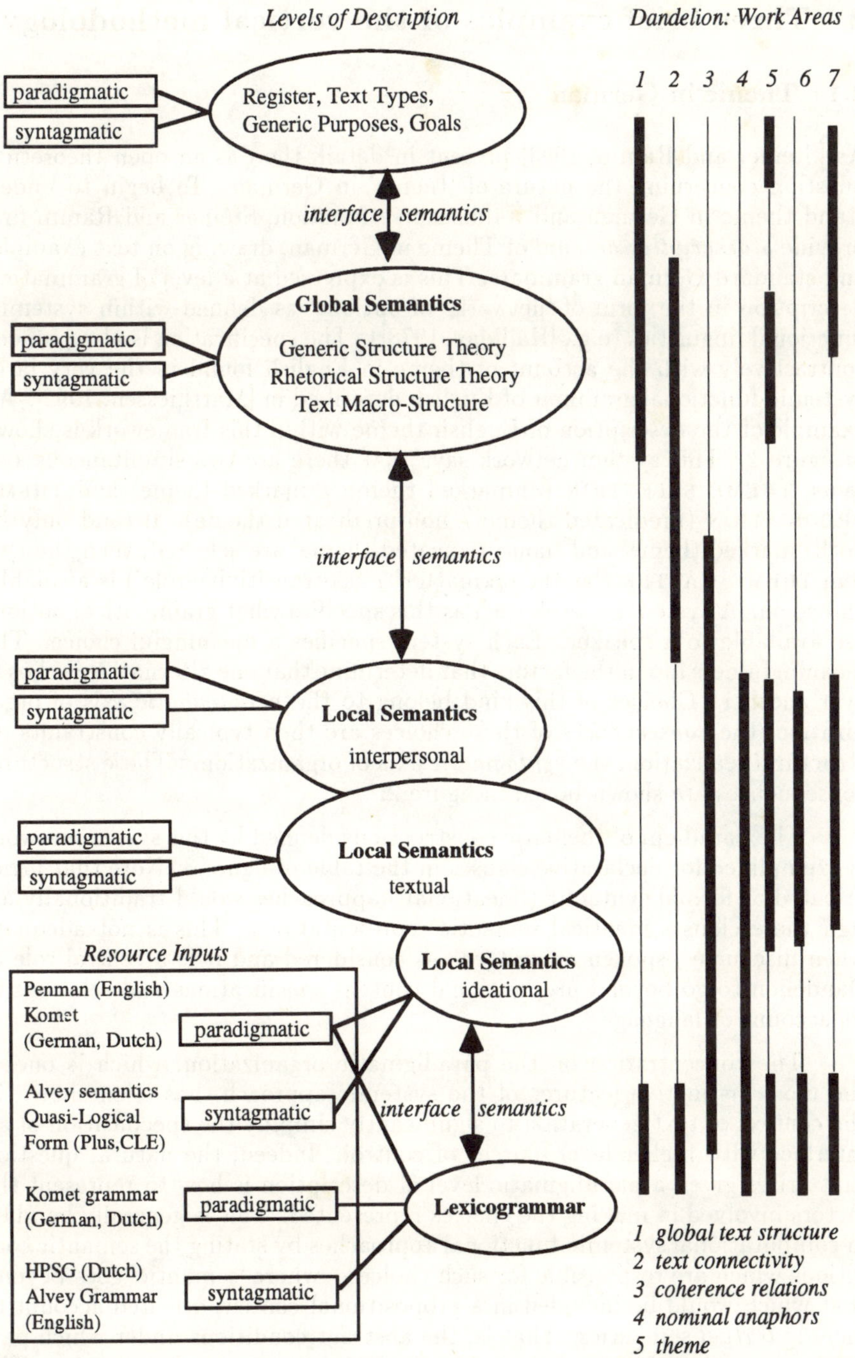


**Figure 1:** Dandelion at a glance: vertical spread

# 2 Three brief examples of the vertical methodology

## 2.1 Theme in German

As [Steiner and Ramm, 1993] present in detail, there is an open theoretical question concerning the nature of 'theme' in German. To begin to understand theme in German and its discourse function, Steiner and Ramm first provide a *descriptive account* of Theme in German, drawing on text examples and standard German grammars. This is expressed at a level of grammatical description in the form of 'networks of options' as defined within systemic-functional linguistics (e.g., [Halliday, 1978]). The specification is also pursued contrastively with the account of theme in English found in the very large systemic-functional grammar of English described in [Matthiessen, 1992]. An example of the description of English theme within this framework is shown in figure 2. This system network says that there are two simultaneous systems, THEME SELECTION (unmarked theme / marked theme) and THEME PREDICATION (predicated theme / non-predicated theme). If (and only if) both 'marked theme' and 'non-predicated-theme' are selected, then the system THEME MATTER ('as-theme-matter' / 'as-transitivity-role') is available; and so on. A system network such as this specifies what grammatical options are available to a speaker. Each system specifies a meaningful choice. The meaningfulness lies in the factors that determine that one alternative is chosen over another. Choices of this kind belong to the *paradigmatic* axis of organization; the *consequences* of these choices are then typically constraints on structural realization, the *syntagmatic* axis of organization.[2] These structural consequences are shown boxed in figure 2.

The paradigm of thematic constructions defined by this system network is exemplified for declarative clauses in the table of figure 3. Note that logic-oriented or formal syntactic ('ideational') approaches would traditionally assign these clauses identical semantic representations. This is not adequate when discourse—spoken or written—is considered and it is a central role of Dandelion to go beyond propositional content specifications and relations in its account of language.

The concentration on the paradigmatic organization, which is one of the most distinctive features of the systemic approach, has been shown in the context of text generation to significantly simplify the specification of an interface with higher level sources of control. Indeed, the natural question that arises given a paradigmatic level of description is how to represent the factors involved in making the choices represented. This is generally handled in computational systemic-functional approaches by stating the semantic conditions which are responsible for such choices—where 'semantic' goes beyond that which would be included in a propositional content oriented account to include *textual* semantics. That is, the abstract conditions under which particular textual options are selected in the lexicogrammatical realization. The recognition of a textual semantics is one step towards decomposing the general

[2]This distinction in systemic linguistics goes back to [Halliday, 1963].

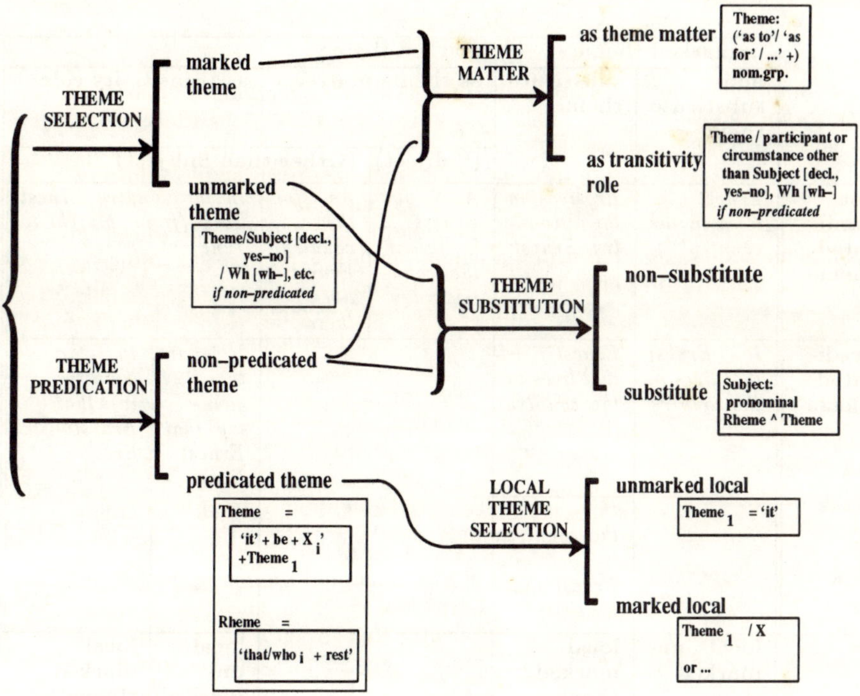


**Figure 2**: Generalized theme systems for English

area of 'pragmatics' more finely; the other vertical levels used in Dandelion represent further such steps.

The textual semantic conditions for constraining lexicogrammatical variation are expressed initially, following a methodology set out in [Matthiessen and Bateman, 1991, pp197-202], in terms of *inquiries*. Inquiries were originally introduced into computational systemic-functional accounts by [Mann, 1983] as a means of cleanly interfacing a grammatical account with various semantics even prior to formalization. Making inquiries, i.e., the 'semantic questions that must be asked in order for a selection of grammatical features to be made', explicit provides a set of hypotheses concerning the more abstract information that needs to be present to functionally motivate grammatical variations. A selection from the set of inquiries posited by Steiner and Ramm for the corresponding German theme network is as follows.

| | |
|---|---|
| **Grammatical Choice:** | marked *vs.* unmarked |
| **Inquiries:** | Which is the foregrounded information ?<br>Is it foregrounded as contrastive<br>and is the mode of the register 'written'<br>and/or is it a new paragraph topic? |

<table>
<tr><td></td><td colspan="2">unmarked theme</td><td colspan="4">marked theme</td></tr>
<tr><td></td><td>non-substitute theme</td><td>substitute theme</td><td colspan="2">as theme matter</td><td colspan="2">as transitivity role</td></tr>
<tr><td></td><td></td><td></td><td>(Subject)</td><td colspan="3">(Other than Subject)</td></tr>
<tr><td>not predicated theme</td><td>Ernest lives in the country</td><td>He lives in the country, Ernest</td><td>As for Ernest, he lives in the country</td><td>As for the country, Ernest lives there</td><td colspan="2">In the country Ernest lives (from March to June)</td></tr>
<tr><td rowspan="2">predicated theme</td><td rowspan="2">It's Ernest that lives in the country</td><td>Ernest it is that lives in the country (i)</td><td colspan="2" rowspan="2"></td><td rowspan="2">It's in the country that Ernest lives</td><td rowspan="2">In the country it is that Ernest lives</td></tr>
<tr><td>In the country it is Ernest that lives (ii)</td></tr>
<tr><td></td><td>local unmarked theme</td><td>local marked theme</td><td colspan="2"></td><td>local unmarked theme</td><td>local marked theme</td></tr>
</table>

**Or:**

**(i)** *As for Ernest, it's him that lives in the country*
**(ii)** *As for the country, it's Ernest that lives there*

**Figure 3**: Examples of thematic options in English

**Grammatical choice:** unmarked as 1st. participant *vs.* circumstance *vs.* textual *vs.* interpersonal

**Inquiries:** Is Theme most central participant of the event?
Is Theme subclassifiable as a time or space description of the current event?
Does the text plan call for 'hanging' this message on the textual relationship (causal, conjunctive, etc.) with some other part of the text?

**Grammatical choice:** simple *vs.* multiple

**Inquiries:** Is your message hung on more than one of

- element of the situation,
- interpersonal expression,
- textual expression?

**Grammatical choice:** interpersonal *vs.* non-interpersonal theme

**Inquiries:** Does the text plan call for:

- addressing some interlocutor by name?
- presenting the text's epistemic or deontic assessment of the proposition?
- asking a W-question?

Although there are several more inquiries relevant for controlling grammatical theme for German, of importance here is the kinds of semantic information that these inquiries *presuppose*. That is, there are clear kinds of textual semantic information that a level of discourse theory needs to provide to support the semantic discriminations called for by these inquiries. Thus, semantic information such as textual foregrounding, rhetorical organization, distinguishing attitudes, the 'register' of the text (see Section 2.3), patterns of paragraph topics, are all directly set up as hypotheses of discourse level constructs that must be supported, refined, or replaced by the empirical studies in the project. More details of this initial study are to be found in [Steiner and Ramm, forthcoming].

## 2.2 Temporal connectives in Dutch

Whereas the previous example of the vertical approach was embedded within a systemic linguistic approach, [Oversteegen, 1993] provides an analysis of the discourse functioning of temporal connectives in Dutch which shows our vertical methodology at work in a context independently of systemic linguistics. This is the more typical situation for empirical work in the project. Oversteegen's analysis is concerned with the interpretation of temporal connectives in their particular contexts of use. As she reports, this '...interpretation appears to depend on various properties of both main sentence and temporal subsentence (tense, event type, agentivity, information status, etc.) and our real world knowledge about their relation (i.e., consequential, contrastive).' In order to explain the interpretations observed for connectives, Oversteegen sets out first to provide context-neutral specifications of the semantic contribution made by particular temporal connectives, followed by an account of their interaction with specified contextual properties. The result of this interaction is then the interpretation in context of the connectives analyzed.

Two Track Structures (TTS) [Oversteegen, 1989] are used as an initial heuristic device for representing the interpretations of the temporal connectives. TTS representations consist of time relations on an S-track (where S stands for the speaker or point of speech) and an E-track (where E stands for event). The S-track has a point structure and harbours points of speech and points of evaluation; the E-track has a dense structure harbouring intervals onto which events are mapped and can split to represent nonactualized, potential time-lines. Within this framework, the main function of tense is to create a bridge between the S-track and the E-track. Examples of interpretations of simple tenses are given in figure 4. The bridge between tracks denotes simultaneity. It is straightforward to re-represent the TTS account in terms of the logical relationships that it entails. The account also includes distinctions in event types (e.g., 'terminative' events, 'process/states', etc.)

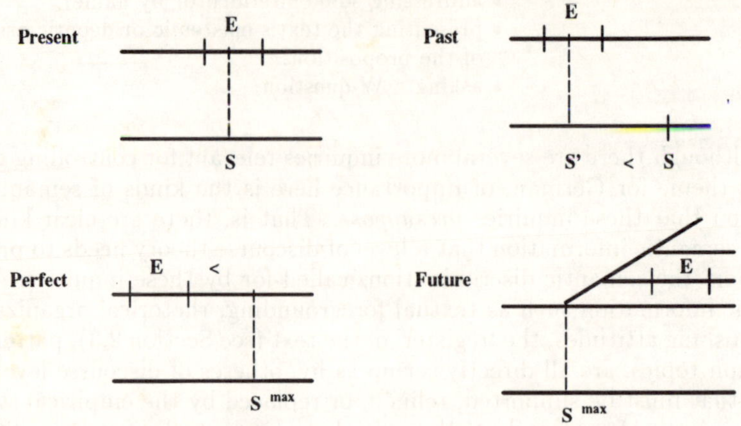


**Figure 4**: TTS examples: basic tenses

such as discussed in [Moens and Steedman, 1988] and elsewhere, as well as many other subtleties beyond the scope of the present paper.

Oversteegen goes on to provide similar TTS interpretations for combinations of events described in texts with particular selections of temporal connectives. In the following four sentences, for example, the connective *voordat* ('before') is used in four different senses:[3]

1. Voordat Nikki binnenkwam at Peter haar tartje op. (Before Nikki came in, Peter ate her piece of cake.) [factual 1]
2. We moesten een nieuwe accu installeren voordat de auto startte. (We had to install a new battery before the car started.) [factual 2]
3. Mathilda stopte met boxen voordat ze bij een match haar neus brak. (Mathilda stopped boxing before she broke her nose in a match.) [counterfactual]
4. Ik verliet het land voordat er iets gebeurde. (I left the country before anything happened.) [non-commital]

When represented in terms of TTS, the situations described can be related to sets of logical properties characterizing their differences. These are summarized in figure 5, drawn from [Oversteegen, 1993, p56-7]. Similar conditions are articulated for the connectives *toen* ('when'), *terwijl* ('while'), *sinds* ('since'), *nadat* ('after') and *totdat* ('until').

The semantic conditions which govern the selection of these temporal connectives then induces an organization over them. It is straightforward to represent this organization in terms analogous to those illustrated

[3]Although these senses largely carry over for English, there are interesting differences between English 'before' and Dutch 'voordat' which Oversteegen also discusses.

**all interpretations:**

- at least one evaluation point for the main sentence event ($E_m$) precedes all evaluation points for the subsentence event ($E_s$);
- the point of speech is not between these two sets;

**temporal interpretations:**

- terminative $E_s$ and $E_m$ leads to pure precedence interpretation;
- terminative $E_s$ and process $E_m$ leads to pure precedence or overlap interpretation;
- process/state $E_s$ and terminative $E_m$ require: inchoative marker in $E_s$, measurement in $E_m$, subsentence in Perfect tense;

**strict temporal interpretation:**

- $E_s$ is presumed.

**mixed temporal/conditional interpretation:**

- $E_m$ leads to $E_s$;
- $E_m$ contains deontic marker.

**non-factual interpretations:**

- $E_s$ is expected (default from context) or intended;
- $E_s$ is evaluated (positively or negatively)

**counterfactual interpretation:**

- $E_s$ does not occur;
- $E_s$ contains epistemic marker;
- $E_m$ does not entail *not*($E_s$);
- $E_m$ is new.

**non-commital interpretation:**

- $E_s$ does or does not occur;
- negative polarity marker present.

**Figure 5**: Semantic conditions for Dutch 'voordat'

in the previous section for theme in German; this is shown in the network extract in figure 6. The particular semantic conditions appear as inquiries on the paths of choice points leading to the selection of particular connectives; two examples for conditions on 'voordat' are shown in the figure. The *content* of those inquiries again provides hypotheses of discourse level constructs that need to be maintained if the use of the temporal connectives described is to be constrained appropriately. These include event types, temporal precedence relations, information status (given, new, presumed/presupposed, counterfactual), agentivity, event comparability, attitudinals, and temporal measurement. Importantly, the full specification of the semantic conditions necessary for selecting particular connectives makes it clear that, here again, the pure temporal relations involved between events are not sufficient. Even for temporal connectives it is essential that discourse considerations are also represented (cf. the distinction for discourse relations in general drawn between 'external'/'internal' [Halliday and Hasan, 1976, Martin, 1992], 'semantic'/'pragmatic' [van Dijk, 1977, Sanders *et al.*, 1993]). Otherwise, there are insufficient discrimination criteria to cover the uses of the connectives that are found in texts.

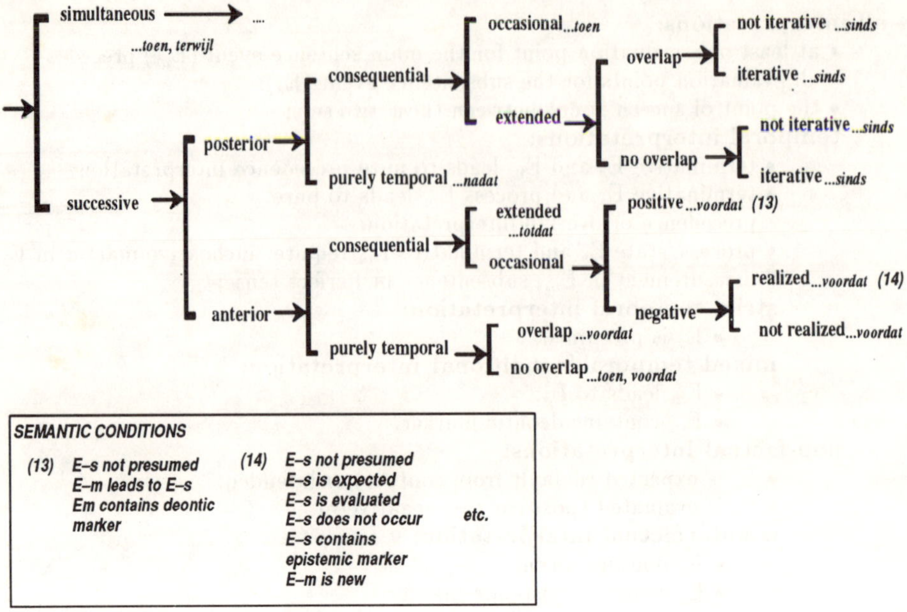


**Figure 6**: Network of Dutch temporal connectives

Supportive of the basic Dandelion tenet that various groups of lexicogrammatical phenomena pattern together in discourse, we can already see here that there is often considerable overlap in the kinds of more abstract information required by different lexicogrammatical phenomena: for example, both temporal connectives in Dutch and theme in German require semantic classifications that include attitudinals, discrimination of agency, and many more. Evidence concerning discourse level semantics can thus be accumulated from distinct sources and organized within a single account.

## 2.3 Context, generic structure and register

The previous two examples of the vertical methodology concentrated on lexicogrammar and semantics; some parts of the project, however, are dealing with issues of global text structure directly. [Lavid, 1993], for example, examines text types in order to set out a framework within which it is possible to state the regularly occurring text structure by which they are recognized as instances of their particular types. This work is building on the notion of 'Generic Structure Potential' (cf. [Hasan, 1984, Halliday and Hasan, 1989]), according to which texts can be decomposed into a sequence of stages. Crucially, each stage has a recognizeable realization in lexicogrammatical patterns that differentiates it from other stages.

Such a level of description is essential since, as has often been observed, patterning of lexicogrammatical and discourse realizations *are* different in different text types and even within particular segments of a text. Recipes offer a standard example of the pervasive effect of this kind of organization: the generic structure of one recipe analyzed by Lavid is shown in figure 7. Here, as Lavid notes, we see a

> '...differentiation in grammatical patterns emerging out of the different elements that configure the text's generic structure. In the **Method** element, the transitivity selections show a predominance of material:action processes (*marinate, drain, brush, preheat, press, boil,* etc.). The participants associated with those processes play the role of Goal in the actions described by those processes and are mostly inanimate and concrete (*lamb, liquid, stock, salt*). The Mood selections are imperative throughout. However, the clauses realizing the **Preliminary Information** element select for indicative:declarative Mood (e.g., *Boneless, heart-shaped chops are pure bliss served with a fruity sauce*). The transitivity selection is of a relational:ascriptive process: the dish is characterized according to the writer's subjective opinion, not acted upon.'

This kind of organization and its relation to the use that is made of lexis, grammar and discourse structure is a central phenomenon of language. The original Dandelion commitment to analyzing phenomena in their discourse context, which includes a classification according to context, is a response to this. Such a classification allows us to relativize discourse conditions as illustrated in the previous sections according to the text types for which those conditions are observed. For example, thematic progression is not identical for all types of texts and it is possible that the semantic conditions on temporal connectives also differ.[4] Indeed, it appears that most of the lexicogrammatical areas that are being examined in Dandelion require reference to be made to aspects of the text type in the specification of their semantic conditions. The further formalization of text type is thus a crucial aspect of the project.

Such a formalization is begun in [Lavid, 1993] by applying the same descriptive methodology that has been used with systemic-functional grammars. That is, the generic structures that are indicative of particular text types are seen as *syntagmatic* structures for which we need to ascertain the conditioning *paradigmatic* choices that give rise to them. Such choice networks are generally taken to describe the situation in which language occurs. The architecture as a whole then sees selections of features at a situational level of description being realized as constraints on the possible selections of features from semantic (including textual semantics) and lexicogrammatical levels of description.

This model draws heavily on [Martin, 1992], where a *stratified* approach to context is adopted. The traditional notion of 'text type', notoriously difficult to define, is here broken down across two strata (genre and register) and across a number of general areas of meaning. [Lavid, 1993]

[4]This latter possibility is currently under investigation within Dandelion.

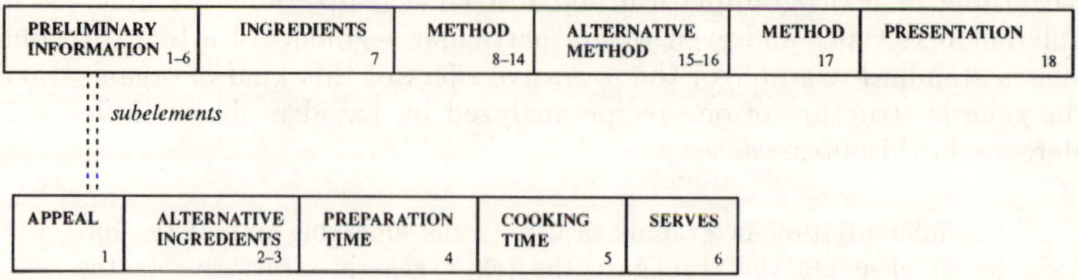


**Grenadine Valentines**

(1) Boneless, heart–shaped chops are pure bliss served with a fruity sauce. (2) (If grenadine is unobtainable, (3) you can use cassis or other red fruit syrup.) (4) Preparation time: 30 minutes. (5) Cooking time: 12 minutes. (6) Serves 4. (7) 4 valentine (boneless) lamb chops; 2 tbs grenadine (pomegranate syrup); 2 tbs Worcestershire sauce; 1tbs grapeseed oil; 1/2 tsp sea salt flakes; 8 tbs lamb stock; 2 tbs guava or crabapple jelly; 225g (8oz) chassela grapes. (8) Marinate lamb in grenadine and Worcestershire sauce for 20 minutes. (9) Drain, reserve liquid. (10) Preheat heavy–based frying pan, (11) brush with a little oil. (12) When pan is very hot, (13) press lamb down with a fish slice for five minutes on each side (14) or until golden outside and pink inside. (15) (If preferred, (16) extend cooking to 12 minutes total.) (17) Meanwhile, in a separate pan, boil the marinade, uncovered, with the stock, salt and jelly for ten minutes to a syrupy glaze. (18) Serve valentines with a pool of sauce.

**Figure 7**: Example of generic structure of a recipe

proposes an initial classification network for genres based on [Martin, 1992, Martin, 1993] as shown in figure 8. In this network, the consequences of choices (shown in boxes as before) are particular 'text types', each with a particular generic structure and specified further general constraints on the lexicogrammar, semantics, and discourse relations that can occur. Filling out those constraints more finely than that suggested in [Martin, 1992] and elsewhere is one of the prime goals of Dandelion.

## 3 Generic situations – bridging the gap between speech and writing

We can now take a brief step beyond Dandelion goals and use the notion of context just introduced to suggest how our work on discourse and a discourse researcher's workbench should also be of relevance for accounts of speech. In general, and as made explicit in our architecture, the forms of language that may be employed vary according to the situation in which language is used. One further aspect of situation is the *mode* of interaction. Now, whereas there are currently attempts to set up the grammar of spoken language as fundamentally different from the grammar of written language, this is in danger of missing the fundamental relationship between situation and language that allows us to relate these modes. Although spoken language will be different from written language because their respective situations are different, the terms 'spoken' and 'written' are not them-

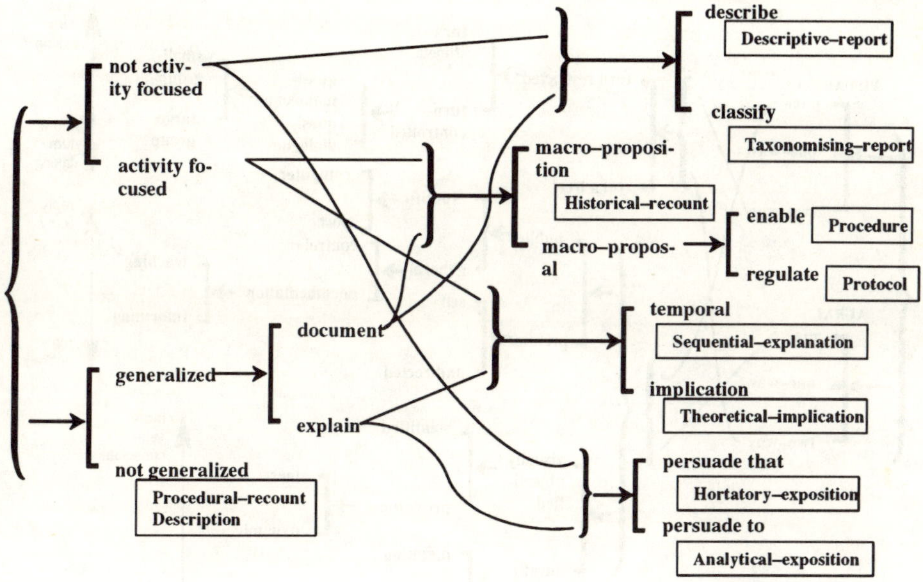


**Figure 8**: Classification of generic purposes

selves theoretically well motivated features from a classification of situations. A finer classification of situations is more revealing. This has been shown empirically by the series of large-scale analyses reported in [Biber, 1986, Biber, 1988]: here we see large-scale similarities that cross-cut the written-spoken classification as well as differences. Also, [Redeker, 1992] proposes a model of textual coherence and its lexicogrammatical realization that similarly cross-cuts the written-spoken divide.

These studies show that the terms 'spoken' and 'written' need to be replaced by a multidimensional classification system. This is, however, precisely what the paradigmatic networks suggested in the previous section for the situational level of description provide. An extract from the relevant area of these networks is shown in figure 9. Here we can see that there are a number of different ways in which speech can resemble writing and writing can resemble speech. Taking the first classification choices gives the table of cross-classification shown in figure 10, where face-to-face interaction and writing are just two extreme cases of a multidimensional continuum. The kinds of grammar that will be found will also vary systematically across this continuum. When spoken language situations share significant features with the situations that we address within Dandelion, then the consequences of those features will also hold for that spoken language. What is essential is that an account spans all kinds of lexicogrammar and shows how they are related; something which compartmentalizing speech and writing is unlikely to achieve.

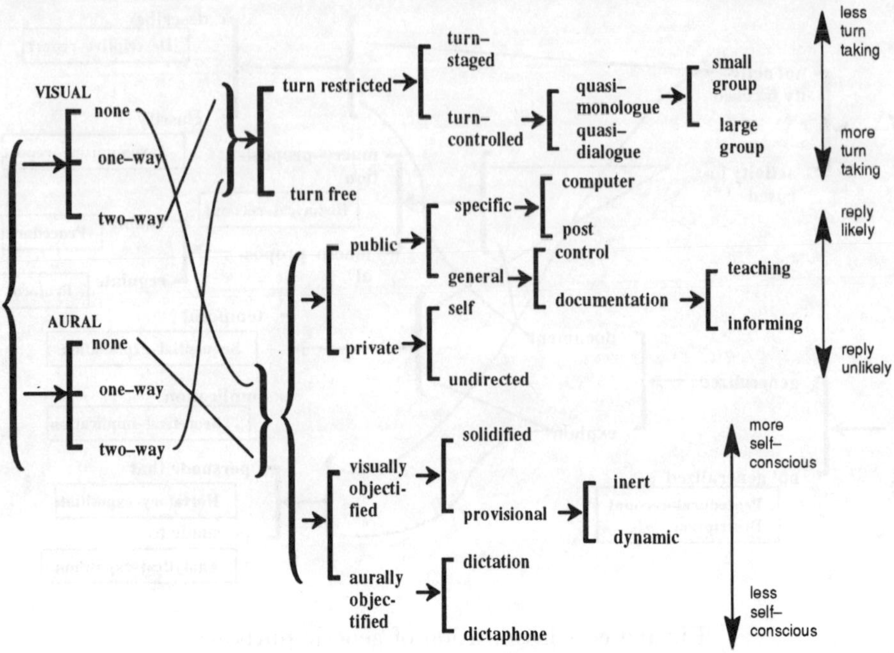


**Figure 9**: Mode situational feature; from Martin (1992: 515)

| | VISUAL CONTACT | | |
|---|---|---|---|
| AURAL CONTACT | **none** | **one-way** | **two-way** |
| **none** | writing | silent movie, home movie, Big Brother (1984) | sign language, mime? |
| **one-way** | radio, audio tape, record | television, movie video prayer | lip-reading (hearing/deaf dyad) sermon, theatre |
| **two-way** | telephone, intercom, short-wave radio, confession | HAL (2001), blind/seeing dyad, video-intercom | face-to-face conversation |

**Figure 10**: Aural and visual contact, cross-classifying mode; taken from Martin (1992: 511)

## 4 Conclusion

In this paper, I have briefly introduced the goals, methods, and some of the work being undertaken in the Dandelion project. I have also tried to describe how our approach to discourse may be of use in the future for work on speech. Although the current focus of the project is written text, our general interest is to account for the relation between different text types, characterized in terms of the situations in which they appear, and the corresponding language out of which those texts are constructed. 'Spoken' language, from this perspective, should be seen as a set of varieties of language whose general properties are largely to be motivated from situation, just as are those of 'written' language. Breaking down the dichotomy between spoken/written allows a clearer view of what aspects of the accounts of either can carry over to the other—thereby motivating principled re-usability of resources/accounts where appropriate.

There is also a potential benefit of our approach for speech in terms of the architecture being constructed. Our attention to vertical relationships has placed inter-stratal mappings at the centre of attention. We have also increased the number of distinct vertical levels over more usual accounts. We expect that this will simplify the inter-level mappings, which is an essential precursor for allowing high-level information to filter out inappropriate low-level hypotheses.

Finally, for high-quality speech synthesis, particularly the generation of intonation, it is well accepted that information concerning the discourse context and speaker intentions is essential. This level of description is precisely that at which Dandelion is aiming to make its main contribution. There are, therefore, many good reasons for interaction between the concerned research communities to continue.

## References

[Bateman *et al.*, 1991a] John A. Bateman, Elisabeth A. Maier, Elke Teich, and Leo Wanner. Towards an architecture for situated text generation. In *International Conference on Current Issues in Computational Linguistics*, Penang, Malaysia, 1991. Also available as technical report of GMD/Institut für Integrierte Publikations- und Informationssysteme, Darmstadt, Germany.

[Bateman *et al.*, 1991b] John A. Bateman, Christian M.I.M. Matthiessen, Keizo Nanri, and Licheng Zeng. The re-use of linguistic resources across languages in multilingual generation components. In *Proceedings of the 1991 International Joint Conference on Artificial Intelligence, Sydney, Australia*, volume 2, pages 966 – 971. Morgan Kaufmann Publishers, 1991.

[Bateman *et al.*, 1993] John A. Bateman, Liesbeth Degand, and Elke Teich. Multilingual textuality: Some experiences from multilingual text generation. In *Proceedings of the Fourth European Workshop on Natural Language Generation, Pisa, Italy, 28-30 April 1993*, pages 5 – 17, 1993. Also available as technical report from GMD/Institut für Integrierte Publikations- und Informationssysteme, Darmstadt, Germany.

[Bateman *et al.*, in preparation] John A. Bateman, Christian M.I.M. Matthiessen, and Licheng Zeng. A general architecture for multilinguality in natural language processing. Technical report, GMD/IPSI, Darmstadt and University of Sydney, in preparation.

[Biber, 1986] Douglas Biber. Spoken and written textual dimensions in English: resolving the contradictory findings. *Language*, 62(2):384 - 414, 1986.

[Biber, 1988] Douglas Biber. *Variation Across Speech and Writing.* Cambridge University Press, 1988.

[Bunt, 1987] Harry C. Bunt. Utterance generation from semantic representation augmented with pragmatic information. In Gerard Kempen, editor, *Natural Language Generation: Recent Advances in Artificial Intelligence, Psychology, and Linguistics*, pages 333 - 348. Kluwer Academic Publishers, Boston/Dordrecht/The Hague, 1987. Paper presented at the Third International Workshop on Natural Language Generation, August 1986, Nijmegen, The Netherlands.

[Caenepeel, 1989] M. Caenepeel. *Aspect, temporal ordering, and perspective in narrative fiction.* PhD thesis, University of Edinburgh, 1989.

[Caenepeel, 1993] Mimo Caenepeel. Aspect and text structure. Technical report, University of Edinburgh, Edinburgh, Scotland, September 1993. (ESPRIT Basic Research Action: Dandelion, EP6665; Deliverable R1.3.1).

[Calder and Humphreys, 1991] J. Calder and K. Humphreys. The PLEUK manual, 1991.

[Degand and Bateman, 1993] Liesbeth Degand and John Bateman. Coherence relations and multilingual text generation. Technical report, GMD-IPSI, Darmstadt, FRG, September 1993. (ESPRIT Basic Research Action: Dandelion, EP6665; Deliverable R1.1.2a).

[Grover *et al.*, 1993] Claire Grover, John Carroll, and Ted Briscoe. The Alvey Natural Language Tools Grammar (4th release). Technical report, Human Communication Research Centre, University of Edinburgh and Computer Laboratory, University of Cambridge, 1993.

[Halliday and Hasan, 1976] Michael A.K. Halliday and Ruqaiya Hasan. *Cohesion in English.* Longman, London, 1976.

[Halliday and Hasan, 1989] Michael A.K. Halliday and Ruqaiya Hasan. *Language, Context and Text: a social semiotic perspective.* Oxford University Press, London, 1989.

[Halliday, 1963] Michael A.K. Halliday. Class in relation to the axes of chain and choice in language. *Linguistics*, 2:5–15, 1963. Reprinted in abbreviated form in Gunther R. Kress (ed.)(1976) *Halliday: system and function in language*, London: Oxford University Press, pp84-87.

[Halliday, 1978] Michael A.K. Halliday. *Language as social semiotic.* Edward Arnold, London, 1978.

[Hasan, 1984] Ruqaiya Hasan. The nursery tale as a genre. *Notthingham Linguistic Circular*, 13:71 – 102, 1984.

[Hovy *et al.*, 1992] Eduard Hovy, Julia Lavid, Elisabeth Maier, Vibhu Mittal, and Cecile Paris. Employing knowledge resources in a new text planner architecture. In *Proceedings of the 6th International Workshop on Natural Language Generation*, Trento, Italy, 1992. Springer-Verlag.

[Hustinx *et al.*, 1993] Lettica Hustinx, Fons Maes, Corine Schouten, and Wietske Vonk. Discourse functions of NP-anaphora: linguistic and text analytic form-function analysis of NP-anaphora. Technical report, Center for Language Studies, Tilburg, Holland, September 1993. (ESPRIT Basic Research Action: Dandelion, EP6665; Deliverable R1.4.1).

[Lavid, 1993] Julia Lavid. Generic structure potential: a functional characterization of global discourse structures. Technical report, Universidad Complutense Madrid, Madrid, Spain, September 1993. (ESPRIT Basic Research Action: Dandelion, EP6665; Deliverable R1.1.1b).

[Maes, 1990] A.A. Maes. The interpretation and representation of coreferential lexical nps in expository texts. *Journal of Semantics*, 7:143–174, 1990.

[Maes, 1991] A.A. Maes. *Nominal anaphors and the coherence of discourse.* PhD thesis, Katholieke Universiteit Brabant, 1991.

[Mann, 1983] William C. Mann. The anatomy of a systemic choice. *Discourse Processes*, 1983. Also available as USC/Information Sciences Institute, Research Report ISI/RR-82-104, 1982.

[Martin, 1992] James R. Martin. *English text: systems and structure.* Benjamins, Amsterdam, 1992.

[Martin, 1993] James R. Martin. A context for genre: modelling social processes in functional linguistics, July 1993. Paper presented at the International Systemic Functional Congress, University of Victoria, British Columbia, Canada.

[Matthiessen and Bateman, 1991] Christian M.I.M. Matthiessen and John A. Bateman. *Text generation and systemic-functional linguistics: experiences from English and Japanese.* Frances Pinter Publishers and St. Martin's Press, London and New York, 1991.

[Matthiessen, 1992] Christian M.I.M. Matthiessen. Lexicogrammatical cartography: English systems. Technical report, University of Sydney, Linguistics Department, 1992. Ongoing expanding draft.

[Moens and Steedman, 1988] M. Moens and M. Steedman. Temporal ontology and temporal reference. *Computuational Linguistics*, 14(2), 1988.

[Oversteegen, 1989] E. Oversteegen. *Tracking Time. A proposal for the representation of temporal expressions in Dutch.* PhD thesis, University of Utrecht, 1989.

[Oversteegen, 1993] Leonoor Oversteegen. Dutch temporal connectives. Technical report, Center for Language Studies, Tilburg, Holland, September 1993. (ESPRIT Basic Research Action: Dandelion, EP6665; Deliverable R1.3.2a).

[Penman Project, 1989] Penman Project. PENMAN documentation: the Primer, the User Guide, the Reference Manual, and the Nigel manual. Technical report, USC/Information Sciences Institute, Marina del Rey, California, 1989.

[Redeker, 1990] G. Redeker. Ideational and pragmatic markers of discourse structure. *Journal of Pragmatics*, 14:367–381, 1990.

[Redeker, 1992] Gisela Redeker. Coherence and structure in text and discourse, 1992. Manuscript. Tilburg University.

[Rothkegel and Villiger, 1993] Annely Rothkegel and Claudia Villiger. Chaining. Technical report, Universität des Saarlandes, Saarbrücken, FRG, September 1993. (ESPRIT Basic Research Action: Dandelion, EP6665; Deliverable R1.2.2a).

[Rothkegel, 1993] Annely Rothkegel. *Textualisieren. Theorie und Computermodell der Textproduktion.* Peter Lang Verlag, Frankfurt am Main, 1993.

[Sanders *et al.*, 1992] Ted J.M. Sanders, Wilbert P.M. Spooren, and Leo G.M. Noordman. Towards a taxonomy of coherence relations. *Discourse Processes*, 15(1):1 – 36, January – March 1992.

[Sanders *et al.*, 1993] T.J.M. Sanders, W.P.M. Spooren, and L.G.M. Noordman. Coherence relations in a cognitive theory of discourse representations. *Cognitive Linguistics*, 4(2):93 – 133, 1993.

[Steiner and Ramm, 1993] Erich Steiner and Wiebke Ramm. Grammatical coverage German. Technical report, Universität des Saarlandes, Saarbrücken, FRG, September 1993. (ESPRIT Basic Research Action: Dandelion, EP6665; Deliverable R2.1.3).

[Steiner and Ramm, forthcoming] Erich Steiner and Wiebke Ramm. On theme as a grammatical notion for German. *Functions of Language*, 1(1), forthcoming.

[Steiner *et al.*, 1988] Erich H. Steiner, Paul Schmidt, and Cornelia Zelinksy-Wibbelt, editors. *From Syntax to Semantics: insights from Machine Translation.* Frances Pinter, London, 1988.

[van Dijk, 1977] T.A. van Dijk. Connectives in text grammar and text logic. In T.A. van Dijk and J. Petöfi, editors, *Grammars and descriptions: studies in text theory and text analysis*, pages 11 – 63. de Gruyter, London, 1977.

[Vonk and Noordman, 1987] W. Vonk and L.G.M. Noordman. On the effect of contrastive signaling in processing text. In G. Lüer and U. Lass, editors, *Fourth European conference on eye movements, vol.I: Proceedings*, pages 39–40. Hogrefe, Toronto, etc., 1987.

[Vonk and Noordman, 1990] W. Vonk and L.G.M. Noordman. On the control of inferences in text understanding. In D.A. Balota, G.B. Flores d'Arcais, and K. Rayner, editors, *Comprehension processes in reading*, pages 447–464. Erlbaum, Hillsdale, NJ, 1990.

# A Friendly Interactive Robot for Service Tasks

Gianni Lazzari
I.R.S.T. - Istituto per la Ricerca Scientifica e Tecnologica
I-38050 Povo (Trento)
Italy

## Abstract

This paper presents the EU-474 Eureka Project "*FIRST*". The project started in 1991 with a 5 year development perspective and a total value of 11 MECU. IRST acts as prime contractor with P&TI in Italy, ITMI and LIRM in France as partners. The "target" system of this project is based on a set of intelligent robots navigating autonomously inside a hospital in a peopled environment. A supervision system provides flexible planning and traffic control strategies, monitoring and teleoperation capabilities. Moreover a set of information stations located in the departments, with natural language understanding capabilities, allow the negotiation of services with the supervision system and the maintenance of environmental and organisational information. The hospital environment is characterised by a complex organisation requiring a variety of transport tasks. Human-machine interaction has a key role in integrating the automatic transportation system with the hospital organisation. The voice input-output capabilities are mainly devoted to qualified operator-robot interaction for delivery/pick-up of objects and to supervisor operator/supervision station for the control and telecontrol of the system.

In the following, the system architecture and a short functional analysis of the system are presented. Then, the motivations of the use of speech technologies are discussed. Finally, the first prototypes of the Automatic Speech Understanding (ASU) unit developed in FIRST is presented together with some future work directions.

## 1. Introduction

Transportation is a very important activity in health care. Studies on hospital organisation show that fetch and carry tasks take up a considerable amount of nursing time [11]. A mobile robot can support nurses, freeing more time for patient care, given that a lot of material has to be delivered or removed:

- meals are delivered to patients and empty trays have to be collected and taken back to the kitchen three times a day;
- linen is changed every day and dirty linen is collected;
- sterilised instruments have to be moved from a central sterilisation station to the various departments and then back for a new cleaning cycle;
- organic samples (e.g. blood test tubes) are sent to the laboratory for analysis;
- documentation and reports of medical examinations have to be moved between different locations in the hospital;
- waste (both normal and dangerous) has to be collected.

In the past, innovative solutions were developed for some of these tasks: pneumatic mail has been used for reports and normal mail delivery, Automatic Guided Vehicles (AGV) operating by means of a network of wires buried or attached to the floor have been adopted for heavy loads. These solutions are characterised by a high degree of rigidity and they require a substantial change in the hospital environment.

In a hospital located in Bolzano (Italy) a fleet of AGVs works 18 hours a day, from six in the morning until midnight, to transport meals, medicines, waste and linen. There are other similar experiences in Europe, especially in France and Germany, but these systems are not yet widely used [1]. In France there are 17 hospitals with about 100 AGVs installed in all.

An alternative approach was recently implemented in the U.S.A. *"Helpmate"*, a hospital transport mobile robot, was introduced and tested in many hospitals. There are 25 units of *"Helpmate"* installed in the U.S.A. *"Helpmate"* navigates in a hospital environment handling uncertainty and unexpected obstacles, requiring slight modifications for any given hospital [2].

Nevertheless, no current commercial system seems to offer a satisfactory level of flexibility to approach the problem of automatic transportation of goods in the hospital environment. The target of the system discussed here is a "Friendly Interactive Transport System". This involves the development of an integrated system managing a fleet of autonomous robots interfaced to the organisation of the hospital in a flexible way, i.e. allowing "out of schedule" tasks and organisational changes.

In the following, the system architecture and a short functional analysis of the system are presented. Then, the motivations of the use of speech technologies are discussed. Finally, the first prototypes of the Automatic Speech Understanding (ASU) unit developed in FIRST is presented together with some future work directions.

## 2. The "Friendly Interactive Transport System"

As previously shown, the hospital is characterised by a rich variety of transportation tasks to be carried out within a very articulated organisation, continuously changing and varying from hospital to hospital. This high degree of complexity of the transportation problem within hospitals calls for the adoption of a set of innovative AI. technologies, like autonomous navigation, multimedia interface, natural language and planning, integrated with more consolidated ones, like mechanics, electronics and control [3].

There follows a short presentation of the requirements and an introduction to the functions of the system.

## 2.1 Requirements

The analysis of the transport requirements seen in a typical hospital led to the definition of the *"mission"* concept as the basic transport operation. A mission is characterised by a set of parameters: starting location, destination, load, priority and temporal constraints. Missions can be classified on the basis of their temporal collocation as:

- routine missions corresponding to transport services performed on a periodic basis like the daily distribution of meal trays, waste collection, linen;
- spot missions, related to single asynchronous requests, like off-schedule transport of medicines, lab and pharmacy supplies, patient's records.

The system must cope with requests for both types of missions.
A key factor for the adoption of an automatic transport system is the amount of effort required to introduce such a system inside the hospital organisation. This implies the development of a "friendly" and "interactive" system, presenting a "natural" interface towards users without requiring a deep knowledge of its internal structure.

The system should include modules allowing users to directly specify missions to be performed and to negotiate the availability of resources. Moreover, the resource status (robot position, scheduled missions, current missions and log of system activities) should be presented to the system operator, giving him the possibility to modify the mission evolution and to make decisions when critical situations (conflicts for resources, delays in mission execution) occur.

Another relevant aspect concerns the "robustness" of the system, given the high degree of unpredictability of the environmental configuration. The system is required to gradually reduce its performances in presence of diminished viability of hospital spaces, avoiding "crash" situations particularly with small disturbances.

Some hospitals are characterised by the presence of suitable "technical areas" with access forbidden to unauthorised persons. This is not quite the majority of cases, so the system must be able to share spaces and technical plants with people present within the hospital.

Finally, the system should have a very limited impact on the environment, in terms of both installation duties and operational "noise" (acoustic and electromagnetic) emissions.

## 2.2 Overall System Architecture

The system is composed of a fleet of autonomous robots navigating in the environment under control of a Supervision System (SS) which is in charge of the planning and traffic control strategies, and provides monitoring and teleoperation functions. Moreover the SS offers a friendly interface with a human operator who interacts with the system to input, and possibly, modify transport requests and to resolve critical situations involving the moving robots.

Finally, a set of Information Stations (IS) displaced in the hospital departments allow enabled personnel to access information related to the transport tasks. All these subsystems are linked by means of a Communication System (CS) based both on a wireless network connecting the robots and a LAN for the IS. The system architecture is schematically represented in figure 1.

Two mobile platforms will be developed in the FIRST project. The main difference between them is related to the maximum load transportable. The French partners will produce a mobile robot targeted for a 250 kg load mainly devoted to routine missions [1]. The Italian partners will develop a more flexible platform targeted for a load of 30 Kg max. mainly carrying out spot missions. The two platforms have different mechanical specifications and use different navigation techniques. Both can be managed by the same supervision station exploiting a complementary function. The exploitation of spot missions requires more interaction between the system and the operators due to the necessity of managing "out of scheduling" tasks. The use of speech technology both for robot operator and for supervision station-supervisor operator interaction will improve the flexibility of the system and system use by the organisation.

## 2.3 System Functions

The main objective of the system is the transportation of goods within the hospital building. This implies the availability of autonomous subsystems capable of moving in the somewhat unstructured hospital environment.

A second key factor for system introduction into a hospital concerns the functions and the interface offered to users. The component subsystems provide a variety of interaction modalities to facilitate co-operation with humans.

- the robots are equipped with a spoken command language interface allowing authorised personnel to perform local control by means of a small set of oral messages (e.g. "turn left", "two meters back" and so on); moreover, robots have specific input peripherals (like badge reader and keypad) for user identification;
- the ISs are characterised by a typed natural language interface;
- the SS is equipped with a multimedia interface (mouse, touch screen, advanced graphics and spoken command language) to allow the operator easy access to the SS functions without having his own attention capabilities saturated. The supervision operator is also able to telecontrol a single robot through the SS man-machine interface when difficult environmental situations are encountered.

The users have been grouped into three main categories:

1. *Untrained users*: patients, visitors, unqualified operators. They neither know the system capabilities nor how to interact with it. Their only interaction is limited to stopping robots in case an emergency arises by means of a push-button or an oral message.

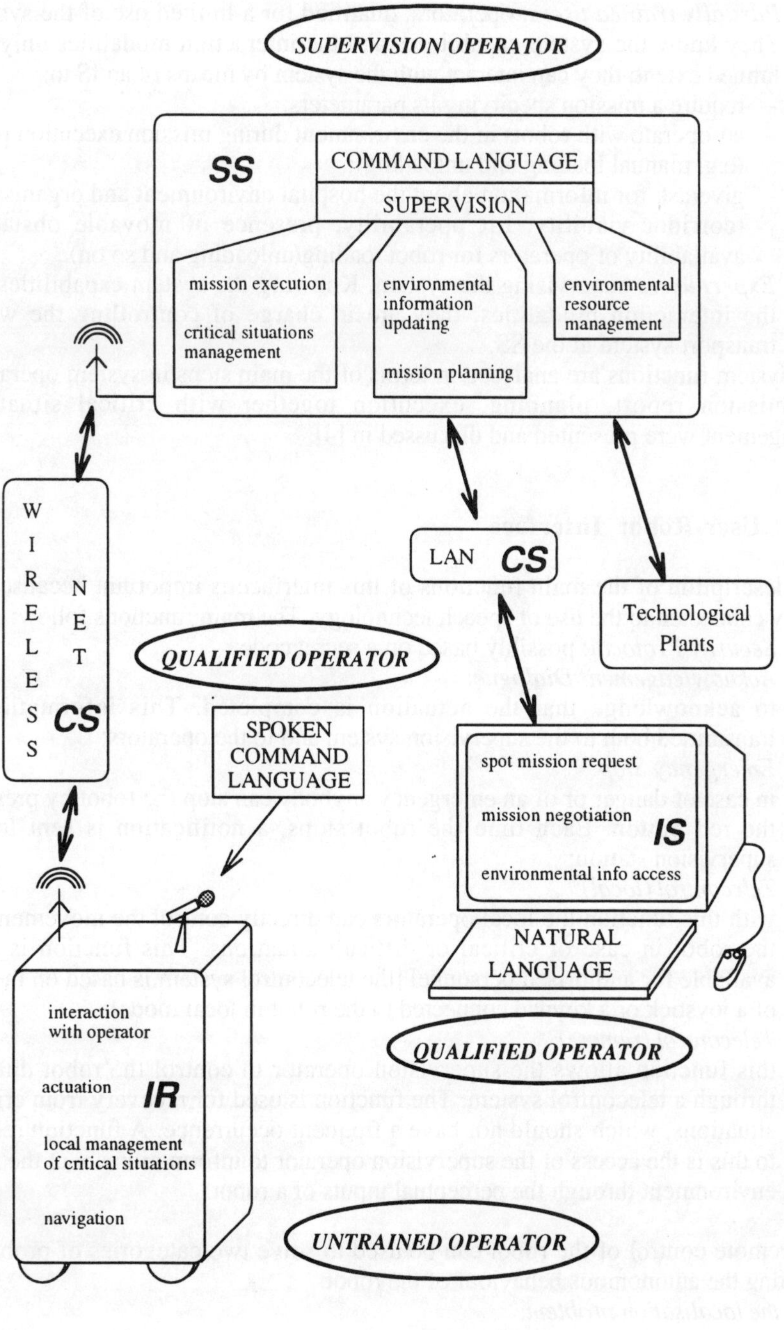


**Figure 1:** Overall system architecture

2. *Partially trained users*: operators, qualified for a limited use of the system. They know the system capabilities and the interaction modalities only to a limited extent; they can interact with the system by means of an IS to:
   - require a mission specifying its parameters;
   - co-operate with robots in the environment during mission execution phase (e.g. manual loading and unloading);
   - give/ask for information about the hospital environment and organisation (corridor viability, lift operability, presence of movable obstacles, availability of operators for robot loading/unloading and so on).
3. *Expert users* supervising the system. Knowing the system capabilities and the interaction modalities, they are in charge of controlling the whole transport system at the SS.

The system functions are analysed in terms of the main steps in system operation, i.e. mission report, planning, execution together with critical situations management were presented and discussed in [4].

## 2.4 User-Robot Interface

The description of the main functions of this interface is important because it is tightly connected to the use of speech technology. The main functions follow:

- *Security Protocol*: possibly based on a secret code;
- *Acknowledgement Dialogue*:
  to acknowledge that the actuation is completed. This information is transmitted both to the supervision system and to the operators;
- *Emergency Stop*:
  in case of danger or of an emergency anybody can stop the robot by pressing the red button. Each time the robot stops, a notification is sent to the supervision station;
- *Telecontrol (local)*:
  with this function the local operators can directly control the movements of the robot in case of critical or difficult situations. This function is only available for authorised personnel [the telecontrol system is based on the use of a joystick or a keypad connected to the robot in local mode].
- *Telecontrol (remote)*:
  this function allows the supervision operator to control the robot directly through a telecontrol system. The function is used for recovery from critical situations, which should not have a frequent occurrence. A function related to this is the access of the supervision operator to information about the local environment through the perceptual inputs of a robot.

The remote control of the robot can be used to solve two categories of problems affecting the autonomous behaviour of the robot:

- *the localisation problem*:
  a robot can estimate poorly its location or have a local representation of the environment that does not correspond to its map. In this case the supervision

operator needs to provide information to allow the robot to localise its position on the map correctly;

- *the problem of a stall situation*:
  the path chosen by the robot can be blocked by an obstacle and the navigation system may not be able to overcome it unless further information is provided by the supervision operator. When a robot gets stuck this way the supervision operator must provide high level guidance to allow re-planning.

The precise form of assistance that the supervision operator must provide has to be defined in relation to the ability and the functionality of the autonomous navigation system. Instead of having direct control of robot movements, the telecontrol system offers a set of elementary commands specified at a rather high level and interpreted by different levels of the system (e.g. a set of commands can be: *move a unit backward, rotate the camera of one unit, re-orient according to the orientation of the camera, free space on your right.*

## 3. Speech Technologies in FIRST

The main goal of the FIRST project, from the scientific point of view, is the integration of different capabilities in order to obtain an "intelligent system behaviour". Intelligent behaviour means a high degree of adaptability to the needs of the hospital organisation. The robot must adapt to the dynamic change of the environment and the system has to cope with the organisation (operators) giving them an effective interface for communicating needs, mission to carry out, environmental changes, organisational changes. As already stated, a major factor influencing the form of human-machine interfaces in FIRST is the specificity of the tasks that must be achieved through the interfaces and the degree to which the users know how the tasks are achieved, or at least, communicated to the system.

The most important outcome of this is that we need to distinguish the different types of users in terms of the extent to which they have been trained to interact with the system. For qualified and supervisor operators it is possible to define Task-action Grammars that specify the sequence of user actions required to achieve a particular task. In this way, users communicate the tasks by learning and applying fixed sequences or actions and by specifying parameters.

The use of voice technologies for human-robot interaction enhances the capabilities of the system in terms of easiness and friendliness of interaction. The robot communicates with the operators using a text-to-speech synthesiser. The robot can also communicate with non-qualified users giving messages and information when necessary. A typical situation can be a crowded corridor, a persistent obstacle or an emergency. The use of voice can be useful to the operator in the installation and debugging phase of the system.

A typical robot mission is based on a loading phase, a navigation phase and finally a delivery phase. The operator- robot interaction for loading/unloading, i.e. meal trays, medicines, reports or blood test vials is mainly manual. This operation needs first of all an acknowledgement and can also be supported by receiving/giving some information (messages) from/to the system operator or the operators of the hospital departments. In this context voice is very useful allowing a high degree of flexibility for robot-operator and inter-operator communication.

Another situation in which the use of speech input-output seems to be very useful is when a robot, during the navigation phase is unable to manage a critical situation due to some unexpected event. In this case, or in some cases already discussed in section 2.4, the supervisor operator can use the telecontrol functionality. When the operator takes direct control of the robot, the system displays the latest position of the robot, the previous path accomplished and what the robot sees through the on-board camera. Having all this information on the screen, the operator can give simple basic navigation commands and try to solve the problems as soon as possible.

The telecontrol operation can be carried out using a multimedia interface, in which a key role is played by a speech understanding system. The operator may carry out different tasks: to give simple navigation commands to the robot, to command a rotating camera on board the robot, to give/receive information related to the status of the system. During this interaction, using a voice input modality, the attention of the operator is focused on the robot behaviour and on the information coming directly from the environment and from the system. A command can be issued by voice:

*"follow the corridor until the first corridor on the right";*

or combining voice and gesture

*"follow the corridor to here"*

pointing on the map to the

*"first corridor on the right".*

In this situation the combination of gestures (touch screen) and voice (microphone) is very useful for easiness, correctness and speed of the user action (the operator simply points to an unambiguous destination issuing an action command by voice). The commands can be given without moving the eyes to different interaction objects.

In both cases, the use of speech modality improves the communication task allowing the operator a more natural interaction with the system.

## 4. The Automatic Speech Understanding (ASU) System of FIRST

In general, ASU systems for robot applications should be speaker-independent, cover spontaneous speech phenomena, and provide fault-tolerant semantic interpretation. These issues can be partially fulfilled by using a pattern-matching approach to semantic interpretation, and a rejection criterion for unreliable recognised sentences.

The first prototype of the ASU system [5] [6] (see Figure 2) for the user-robot interface has a cascade architecture with three modules: an Automatic Speech Recognition (ASR) module that receives an input signal and returns the recognised sequence of words, a Rejection module that rejects unreliably recognised sentences, and an Interpretation module that tries to extract a meaning from the recognised and accepted sentences. Training and testing of the system was based on speech data collected by means of Wizard of Oz simulation [7].

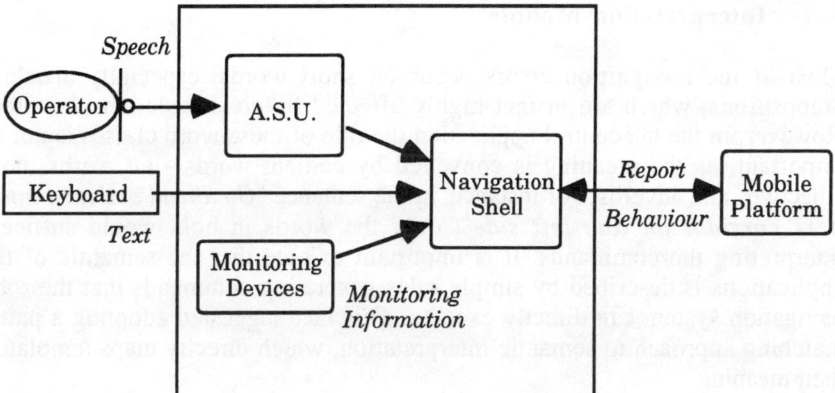


**Figure 2**: Telecontrol Architecture

## 4.1 ASR Module

The ASR module is based on the use of 3-state left to right continuous Hidden Markov Models (HMMs). The probability density functions are defined by means of a linear combination of 16 Gaussian densities per transition. HMMs of 37 phonetic units, trained on a phonetically rich speech data base collected at IRST [8], were used to model a vocabulary of 205 words.

To constrain word sequences, a class based bigram Language Model (LM) was used. The available material was labelled with 35 classes corresponding to a mixture of Parts of Speech (POS) and lemmas. Recognition performance was computed by aligning recognised sentences with their transcription. Results reported in Table 1 were obtained with the leave-one-out testing method.

| Word Accuracy | Sentence Accuracy | Sentence Interpretation Accuracy |
|---|---|---|
| 3823/4445<br>86.0% | 652/1024<br>63.7% | 931/1024<br>90.9% |

**Table 1**: Recognition and Interpretation Rates

A careful analysis of the wrongly recognised sentences revealed that many errors do not corrupt the meaning. This suggested that many of the recognition errors could be recovered during the interpretation phase.

### 4.2 Interpretation Module

Most of the recognition errors occur on short words, especially articles or prepositions, which are in fact highly affected by co-articulation phenomena. However, in the telecontrol application the role of these word classes is not very important, as the meaning is conveyed by content words - i.e. verbs, nouns, adjectives and adverbs. For instance, in the sentence "***Go ahead** and **turn** into the **next corridor** on your **left** side*", only the words in bold would suffice for interpreting the commands. It is important to note that the semantic of these applications is described by simple rules generating commands that the robot's navigation system can directly execute. This fact suggested adopting a pattern-matching approach to semantic interpretation, which directly maps templates to their meaning.

Two versions of the ASU system have been implemented. A first one used in the qualified operator-robot interface exploits the acknowledgement of the load/unload operation together with simple message voice handling. This recogniser runs in almost real time on a PC-486 66 MHz under a Unix operating system. It requires only a low cost A/D converter like ProAudio or SoundBlaster. A second one used in the telecontrol functionality exploits the robot remote control. The ASU runs on a HP 735, in real time, using the A/D facilities of the HP 735. The same software also runs on a Sparc Workstation 10.

## 5. Future Work

This project is in an ongoing phase; some required features for the first ASU prototype have been achieved, as follows: it is speaker independent, allows continuous speech, has 200-word vocabulary, and the real time capability. A key role for the feasibility of the project, from the speech technology point of view, is played by the user. The user can be trained to interact with the system and this improves the system's performance. Finally, in order to improve the robustness of the ASU systems, the project requires more work in the future on two important issues:

- Development of a voice acquisition module that allows a natural interaction with the system, a "microphone free interaction" from the user point of view. Automatic speech recogniser performance often degrades drastically when employed in conditions that are different with respect to those for which they were designed. One reason for this is environmental noise. Another reason can be an inconsistent use of the acoustic transducers during message acquisition. For example, a substantial decrease in performance can be caused by a non adequate position of the talker's mouth with respect to the microphone. Head-mounted, hand-held or fixed-position microphones do not solve this problem completely.

In the last decade, some research efforts have been devoted to microphone array processing techniques, especially for teleconferencing and large room recording, but also for speech recognition purposes [9]. Microphone arrays represent an attractive solution to the need for normalising speech information with respect to the above mentioned factors. Furthermore, using this technology allows investigation of ambitious tasks such as talker localisation and talker tracking, that can imply new scenarios for future speech applications [10].

• Development of techniques for rejections for unreliable recognised sentences, out-of-domain sentences and generally ASU systems. Techniques for computing a *confidence* of the recogniser's output have to be also investigated. A typical problem with the statistical approach to ASR is to introduce valid criteria for rejecting out-of-domain sentences as well as mistakenly recognised ones [5].

## 6. Conclusion

This paper has described and discussed the EU-474 Eureka Project "FIRST" of a Friendly Interactive System for Service Tasks. The design criteria and functional analysis of the system were presented together with a short description of the state of the art in the field.

The Speech technology used in the project was discussed. The first prototype of the ASU system architecture was presented together with the directions of future work: the development of a voice acquisition module allowing a microphone-free interaction and the development of techniques for rejection of unreliable sentences.

There is a strong demand for flexible and robust systems to manage the different needs of hospital transportation. Flexibility, complexity and robustness, the major requirements of such systems, will be achieved by integrating innovative artificial intelligence technologies such as autonomous navigation, multimedia interface, natural language and planning, and speech understanding, with more consolidated ones.

## References

1. Proceedings of "Les Robot Mobiles dans l'Industrie et les Services", Grenoble, France, October 14, 1992.
2. Evans J., Krishnamurthy B., Bardows B., Skewis T., Lumelsky V., "Handling Real World Motion-Planning: a Hospital Transport Robot", IEEE Control Systems, pp. 15-20, February 1992.
3. Stringa L., "Il Progetto MAIA", Le Scienze - Italian issue of Scientific American, No. 290, pp.86-97, October 1992.
4. Collini G., Flor R., Lazzari G., "A Friendly Interactive Transport System for Hospital Environment". IRST Technical Report 9301-10. In *Proceedings of the 24th International Symposium on Industrial Robots* [ISIR 93], Tokyo, Japan, November 4-6, pp. 487-493, 1993.
5. Antoniol G., Cettolo M., Federico M., "Techniques for Robust Recognition in Restricted Domains". IRST Technical Report 9307-15. In *Proceedings of the 3rd European Conference on Speech Communication and Technology* [EUROSPEECH 93], Berlin, Germany, September 21-23, Vol. 3, pp. 2219-2221, 1993.

6. Antoniol G., Cattoni R., Cettolo M., Federico M., "Robust Speech Understanding for Robot Telecontrol". IRST Technical Report 9302-19. In *Proceedings of '93 International Conference on Advanced Robotics* [ICAR 93], Tokyo, Japan, November 1-2, pp. 205-209, 1993.
7. Corazza A., Federico M., Gretter R., Lazzari G., "Design and Acquisition of a Task-oriented Spontaneous Speech Database". IRST Technical Report 9204-05. To appear in: V. Roberto (ed.), 'Research Topics on Intelligent Perceptual Systems', Lecture Notes in Artificial Intelligence, Vol. XXX, Springer Verlag, Heidelberg, 1993.
8. Angelini B., Brugnara F., Falavigna D., Giuliani D., Gretter R., Omologo M., "Automatic Segmentation and Labeling of English and Italian Speech Databases". IRST Technical Report 9307-20. In *Proceedings of the 3rd European Conference on Speech Communication and Technology* [EUROSPEECH 93], Berlin, Germany, September 21-23, Vol. 1, pp. 653-656, 1993.
9. Silverman H.F., "Some Analysis of Microphone Arrays for Speech Data Acquisition", IEEE Trans. on Acoustics, Speech and Signal Processing, Vol. ASSP-35, n.12, December 1987.
10. Omologo M., Svaizer P., "Talker Localization and Speech Enhancement in a Noisy Environment Using a Microphone Array Based Acquisition System". IRST Technical Report 9307-19, Patent Pending No. TO92A000855, October 1992. In *Proceedings of the 3rd European Conference on Speech Communication and Technology* [EUROSPEECH 93], Berlin, Germany, September 21-23, Vol. 1, pp. 605-608, 1993.
11. Engelberger J.F., "Automazione e Trasporti Automatici nei Servizi Sanitari", Personal Communication, Milano, Italy, October 13th, 1992.

## Acknowledgements

The author wishes to thank the researchers of Vision, Reasoning and Computational Logic, Architecture and System Engineering Labs involved in this project. A special thank to the Acoustic and Speech Lab that developed the FIRST ASU prototype and to Stephen Trueman for supporting the management.

# Architectural Design of the PLUS Dialogue System

J.-M. Lancel, X. Briffault, F. Dols, C. Godin,
L. Horel, K.Jokinen, G.Tabuteau
CAP GEMINI INNOVATION
86-90 Rue Thiers, F-92513 Boulogne-Billancourt, France

## Abstract

The aim of the project is to achieve robustness in cooperative natural language dialogue. The target of PLUS is to produce an environment for developing intelligent natural language interfaces for information-seeking dialogue systems. A first demonstrator, interactive Yellow Pages, has been developed, allowing access in English and French to the Electronic Telephone Directory application. A modular architecture with a replaceable application model enables new applications to be produced. The emphasis on language-independent reasoning, and the resulting modularity of the language-specific knowledge bases facilitate the adaptation of the system to new languages and multi-lingual use.

## 1. PLUS Project

The aim of the PLUS project [4] is to produce a robust natural language understanding component, which allows a flexible and efficient Human-Computer Interaction. Robustness is achieved by treating natural language as a communicative activity whose essential characteristic is to convey a meaning, that is both appropriate and relevant contextually.

The system is tolerant to faulty input and flexible enough to allow a real dialogue with the user [1], using contextual [5] and pragmatic knowledge. The PLUS system is a natural language dialogue handler, which allows the integration of natural language interaction facilities in different applications, at a reasonable cost. This relies on a modular architecture, which clearly separates the topics specific to the language, the application specific parts, and the general topics. It also provides a framework for integrating new languages and new applications.

The system is used to access information in the domain of interactive Yellow Pages in order to demonstrate the capabilities of the PLUS facilities, and to assess the feasibility of natural language interaction in real-size applications. PLUS is an ESPRIT project with a duration from November 1990 to May 1993. The participating organisations are: CAP GEMINI INNOVATION, Paris (coordinating contractor); CAP debis, BeCom, ITK, Omega Generation, LIMSI-CNRS, University of Bristol, UMIST, University of Göteborg. The project leader is Jean-Marie Lancel.

# 2. PLUS Architecture

## 2.1 Overview

A standard natural language interface consists essentially of a lexicon, a grammar and a parser. It usually fails when confronted with input which has not been in some way explicitly modelled in the grammar by the system developers. A robust natural language interface must include the standard components, but must also have the capability of reacting appropriately in problematic situations. This is achieved in PLUS by focusing on the nature and structure of the discourse context.

The design of the PLUS architecture relies on an explicit modelling of this notion of context. A set of high level knowledge sources is defined to act on this context in order to allow a cooperative interaction with the PLUS system user. The system makes use of background knowledge [3], which represents the system's knowledge about following items: the world, the application, the language and the relationship between them. To drive these knowledge sources a general and flexible control mechanism has been defined.

## 2.2 Control

The architecture of the system is based on the notion of *module*. A module is an entity that has the ability to perform certain classes of operations, and also to achieve the specified goals. This can be regarded as the *task* of each module. For example, a "parser" performs some operations on a string, and is able to provide a syntactic analysis of this string.

A "cognitive analyser" is able to give the meaning of the sentence by using this syntactic analysis. A "user goal analyser" works on the meaning of the sentence in order to determine the goal of the user. A module *B* can be asked by another module *A* to execute a task. In this case, we will say that the module *A* controls *B*. Two kinds of modules are defined as follows:

- simple modules (SM), that are procedural or declarative implementations of specific tasks. They do not control any other modules.
- compound modules (CM), which control several SM-modules, and can trigger these modules to get data.

The Dialogue Manager, the Cognitive Analyser, the Goal Formulator, and the Response Planner of the PLUS system are examples of compound modules. Modules computing the communicative functions of the user's contribution, its topics, and its discourse referents are illustrations of simple modules controlled by the Cognitive Analyser. A compound module needs following functional capabilities in order to perform its task:

[1] *Knowledge of the task to be performed:*
Since a module has a task to perform, a part of its knowledge is dedicated to the "description" of its task. This description can be implemented in form of declarative rules (or procedural code if needed), and includes indications about the results which should be provided, what data is needed, and which operations must be performed. This knowledge is called "control rule" in the PLUS architecture.

[2] *Inference mechanisms to perform its task:*
Different kinds of reasoning exist, which can be used to perform a task, and the system should be able to use these mechanisms in an appropriate way.

[3] *Knowledge of the controller modules:*
A compound module must know what kind of operation the controlled modules are able to perform, and what data they can provide. Additional knowledge is needed in oder to decide how the controlled modules can be used in order to perform a task, and what kind of operations they are able to perform, and also what data they can provide. The functional representation of a module cannot be the module itself, it is expressed by the module abstraction, i.e. by its functional specifications.

[4] *Ways to communicate with its controlled modules:*
Since a module can exchange messages with the modules it controls, we must define how they can communicate.

[5] *Ways to communicate with other modules:*
A module can also exchange some messages with the other modules of the system. A communication protocol must be defined.

[6] *A memory area in which it can perform its own computations:*
Some results of the computations of a module are of no interest for the other ones. Hence, it is interesting to have local, private memories which can be accessed only by the owner of this memory.

[7] *A memory area in which the modules of a CM can read and write:*
The computation results of a module can be useful to other modules, and each CM needs the access to the results of its controlled modules. A common memory area ("blackboard") can be used to read and write data that is shared by the modules.

## 2.3 Dialogue Manager

What drives the dialogue in the PLUS system ? This section gives answers to this question by providing a general view on the role of the dialogue manager in PLUS. It describes how a cooperative dialogue between the user and the system derives from the system processing principles, and the use of pragmatic knowledge.

### Description of the Dialogue Manager Architecture

Basically, one can consider the PLUS system as a hierarchy of modules with a top module as the Dialogue Manager. As other modules it is organised as already described in chapter 2.2. A control mechanism provides the plans and also triggers different actions carried out by its corresponding submodules. The submodules of the Dialogue Manager are as follows:

- the Parser,
- the Cognitive Analyser,
- the Goal Formulator,
- the Response Planner,

- the Surface Generator, and
- the User Interface.

The core component of the Dialogue Manager is the Goal Formulator (GF). This module is the expert of the application. If several applications were available in the system, the Goal Formulator would also be the single interface to all of them. The Goal Formulator has to query the application database and to provide the user with the desired information. In the current PLUS system, the Goal Formulator aims at providing the list of YP-entries corresponding to the user's general query.

Two modules have been implemented, the Cognitive Analyser (CA) and the Response Planner (RP) in order to support the interaction with the end-users (the end-users are using natural languages). These modules are able to map the surface meaning of dialogue utterances onto their deep semantic representation. The Parser (P) and the Surface Generator (SG) map in a context-independent manner these surface meanings onto the verbatim representation of utterances. The Dialogue Manager controls [7] these different modules in order to react appropriately to the different discourse situations.

Thanks to their pragmatic knowledge, each module (including the Dialogue Manager) is able to read and write information in a global and dynamic Knowledge Base, which is called the Discourse Model. As a whole, this Discourse Model contains all the different pieces of information, at different knowledge levels, which have been computed during the dialogue. It represents the discourse context in which new utterances have to be interpreted.

## What Drives the Dialogue?

One of the aims of PLUS system is to explain why and how a dialogue can be generated between a person and a machine, in order to allow an efficient use of the machine as a tool. Several questions can be raised:

- What is the basic mechanism which drives the dialogue?
- What is the PLUS fundamental principle which explains and justifies the existence of a cooperative dialogue between the system and the user ?

The dialogue of the PLUS system can be seen as a surface phenomenon generated by a deeper and more complex internal process, which is trying to access the relevant information in a database, called Information Database. This internal process is a component of the Goal Formulator, and basically consists of the following three generic steps:

[1] Build the system's query to the Information Database (which reflects the user's latest specification of the problem).
[2] Use this internal form of the user's query to access the Information Database.
[3] Evaluate the relevance of the answer returned from the Information Database assuming a general cooperative behaviour of the system.

If the evaluation is positive, the task of the Goal Formulator is completed while if it is negative, the sequence 1, 2, 3 has to be iterated again and again, in order to converge to a positive evaluation, and to complete the Goal Formulator task. These steps can be seen as general steps of a module which has the expertise on a given application domain.

According to this description, two additional questions can be raised:

- Why should the Goal Formulator be considered the heart of the dialogue explanation ?
- Why is the Goal Formulator precisely "formulating goals" ?

Both these questions can be simultaneously answered with the following description of the Goal Formulator processing: the Goal Formulator is an application expert, and the Goal Formulator is triggered by the system, i.e. by the Dialogue Manager.

Depending on the current state of the discourse context, the Goal Formulator might be able to build more or less completely a query to the Information Database. If the query cannot be built, the first submodule is obliged to suspend its processing and to ask for the missing information from its controller, i.e. the Goal Formulator controller.

The Goal Formulator controller has now basically three options:

- Either one of its (other) submodules knows how to get the required information, and it can activate that module,
- Discard the suspended module and trigger another one which would also lead to satisfy the general task which has to be carried out by the Goal Formulator.
- Pass the question to its father module, i.e. the dialogue manager.

In the first option, the required data is obtained from the relevant module and then passed back to the suspended module, which can then continue normally. The second option consists of changing the strategy if possible to reach the same final goal. The third option goes precisely straight to the heart of the dialogue and its motivation. The Goal Formulator is in this case not able to manage itself to get the relevant information. Then it suspends its processing and passes the problem to the Dialogue Manager. Here, as a recursive mechanism, the dialogue manager has one of two options:

- Either one of its (other) submodules knows how to get the required information and this module can be triggered,
- Else discard the suspended module and trigger another which would also satisfy the general task which has to be carried out.

In this case it is no longer possible to have a third option, namely to pass the problem to the Dialogue Manager in charge, since the dialogue manager is now the top-level module of the system. At the level of the dialogue manager, potentially all problems can be solved, even if this means that the user has to solve the problem.

The goal of obtaining this missing information is converted by the Dialogue Manager into a system's communicative intention, if the original missing information cannot be obtained from the discourse context. Note that the Goal Formulator and its first submodule are in pending state during the the interaction with the user with the aim of providing the missing information.

If the user gives relevant answer, which can be correctly analysed by the system, the Dialogue Manager will get the answer to its original problem, i.e. will accumulate the missing information. It can then be in the position of providing the information requested by the Goal Formulator, which then will pass back the information to the submodule which initiated this question (in our example the first module of the Goal Formulator). This submodule then continues its processing to build the system's query to the Database.

We have here enlightened the basic processing principle of the system, which is responsible for the dialogue. As a side effect, the Goal Formulator tries to carry out its goal, which consists in querying the database and providing relevant information to the user. During this process, some relevant data may appear to be needed at some level of processing, and cannot be found in the discourse context. This kind of internal "quasi-failure" will result, if necessary, in creating a communicative goal, whose purpose is precisely to get the missing information from the user.

Once the data has been obtained, it is sent back to the calling module, which originated the problem, so that the process of querying the database can continue. The goal formulator can be regarded as a dynamic planner, which creates (dynamically) subgoals in order to complete its task. Some goals need to be solved by the user himself and this leads the dialogue manager to create corresponding *application-oriented* communicative goals. The general control flow in the system can be regarded as an attempt to solve subgoals generated by the Goal Formulator.

Yet, the explanation of what drives the dialogues in the PLUS system is not completed. Dialogues also contain communicative goals which are not application-oriented. How does the PLUS design cope with these goals ?

Simply by extending the recursive suspending/querying mechanism described for the Goal Formulator to all the modules of the Dialogue Manager. The Parser, CA, Response Planner, and SG, and UI, can be seen as modules which help the goal formulator to communicate with the user through a natural language [6].

This help is organised by an expert in man-machine communication in natural language, namely the Dialogue Manager. In achieving this help, it may occur in one of these modules that some information is needed to complete a given subtask of interpretation, or generation. For instance let us assume that the Cognitive Analyser cannot resolve a problem with the user's contribution, which prevents it from computing the user's current contribution intention. Then, by applying exactly the same suspending/querying mechanism as previously described for the Goal Formulator case, the module passes on the problem to the Dialogue Manager. The top-level module considers the communication problem raised (by the CA in our example), and if none of it submodules can help in solving this problem, the dialogue manager ultimately creates a *dialogue-oriented* communicative goal.

In our example, the dialogue manager will ask the user about the referent which is unclear. The Goal Formulator is responsible for the discourse segments dealing directly with the application domain, i.e. the application-oriented communicative goals. The suspending/querying mechanism applied in the parser, the cognitive analyser, the response planner, the surface generator and the user interface modules are responsible for the dialogue-oriented segments, i.e. segments whose topics are focussed on the dialogue itself. The system strategy thus relies essentially on a homogeneous control mechanism, which is applied to every module of the system.

This mechanism consists of *not failing* whenever a data is improper or incomplete. Execution suspendes in this case the current processing of the concerned module, and passes on the problem to the supermodule. The supermodule then tries to solve locally this problem, thanks to its pragmatic knowledge of how to try to solve the problem, and in case that it doesn't succeed, it passes the problem on to its own supermodule, and waits for an answer. At the top level, the Dialogue Manager may decide, as an ultimate solution, to ask the user to solve the problem. The dialogue derives from that generic process. We can summarise the overall system's strategy as follows:

> *The dialogue manager is mainly willing to help the user to get the desired information from the Application Database.*

To achieve this goal, the dialogue manager triggers the Goal Formulator, which is the application expert, and which initiates a dynamic planning mechanism.

The basic strategy of the Goal Formulator is to build a query representing the user's expression of the problem, to query the Application Database and to evaluate the answer returned from the database in order to respect the communicative principles. During this iterative process, some data may be missing in order to achieve the Goal Formulator goal. The problems that cannot be solved locally are passed on to the Dialogue Manager, which evaluates the importance of the problem, and if possible solves it.

There are two basic ways for the Dialogue Manager to solve a problem: either making use of the already collected discourse context or by asking directly the user. This behaviour explains the dialogue: when the dialogue manager has identified an important goal to achieve in its goal agenda, and if this goal cannot be solved by the system, the Dialogue Manager creates a corresponding *application-oriented* communicative goal.

Similarly, the dialogue-oriented communicative goals are generated by problems raised by the *communication-dedicated* dialogue manager, such as Cognitive Analyser, Response Planner, Parser, Surface Generator and User Interface, in case that the Dialogue Manager cannot solve the problem with its own resources. The dialogue can here be regarded as an ultimate step to achieve a *robust* computation of the user's query, i.e. a computation which is not permitted to fail. In this way, robustness based on dialogue processing, which is used in the PLUS system simply derives from a more general form of robustness towards computing problems (e.g. database information retrieval).

## 2.4 Cognitive Analyser

The Cognitive Analyser has four submodules, corresponding to the four phases mentioned above, and is dealing with following aspects of analysis:

- Determination of semantic content (conceptual analysis, quantors, anaphora and ellipsis, metonomy, and unknown aspects).
- General disambiguation.
- Assignment of Communicative Functions (direct and indirect attitudes).
- Determination of discourse referents.
- Determination of topic and focus information.
- Determination of goals of the speaker and other related information.
- Dealing with corrupt input.

## 2.5 Goal Formulator

The task of the Goal Formulator is to provide database information corresponding to a database query. As there is only onedatabase in the PLUS system, the Yellow Pages database, the ultimate goal of the Goal Formulator is to "give a list of name/address/telephone number of service suppliers to the user".

### Input/Output

The input of the Goal Formulator is the system deep goal expressed as

*Achieve* (Goal Formulator, System, Provide_Data).

This goal is put in the Goal Formulator agenda by the Dialogue Manager at the beginning of the dialogue. The output is the list of database information to be presented to the user. This is given to the Dialogue Manager who triggers the modules allowing to present the list to the user.

### Description

The Dialogue Manager triggers the Goal Formulator by sending the goal

*Achieve* (System, User, Provide_Data)

which initiates the Goal Formulator agenda. As the Goal Formulator is an application expert, it is able to achieve this goal. To achieve it, the Goal Formulator has a set of task parameters to instantiate. They are used to access the Yellow Pages Data Base. They can be classified in three classes:

- *obligatory* parameters: there is only one (the heading) in the YP application,
- *optional and independent* parameters: These parameters are independent from other parameters (e.g. location).
- *optional and context dependent* parameters: This kind of parameter can be instantiated only for a special set of headings (e.g. speciality of some service suppliers).

Database queries can be built by instantiating these parameters. As they are not known to the user, the user can't give direct values for them. Instead, the Goal Formulator can obtain these values by querying the user or by accessing the discourse context. For the Goal Formulator, the control is simplified, because the triggering of modules is performed in procedural way. To achieve its goal, the Goal Formulator has to build a query to access the database, and this query must reflect the user´s request. The result of the query is evaluated. If the evaluation is positive, then the task of the Goal Formulator is completed, and data can be provided to the Dialogue Manager, and then to the user. If the evaluation is negative, the Goal Formulator will try to modify the query in order to converge to a positive evaluation. This will be re-iterated as longer as necessary. This algorithm has the following steps:

*Select* the application concerned with the user request,
*Find* parameter values to build the database query,
*Access* the application, and
*Evaluate* this access.

If the evaluation is acceptable, the Goal Formulator was successful, otherwise it returns to the activity of building the query.

## 2.6 Response Planner

The task of the *Response Planner* (RP) is to generate a meaningful representation for the next system contribution, from a system goal formulated by the Goal Formulator. This task is two-fold: the Response Planner decides how to express the system goal by specifying the communicative function of the response, and also how the content will be realised on the surface level. Lexical entries and pragmatic features are here used, but there is no decision concerning the question "how the actual surface string is generated".

**Input**

The Response Planner Controller gets as an input the system's communicative goal, which is represented by a set of attitudes. The Goal Formulator creates an instance of the CML class "Contribution" with one "Dialogue Unit" and one "Dialogue Act", and with the property *trigger* instantiated to the system's intention. For example, the Response Planner input for the generation of the question

*Where?*

is implemented by following instances:

```
1.      INSTANCE Contribution12  IN  Contribution
        WITH
                previous = Contribution11
                speaker = system
                dus = DialUnit34
        END_INSTANCE

2.      INSTANCE DialUnit34  IN  DialogueUnit
        WITH
                dacts = DialAct43
        END_INSTANCE

3.      INSTANCE DialAct43 IN DialogueAct
        WITH
                trigger = Attitude56
        ENDINSTANCE

4.      INSTANCE Attitude56  IN  Attitude
        WITH
                content  = wants (system,know (system
                         , [propval (location,carHireCo,\X)]))
                state = active
        END_INSTANCE
```

**Output**

The output of Response Planner is the grammatical unit that expresses the system's goal.

```
INSTANCE gu75 IN GrammaticalUnit
WITH
        feature_structure = fstr98
        quasilogical_form = qlf21
        pragmatic_features = prftr43
END_INSTANCE
```

The values of the three properties are translated into an appropriate conjunction of predicates which is the input to the Surface Generator. The translation is parallel to the interface between the parser and the Cognitive Analyser. The Response Planner also updates the context as a by-product of the completion of Grammatical Units.

## 2.7 Pragmatic Knowledge Bases

Three kinds of pragmatic knowledge are distinguished, *static contextual knowledge, dynamic contextual knowledge*, and *pragmatic rules*.

The static contextual knowledge includes general knowledge about the world and about the information-seeking activity in which the system is involved. This knowledge is stored in the World Model and in the Application Model.

The dynamic contextual knowledge derives from interpreting the user's contributions, from querying the database, from planning the system's responses, etc. It is built up and modified as a dialogue procedure, and it is stored as the Discourse Model.

Pragmatic rules are rules for using contextual knowledge (both static and dynamic) in order to interpret the user's contributions and plan the system's responses in a way that produces robust and cooperative dialogue behaviour.

**Static Knowledge Bases**

There are four Static Knowledge Bases developed in PLUS. They are as follows:

- the World Model (World Model),
- Application Model (Application Model) ,
- Yellow Pages Database (YP), and
- the Conceptual Lexicon (CL).

The PLUS world and application knowledge bases (KB's) are designed with a concern for portability of the future PLUS applications. The most straightforward extension to PLUS involves changing the underlying YP database. In order to ensure that the PLUS system is indeed portable to other YP databases it is needed to separate the KB's into an

- Application Model, and a
- World Model.

The interprocess communication between the backend YP database and the application process is controlled by the Data and Inquiry Servers.

The Application Model itself encapsulates all concepts related to the specific underlying database, i.e. knowledge about the structure of the information available in the database and knowledge about "how to retrieve this information". The YP database is basically accessed by giving *headings* under which entries are stored. The Application Model, which is implemented in CML, makes use of a Prolog interface to the YP. In addition, the Application Model contains mapping between database concepts and application concepts. The headings in the Application Model are mapped to concepts in the World Model representing their meaning. Thus a change of the YP database only requires exchanging the Application Model.

The World Model comprises common sense knowledge that the system accesses in making inferences based on contextual information. It contains concepts which are relevant for the selected domains of discourse. The World Model is built to be as general as possible, and therefore contains general concepts such as Events and Objects, as well as specific concepts like Hiring, Travelling, Repairing, Buying, and Service. This enables the extension of the World Model to other Domains of Discourse. Such general concepts in the World Model can be adapted to many Domains of Discourse. This is achieved by making use of the object-oriented modelling features of CML.

**Discourse Model**

The Discourse Model can be considered as the backbone of the PLUS architecture. Data in the Discourse Model are grouped in *context independent,* and *context dependent* information.

Context independent information is computed on the dialogue referring to previous information stored in the Discourse Model. Typically, this refers in PLUS to the data computed by the Natural Language Engine (NLE). Context dependent information is computed by the different knowledge sources of the Dialogue Manager, which makes use of the discourse model´s previous information. The Discourse Model is a structured knowledge base, represented in CML, which contains different types of information:

- *Context independent information:* verbatim input representations, grammatical properties of user and system contributions, quasi-logical form, pragmatically relevant features of grammatical form, and discourse referents,
- *Context dependent information:* dialogue structure, attitudes, topic information, semantic representation, and communicative function.

These pieces of information are computed by elementary knowledge sources, or modules, during the analysis and generation process. These elementary modules are able to compute new elements of the Discourse Model on the basis of static knowledge (world and application knowledge, pragmatic rules) and previous information collected about the dialogue, which is stored in the Discourse Model. For instance, during the user's contribution analysis, topic information is computed by a specialised module on the basis of the semantic representation of the contribution, using world knowledge.

**Pragmatic Rules**

Following Bunt and Allwood (see [2], pragmatic rules are globally seen as the superset of rules that determine the system's behaviour. As a first approximation, Bunt & Allwood distinguish three types of pragmatic rules:

1. Interpretation rules: rules that interpret what communicative acts are conveyed by the contributions. These rules are simultaneously rules of attitude extraction.
2. Processing evaluation rules: rules that help the CA to evaluate whether sufficient perception and understanding has been attained. They also help the Goal Formulator and Response Planner decide on the best appropriate responses, given the analysis of the expressive and evocative features of the user's contribution and the state of the dynamic update modules.
3. Response planning rules: rules that plan what communicative acts and referential content should be expressed in the response, given an abstract goal formulation.

The pragmatic rules defined in PLUS are as follows:

- *General Rules:* Obligation Fulfillment Rule, Belief Transfer Rule, and Cooperation Rule
- *Activity & Role Analysis Related Rules:* Intention Expectation Rule, and Information Seeking Rule
- *Rules for determination of Communicative Functions:* Communicative Function Assignment, and Communicative Function Definitions
- *Topic Shifting Rules:* Smooth Topic Shifts, Awkward Topic Shifts, and Tracing Topics
- *Reference Rules:* Identity: Pronoun Anaphoras, Identity: Full NP Anaphoras, Association, and Set-element Relation
- *Explicitness and Implicitness*
- *Dialogue Structure Rules:* Dialogue Structuring Constraints, and Updating Rules
- *Derivation of Expectations*, and
- *Feedback Rules.*

## 3. The PLUS Achievements

The first six-month phase of the PLUS project has been devoted to training, evaluation of reusable components, corpus collection, external requirements and system design. In the second phase, work was devoted to the detailed design of the system components, the prototyping of the PLUS system, and the conceptual modelling of selected Yellow Pages sub-domains. The PLUS partners successfully achieved the definition of a suitable architecture for cooperative dialogue integrating, while enhancing the different approaches to pragmatics in the consortium. In the third phase, the partners developed the PLUS system, which allows to access in English and French the Electronic Telephone Directory.

## References


[1] Bilange B. "Dialogue personne-machine, Modélisation et réalisation informatique", Editions Hermes, 192 pp., 1992.

[2] William J. Black, Jens Allwood, Harry C. Bunt, Frens J.H. Dols, Carlo Donzella, Giacomo Ferrari, John Gallagher, Rainer Haidan, Bill Imlah, Kristiina Jokinen, Jean-Marie Lancel, Joakim Nivre, Gérard Sabah, Tom Wachtel "A Pragmatics-based Language Understanding System", PLUS Project Report, 1992.

[3] Haidan R. and R. Meyer "Requirements Modelling and SystemSpecification in a Logic-based Knowledge Representation Framework", DAIDA (ESPRIT 892) Project Report.

[4] Lancel, J.M., Allwood, J., Bilange, E., Black, W.J., Bunt, H.C., Dols, F.J.H., Donzella, C., Gallagher, J., Haidan, R., Sabah, G., Wachtel, T. "PLUS Technical Annex", Part II, October 1990.

[5] Black, W.J. (ed). "ABC: Abduction, Beliefs and Context", Second PLUS Workshop, Alghero, Italy, September 1992.

[6] Dols F. and K. van der Sloot "Modelling Mutual Effects in Belief-based Interactive Systems", Proceedings of the 3rd International Workshop on User Modelling, UM 92 Conference, Dagstuhl, Germany, IBFI, August 1992.

[7] Underwood N. "Dialogue Management in a Pragmatics-Based Natural Language System", Proceedings of the BCS Colloqium on Information Retrieval, Springer-Verlag, 1993.

# WERNICKE: A Neural Network-Based, Speaker-Independent, Large-Vocabulary, Continuous-Speech Recognition System

Hervé Bourlard
Lernout & Hauspie, Speech Products
Koning Albert I laan 64, B-1780 Wemmel, Belgium

## Abstract

The goal of this paper is to describe the research underway for the ESPRIT WERNICKE project. This project aims at extending the state-of-the-art for hybrid hidden Markov models/artificial neural networks approaches to large vocabulary, speaker independent, continuous speech recognition. The projects brings together a number of research teams from Europe and the US and focuses on several aspects of the problem, including new theoretical works, practical development of a common software, development and use of common hardware, and assessment of results on standard reference databases. This paper describes the specific goals and workpackages of the project and briefly presents some of the results achieved so far.

## 1 Introduction

WERNICKE is a 3-year ESPRIT Basic Research project which started in October 1992. The main objective of this research project is to learn how neural networks can be used for continuous speech recognition to significantly improve state-of-the-art systems and, using dedicated hardware, to develop fast implementations of the resulting algorithms, i.e., real-time recognition and

[1]Pioneer of neurology whose name is now applied to an area of the brain concerned with language processing.

[2]The work reported here (as well as parts of text) is the result of a collaborative effort between several people including (but not limited to): M. Hochberg, D. Kershaw, S. Renals, and A.J. Robinson from CUED, L. Almeida and J.P. Neto from INESC, P. Kohn, Y. Konig, and N. Morgan from ICSI, and S. Accaino, J.M. Boite, and J. Vantieghem from L&H. A short version of this paper can be found in [16].

fast turnaround of training. More specifically, this project addresses to problem of improving state-of-the-art, Hidden Markov Model (HMM)-based, large vocabulary, speaker independent, continuous speech recognition systems by using, jointly with HMMs, Artificial Neural Network (ANN) techniques. In the following, this kind of system will be referred to as HMM/ANN hybrid. The kinds of ANNs which are investigated here mainly are Multilayer Perceptrons (MLPs), Recurrent Neural Networks (RNNs) or any other intermediate or alternative solutions which could result of the collaboration or comparisons performed in the framework of this project. Other aspects of the project address closely related problems (robustness, lexical access), or more general ones (speaker adaptation) and hardware implementation on special parallel architectures.

The projects brings together partners with existing skills and baseline systems in the area: L&H Speech Products (L&H: a Belgian company, as prime) and International Computer Science Institute (ICSI, Berkeley, US) for hybrid HMM/ANN structures with feedforward networks, Cambridge University Engineering Department (CUED, UK) using recurrent neural networks for hybrids, and Instituto de Engenharia de Sistemas e Computadores (INESC, Portugal) for ANN training and speaker adaptation. In addition, ICSI provides the computing environment which is necessary for the computationally expensive research and which is used as a standard hardware (and software) platform to the project. In this framework, all partners are implementing their algorithms on the ICSI Ring Array Processor (RAP) hardware [10] that provides about 0.5 Gflops and allows for fast processing (which is a necessity for highly CPU power demanding ANN training and, consequently, to reduce the research and testing cycle). Later on, a new hardware based on the Synthetic Perceptron Trainer (SPERT, a single custom VLSI chip) will also be used in the project.

## 2 Hybrid HMM/ANN Speech Recognition

Hidden Markov Models (HMM) are widely used for automatic speech recognition and inherently incorporate the sequential and statistical character of the speech signal. However, standard HMMs also suffer from several weaknesses [3] including:

- Poor discrimination due to the training algorithm which maximizes likelihoods [Maximum Likelihood Estimate (MLE) criterion] instead of a posteriori probabilities [Maximum a Posteriori (MAP) criterion].

- A priori choice of model topology and statistical distributions, e.g., assuming that the emission probability density function associated with each HMM-state can be described as a multivariate Gaussian density or as a mixture of multivariate Gaussian densities.

- Assumption that the state sequences are first-order Markov chains.
- No contextual information is taken into account and the possible correlation of the successive acoustic vectors is overlooked inside each HMM state.
- For the sake of storage and computational efficiency, the need to treat as independent certain processes or acoustic features that are not truly independent.

Finally, the hypotheses that provide the strength and computational efficiency of HMMs also are at the origin of their fundamental limitations, since the underlying assumptions are generally not correct.

Recently, it has been shown that Artificial Neural Network (ANN) could provide an alternative to the problem of (discriminant) learning, feature extraction and classification, which might be useful for speech recognition. Their main advantages include:

- They are learning machines (as are HMMs).
- They provide discriminant-based learning (that is, models are trained to suppress incorrect classification as well as to accurately model each class separately).
- Because ANNs are capable of incorporating multiple constraints and finding optimal combinations of constraints for classification, features do not need to be treated as independent. In other words, there is no need of any particular assumptions about statistical distributions and independence of input features.
- Using the interpolative capabilities of the MLP, statistical pattern recognition can be performed over an undersampled pattern space without many restrictive simplifying assumptions.
- ANNs are highly parallel structures, which makes them especially amenable to high-performance architectures and hardware implementations (such as VLSI).

Unfortunately, ANNs also have certain weaknesses and most previous applications of neural networks to speech recognition have depended on severe simplifying assumptions (e.g., very small vocabularies, isolated words, known word or phoneme boundaries ). However, the major drawback of ANNs is their inability to deal easily with dynamic signals and the time sequential nature of speech.

The hybrid HMM/ANN approach (first proposed in [1] and extensively described and discussed in [3]) combines the temporal modelling structure of the HMMs with the pattern classification capabilities of ANNs. As in HMMs, a Markov process is used to model the basic temporal nature of the speech signal. This provides the structure for specification of a language model and incorporates constraints on the duration of the modelled words. The connectionist structure is used to model the local (in time) acoustic signal conditioned on the Markov process andto estimate local (emission) probabilities of the HMMs. This makes use of the result that connectionist networks used in classification mode can, under certain conditions, be used as effective estimators of a posteriori probabilities of output classes conditioned on the input pattern [1], [3].

The advantages of this HMM/ANN hybrid approach are then numerous for speech recognition:

1. natural structure for discriminative training,
2. phone models are combined resulting in parsimonious use of the parameters,
3. better robustness against under-sampled training databases,
4. acoustic correlation can efficiently be modelled (by using contextual input windows in the MLP or recurrences in the RNN),
5. correlations (even high order) between different features can be exploited without severe distributional assumptions.

There are two basic connectionist architectures currently tested and compared in the WERNICKE hybrid systems. Work at L&H, ICSI and CUED has investigated the multi-layer perceptron (MLP) as a phone probability estimator [11]. This structure employs the MLP as a static pattern classifier where temporal acoustic context is modelled via a multiple frame input layer. The second architecture under evaluation as phone probability estimator is a recurrent neural network (RNN). This CUED developed system models acoustic context via a fully recurrent set state nodes [15]. Both systems achieve performance results comparable with other state-of-the-art speech recognition systems (see, e.g., [14], [16]) with significantly fewer parameters on international reference databases.

## 3 Research Topics Addressed in the Project

This project is basically split into two parts, with very strong relationships and inter-dependencies:

- Development and evaluation of theories and methods to improve the hybrid HMM/ANN systems for continuous speech recognition; this includes comparison of the different hybrid approaches with possible convergence to a solution mixing advantages of both RNNs and MLPs and significantly improving state-of-the-art speech recognition systems for difficult and realistic tasks.

- Adaptation of ICSI hardware and software tools to help the research and to implement resulting algorithms. This hardware is used by all the partners for their developments as a common hardware (and software) platform.

The first part of this project thus focuses on important issues related to the improvement of the baseline HMM/ANN systems, namely:

1. Multilayer Perceptrons (MLPs) — Although it has already been shown [11], [14] that hybrid HMM/MLP approaches can improve standard HMM systems, it is expected that further investigation could lead to additional improvements.

2. Recurrent Neural Networks (RNNs) — Given the good results obtained at CUED with recurrent neural networks, it is particularly interesting to further investigate this approach and to compare its recognition performance with HMM/MLP hybrids.

3. Development of better acoustic features — As for standard HMMs, development of features that neural networks can use to give recognition performance that is robust in speaker independent mode and in the presence of unpredictable variability in the acoustic input is an important area of investigation. Different approaches are being developed and compared in the framework of hybrid HMM/ANN systems.

4. Context-Dependent Neural Networks (CDNNs) — State-of-the-art recognizers now use context-dependent phonetic units to improve their performance. However, it is still not clear how one could use the same approach in an HMM/ANN approach. Approaches capable of dealing with this problem should be investigated here and compared with standard HMMs.

5. Training Procedures — The procedures presently used for the neural network training as well as the embedded HMM/ANN training still require improvement. For neural networks alone, better and faster training procedures are required. For the embedded HMM/ANN training, methods avoiding any a priori phonetic segmentation of the training material are necessary. Also, better training criteria minimizing the error rate directly should be investigated.

6. Speaker Adaptation — Several speaker adaptation techniques have been developed for standard HMM approaches. It is the goal of this task to investigate and compare different speaker adaptation schemes for hybrid HMM/ANN recognizers as well as the possibility of incremental training of speaker independent systems.

7. Reference decoder (Y0) — Although each partner develops its own training and recognition systems, a reference decoder is constantly maintained as a basis for comparisons and evaluation. Each time possible improvements have been defined, and when agreed by all the partners, this reference decoder is updated according to the new specifications.

8. Evaluation — The reference decoder is evaluated at each stage on international databases.

The second part of this project is devoted to the transfer and adaptation (at the software and system level) of the hardware and software systems that are developed at ICSI and that is necessary to support this project. In this framework, ICSI has been subcontracted to design all its software primitives so that the partners of this project can take advantage of further developments (even beyond RAP). This primarily consists of software for both the RAP and the possible required adaptations of a smaller new hardware, the Synthetic PERceptron Trainer (SPERT), a single-board system with a single custom VLSI chip consisting of a microcoded SIMD array[3]. In this framework, ICSI has manufactured one RAP system for each of the partners and help them to port and exploit hardware and software tools. At the end of the first year of this project, all the RAP systems had been delivered to the partners and are up and running with different baseline systems (see Section 4.1).

# 4 Workplan of the Project

The workplan has been broken down into five work packages (WP) that are briefly described below.

## 4.1 Work Package 1: Setting up

This WP involved the selection of common speech databases and the implementation of initial systems on each site.

To allow realistic comparison studies regarding the improvements made in the different tasks, it was agreed to define a single reference decoder referred to as Y0[4] (Section 4.2.6). Y0 is a decoder (not a full recognizer) which takes

[3]This new hardware is currently developed under other funding but will be helpful later in this project period.

[4]Pronounced “Why nought”.

HMM emission probabilities generated by the RAP (from any kind of ANN) as inputs and outputs the most likely word sequence. Y0 can also be used to performed the forced Viterbi matching required during training. It was however agreed that the partner would have the flexibility to develop their own training systems.

For what databases are concerned, the consortium worked on the ARPA Resource Management (RM) database [13] as initial database, and comparative results were reported at the end of the first year of this project [16]. Although RM will remain a standard development database, work has now started on the ARPA Wall Street Journal (WSJ) database [12] which is a more challenging task (5K or 20K lexicon words, speaker independent, continuous speech) and which is now considered at the international level as the new standard for the comparisons of speaker independent, large vocabulary, continuous speech recognition systems.

Another important issue involved in this project is the common use of the same hardware platform, i.e., the Ring Array Processor (RAP) developed by ICSI and its software library (Section 4.4). Providing a significant increase in processing power (and, consequently, reducing research cycles), the RAP however required a substantial effort in the porting of existing systems. At the end of the first year of this project, the RAP was installed and used by all the partners, and a common reference decoder was defined, implemented and running on each site.

## 4.2 Work Package 2: Improvements

This WP represents the core of this project and is concerned with all the possibles improvements, comparisons and extensions of the different hybrid HMM/ANN systems. After the initial work of porting the different baseline systems available by the partners to the RAP, much of the remaining WERNICKE project effort is focused on improving these baseline systems. The overall goal is to extend the state-of-the-art in these hybrid systems through research in the neural network and speech recognition areas. This workpackage is split into several tasks.

### *4.2.1 Feedforward Neural Networks*

Hybrid approaches using multi-layer perceptrons (MLPs) to generate emission probabilities for hidden Markov models (HMMs) have recently been shown to yield state-of-the-art recognition performance [14]. However, this approach is still a new technology with many open issues still requiring further research.

In this hybrid HMM/MLP approach, emission probabilities of HMMs are estimated via a multi-layer perceptron with acoustic context at the input containing typically 7 or 9 frames of acoustic parameters (possibly with their time derivatives).

During the first year, L&H has developed its own HMM/MLP training and recognition systems using the RAP hardware and software libraries. Also, the reference decoder Y0 has been installed and tested. The MLP code on the RAP can be used for training and recognition. Similar work has been done independently at ICSI and CUED, where MLP trainings have been initialized by running a forced Viterbi alignment on the RM database using a network trained phonetically on the hand-labeled TIMIT database. Training on these new labels yields results that are essentially the same as those obtained in the L&H experiments (see Section 5, Tables 1 and 2).

### *4.2.2 Recurrent Neural Network*

In the hybrid HMM/RNN approach (described in [15]), the acoustic probabilities are estimated with a recurrent network. The advantage of this approach is that acoustic context is implicitly and automatically modeled by the recurrent structure of the network. Furthermore, preliminary tests suggested that RNNs require fewer parameters than MLPs to achieve similar recognition performance. The purpose of this task is to identify and investigate improvements to this hybrid HMM/RNN approach.

During the first year of the project, much of the work has focused on porting the original CUED Transputer-based system to the RAP. In the process, a number of minor improvements have been investigated and implemented, and a number of areas have been identified for future work on HMM/RNN hybrids. The initial improvements which have been implemented to date in the HMM/RNN hybrid system include: (1) modifications to data access procedures to allow for training on larger databases (WSJ), (2) duration and pause modeling[5], and (3) optional differenced parameters to the input representation. For preliminary results and comparisons with HMM/MLP hybrids, see Table 1 in Section 5.

One piece of new work is the application of the HMM/RNN system to the Wall Street Journal task on which very preliminary results have been obtained. A 12.6% word error rate has been achieved on the ARPA November '92 5.000 word, non-verbalized pronunciation task.

### *4.2.3 Acoustic Vectors*

Our major current interest in features (input representation) is the development of representations that are quite speaker independent and which neural networks can use to obtain robust recognition performance in the presence of unpredictable variability in the acoustic input and in noisy environments.

[5]The duration model employed at L&H and ICSI (pseudo-Poisson distribution) along with the pause modeling was found to give slightly better results on the RM task (7% to 5% on the ARPA RM feb89 task)

One area under investigation at L&H and ICSI is representations which are resistant to variation in the gross spectral shape arising from variability across microphones, microphone position, and communications channel. Recently, an approach using ANNs together with a particular class of auditory spectral parameters, referred to as Perceptual Linear Prediction (PLP) coefficients [5], has been shown to be particularly robust in a speaker independent mode. Additionally, simple approaches using on-line temporal filtering of auditory spectral parameters (called RASTA filtering [6]) are also investigated in the framework of this project.

To make comparisons easier, L&H has developed a very modular software referred to as "Object Oriented Speech Toolkit" which is an HMM-based system designed to accommodate easily Gaussians, multi- (or tied multi-) Gaussians, discrete or continuous hybrid HMM/MLP systems. The program is designed to handle several kinds of features on demand, including LPC-derived cepstra, PLP, RASTA-PLP, energy, and first and second time derivative of these features. Additional features and capabilities of this toolkit will be added in the course of this project. This toolkit will allow easy comparisons of different approaches (including, among others, acoustic features, HMM topologies, HMM approaches) just by changing one set up file. Particular attention is paid to the compatibility of this software with the RAP libraries.

Another area of research at CUED into the acoustic representation involves the systematic comparison of different front-ends (mel-scaled filter banks, PLPs, mel-frequency cepstral coefficients) applied to the different HMM/ANN hybrids. Preliminary results are presented in Section 5 (Table 1).

### *4.2.4 Context-Dependent Neural Networks*

For the past few years, context-dependent modeling has been used in HMM-based speech recognition systems with a great deal of success [18]. Integration of context-dependent modeling with the hybrid recognition approach could result in similar improvements for the HMM/ANN systems. However, applying the standard context-independent neural network approach as such to context-dependent modeling is difficult, as the number of ANN output units (and, consequently, the number of parameters) quickly becomes too large to be reliably estimated from current speech databases. Recently, solutions to the problem of applying MLP techniques to context-dependent HMMs have been presented [2], [4]. The goal of this task is to pursue the development and testing of this new approach on large vocabulary tasks. Since this latter approach is more complex to implement and more CPU intensive, simpler alternative methods (such as using standard hybrids with limited context dependencies) will also be implemented and assessed.

### 4.2.5 *Training Procedures*

The goal of this task is to investigate new training procedures for both the MLP and RNN based speech recognition systems. The main issues addressed here include speed of training, stability of the training procedure, and resulting recognition performance.

The issue of training time is very important for the hybrid HMM/ANN systems. Consider the ARPA RM task with 3.990 training sentences. Training of both the basic HMM/MLP and HMM/RNN systems takes approximately 24 hours on a RAP with 4 boards (0.5 GFlops). On the 7.240 sentence ARPA Wall Street Journal (WSJ0) training set, it takes on the order of 5 days to train the RNN system. The time required to train becomes prohibitive for larger databases such as the 37.000 sentence WSJ1 training set. In addition, cycling through these data requires more than a linear increase in computation, as the estimators themselves should (ideally) be expanded to a greater number of parameters in order to take advantage of the increased coverage in the training materials.

In this task, L&H and CUED are investigating different approaches to speed up the HMM/ANN training. A possible approach under consideration at L&H is the utilization of parallelism in training. In this case, multiple estimators are trained on disjoint elements in the training set and then combined in an appropriate manner to generate the best estimate of HMM emission probabilities during recognition. Additionally, there is some hope that the right partitioning and weighting of the separate estimates could provide some improvement in performance[6]. Initial improvements allowing for a better training by merging two MLP networks trained separately have been obtained at L&H (Section 5, Table 3).

CUED's approach to RNN training speed relates directly to the implementation of the training algorithm. The training algorithm, specified in [17], is controlled by various parameters which determine learning rate. The main effort has been to quantify the relationship between the various factors which contribute to both the learning rate and training stability. This work has led to the selection of appropriate training parameters for the current tasks and is expected to guide the effort to improve the learning algorithm.

Of course, the bottom line is recognition performance. One area of research is the use of better optimization criteria. Embedded training of hybrid HMM/ANN models is usually based on a maximum likelihood (ML) criterion or maximum a posteriori probability (MAP) criterion optimized by a Viterbi algorithm (considering the best path only). However, in standard HMMs, training is usually done by the Baum-Welch algorithm which optimizes the actual likelihood (taking all paths into account). The possibility of using

[6]For instance, separating male and female training data has some demonstrable advantages in standard HMM systems.

this formalism in our hybrid approaches will be investigated. Also, criteria directly minimizing the error rate at the word level will be considered.

Another issue is the robustness of the trained system. Bayesian regularization or smoothing methods to MLP training are currently under investigation at CUED.

#### *4.2.6 Lexical Access*

The basic interest in this task is the decoding of word sequences from local phone probabilities. This work links the advances achieved in the improved acoustic modeling from the connectionist structures to the problem of connected speech recognition.

This task thus involves the implementation of efficient, high quality decoders. To this end, the Y0 decoder – originally developed at ICSI – has been improved and distributed to all the partners. Y0 is a time-synchronous Viterbi decoder which takes phone probabilities generated by the RAP (from a MLP or a RNN) as inputs and outputs the most likely word sequence. It was originally developed for RM but has been extended to other tasks. It handles multiple pronunciations. Changes to Y0 include additional pruning capability, forced Viterbi alignment for embedded training, and incorporation of back-off bigram language model with cache.

The availability of a common, sophisticated decoder has facilitated the comparison of results between sites and allows research into more challenging speech recognition areas (e.g., Wall Street Journal). The Wall Street Journal task requires the application of trigram or more sophisticated language models. As a consequence, continued work on Y0 will primarily be the extension to more complicated language models, and the study and improvement of its scaling properties to larger lexicon tasks.

### 4.3 Work Package 3: Speaker Adaptation

Speaker adaptation has been explored with relative success in classical HMM-based recognition systems. However, in the case of connectionist and hybrid HMM/ANN recognizers, virtually no work exists on speaker adaptation yet. The goal of this WP is to investigate speaker adaptation techniques which can be used in the hybrid HMM/ANN systems that are developed in this project.

Two basic classes of adaptation techniques are studied in this project:

- Transformation of the speaker independent emission probabilities into speaker dependent (adapted) emission probabilities. In a preliminary experiment, this has been achieved by extending the standard speaker independent ANN (generating emission probabilities for the HMMs) with an additional layer which weights are optimized to better match the adapted speaker. Actually, this additional layer is trained (by a minimizing a constrained least mean square procedure) to optimize a stochastic transformation matrix.

- Adaptation of the HMM/ANN parameters themselves from a speaker independent model. This can be achieved, e.g., by a fast retraining or adaptation of the whole set or a subset (e.g., only the biases) of the ANN parameters.

Alternative approaches, more directly related to ANN are also investigated in this WP.

These different adaptation techniques will be compared in terms of required adaptation speech material (i.e., in terms of free parameters to be adapted) and performance for both on-line and off-line training procedures. The possibility of performing HMM/ANN hybrid incremental training should also be investigated in the framework of this task.

## 4.4 Work Package 4: System Development

The aim of this WP is to adapt the ICSI hardware and software tools that are required to support the research described in this project. This primarily consists of software (such as object-oriented library classes) for both the RAP and the SPERT (high speed and low cost permitting several users at the same site to simultaneously develop algorithms).

During the first year of this project ICSI has extended the RAP software to support algorithms needed by the partners, and to ensure compatibility for remote procedure calls on the SUN SPARC, the RAP, as well as the SPERT.

By the third year, much of this effort will be focused on software to support the final demonstration systems.

### *4.4.1 Extension to RAP Software*

The RAP [10] is a highly versatile, high-speed multi-DSP computer that has successfully aided connectionist research in the USA since mid-1990. ICSI has developed Remote Procedure Call (RPC) mechanisms for the RAP that permit users to insert simple calls to RAP hardware in C and C++ programs that otherwise run on the SUN. During the first year of this project, ICSI has developed this software further. Also, a new form of object-oriented class libraries (BOB – Boxes Of Boxes) has been developed to permit easier coding for a wider class of programmers. It is expected that BOB will be used on both RAP and SPERT systems in the future.

### *4.4.2 SPERT Software Environment*

Over the last few years, ICSI and UC Berkeley researchers and students have been working on developing VLSI circuits and architectures for the next generation of neurocomputing engines. As part of WERNICKE, ICSI has been working on the elements necessary to provide such tools for the later parts of the project. The Synthetic Perceptron Trainer, or SPERT, is an S-Bus card that includes a custom chip that does both general-purpose operations and specialized fixed-point vector operations commonly used in connectionist computation. For this new hardware (which should be available at the end of the second year of this project), the required VLSI design tools and building blocks are funded by a US grant from the National Science Foundation. However, ICSI will make these developments (SPERT hardware and software tools) available to the partners and the work involved in this project will mainly be concerned with the (hardware and software) adaptations of the final boards (at least in terms of low level software) as required for effective use by the partners. As of today, SPERT appears to be on schedule and could be distributed to the partners by the end of the second year of this project.

## 4.5 Work Package 5: Evaluation and Demonstration Systems

The main goal of this WP is to assess and demonstrate the performance of the different systems which are developed in this project. This takes two forms: (1) formal evaluations and comparisons of the different hybrid systems on the agreed reference databases, and (2) more informal evaluations under the form of demonstration systems.

One of the advantages of the investigated hybrid HMM/ANN approaches seems to be their simplicity (e.g., fewer parameters and good recognition performance achieved with single state, context-independent phonemic HMMs) and their better adaptability to new databases. Our current experience suggests that, despite the large computational requirements for training with these methods, recognition is perhaps even simpler than for conventional HMM systems. For this reason, many of our systems may not require a high-performance system like RAP or SPERT for recognition. As a consequence it is planned to produce a (realtime) demonstration system by the conclusion of the project that is expected to run on a DSP-based board that plugs into a PC. Another potential advantage of the developed hybrid approaches which should also be tested and demonstrated here is their better adaptability and robustness to new tasks (containing words which were not encountered in the training set).

## 5 First Year Status and Results

At the end of the first year of the project, the common reference databases have been defined and are now available on each site. Also, three RAP systems have been delivered by ICSI: a 4-board system for L&H and CUED and a 3-board system for INESC.

After a relatively short training period all the partners were able to implement their baseline system (using their own algorithms in conjunction with the RAP software library) on the RAP. At the end of the first year, different baseline HMM/ANN systems were implemented by each of the partners and the reference decoder was up and running at each site. Also, each partner has developed its own training system that has been evaluated on the reference decoder to insure that they all lead to (approximately) the same performance. These baseline systems provide the partners with a reference point from which to evaluate the effectiveness of their research. There are slight variations between the baseline systems at the different sites, but all have been developed with common software.

This process enabled the consortium to:

- Define a common phone set and pronunciation dictionary,
- Debug (as much as possible!) the different codes by cross-comparison of sub-modules and general performance of the recognizers,
- Improve each of these systems,
- Define and implement a common decoder (Y0) which is constantly maintained on one site (so far CUED) and which is used as a basis for comparisons and evaluation. This reference decoder is regularly updated according to the progress made in the project.

Based on this, preliminary research work has been carried out in several directions, including:

- Comparison of different acoustic features and different kinds of hybrid HMM/ANN systems (see Table 1),
- Improvement of the reference decoder which can now handle multiple pronunciations and pauses between words,
- Preliminary results for speaker adaptation in HMM/ANN hybrids,
- Improvement of probability estimation with ANNs,
- Combination of independently trained neural networks in view of: (1) separate training in case of very large training databases, and (2) better performance.

| Net | Pre-Processing | Error Rate % feb89 | oct89 | feb91 | sep92 |
|---|---|---|---|---|---|
| RNN | MEL+ 16/32 | 4.8% | 6.1% | 5.4% | 10.7% |
| RNN | MFCC 10/20 | 6.1% | 7.6% | 7.4% | 12.1% |
| RNN | MFCC 16/32 | 5.9% | 6.3% | 6.1% | 11.5% |
| RNN | PLP 16/32 | 4.4% | 5.9% | 5.1% | 10.8% |
| MLP | PLP 10/20 | 5.1% | 5.7% | 5.8% | 12.2% |
| MLP | PLP 16/32 | 5.6% | 6.7% | 6.1% | 12.9% |
| MLP | MFCC 10/20 | 5.7% | 7.1% | 7.6% | 12.0% |
| MLP | MFCC 16/32 | 6.6% | 7.8% | 8.5% | 15.0% |

Table 1: Comparisons of HMM/RNN and HMM/MLP approaches on RM task with different front ends and Y0 as obtained at CUED.

Results obtained to date at CUED for different acoustic representations and architectures evaluated on the RM task are shown in Table 1 [16]. The MLP had a seven frame input, 1.000 hidden units (250.000 parameters) and the input was augmented with difference coefficients. The RNN had 220 state units (70.000 parameters). Both the MLP and the RNN had 61 phonetic output units. The RM feb89 test set was used to set the word transition penalty for the MLP recognizer and was used as a cross validation set for the RNN recognizer. The front end options were:

**MEL+** a 20 channel mel-scaled filter bank with voicing features

**PLP** 12th order perceptual linear prediction and energy

**MFCC** 12th order mel-frequency cepstral coefficients and energy

The two numbers associated with processing type in Table 1 are the frame rate and width of the Hamming window in milliseconds. The results obtained at L&H with HMM/MLP hybrids (Table 2) are comparable to the CUED ones, except for the RM sep92 test, which was a difficult one, where they are better (9.9% word error rate instead of 12.2%). The reason of this difference is not explained. Otherwise, results obtained at CUED and L&H showed a slight advantage for the HMM/RNN approach over the HMM/MLP one.

In view of the WSJ task [12], work has started on splitting databases among separate networks that can be trained independently. The networks are recombined (properly) during recognition to generate the required probabilities [7]. The goal of this work is twofold: (1) to investigate how the HMM/ANN approach performs on split training data (to speed up training on large databases), and (2) to see whether improvements can possibly be expected from such a split training. After some theoretical work, initial experiments on RM have shown that it was possible to split the training data

| Test set | Scores % | | | | |
|---|---|---|---|---|---|
| | Error Rate | Substitutions | Deletions | Insertions | Sent. Err |
| feb89 | 5.1 | 3.6 | 1.1 | 0.4 | 31.3 |
| oct89 | 6.0 | 4.1 | 1.5 | 0.4 | 30.0 |
| feb91 | 5.9 | 3.9 | 1.3 | 0.6 | 28.7 |
| sep92 | 9.9 | 5.8 | 2.4 | 1.7 | 42.0 |

Table 2: RM recognition results obtained with the L&H trained HMM/MLP system used in Y0. The MLP contained 7 frames of PLP 10/20 parameters, 1.000 hidden units and 61 phonetic ouptut units.

| Network description | Scores % | | | | |
|---|---|---|---|---|---|
| | Error | Sub | Del | Ins | S. Err |
| Standard L&H MLP only | 5.1 | 3.6 | 1.1 | 0.4 | 31.3 |
| +2nd net with no hidden units | 5.0 | 3.5 | 1.1 | 0.4 | 30.7 |
| +2nd net: 3 frames, 2.000 hidden | 4.8 | 3.3 | 1.2 | 0.4 | 30.3 |
| +2nd net: 9 frames, 100 hidden units | 7.4 | 4.9 | 1.9 | 0.7 | 40.7 |

Table 3: RM feb89 test results for the case of the L&H standard MLP (9 frames of input) merged during recognition with a 2nd net (with 3 or 9 frames of input) and with optimization of the blending weigthing factors according to a mean square error criterion.

across two smaller nets without any significant loss in recognition performance. Table 3 shows preliminary results obtained at L&H with the merging of two MLPs trained on a random split of the training data.

## 6 Future Work

The work completed in the first year of the project provides all the members with state-of-the-art HMM/ANN baseline systems. From this vantage point, it is now possible to extend the systems to new areas of research. Some of the important issues which will be addressed in this project are listed below.

### 6.1 Extension to Larger Databases

Work to date has shown on the RM task that the hybrid HMM/ANN approach using simple context-independent phoneme models is competitive with state-of-the-art HMM systems using multiple pronunciations and context-dependent phoneme models. However, the limitations with the RM task has led the project to undertake the Wall Street Journal (WSJ) task. This change in databases is desirable for a number of reasons:

- research into multiple pronunciation word models and appropriate use of acoustic context will require a substantially greater amount of training data than is available with the RM task.
- the WSJ task, with substantially more variation in acoustic context, will show how well the acoustic context which is implicitly modelled in hybrid approaches scales to a larger database.
- the WSJ task will show whether context-independent phoneme models are still a viable solution for very large lexicon tasks or whether one has to go to context-dependent HMM/ANN phoneme models.
- evaluation on the WSJ task allows for direct comparisons of the hybrid approaches with other state-of-the-art systems.

## 6.2 Better Training Algorithms

The transition to a larger database will directly lead to research in the area of network training since achieving adequate turn-around time on training runs will require a substantial speed-up in the training algorithms. In this regard, connectionist systems are currently at a disadvantage in that they take about an order of magnitude more computation to train than pure HMM-based systems. Thus faster training procedures would allow connectionist systems to be applied to larger databases and receive better acceptance in the speech recognition community.

We currently avoid overtraining the ANNs used to estimate state output probabilities using a cross-validation technique [3]. We are investigating the use of an explicit parameterised prior on the weight matrix, and the use of an objective Bayesian procedure to set the regularisation parameters. This is referred to as "regularised training" [16].

## 6.3 Split Networks

In view of the WSJ task, work has started on splitting databases among separate networks that can be trained independently (mixture of statistical experts [7]). More generally, this is related to the problem of combining probability estimates from several sources (e.g., from two types of network or data). After some theoretical work, initial experiments on RM have shown that it was possible to split the training data across two smaller nets without any significant loss in recognition performance. This approach should be investigated further on larger databases (WSJ) and could be used not only to speed up training but also to get improvements of recognition performance. In theory, such improvements can be expected in two cases: (1) random split of the training data used to train MLPs with different properties (e.g., different architectures or different training criteria), and (2) MLPs with the same architecture trained on data with different statistical properties (e.g., training data split according to gender or speaker clusters). This approach should also be tested on speaker adaptation problems (by on-line or off-line adaptation of the gating network [7] parameters generating the weighting factors).

### 6.4 Context-Dependent Phone Models

State-of-the-art HMM-based recognizers now use context-dependent phonetic units to improve their performance. On the other hand, it has been shown that context-independent, single-state phonemic HMM/ANN approaches perform nearly as well as context-dependent, multi-state HMM systems. However, it is still not clear how well this is going to scale (in terms of performance) on more difficult tasks like WSJ and what additional improvement one can expect from context-dependent hybrid systems.

### 6.5 Alternative Approaches

In the framework of this project, alternative hybrid approaches (which are not directly addressed in this project) will also be considered and tested. Among these, we have:

- Predictive Networks – There is a relationship between predictive networks (as proposed in [8]) and nonlinear autoregressive modelling. Although they are also very attractive from the theoretical point of view, they have their own weaknesses (e.g., no discrimination, and very noisy estimate of probabilities) which make it difficult to actually get significant improvements out of them. A (theoretical) solution could be to merge both predictive and discriminant approaches.

- Output Feedback – In the initial theory of the hybrid HMM/MLP approach [1] it was suggested to have contextual inputs but also feedback from the output units to the input layer (to model correlation at both the acoustic vector and HMM state level). This initial architecture can be implemented and leads to the investigation of approaches mixing RNN and acoustic input context.

# 7 Conclusion

The WERNICKE project is a substantial effort in research into the problem of speaker independent, large vocabulary, continuous speech recognition. The HMM/ANN is an approach with a great deal of potential for this kind of task. Work to date has shown that the approach is competitive with HMM-based systems, although there has been substantially less research in the HMM/ANN field. The project has the potential to further improve the most advanced HMM-based speech recognition systems by adding a neural component to the existing HMM technology. After initial developments and tests on the ARPA RM database, the consortium is now moving to the more ambitious WSJ task.

# References

[1] Bourlard, H., & Wellekens, C.J., "Links Between Markov Models and Multilayer Perceptrons", *IEEE Trans. on Pattern Analysis and Machine Intelligence*, vol. 12, no. 12, pp. 1167-1178, 1990.

[2] Bourlard, H., Morgan, N., Wooters C., & Renals, S., "CDNN: A context dependent neural network for continuous speech recognition", *IEEE Intl. Conf. on Acoustics, Speech, & Signal Processing*, San Francisco, pp. 349-352, 1992.

[3] Bourlard, H. & Morgan, N., *Connectionist Speech Recognition - A Hybrid Approach*, Kluwer Academic Press, 1994.

[4] Cohen, M., Franco, H., Morgan, N., Rumelhart, D., & Abrash, V., "Hybrid Neural Network/Hidden Markov Model Continuous-Speech Recognition", in *Proc. Intl. Conf. on Spoken Language Processing*, Banff, Canada, 1992.

[5] Hermansky, H., "Perceptual Linear Predictive (PLP) Analysis of Speech", *Journal of the Acoust. Soc. Am.*, 87(4), pp. 1738-1752, 1990.

[6] Hermansky, H., Morgan, N., Bayya, A., & Kohn, P., "RASTA-PLP Speech Analysis Technique", *IEEE Intl. Conf. on Acoustics, Speech, & Signal Processing*, San Francisco, pp. I-121-124, 1992.

[7] Jordan, M.I., & Jacobs, R.A., "Hierarchical Mixtures of Experts and the EM Algorithm", submitted to *Neural Computation*, 1993.

[8] Levin, E., "Hidden Control Neural Architecture Modeling of Nonlinear Time Varying Systems and its Applications", *IEEE Trans. on Neural Networks*, vol. 4, no. 1, pp. 109-116, 1993.

[9] Morgan, N., & Hermansky, H., "RASTA Extensions: Robustness to Additive and Convolutional Noise", *Proceedings of Workshop on Speech Processing in Adverse Conditions*, pp. 115-118, 1992.

[10] Morgan, N., Beck, J., Kohn, P., Bilmes, J., Allman, E., & Beer, J., "The Ring Array Processor (RAP): A Multiprocessor Peripheral for Connectionist Applications", *Journal of Parallel and Distributed Computing*, vol. 14, pp. 248-259, 1992.

[11] Morgan, N., Bourlard, H., Renals, S., Cohen, M., & Franco, H., "Hybrid Neural Network/Hidden Markov Model Systems for Continuous Speech Recognition", *Intl. Journal of Pattern Recognition and Artificial Intelligence*, vol. 7, no. 4, pp. 899-916, 1993.

[12] Pallett, D.S., Fiscus, J.G., Fisher, W.M., Garofolo, J.S., Lund, B.A., & Pryzbocki, M.A., "1993 Benchmark Tests for the ARPA Spoken Language Program", *Proc. ARPA Workshop on Human Language Technology*, 1994.

[13] Price, P., Fisher, W.M., Bernstein, J., & Pallett, D., "The DARPA 1000-word Resource Management Database for Continuous Speech Recognition", *Proc. of the IEEE Intl. Conf. on Acoustics, Speech, and Signal Processing*, 1988.

[14] Renals, S., Morgan, N., Bourlard, H., Cohen, M. & H. Franco. H., "Connectionist Probability Estimators in HMM Speech Recognition", in *IEEE Trans. on Speech and Audio*, vol. 2, no. 1, pp. 161-174, 1994.

[15] Robinson, T., "A Real-Time Error Propagation Network Word Recognition System", *Proc. of the IEEE Intl. Conf. on Acoustics, Speech, and Signal Processing*, 1992.

[16] Robinson, T., Almeida, L., Boite, J.M., Bourlard, H., Fallside, F., Hochberg, M., Kershaw, D., Kohn, P., Konig, Y., Morgan, N., Neto, J.P., Renals, S., Saerens, M., & Wooters, C., "A Neural Network Based, Speaker Independent, Large Vocabulary, Continuous Speech Recognition System: The WERNICKE Project", pp. 1941-1944, *Proceedings EUROSPEECH'93*, September 1993, Berlin, Germany, 1993.

[17] Robinson, T., "The application of recurrent nets to phone probability estimation", to appear in *IEEE Trans. on Neural Networks*, 1994.

[18] Schwartz, R., Chow, Y., Kimball, O., Roucous, S., Krasner, M., & Makhoul, J., "Context-dependent modelling for acoustic-phonetic recognition of continuous speech", *IEEE Intl. Conf. on Acoustics, Speech, & Signal Processing*, Tampa, pp. 1205-1208, 1985.

# Contributors

# Springer-Verlag and the Environment

We at Springer-Verlag firmly believe that an international science publisher has a special obligation to the environment, and our corporate policies consistently reflect this conviction.

We also expect our business partners – paper mills, printers, packaging manufacturers, etc. – to commit themselves to using environmentally friendly materials and production processes.

The paper in this book is made from low- or no-chlorine pulp and is acid free, in conformance with international standards for paper permanency.

Printing: Weihert-Druck GmbH, Darmstadt
Binding: Theo Gansert Buchbinderei GmbH, Weinheim